The Book that Doesn't Even Matter

The Book That Doesn't Even Matter
Printed in the United States of America
Copyright © 2013 by **Marc Marcel**
ISBN 978-1-300-68173-1
First Edition

All rights reserved. No part of this publication may be reproduced, distributed, or transmitted, without the prior written permission of the publisher, except in the case of brief quotations embodied in critical reviews and certain other noncommercial uses permitted by copyright law. For permission requests, contact author.

Author: **Marc Marcel**
Editor in Chief: **Nehemiah Clark**
Editor: **Guy Bragg**
Editor: **Kalia Glover**
Editor: **Sara Gray**
Cover and book design by **Marc Marcel**

Marc My Words Productions
www.marcmywordsproductions.com
www.marcmarcel.com

This book is dedicated to **You**!

Diana,
get started
the world is
your canvas.

TABLE OF CONTENTS

DEDICATION..I
TABLE OF CONTENTS..III
PREFACE...IX
PREAMBLE...XVII

CHAPTER ONE – Remembering..................................1
   (Introduction to Remembering)..................................1
   (Thoughts)...2
   (The Brain)..3
   (The Pineal Gland)..6
   (Levels of Consciousness)...7
   (Stretch Your Thinking)..13

CHAPTER TWO – Language......................................17
   (Introduction to Language)......................................17
   (Origins of Speech)...18
   (Words & Terms)..21
   (Creating Language)...23

CHAPTER THREE – The Cosmos..............................25
   (Introduction to the Cosmos)..................................25
   (The Universe)..26
   (Astrology)...30
   (The Solar System)...38
   (Extraterrestrial Life)..43

CHAPTER FOUR – Ancient Civilizations.................48
   (Introduction to Ancient Civilizations)...................48
   (Sumer)...49
   (Egypt)..54
   (Maya)..63
   (Inca)..68

CHAPTER FIVE – Ancient Unknowns..................72
(Introduction to Ancient Unknowns)..................72
(Ancient Baghdad Electric Batteries)..................73
(Great Pyramid of Giza)..................74
(Stonehenge)..................76
(Moai of Easter Island)..................78
(Pumapunku)..................79
(Machu Picchu)..................80
(Nazca Lines)..................82
(Coral Castle)..................84
(Bosnian Pyramids)..................86
(Ancient Astronauts Rounding Theory)..................88

CHAPTER SIX – Religion..................94
(Introduction to Religion)..................94
(Beliefs in God)..................95
(Evolution of Religion)..................97
(Hinduism)..................99
(Buddhism)..................105
(Judaism)..................111
(Christianity)..................119
(Islam)..................129
(The Effects)..................135

CHAPTER SEVEN – Human Evolution..................141
(Introduction to Human Evolution)..................141
(Evolution Theory)..................142
(Planet Migration Theory)..................146
(Alien Creation Theory)..................153
(Theory of Us All)..................157

CHAPTER EIGHT – What You Really Are..................158
(Introduction to What You Really Are)..................158
(The Reconstructing Body)..................159
(The Mind)..................160
(You're Higher Self)..................163
(The Eyes)..................166

IV

CHAPTER NINE – The World of Question.....................168
   (Introduction to the World of Questions)........................ 168
   (Creation from Thought)...169
   (Atoms)..171
   (Paintings, Symbols & Numbers)...................................174
   (Sacred Geometry)..175
   (Complex Hologram)...179
   (Colors)..180
   (Running in One Place)...182
   (Hallucinogenic)...185
   (Oxygen)..189
   (Particle inside You)..191

CHAPTER TEN – The World of Answers..........................192
   (Introduction to the World of Answers)..........................192
   (Dreams)..193
   (Déjà Vu)...195
   (The Moment of Transition)..196
   (Death and the Panoramic Life Review)........................199
   (Healing Process)...202
   (Inside the World of Answers)...204
   (Spirit Workers)...208
   (Soulmates)..211
   (Akashic Records)...214
   (Where does it Exist)...219

CHAPTER ELEVEN – God...221
   (Introduction to God)...221
   (How God came to Existence)...222
   (Forgetting Everything)...224
   (What is Love)...227
   (How You relate to God)...230

CHAPTER TWELVE – The Game......................................232
   (Introduction to the Game)..232
   (Why Play)...233
   (Wisdom & Problems)...236
   (Reincarnation Process)...238

(The Laws of Forgetting)..241
(Destiny)..243
(Parallel Universes)...244
(Levels of the Physical)..247
(Levels of the Soul)..251
(The Yin-Yang)...260

CHAPTER THIRTEEN – Tools.. 263
(Introduction to Tools)..263
(Adversary)..264
(Karma)..268
(Frequencies)...273
(Prayer)..274
(Ho'oponopono)...276
(The Om)..278
(Chakras)...280

CHAPTER FOURTEEN – Decoding the Past.....................288
(Introduction to Decoding the Past)....................................... 288
(Genesis)..290
(Moses & Mises)...300
(Yeshua, the Jmmanuel)...305
(Psychedelic Prophets)..321
(Revelation)...323

CHAPTER FIFTEEN – Encoding the Future.....................327
(Introduction to Encoding the Future)...................................327
(Future Type 1, Type 2, Type 3 Civilizations)......................328
(Alien Interaction)...331
(Have We Done This Before)..332
(Future Higher Conscious)...336

CHAPTER SIXTEEN – Tomorrow......................................338
(Introduction to Tomorrow)..338
(Senses & the Body)..339
(Writing System)...342
(Technology)..343
(Money)..346
(Government)..351

VI

(Prejudices)..353
(Family Structure)..355
(Earth & Expansion)...356
(God of Our Future)..358

CHAPTER SEVENTEEN – The Continue......................... 360
(Introduction to the Continue)..360
(The Beautiful)...361
(For The Better)...364
(Forever)...365

AUTHOR'S CLOSING STATEMENT................................**XV**
APPENDIX: FOOTNOTES & REFERENCES...............**XXXI**

PREFACE
By: **Marc Marcel**

The purpose of this book is to help you remember what you already know. This book will not save you, you cannot be saved, because there is nothing to save you from.

The information you are about to read, you already know, everyone already knows. The only difference in myself and someone who may think they don't know, is that I have 'Chosen' to see behind the veil. I am not special, gifted, more enlightened or smarter than anyone else, I am just sharing what I have made myself 'Aware' of. Much like many before me, this will be done again and again, many people after me will continue this process of sharing with 'You' who you really are.

What I am doing now, is sharing with those that desire to understand who, how, why and what they are doing here. Truly, no one is making you read this, whether someone suggested this book to you, or you were intrigued to pick it up from the cover design, this book will be read only by your choice, by your 'Free Will.'

This book is a composite of information that has been accumulated through **Out-of-Body Experiences**, **Astral Projection**, **Shamanism**, **Conversations**, **Historical References**, studies of **Philosophies** and by the simple thought of…**Remembering**. There were many hours in which I found myself secluded in thought, reflecting in silence, listening and making sure that I could correctly hear my truest self. During the writing process for this book, I asked that only the truth come forth. The last thing I desire is to mislead someone. My purpose is to help those that wish to become more informed of their awakening.

To understand who you truly are, there are certain subjects that should be addressed, some more heavily than others. Processing the information can be a handful, therefore I outlined the book in a chronological format that may be digestible to even the most skeptical person. At times, it may be best to feed people slowly, without shoving the whole meal in their mouth.

The book opens with a basic outline of our **Thoughts**, and then addresses the uses of **Language**. From there, I begin to expand in a brief course of the **Cosmos** and the possibilities that exist in Universe, before exploring the mysteries of the **Ancient Civilizations** that inhabited this Earth. After covering a history of **Religions**, I found it appropriate to go deeper into the many theories of how **Human Beings** came into existence, addressing some inaccuracies, but giving aid to all probabilities and theories. From there, I begin to go deeper into what '**You**' are, and where you come from. After explaining how the Body and the Universe came to be, the book takes a turn from the Physical, to the Nonphysical. I address and explain how the **Physical Realm** came to be, in a section entitled the '**World of Questions**.' After going over the **Afterlife**, in a chapter entitled the '**World of Answers**,' I then explain what most people have wondered about all their life, '**God**.' Our connection to God, leads into the next chapter which I entitled, '**The Game**,' here is a final rundown of what we are all doing here, and why. But this doesn't come without rules and consequences, so it is important to explain certain energies while playing the 'Game,' which is placed in the chapter entitled '**Tools**.' After retouching on a few subjects to clarify certain meanings, I then address the '**Changes to come**.'

The material you are about to take in, would not have been possible without the energy and assistance of others. I extend gratitude to those that have partaken in our '**Remembering Courses**,' and the people that would simply listen to my rants on 'Life' and 'Higher Consciousness.' Their ears and input have all made this possible.

While many friends affected this process, a portion of the conclusions to this information are due to some of my most trusted friends, **Travis James Connell**, **Nehemiah Clark** and **Palmetto Starr**. I deeply thank them for embarking on a journey with me 'Down the Rabbit Hole.' They played a significant part in helping pieces of the puzzle be placed together. Many nights we would discuss the knowledge and findings that rediscovered. If not for them, I may have found myself bottling up a lot of what I was going through, or possibly feeling as though I was losing my sanity. I was thankful that out of the things I had witnessed, there were a few people I knew personally that could fully understand the course my thoughts were taking.

It has been a beautiful journey of remembering. I cannot stress that point enough, remembering. Therefore, I will not be revealing one new thing to you, you already know '**EVERYTHING.**' I'm just reminding you of what you've forgotten.

In turn, I hope this book does not become something you feel the need to read every day, or something that you feel you can't do without. Frankly, when thinking of your favorite books, I wish that so many others will come to mind. My only wish is that this book becomes just a minor footnote, in your extraordinary growth. The power to affect the world lies in your hands. Essentially, this book can do nothing for you. This book is not important. The book doesn't even matter. You are what matters! You are important! Therefore, this book will not change your life, **YOU** will!

Marc Marcel

"God loves each of us as if there were only one of us."
-St. Augustine-

XIV

CHAPTER ONE
(Remembering)

"Reality is merely an illusion, although a very persistent one."
- Albert Einstein -

Remembering: (Introduction)

You've probably read this before.

Perhaps this was written in so many ways, in various different forms, with more than one conclusion, so there's a chance you've already read this. Maybe somewhere on an airplane, or sitting at home in your favorite chair, somewhere on a park bench, or resting on one of the shores, these words may have previously once filled you, surely you already know how this ends. Maybe this is something you've given yourself to experience...again.

Hard to remember? It must be, but the world has to have started to look familiar to you. The horizons, landscapes, oceans, events, situations, your problems and the faces of people, they all must seem like something you already know.

Strangers, people you've never met before, if the picture got any clearer they'd reveal their prior connection with you, on what you think is your first encounter with them, and tell you a story of an experience that the both of you once shared in a previous existence, just to remind you. It shouldn't be this difficult to remember, who you are, why you are here, and where you come from.

How many times have you wondered 'Why are we here?' How many lives have you lived? This can't be your first lifetime, and surely you must have been somewhere before this. You didn't just 'Come out of nowhere' when you were born from your mother's womb, so where did you come from? What were you doing before you were here? What were you before you were here? Why can't you remember? How many times have you done this, over and over again, once...twice...maybe several, even hundreds?

Surely these words have already filled you. How many times have you learned something new, just to feel like you've actually known it all along? How many times have you come across the information you are about to intake, again, for the first time? The answer to the question is...possibly countless.

The information in this book will seem to reveal new doors to you, but in the end, you will find the only thing you are doing is remembering all that you already know. What you are about to process has been known by everyone, but forgotten by most. The answers to EVERYTHING have always been right before your eyes. Now is the time to look!

Remembering: (Thoughts)

Our **'Thoughts'** are drastically underappreciated. Certain belief systems stress our thoughts are of the type of power that can move mountains, split a sea, walk on water, but yet we do not seriously give thought to these types of things. We imagine thinking this way is extreme or unrealistic, not realizing it was once unrealistic to think of airplanes made of steel flying across the sky from city to city. It was once unrealistic to think we could sit at a table in a restaurant in New York City and get a phone call from someone on a beach in the Virgin Islands. It was once unrealistic to have 'Space Shuttles' that can break through Earth's orbit and go into Outer Space. It was once unrealistic to do so many things we now take for granted in our evolution of thought.

Why? If certain things were once unthinkable, but have happened right before our eyes, then why is it unrealistic to believe **Human Beings** will do the unthinkable again, even right this moment? For example, think of **Thomas Edison** and his invention of the **'Light Bulb,'** which famously took him over **10,000** experiments to finally create. He drastically changed the world forever, nothing since brought as much overnight success and benefit to people. 'Thought' created the possibility of

Edison's action. One could argue, just by the mere thought of thinking he was going to achieve such a thing, in turn he had already achieved it.

Our 'Thoughts' are the things that shape, mold, and create the life around us. In **2005**, a film documentary called **'What the Bleep Do We Know,'** discussed how the molecular structure in water is affected by conscious thought. Japanese author **Masaru Emoto** held experiments, in which he printed words and placed them on bottles of distilled water, left them overnight and found that the molecules transformed into new exciting designs that mostly resembled patterns of a snowflake.

This is how we live our lives; our thoughts are more powerful than we realize. Thought manipulates water. Why can't our thoughts manipulate the world around us as well? It can, and it does! Every single fraction of a second, our world is being manipulated by our thoughts. Our thoughts are what keep this world together, and the mere notion of wanting it here is enough to do so.

In contrary to popular belief, there is no such thing as 'Supernatural.' Everything that occurs, no matter how incredible the event might seem, if it is able to exist, then it is not supernatural. It is a part of nature and the ebb and flow of the Universe; it is natural. There is no such thing as 'Unordinary' in life. There is no such thing as 'Weird' or 'Strange,' there is no such thing as the 'Unbelievable,' everything you can conspire to think of is an action waiting to happen.

Your thoughts are the root to change. If you 'Think' you can do something, then 'Know' you will do something…you will in turn do something. Your thoughts are the greatest thing you have, your thoughts can inspire you to create the light bulb, it can motivate you to walk on water or split a sea, it has the power to change your life and the world you exist in.

Remembering: (The Brain)

The **Brain** is one complex piece of machinery. To make things simple, it is like the hard drive on a computer. Every button means something, and if rewired incorrectly it could lead to all kinds of complications. Controlling all organ systems of the body by activating the muscles or releasing of chemicals such as hormones and neurotransmitters, the **Human Brain** contains the same structures as the brains of other mammals (Animals), but is larger in proportion to its body size. This enlargement is thought to have been caused from a massive expansion of the **Cortex**, from focusing on such parts as visualization and premonition.

Our brain, like the rest of our anatomy, is made up of two halves, a **Left** brain and a **Right** brain. It is divided into halves with a distinct fold that separates the two. At the base of each half brain, it is connected by a cable of nerves, called the **Corpus Callosum**. In comparisons to a computer, it resembles an Ethernet Cable, designed to connect each half through the wiring system.

The Left side of our body is wired to the Right side of our brain, and the Right side of our body is wired to the Left side of our brain. Our eyes even process a major portion of its sensory data from the opposite sides of the brain. The idea of our body's framework doing this form of crossing seems understandable when thinking of how everything is connected to something else.

The 'Left' and 'Right' sides of the brain perform in a variety of ways. Artistic abilities are connected to the Right side of the brain, as is depression, arousal and self-reflection, while the Left side is connected to processing pleasurable experiences, and decision making. It is said the Right hemisphere is more involved in processing uncommon situations, and the Left hemisphere is most involved with routine processing. The Left side is also the function of direct fact recovery. Both sides connect to and comprehend numbers, the Left deals with exact calculation, numerical comparison and estimation, while the Right deals with approximate calculation, numerical comparison, and estimation. Both sides also deal with Language, with the Left half focusing on grammar, vocabulary and literal speech, while the Right focusing on intonation, accentuation, prosody, pragmatic and contextual. Behaviors of the Left and Right side of the brain are listed below:

Left Brain Functions		Right Brain Functions	
Reality	Organized	Fantasy	Conceptual
Knowing	Safe	Believes	Risk Taking
Logical	Strategies	Imaginative	Possibilities
Objective	Words	Subjective	Symbols
Acknowledges	Language	Appreciates	Images
Literal	Math	Figurative	Philosophy
Repetitive	Scientific	Intuitive	Heuristic
Present	Past	Present	Future

There has been a serious misconception about the brain, many have believed humans access only 10% of their brain, but that theory is believed to be either a misquote of **Albert Einstein**, the misinterpretation of **Jean Pierre Flourens**'s work in the **1800s**, or an idea someone published in a newspaper in the **1920's**. There are a few other theories of where it may have originated, however, it is an urban legend that got picked up and passed down from person to person.

Humans actually access all of their brain. It is known through taking MRI's, PT scans, and other brain scans. Scientists find that while all of the brain is used, not all the neurons in our brain are operating at the same time. This may lead someone to say we only use 10% of the brain at one time. If all neurons fired at the same time you could get conflicting messages and overloaded with a large number of multiple thoughts, therefore, not accessing all of our brain at all times actually aids your thought process.

It is not certain how much of our brain we use, but what is true is that we do not occupy the extent of its capability. We constantly fool ourselves regarding what our brain is capable of.

One movie in particular '**Defending Your Life**' in a very amusing way, describes our use of the brain, as '**Little Brains**.' A character, **Bob Diamond** played by **Rip Torn**, is defending the main character, **Daniel Miller** played by **Albert Brooks**, for his progression onto the next stage of his evolution, based how well he did with the life he recently lived. **Daniel Miller** acts out in ways of asking question after question, wondering what the whole process is about, why, and how come, while **Bob Diamond** replies that this is just a simple process. Further explaining that he uses **48** percent of his brain, while Daniel only uses **3** percent, **Bob** reveals people on Earth use **3** to **5** percent of their brain, and if they used more than that percentage then they would not want to be on Earth anymore. He and his colleagues of superior thinking brains, referred to the people on Earth, as **'Little Brains.'**

Remembering: (The Pineal Gland)

While there are many important facets of the brain, there may be none more important than the **Pineal Gland**. The pineal gland (Also called the **Pineal Body, Epiphysis Cerebri**, or the **'Third Eye'**) is a small endocrine gland shaped like a tiny Pine Cone, located near the center of the brain, tucked in a groove between the two thalamic bodies (Left & Right side of the brain). The pineal gland is reddish-gray and about the size of a grain of rice. It produces the serotonin derivative **Melatonin**, which is a hormone that affects the modulation of wake, sleep and death.

The activity of the pineal gland is mildly understood, and the natural function of its widespread presence is not fully determined, but it is said to be a **'Mystery Gland,'** and a gateway to the **'Afterlife,'** or the **'World of Answers.'** Its importance is historically stressed by philosophers and shamans. **René Descartes**, a French philosopher who studied the pineal gland, called it the **'Seat of the Soul.'** He believed it is the point of connection between the intellect and the body. Descartes gave significance to the gland because he believed it is the only part of the brain which existed as a single part, instead of it being one half of a pair.

It has been hypnotized that a substance known as **Dimethyltryptamine** is either found, released from the pineal gland, or activates the melatonin in it. Dimethyltrypatmine is found in almost every living organism, plants, animals and humans, and is a naturally occurring psychedelic compound of the **tryptamine** family. This element is important because of the effects many believe it has for operating the pineal gland.

There are many myths, superstitions and theories surrounding the pineal gland's functions. Being similar in shape to a Pine Cone, hence the word, it's symbolism can be found in almost every religion. Along with a pine cone on the Pope's Staff, there is also a large structure of a pine cone in Vatican City. One has to wonder, why artifacts of a pine cone? Could it symbolize more than what churches have told you?

Remembering: (Levels of Consciousness)

Even though the concept has been around since the dawn of time, Austrian Psychologist **Sigmund Freud** is viewed by many as the first to bring the concept of '**Three Levels of the Mind**' into mainstream society. Freud separated the Mind into 3 tiers or sections, the **Conscious**, the **Subconscious**, and the **Unconscious** Mind which is also known as, the **Superconscious**.

Limited by its analytical nature, the **Conscious** Mind sees all things as separate and distinct. When we are puzzled, confused, or in shock, it is because it seems unrelated to other events, therefore it becomes difficult to respond. By contrast, because the **Superconscious** mind sees all things as part of a whole, it can immediately draw solutions. The problem and the solution are seen as one, in the **Superconscious** mind. The solution is seen as a natural outgrowth from the problem, all things are relative in the **Superconscious** mind.

Your **Conscious** mind only holds a small portion of space, representing about **10%** of your brain capacity, while your **Subconscious** accounts for **50-60%**. The **Subconscious** mind is extremely more powerful, and responds much faster than the **Conscious**. It is believed Humans operate from **Subconscious** levels of mind approximately **95%** of the time. For instance, when you drive to a destination, most of the time you aren't taking notice of your travels, doing so routinely. Whether it is cooking, preparing for bed, or waking up in the morning getting ready for work, most of us operate **Subconsciously**, not taking **Conscious** awareness of what we are doing.

The **Superconscious** occupies **30-40%** of your brain capacity. It is vast and deep, much like the depths of Space, and largely inaccessible to the **Conscious**. The **Superconscious** holds and stores all our memories, those forgotten and those we have repressed and don't wish to recall. Certain psychoanalytical methods are known to bring back these memories, hypnosis, meditation, or it can be triggered by a particular event, a scent, familiar place, something someone says, similar situation, etc. The **Subconscious** is almost the same as the **Superconscious**, except the major difference is we can choose to remember. The memories are a lot closer to the surface and easier to access than it is in the **Superconscious**.

For example, if someone were to ask you the date of your birthday, you could easily bring that into **Conscious** thought. It is available and ready for recall, stored in your **Subconscious**, because you may need to remember it quite regularly. If it wasn't important to recall your own birthday, then it would be stored much deeper, in the Superconscious, and as a result when someone asks you to recall your birthday, you may struggle to remember it.

The Conscious Mind

The **Conscious** mind is the **Decision Maker**. It is aware, and controls your actions, creates your habits, decides your thinking patterns, analyzes, imagines, learns, reasons and also pilots the **Subconscious** mind. The two main abilities of the **Conscious** mind is **Focus** and to **Imagine** which is and not real. The **Conscious** mind communicates to the outside world and the **Inner Self** through speech, writing, physical movement, art and thought.

Our habits control our lives, whether it is waking up in the morning, walking the dog, certain things we like to do, our routines are played out from our **Subconscious**. We do most of these things without thinking, going along with the course of our day. Even when particular situations come upon us, we program ourselves to react in a specific way each time. This is referred to as being asleep. To be awake, is to take control of your **Conscious**, and be aware of your surroundings and situations. Since our actions, habits and thinking patterns are stored in the **Subconscious** level, it is important to use your **Conscious** mind to its full possible potential. It is what you do **Consciously** that gets pushed into your **Subconscious** mind, which in turn controls how you will routinely react.

Another important ability of the **Conscious** mind is the use of **Visualization**. Your mind has the potential to imagine something that is literally 'New and Unique,' something you've never physically experienced, or mentally thought of before. By contrast, your **Subconscious** can only offer accounts of memories it has stored from your experiences, therefore when you are imagining something new, or possibly creating a piece of art, your **Conscious** is in turn tapping into your **Superconscious**, which holds all information. When compared to the **Superconscious**, the **Conscious** only scratches the surface of what the 'Overall Mind' is capable of.

The Subconscious Mind

Your **Subconscious** mind plays many different roles in your life. It is the place of your dreams, instincts, personal and ancestral memories, emotional awareness and belief systems, while ensuring you have everything you need for quick recall. All our automatic processes and responses are controlled **Subconsciously**.

The **Subconscious** mind is the storeroom of all your past memories and experiences, both from repression of trauma and those that have consciously been forgotten for the simple reason of a lack of personal importance, however, it's from these memories and experiences that our habits, beliefs and behaviors are formed. Features of the **Subconscious** are as follows:
- Mega-Memory bank, stores all your past experiences.

- Controls your behaviors, daily habits, and moods.
- Attract things that resonate with its beliefs.
- Maintains and balances the well-being of our body.
- Protects you from emergencies and dangers.
- Connected to your **5 Senses**.
- It is like radar, which not only connects to the **Conscious Mind**, but extends to the information held in the **Superconscious**.

According to the **NLP** (Neuro-Linguistic Programming) communication model, our mind is bombarded with over **2 million bits of data every second**. Your **Conscious** mind cannot handle all that data at once, you would not be able to function throughout your day normally, therefore it is retained in the **Subconscious**.

Your **Subconscious** filters out all the unnecessary information and delivers what is needed at that moment in time, which is believed to be around seven bits of information. You are not aware of this, but behind the scenes it is working so you can perform and go about your day undisturbed. The **Subconscious** doesn't communicate in words, it communicates into **Consciousness** through emotions, feelings, sensations, images and dreams.

The Superconscious Mind

The **Superconscious** mind is the 'Ultimate Computer,' consisting of all the other computers that ever could exist. It orchestrates the activities in every little computer it is connected to it. The **Superconscious** mind is linked to higher potential, intuition, quantum reality and spiritual awareness. The **Superconscious** constantly communicates with the **Conscious** mind through the **Subconscious**. It provides us with the meaning to all our interactions with the world, and communicates through feelings, imagination, sensations, and dreams.

The **Superconscious** mind is similar to the **Subconscious** mind in dealing with our memories. The difference is that the **Superconscious** sits a layer deeper in the mind, it is the cellar to the **Subconscious**, the underground library of everything, every memory, habit, feeling or behavior, and extends to what you haven't witnessed through your own **Conscious**. In fact, it holds the experiences to all and every **Consciousness**. While the **Subconscious** is the **Storeroom**, the **Superconscious** is the **Storehouse**.

The **Superconscious** deals with many tasks as the **Subconscious**, but the **Superconscious** is the source of all the programs your **Subconscious** uses. It is the place where all your memories and experiences since the moment of your birth is stored, and beyond. It literally holds every bit of information in your life. A traumatic memory blocked out from when you were a child or something very distant like the clothes you had on the first time you ever went to the playground is stored in the **Superconscious**. It is all there, though we cannot remember it no matter how hard we try.

The **Superconscious** mind is often associated with the **Collective Conscious**, which we all have access to in the quantum field. This is where we find the answers to all our problems. If you want significant change on the **Conscious** level, the **Superconscious** level is the place to focus. Features of the **Superconscious** are as follows:

- All minds are connected to the **Universal Mind**, which is the **Superconscious Mind**.
- Has the answers to all, helps you to make good decisions, and has **Infinite Intelligence**.
- It is the source of all true invention. Art comes from connecting to the **Superconscious**.
- It assists you, constantly connecting to you through the **Subconscious**.

How the Three Operate Together

Your **Conscious** mind is like the '**Driver**' in a **NASCAR** race. You're making all the moves, twisting and turning on the track, but it's your crew, who has to give you tune ups and makes sure the engine is functioning on your pit stops. The **Crew** is the **Subconscious**. The Driver gets to race, but it is the Crew that makes sure the car is functioning well, providing it with all it needs to run properly.

Your **Subconscious** mind has a much stronger sense than your **Conscious** sense of awareness, it is always switched on, even through sleep. Another great thing about the **Subconscious** is that it obeys you! Your **Conscious** mind gives orders, and the **Subconscious** distributes the emotions you continuously think about. If all you do is focus your **Conscious** mind on negative things, then your **Subconscious** will deliver those experiences through feelings, from the type of thinking you brought forth **Consciously**. It is important to know this because too many people are caught in negative cycles they have placed upon themselves, whether from fear, jealously, anxiety or constantly focusing on the bad in every situation. The **Subconscious** mind does not distinguish between that which the **Conscious** mind imagines and that which is real, therefore whatever the **Conscious** mind imagines, brings into focus all of the emotions and feelings that are associated with what the **Conscious** mind assesses.

Imagination is important because it is the key to opening our creations. For example, in a popular sporting study conducted by **Dr. Judd Blaslotto** of the **University of Chicago**, he took **3** groups of people to test their improvement with a free throw accuracy experiment. They were tested at the start and at the end of the experiment.

The **First Group** was to practice free throws for **20** days in a row. The **Second Group** was not allowed to train at all. The **Third Group** spent **20** minutes a day getting into a relaxed state, only being able to image themselves shooting the free throws. The **Third Group** was also instructed if they missed in their minds, to adjust their thinking, and see themselves making it the next time.

The results were astonishing. The **First Group** that physically practiced each day improved their score by **24%**. The **Second Group** who didn't practice didn't improve at all. The **Third Group**, who were only allowed to visualize themselves shooting, actually improved their score by **23%**, almost as much as the **First Group**. Don't under estimate the power of the **Conscious** mind.

By being in charge of your own thoughts, using visualization and imagination to control your **Subconscious** mind, you influence the change you so desire. Our mental thoughts are the one true freedom we have in this world we can control. If you want to affect change in your life, you will work on the programs held in the **Subconscious** mind. The place to start doing that is in the **Conscious** mind. Reprogram your **Subconscious** representation by using your **Conscious**. Do this often and enough, and it will it become a part of your 'Way of Life.'

Remembering: (Stretch Your Thinking)

Before we go further, it is important to understand that most people today, live their lives by ideals, morals and traditions by those before them. For some reason people tend to think the best way to go about their existence is from those that aren't here now.

Most tend to think they are progressing from their forefathers or ancestors ways of thinking, but in fact remain stagnate, as if their forefathers may have a better understanding as to how 'You' should live in the present, when they haven't walked this Earth for **50**, maybe a **100**, or even thousands of years.

We are all products of our environment, if you took someone who grew up in Wichita Kansas, more than likely they may be of a **Christian** faith. Imagine that same person was born and raised in Riyadh, Saudi Arabia, being of a Christian faith would be very rare. The population of the country in **Saudi Arabia** is over **19** million, and the percentage of **Muslims** that occupy the land is believed to be over **99.99%**. How likely would it be for that person from **Wichita** to still be of a Christian faith, had they been born in **Saudi Arabia**? Not likely at all.

People are victims to repetitive nature by more than their religious upbringings. You can see this repetitive nature in many facets of life, whether it be school, jobs, marriage or their relationships with people, friends or strangers. How many times have you felt burdened to do something just because it is what your parents wanted, or because it's what someone else did?

For instance, modern day society has a basic structure to life, go through years of schooling, graduate, get a job, get married and have kids. To most, this is how life should be. Why? Mostly due to what was constructed in writings and traditions from their forefathers, ancestors and leaders, hundreds and thousands of years ago. More importantly, who is to say they are right? How can people who lived thousands of years before you, who did not see the world you live in today, provide you with a **100** percent accurate outline on a way of life that would resonate to you right now at this moment?

How many times can you think of an instance when you had a disagreement with your friends about a particular situation, and you may've thought to yourself you understood the circumstances better than they could comprehend, because you were the one who was actually a part of the situation, and they were not? How many times did you take their advice, and how many times did you not? The times you didn't take their advice and it worked out in your favor, how satisfying was it that you made your own outcome? This goes beyond a disagreement with your friends. This goes with the way you view the World as well.

It is important to know this because it will give you an idea of the model others have created for you, to break. While technology has advanced at an alarming rate, many of us still live out our lives by codes of yesterday, in which some codes of yesterday may not be relevant today. For instance, just **50** years ago, it was illegal to interracially marry, that way of thought seems like a primitive concept now. Surely there are other barriers people will eventually break.

How would you have made the rules? Have you ever thought what if you were born before these people, how would you have done this? How would you have imagined life for you, what traditions, rituals or path for a successful life would you give yourself or suggest others to use? How would you write the blueprint for your own life?

It is time to stretch your thinking. It is time to leave primitive thoughts behind. It is time to catch up with the times and realize the many possibilities that are awaiting you, but first you must release yourself from this 'Box' or 'Walls' you have surrounded yourself in.

Some people are quick to think what they 'Know' right now is the only truth there is to know, as if their perspective could not be changed, no matter what is presented for them to see. Unfortunately some people do not leave a door cracked for them to enjoy being wrong, making it incapable for them to see direction. When the door is closed to new information, the only thing you see is a 'Dead End.'

People have made this mistake so many times before. The Earth being flat is one example of how what we once believed true, was indeed the furthest thing from the truth. People also once believed the sky was a solid dome, and the stars were holes in the sky, and the earth was motionless, they once believed incest maintained purity of bloodlines, and disease was caused by evil spirits. People once believed the Earth was the center of the Universe, with the Sun revolving around it, and that it was just a few thousand years old. We now know all this not to be true. Most would look at people as foolish for believing this.

The **Moon** shows itself as a full circle once a month and **13** times a year, so how could people be so thoughtless as to think the Earth was flat? The answer was right there in front of their face, staring at them once a month, **13** times a year. The Sun has remained round since the dawn of time, the answer was right there, staring at them in front of their face, daily. Most of the answers that will be revealed to you in your life are answers that are already there, right in front of your face. Truly there is nothing 'New' under the Sun. You will not discover anything, you will only rediscover which already is.

There is much to remember in order to progress past certain ideals that are limiting some people. The closer you get to understanding the 'True You,' the more it will tear down principles and beliefs you think to be true. What beliefs of today will be looked at as ridiculous tomorrow? Will people one day look back on this time, and wonder how could people not believe in Aliens? Will they think it was foolish for us to think 'Man' is of sin, or for religion to have divided us the way it does now? Will we be looked at as ignorant for our combative racial histories or sexual gender issues? Will tomorrow's people look at those today as silly or naïve for having democracies or governments, or even money systems?

There is much that your mind is about to open up to. The rabbit hole is endless, and you have just cracked the door open.

CHAPTER TWO
(Language)

"Use what language you will, you can never say anything but what you are."

- Ralph Waldo Emerson -

Language: **(Introduction)**

Communication amongst one another is extremely vital for our cohabitation. In order for us to understand one another, we communicate, and we must express ourselves with clarity, and precision.

Think of how many times you had a conversation with someone and you may have felt somewhat misunderstood, due to the choice of words you may have used. Unfortunately, this scenario often happens, but for the most part, it is not the lack of a person's vocabulary that causes this, it is instead their lack of thoughtfulness with their choice of words. Frankly, there are so many words to choose from.

The words accompanied with many of the different languages can sometimes lead one to taking the easiest route possible, finding a word that can quickly give an overall assumption of their thought. This can lead to someone not understanding you exactly how you wished to be understood.

With the variety of languages in the world today, it should be clear why some people might be misunderstood. A lot of times people who may've migrated from a different part of the world find themselves having to learn a new language. Surely some of these people try to find the closest word they can think of at the moment when trying to express themselves.

The number of languages that exist in the world today may surprise you, mostly because people tend not to realize the many languages outside of their own surroundings. A **1911** version of the **Encyclopedia Britannica** first implied there were roughly **1,000** languages. Throughout the century that figure grew as experts broadened the definition of **'Language.'** Today, it is believed there are **6,500** to **7,000** distinct spoken languages in the world, with about **2,000** of those languages having fewer than **1,000** speakers. A chart below displays the Top Ten **'Most Widely Spoken Languages'** in the world today:

Language	Number of speakers
Chinese (Mandarin)	880 - 1,213 million
Arabic	205 - 425 million
English	315 - 380 million
Spanish	325 - 329 million
Hindi	182 - 185 million
Bengali	180 - 181 million
Portuguese	175 - 178 million
Russian	144 - 146 million
Japanese	122 - 130 million
German	90 - 95 million
Courtesy of Various sources	

Language: (Origins of Speech)

With the many different languages, there is something more important than words, it is your expression, your tone. Your tone sets the mood of the conversation. You can say the most polite thing to someone, but if you do it in a negative connotation, then it will not be received to match the definition of those words, therefore it is not so much the words, but the feeling behind the words that helps someone understand you, the 'Sound' or the 'Tone' of your voice.

Spoken language requires the development of the vocal tract used for speech production, and the reasoning abilities essential to understand and produce linguistic utterances. The key feature of human language is the capability to ask questions. Long before children start using syntactic structures, they are able to ask questions using intonation at the babbling period of their development. Even though babies require their native language from their own social environment, all languages of the world use similar 'Question intonation' for **Yes/No** questions.

One of the most important abilities language users have is **High-Level Reference**. High-Level Reference allows us the ability to refer to a state of being that is not in the environment of the Speaker. This ability is often related to a **'Theory of Mind,'** or an awareness of the other (Person) as a being like the self (You) with individual wants and intentions. According to **Noam Chomsky**, there are six main facets of this High-Level Reference system:

- Theory of mind
- Capacity to acquire nonlinguistic conceptual representations
- Referential vocal signals
- Imitation as a rational, intentional system
- Voluntary control over signal production as evidence of intentional communication
- Number representation

There is some agreement within the scientific field that a 'Theory of Mind' is necessary for humans to have language use. Many primates show some tendencies toward a 'Theory of Mind,' but not a full one, like humans have. The development of a full 'Theory of Mind' in humans was necessary to have full use of spoken language.

Some scholars believe the development of **Proto-Language** (Primitive language systems) developed with the **Homo Habilis**, while others concede that the development of primitive symbolic communication came with the **Homo Erectus**, or the **Homo Heidelbergensis**, all before the expansion of proper language with Homo Sapiens less than **100,000** years ago.

Scholars believe **3.5** million years ago features of **Bipedalism** (The condition of having two feet or of using only two feet for locomotion), which developed in

Australopithecines would have brought changes to the human skull, allowing for a more L-shaped vocal tract. The **Larynx**, a structure unique to the human vocal tract, is vital to the development of speech and language. The shape of the tract and a Larynx positioned relatively low in the neck are needed conditions for many of the sounds humans make, mainly vowels. Other scholars contend that based on the position of the **Larynx**, not even **Neanderthals** had the anatomy required to produce the full range of sounds modern humans make today.

Neanderthals may have physically been able to speak, but paleoanthropologist **Richard G. Klein** doubted they possessed a fully modern language. Klein argues the Neanderthal brain may not have developed the level of complexity necessary for modern speech, even if the physical apparatus for speech was well evolved.

The most important step in the evolution of language was the progression from primitive, pidgin-like communication to a creole-like language with all the grammar and syntax of modern languages. Some scholars believe this step could have only been obtained with some biological change to the human brain. It has been proposed that a gene called **FOXP2** may have endured a mutation allowing humans to communicate verbally. Recent genetic studies have shown that **Neanderthals** shared the same **FOXP2** allele with **Homo Sapiens**, however, this does not imply a unique mutation to Homo Sapiens, instead it insinuates this genetic change precedes the **Neanderthal /Homo Sapiens** split. There is a debate as to whether language developed steadily over the years or whether it suddenly appeared.

Writing brought a measure of validation to human knowledge. Around **5000** years ago, the speed of technology intensified due to the development of writing. Symbols in which later became words made effective communication possible. Writing is believed to have first been invented in **Sumer** or **Ancient Egypt**, and was primarily used for accounting, then later to record their histories.

Writing was a major part to sustaining and expanding organized religion. In primitive civilizations, religious ideas were passed through oral tradition mostly articulated by Shamans, and remained limited to the collective whole of that culture's inhabitants. With the emergence of writing, information that was hard to remember could then easily be reserved in sacred texts, which were maintained by a select group, or clergy.

Language: (Words & Terms)

If you wish to see beyond the curtain, there are clues all around that exist. Some of those clues come in the form of language. For centuries man has hidden clues and codes in their language, mostly so the particular parties involved could freely communicate amongst themselves, and to do so without the worry of persecution.

Many scholars throughout the years have revealed many underlined messages in coded language, mostly deciphering the text with calculations of word patterns. While most coded messages rely on a pattern of a form of more than one word, in turn focusing on the word itself can reveal so many doors into a world of new mystery.

For example, the English language, which is very much like the food, 'Gumbo,' as far as it having a mixture of a lot of different influences throughout the languages of the world, has hints and clues written all over it. **English** originates from **Anglo-Frisian** dialects in a **West Germanic** language. While the English language once had an extensive grammar structure similar to Latin, Icelandic and Modern German, the introduction of Christianity added another surge of Latin and Greek words. English spelling is variable, so the chances of mispronouncing a word are high. For instance, in the common phrase as 'Tomato,' some pronounce it *'Toh-May-Toh'*, while others say *'Toh-Mah-Toh.'* The English language is still continuing to grow, due to new industrial inventions and the language constantly adopting foreign words from different countries that may start off being used as 'Slang,' in its English context.

While English shows roots in many other languages, the words also spell out words and meanings all into themselves. There are many double meanings, or words inside the words. The list could go on, but several examples are shown below:

- **Good / God**

    Remove the letter 'O' out of '**Good**' and it leaves '**God**.' God is in Good.

- **Devil / Evil**

    Remove the first letter '**D**' from '**Devil**' and you have evil. Evil is in the Devil.

- **Universe / U-N-I-Verse**

    The '**U**' in '**Universe**' represents, '**You**' or '**Them**.' The '**N**,' represent '**And**' or '**Both**' and the '**I**' represent the '**Self**,' while the '**Verse**,' represents the experience both will entail.

- **History / His Story**

    Part '**History**', and add an '**S**,' it becomes '**His Story**.' History has mostly been taken into account by the ruling civilization of that time, therefor, history becoming 'His Story.'

- **Justice / Just Us**

    Pronouncing the word '**Justice**,' sounds similar to saying '**Just Us**.' Many in today's world have felt like it is just them against a corporate establishment, or oppressive government.

- **Realize / Real Lies / Real Eyes**

    Separate the word 'Realize,' with, '**Real**,' being at the forefront, one can then hear the sounds of '**Lies**' or '**Eyes**,' coming afterwards. When you 'Realize,' truth, the 'Eyes' can see pass the 'Lies.'

- **Santa / Satan**

    Rearrange the letter '**N**,' to the end of '**Santa**,' and it becomes '**Satan**.' Take the sound of the last name of Santa, '**Claus**,' and it becomes '**Satan Clause**.'

- **Alone / All One**
  > Separate the word, add an 'L,' and it becomes '**All One**.' Many theologies that we are 'All' connected as 'One.' If you are 'All One' then surely you are really just 'Alone.'

This word 'Alone' or 'All One' may begin to have a more significant meaning to you once reading further. Also, do not jump out of your seats, but analyzing the word 'Santa,' for its double meaning of 'Satan,' does not necessarily mean you need to stop celebrating Christmas or holidays, it means that you need to have a better understanding of the words you use, and why you use them.

These types of words are hints, clues, signals to remind you, to reawake you, make you think, make you question. There is no better reminder than to put it right in front of you, for you to use every day, with our words. Our words are powerful. Use them carefully, and wisely. They not only have the power to, but they will bring into your life the exact essence in which you use them.

Another double meaning by an unknown author can sum it up best, quoted, *"No God, no peace. Know God, know peace."*

Language: (Creating Language)

For the most part, a 'New Language' is created by those that take the Original Language, and use it as a foundation to build on an easier communication amongst themselves. For example, Mexicans, while they speak the same language as Spaniards, there are still some drastic differences in the words. Some Spaniards have thought the way Mexicans use the Spanish language to seem broken, or illiterate. At the time of this transformation, most Mexicans were ridiculed for the use of the language, now it has become more commonplace.

It is also important to realize that the foundations of new languages are being created every day. Many are being ridiculed for what people believe is their misuse of language, but again, it will become commonplace. What some call slang, could in turn be the root to a whole new language. It is the point which progresses from randomly using new words, and into communicating strictly by these new words, that makes it a new language. If these words remain in context of the original language when being used, then it is more commonly referred to as slang. Slang should not be looked upon negatively, slang has the potential to be the next creation of communication.

We are creating our own language, whether we realize it or not. Surely some of your friends may have certain 'Codes' or words that mean something more to the parties involved than it may to others who are unaware of their terminology. Many take joy in having their own dialogue with a friend, sometimes they refer to it as, 'Their own Language.' They are correct in all the senses of the word.

Quite frankly creating a new language is simple, it's as simple as not conforming to the ideas of the founding language. This can mean taking words from a language and manipulating it into new words, or creating new words all together, with no relation to a language before it. Words are simply a choice of what we think it to mean.

Who says something is the color '**Blue**?' Why Blue? Why can't someone refer to that same color as being '**Dushable**,' or whatever made-up word you think it should be called? The only reason is because someone else has told you to call that particular color 'Blue.' Words can truly mean anything you want them to. It is the sound or tone one has when pronouncing that word which is the most important attribute for making someone understand its definition.

CHAPTER THREE
(The Cosmos)

"The universe is a pretty big place. If it's just us, seems like an awful waste of space."

- Carl Sagan -

The Cosmos: (Introduction)

    To fully comprehend who you are, you need 'Others' in order for your personality, needs, wants, desires and gestures to take course. Without others around you in your life, you could not truly know who you are. If you were the only person that existed, you would not know how you would react to love, pain, joy, grief, anger or any emotion that comes to you. You would not know who you are without an outlet for these emotions to take place, without others to receive and react to those feelings and actions. You are the **'Relationship'** you have with others, this is what defines your personality. Without others, you cannot act, or react. You 'Need' others in order for you to 'Know' who you are.

    The same thing can be said of the **Universe**, the **Stars**, the **Sun** and the **Planets**. To fully understand what you are capable of, it is best to understand everything around you. The more you understand your surroundings, the more you understand you. Surely, your surroundings are more than the neighborhood you grew up in, the school you went to, the job you have, the places you go to relax or travel. Surely your surroundings reach to the Stars and Sun above you. You must have relationships with them just as you do everything else. Something so far away, nevertheless is as close to you as your eyelashes.

    From the beginning of time, man has wondered about the unknowns in **Outer Space**. From the drawings of the Stars on ancient cave walls, to explorations on the Moon, man has tried to explain and search for 'What else is out there?'

With the spread of Christianity throughout the West, the **Ptolemaic System** (Earth is at the center of the Universe) became widely accepted. Eventually this concept started cause for debate when **Nicolaus Copernicus** developed a mathematically predictive **Heliocentric System**, a system based on the Sun being at the center of the Solar System. This gradually led to his **17th Century** successors, **Galileo Galilei**, **Johannes Kepler** and **Isaac Newton**, being inspired by his theory, and expanded concepts that the **Earth** moves around the **Sun**, and the other **Planets** are governed by the same physical laws that governs our **Earth**. **Galilei**, an Italian Astronomer who played a major role in the **Scientific Revolution**, made extraordinary advancements for his time when he made improvements on the telescope, which was first invented by a German spectacle maker, **Hans Lipperhey**, in **1608**. **Galilei** is thought to be the first to use the telescope for astronomy purposes, in which his achievements helped solidify astronomical observations in support for **Copernican** (The belief that the earth rotates daily on its axis and the planets revolve in an orbit around the Sun).

For thousands of years, humanity did not recognize the existence of the Solar System. The invention of the telescope and progress into new inventions and more efficient telescopes has discovered further planets and moons in other solar systems. Unmanned space shuttles have landed on planets such as **Mars** and discovered mountains and craters and ice caps.

What will they find next?

The Cosmos: (The Universe)

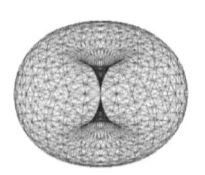

The word **Universe** comes from the Old French word **Univers**, which is derived from the Latin word **Universum**. The Latin word stems from the poetic contraction **Unvorsum**, first used by **Lucretius**, in his book 'De Rerum Natura' (On the Nature of Things). The **Universe** is defined as the totality of everything that exists, including **Space**, **Time**, **Matter**, **Energy**, **Planets**, Stars, **Galaxies**, **Intergalactic**

Space, and beyond. It is believed the Universe has been governed by the same physical laws and constants throughout most of its history.

The **Big Bang**, which is the most common scientific model of the Universe, is the theory that the Universe expanded from an extremely hot, dense phase called the **Planck Epoch**, in which all the matter and energy of the Universe was concentrated. The Universe has been expanding ever since to its present form, and is still continuing to expand. Recent observations suggest this expansion is increasing, and going faster because of **Dark Energy**, which is a hypothetical form of energy that is believed to accelerate the expansion of the Universe. Most of the matter in the Universe may be in a form that is not detectable by present day inventions, therefore it is not accounted for in the present models of the Universe, this is called **Dark Matter**. The properties of Dark Energy and Dark Matter are mostly unknown. What is thought to be Dark Matter, gravitates as **Ordinary Matter** and works to slow down the expansion of the Universe, caused by Dark Energy.

The age of the Universe is believed to be between **13** to **15** billion years. The region visible from Earth, which is known as the '**Observable Universe**,' has a diameter of at least **93** billion light-years. According to general relativity, space expands faster than the speed of light. Since we are not currently able to observe space beyond the limits of light, it is uncertain whether the Universe is finite or infinite, although common belief is that it is infinite and growing.

The massiveness of our Universe can be overwhelming at times. **1** light-year is roughly the distance of **6** trillion miles. To begin to understand how long a light-year is, it is best to explain it on a smaller level. If you were standing on the moon and decided to flash a light, it would take around **5** seconds for it to become able to be seen by someone on Earth. Basically it would take **5** seconds for that light to travel **238, 854** miles, the average distance between the Earth and the Moon.

Our **Galaxy**, the **Milky Way**, is roughly 100,000 light-years in diameter, and holds well over **100** billion Stars. It is not known how many Solar Systems (Planets that orbit around a Sun) exist in the Universe, but our nearest sister galaxy, the **Andromeda Galaxy**, is located roughly **2.5** million light-years away. There are believed to be more than **100** billion Galaxies in the **Observable Universe**. This estimate would imply there are around **Sextillion** Stars in the Observable Universe; which is a number that looks like **6,000,000,000,000,000,000,000**, although a **2010** study by astronomers resulted in a much larger figure of **300** Sextillion (3×10^{23}). The diameter of a common galaxy is 30,000 light-years, while the typical distance between two neighboring Galaxies is 3 million light-years.

Recently, the **WMAP** (Wilkinson Microwave Anisotropy Probe) seven year analysis gave an estimate of the Mass-Energy of the Universe, which appears to consist of **72**% Dark Energy, **23**% Dark Matter and **4.6**% Ordinary Matter (Atoms).

The Universe seems to have a smooth space-time continuum, consisting of three spatial dimensions and one temporal dimension, **Time**. Space is observed to be nearly flat, close to zero curvature, this leading many scientists to believe that the Universe is flat. Even with many of their educated theories, this way of thinking is reminiscent of those in the days of **Christopher Columbus** when people thought the Earth was flat, because that is all they could see. The sole reason some Scientist think the Universe is flat, is because their telescopes aren't designed to see around the curve. Meaning, the Universe is so large, we can't see that it curves, just like you can't see the Earth's curves with human eyes while standing on its surface. It only looks flat, because it is so big.

To imagine the shape of the Universe, first you need to recognize the objects that reside in it. The Stars and planets that inhabit the Universe are of circular formations, shape-like spheres, with a hollow core. This observation should lead one to seeing that the Universe should reflect what it consists of, meaning it should also resemble something of a circular formation. It is believed the Stars and planets have a hollow core, thus leading one to think the Universe may have this same feature, a hollow core. This would conclude the Universe to resembling something of a donut, in geometry this would be called a '**Torus**.'

In **1277** Bishop **Étienne Tempier** of Paris, declared, "God could create as many Universes as he saw fit." There are also various **Multiverse** theories, in which physicists have suggested the Universe is one of many Universes that exist amongst each other. Some physicists propose that this Universe is but one of a set of many disconnected Universes, collectively making up the Multiverse. Multiverse theories range in concepts such as Alternate Planes of consciousness and Simulated Realities.

In **1854**, translated from original German, **Bernhard Riemann** said, "Space has no boundary that is empirically more certain than any external observation. However, that does not imply that space is infinite."

While the Universe consists of many gases and dust, there are a few substantial to everything here, one being **Stardust**. Stardust is refractory dust grains that condensed from cooling ejected gases from individual **Presolar Stars**. Many different types of Stardust have been identified by laboratory measurements, with each Stardust grain existing before the Earth was formed.

Stardust is less than **0.1%** of the mass of total interstellar solids, and is but a modest fraction of the condensed **Cosmic Dust**. Cosmic Dust is a type of dust made-up of particles in space, which are a few molecules to **0.1** mm in size. In our own Solar System, interplanetary dust causes the **Zodiacal Light**, which is a faint, roughly triangular, whitish glow seen in the night sky that extends up from the vicinity of the Sun along the ecliptic or zodiac.

All elements with an atomic number higher than helium are believed to be formed in the core of Stars through stellar nucleosynthesis and supernova nucleosynthesis events, therefore, all elements that exist can be considered a form of 'Cosmic Dust,' this includes the Sun, our planets, and our bodies. Our bodies consist of the same fabric and material makes-up of the Sun, Stardust. Your bodies are nothing more than the dust from the Sun.

The Cosmos: (Astrology)

A **Constellation** is a group of Stars or celestial bodies, unequal in size, that form a pattern or image in the sky. In **1922**, **Henry Norris Russell** assisted the **IAU** (International Astronomical Union) in dividing the celestial bodies into **88** official Constellations, in the Observable Universe. **12** of these Constellations are drawn from Star to Star to make the figures in the **12 Zodiac Signs**.

Astrology is the study of the movements of our zodiac signs, and how their positions influence human affairs. The central principle of astrology is the relationship with the cosmos. The individual, viewed as a single organism, has a connection with certain Constellations, which in turn affect their behavior and feelings, due to the time of their birth. Through cycles of change that are observed in Outer Space, the zodiac signs are reflective to the course of our Day, as well as our characteristics.

The study of Astrology has been around for thousands of years, evidence of this appears as early as **25,000** years ago, with lunar cycles being marked on cave walls. From the dawn of written language, man shows records that it has made attempts to measure, note, predict and record seasonal changes with an astronomical cycle. Since, there has grown to be many different philosophies about our Cosmos and the zodiac.

The tropical zodiac began its development around **700 BCE** (Before Common Era) as **Calendrical Calculations** to align to the **Equinoxes** and **Solstices**. An **Equinox** occurs twice a year, when the tilt of the Earth's axis is inclined neither away, nor towards the Sun, in **Spring** and **Autumn**. A **Solstice** is when the Sun is at its greatest distance from the celestial equator, which is twice a year, in **Summer** and **Winter**. The full circle of the zodiac is divided from **360°** of celestial longitude, and then subdivided into twelve equal **Astrological Signs** of **30°**, which roughly corresponds with the ancient year's division into the modern calendar, of **12 Months**.

Historically the symbolism attached to each zodiac sign is reflective of the seasonal changes that occur in the '**Northern Hemisphere.**' Its measurement begins from the **Vernal Equinox**, when the **Sun**'s path crosses the **Earth**'s equator in March of each year, which in turn determines the first day of **Spring** in the Northern Hemisphere, therefore in Western Astrology the order of the zodiac begins with **Aries**, and is followed in order by **Taurus**, **Gemini**, **Cancer**, **Leo**, **Virgo**, **Libra**, **Scorpio**, **Sagittarius**, **Capricorn**, **Aquarius** and **Pisces**. These **Astrological Signs** represent twelve equal divisions or segments of the zodiac, which are then placed into categories of the '**Four Elements**,' which are **Fire**, **Air**, **Earth** and **Water**.

Empedocles, a 5th **Century BCE** Greek philosopher, explained the nature of the Universe as an interaction of two opposing principles called **Love** and **Strife** manipulating the **Four Elements**. He stated that each of these elements are all equal, of the same age, rules its own province and possesses its own individual character. Different mixtures of these elements produced the different natures of things.

These Four Elements have also been taken into account with Astrology. **Fire** and **Air** signs are considered **Positive**, **Extrovert** and **Masculine** Signs, while **Earth** and **Water** are considered **Negative**, **Introvert** and **Feminine** Signs. A listing of each zodiac sign's selected Element is as follows:

- **Fire Signs** (Aries, Leo, and Sagittarius)
- **Air Signs** (Gemini, Libra, and Aquarius)
- **Earth Signs** (Taurus, Virgo, and Capricorn)
- **Water Signs** (Cancer, Scorpio, and Pisces)

The **Sun** and **Moon** are characterized as planets in Astrology. The 'Seven Traditional' planets comprise of the Sun and Moon along with **Mercury**, **Venus**, **Mars**, **Jupiter**, and **Saturn**. In **Traditional Western Astrology**, each Sign is ruled by one of the seven visible planets. Traditional Astrology also maintains references to **Pluto**, **Uranus** and **Neptune** as being an astrological planet as well.

Various approaches to measuring and decoding the sky are used by differing systems of astrology, though the traditional names and symbols of the zodiac remain consistent. While all Signs are ruled by one at least one planet, there are a few which are ruled by two.

There is a drastic misunderstanding of astrology for some. Most people, unfamiliar with the science, only know of their 'Birth Sign,' which if one was born on **February 2nd**, they would be an **Aquarius**, and as astrology teaches, an Aquarius represents the traits of 'Who they Are.' This is where they fail to understand the depths of astrology.

The **Sun Sign**, which represents your 'Individuality' or 'How you think,' is the sign associated to you according to the day in the twelve astrological periods you are born. For instance, if you were born in the time of a **Libra**, then you would have the traits of someone that 'Thinks' like a Libra. The **Moon Sign**, which represents your 'Personality' or 'How you feel,' is assigned to you according to where the Moon lies in your birth chart during that year. If you had the Moon of a **Leo**, you would 'Feel' like a Leo. The **Rising Sign**, which represents 'How you are perceived,' and is determined by the time of your birth, does not represent your personality so much as it does how others view you, it is more so how you come across to people. If you had the Rising Sign of a **Taurus**, people may think you are a Taurus when they meet you, even though you may really be a Libra. Astrology goes deeper in describing many more character subjects and their attributes, but this is a basic understanding of its depth. The table below shows the zodiac names, symbols and time period, for Traditional Western Astrology:

Sign	Element	Planet	Period
Aries	Fire	Mars	**March 21 - April 20**
Taurus	Earth	Venus	**April 21 - May 20**
Gemini	Air	Mercury	**May 21 - June 21**
Cancer	Water	Moon	**June 22 - July 22**

Leo	Fire	Sun	July 23 - August 23
Virgo	Earth	Mercury	Aug. 24 – Sept. 22
Libra	Air	Venus	Sept. 23 – Oct. 22
Scorpio	Water	Mars / Pluto	Oct. 23 - Nov. 22
Sagittarius	Fire	Jupiter	Nov. 23 – Dec. 21
Capricorn	Earth	Saturn	Dec. 22 – Jan. 20
Aquarius	Air	Saturn / Uranus	Jan. 21 – Feb. 19
Pisces	Water	Jupiter / Neptune	Feb. 20 - March 20

All twelve signs represent twelve basic personality types and characteristic modes of expression. Their capability among one another depends based on the location of other planets to the planet their Sign is ruled by. A brief description of the Signs and their compatible Signs are listed below:

Aries:
> **Positive Attributes**:
>> Adventurous. Generally self-willed and courageous. Clever and confident. Direct. Quick to forgive and forget. Outspoken and uncomplicated.
>
> **Negative Attributes**:
>> Short-tempered, occasionally impatient. impulsiveness and quick temper can lead to potential enemies. Can strike out both mentally and physically.
>
> **Compatible Signs**:
>> Gemini, Leo, Sagittarius, Aquarius

Taurus:
> **Positive Attributes**:
>> Romantic. love for style. Warm at heart, prefers being secure in life. Trustworthy, helpful, handles finances well, despite being spendthrifts.
>
> **Negative Attributes**:

Love money, wealth, and status. Likes to be seen as one who has everything. Can be possessive about everything they have. This may translate to selfishness and greed.

Compatible Signs:

Cancer, Virgo, Capricorn, Pisces

Gemini:

Positive Attributes:

Versatile, quick-witted., spontaneous in communication. Comes across as intelligent. Love for life is evident. Life may appear to be chaotic, but this is preferred.

Negative Attributes:

Tend to worry too much on certain issues. Fail in managing their stress. Form opinions pretty quickly. Sometimes appear to look superficially at life.

Compatible Signs:

Leo, Libra, Aquarius, Aries

Cancer:

Positive Attributes:

Loving and caring, but cautious in their actions. Very protective towards loved ones. Imaginative and artistic. Though careful with money, they are generous.

Negative Attributes:

Deep emotions and fathomless longings. Varying moods. Overly emotional nature needs to be worked on. Rather than take a risk, prefer to wait and watch.

Compatible Signs:

Virgo, Scorpio, Pisces, Taurus

Leo:

Positive Attributes:

Generous and open-minded. Knack of taking everyone along. Possess a dominating nature. True leaders. Open-minded and openhanded. Honest love life.

Negative Attributes:

Egoistic and bossy. Lose temper easily. Proud and regal, fiery and determined, and a deep love for magnificence and luxury.

Compatible Signs:

Sagittarius, Aries, Gemini, Libra

Virgo:
Positive Attributes:
Intelligent, logical, and clever. Base conclusions on long thought process and deep analysis. Happy to remain in the background. Unidirectional talents. Purists.
Negative Attributes:
Overly think on any given subject. Obsessive. worrying overcritical nature can be very irritating to other signs. No sign is more critical or more demanding of itself.
Compatible Signs:
Capricorn, Taurus, Cancer, Scorpio

Libra:
Positive Attributes:
Serenity. Balanced in nature. Keep cool at all occasions. Reasonable and thoughtful. Appear aloof, but attached to loved ones. Sense of order.
Negative Attributes:
Difficult to be expressive. Influenced by others. Indecisive. Becomes surprised at the slightest hint of trouble. Can turn hard, cold.
Compatible Signs:
Gemini, Leo, Sagittarius, Aquarius

Scorpio:
Positive Attributes:
Demands respect. Passionate and magnetic. Clever and courageous. Clarity of thought and expression. Hardworking, dedicated to finishing task.
Negative Attributes:
Forcefully goes by their opinions. Possessive nature. Easily becomes jealous. Resentful, obsessive, and revengeful towards wrongdoers.
Compatible Signs:
Capricorn, Pisces, Cancer, Virgo

Sagittarius:
Positive Attributes:

Intelligent and philosophical. Blunt. Able to forgive and forget. Sense of humor. Interesting. Fun-loving in nature. Regarded as the luckiest sign of the zodiac.

Negative Attributes:

Sometimes excessive optimism can make them behave carelessly. Their moods and whims can be bothersome. Concentration is not strong point.

Compatible Signs:

Aquarius, Aries, Leo, Libra

Capricorn:

Positive Attributes:

Prudent and practical. Upfront, ambitious and vigilant. Plan ahead. Reliable, honest and hardworking. Sense of responsibility toward themselves and others.

Negative Attributes:

May come across as sadistic, orthodox and rigid.

Compatible Signs:

Taurus, Virgo, Scorpio, Pisces

Aquarius:

Positive Attributes:

Intelligent, deep, independent thinkers. Originality in thoughts. Sense of humor. Loyal, honest, helpful and compassionate. Enigmatic, sociable in large gatherings.

Negative Attributes:

Difficult to understand, and different from everyone else. Friendly, yet detached personally. Unsociable at smaller events. Play on gain of power and attention.

Compatible Signs:

Aries, Gemini, Libra, Sagittarius

Pisces:

Positive Attributes:

Sensitive, sympathetic, kind and helpful. Excellent friends. Quiet and introspective, preferring to watch. Often console Oneself in private.

Negative Attributes:

Often vague in thinking and behavior. Idealism is their true differentiator. Rarely content. Not very determined

or courageous. Gullible and easily tempted. Hard to express their feelings.
Compatible Signs:
Taurus, Cancer, Scorpio, Capricorn

Another extraordinary observation is that our Constellations are moving, meaning they are not in the same place they were thousands of years ago, when they were aligned to our daily habits and characteristics. What this means is that the Astrology Sign you think you are aligned to right now, in turn, might not be so.

The Constellations have a loose association with the signs of the Zodiac, and overall do not coincide with them. In **1930**, the **International Astronomical Union** redefined the Constellation boundaries with the path of the ecliptic (Path of the Sun) now passing through **13 Constellations**. **Ophiuchus**, which means 'Serpent-bearer,' is a large Constellation located around the celestial equator, at the bottom in between **Scorpio** and **Sagittarius**. Aligning this Sign with the other zodiacs would place it during the calendar days of **November 29th** through **December 17th**. This also would cause the other zodiacs to have a shorter duration through the calendar year, which would force some people to have a new Sun Sign, and all people to have different connections to their entire Astrology Chart, being that one affects the other.

While Ophiuchus isn't typically referred to as a zodiac, it is however recognized as an ancient Constellation. It is believed by some the ancients may have even used this Sign, which would give them **13** zodiacs for **13** Moon cycles during the calendar year. Through time, cultures may have done away with this sign so that there could be a round number of **12** zodiacs, as we have **12** months.

Astrologers have long debated the degree and depth that is determined by our relationship to these zodiac signs (Constellations). Some believe the celestial movements control destiny and fate, while others believes they only determine our disposition and potential. This will continue to remain up for debate, it is something that for the most part lies in the views of the individual.

In '**The Spirit of Man, Art and Literature**,' C. G. Jung, a **19th Century** Swiss Psychiatrist wrote, *"The fact that it is possible to reconstruct a person's character fairly accurately from the birth data shows the relative validity of astrology. It must be remembered however, that the birth data are in no way dependent on the actual astronomical constellations, but are based on an arbitrary, purely conceptual time-system...If there are any astrological diagnoses of character that are in fact correct, this is not due to the influence of the stars but to our own hypothetical time qualities. In other words, whatever is born or done at this moment in time has the quality of this moment in time."*

In other words, the Stars aren't here just for you to gaze, they reveal many things about one's self.

The Cosmos: (The Solar System)

Our **Solar System** consists of the Sun and the astronomical planets and objects gravitating in orbit around it, all of which is believed to have been formed from the collapse of a giant molecular cloud approximately **4.6** billion years ago. Of the many objects that orbit the Sun, eight relatively solitary planets orbit in an almost circular rotation, lying within a nearly flat disc called the **Ecliptic Plane**.

The Solar System is also home to planets **Mercury**, **Venus**, **Earth**, **Mars**, **Jupiter**, **Saturn**, **Uranus** and **Neptune**, as well as a number of other smaller objects. The **Asteroid Belt**, which lies between Mars and Jupiter, is composed mainly of rock and metal. Beyond Neptune's orbit lies the **Kuiper Belt**, composed mostly of ices such as water, ammonia and methane.

Beyond the outer planets consist of five individual objects, **Ceres**, **Pluto**, **Haumea**, **Makemake** and **Eris** are recognized as large enough to have been rounded by their own gravity, thus they are termed **Dwarf Planets**. Six of the planets and three of the Dwarf Planets are orbited by natural satellites, which are termed a '**Moon**.' Various other small body populations, such as **Comets**, **Centaurs** and **Interplanetary Dust**, freely travel throughout the regions of the **Solar System**.

Our Solar System is located in the **Milky Way** galaxy, a barred spiral galaxy with a diameter of about **100,000** light-years, with our Sun residing in one of the Milky Way's outer spiral arms, known as the **Orion Arm** or **Local Spur**. It is believed that the Solar System's location in the galaxy is a likely factor in the evolution of life on Earth. Some scientists hypothesized a recent supernova may have affected life in the last **35,000** years by pieces of stellar core being flung towards the Sun as radioactive dust grains and larger comet like forms.

The Sun

The Sun, which is the brightest object in the sky with an apparent magnitude of **−26.74**, lies between **25,000** and **28,000** light-years from the **Galactic Centre**. Its speed within the galaxy is about **220 kilometres** per second, and completes one rotation (One orbit of the galaxy) every **225–250** million years, which is known as the Solar System's galactic year.

The **Solar Apex**, which is the Sun's path through interstellar space, is near the constellation of **Hercules** in the direction of the current location of the star **Vega**. The plane of the ecliptic (The plane of the earth's orbit around the Sun) lies at an angle of about **60°** to the galactic plane. There are fairly a few stars within **10** light-years of the Sun, with the closest being a triple star system named **Alpha Centauri**, which is about **4.4** light-years away. **Sirius** is the largest star within **10** light-years of our Solar System. It is **8.6** light-years away, roughly twice the Sun's mass, and is orbited by a white dwarf called **Sirius B**.

The Sun accounts for about **99.86%** of the total mass of the Solar System. It is classified as a type **G2** Yellow Dwarf, with a diameter of about **1,392,000 km**, which is about **109** times that of Earth, and its mass is about 2×10^{30} kilograms, **330,000** times that of Earth. The Sun is not solid, it consists of a plasma, and rotates faster at its equator than at its poles. Astronomers once regarded our Sun as a small and insignificant star, but now believe it to be brighter than about **85%** of the stars in our galaxy, most of which are Red Dwarfs. The Sun's stellar classification based on spectral class, is **G2V**, and is designated as a **Yellow Dwarf** because of its visible radiation.

What color is the Sun? Many people may instantly answer this question as it being 'Yellow' or 'Orange' but this is not totally true, nor incorrect. The answer to the question is that it doesn't have an answer, it has an explanation. The Sun doesn't produce just one color, it produces many of colors. Following is a listing of the Sun's color scale:

Light radiated by the Sun in Nanometers			
Ultraviolet	<380nm	Yellow-Green	550-570nm
Violet	380-450nm	Yellow	570-600nm
Blue	450-500nm	Orange	600-630nm
Blue-Green	500-520nm	**Red**	630-680nm
Green	520-550nm	**Infra-Red**	>680nm

The reason the Sun appears yellow or orange is because the Sun produces light in all its visible spectrum. When we see the Sun during sunrise or sunset, it may appear yellow, orange, or red, but that is because its short blue and purple light rays are being scattered out by the Earth's atmosphere. When the Sun's differently colored wavelengths of light are combined they produce white. All forms of light and energy are part of the same phenomena, the electromagnetic spectrum. Our eyes can only detect a small amount of this energy, the portion we call 'Visible Light.

The brightest part of this spectrum or peak is at **539nm**. According to this table above, **539nm** is green, therefore the answer to what color is the Sun, can also be 'Green.' Actually the color of the Sun is green or any color that corresponds to a wavelength between **250-2500+** nanometers. The yellow 'Curve' is the Sun's radiation that has been intercepted by the Earth at the top of its atmosphere. On its way to the ground, some of the radiation is absorbed or scattered. The amount of radiation left for us to see on the ground is the red 'Curve.'

Evidence suggests the Sun is currently in the 'Prime of Life,' for a star, being that it has not yet exhausted its store of hydrogen for nuclear fusion. Even though the Sun is growing brighter, in its early history it was **70** percent brighter than it is today.

The Planets

The **'Four Inner'** planets, **Mercury**, **Venus**, **Earth** and **Mars**, also called the **'Terrestrial Planets**,**'** are primarily composed of rock and metal. The **'Four Outer'** planets, known as the **'Gas Giants**,**'** are considerably more massive than the terrestrials. The two largest planets, **Jupiter** and **Saturn**, are composed mainly of hydrogen and helium, the two outermost planets, **Uranus** and **Neptune**, are made up mostly of ices, such as water, ammonia and methane, and are more so separately referred to being called the **'Ice Giants.'** A listing of the planets and some of their attributes are as follows, the ones capable of containing organic life are noted:

Mercury

Mercury is the closest planet to the Sun and the smallest planet (Other than Pluto, which as of **2006** is now considered a dwarf planet) in the Solar System. It is **0.055** of Earth's mass. Mercury's only known geological features besides impact craters are lobed ridges or rupes, thought to have been produced by a period of contraction early in its history. It has a large iron core, and thin mantle. Mercury has no natural satellite (Moon).

Venus

Venus is the second closest planet to the Sun, and closest in size to Earth, about **0.815** of its mass. Like Earth, it has a thick silicate mantle around an iron core, and its substantial atmosphere is evidence of internal geological activity. It is the hottest planet in the Solar System with surface temperatures over **400** °C. Venus is the only planet in our Solar System that spins in the opposite direction. It has no natural satellite.

- Scientists have speculated about this planet being able to contain life, and the existence of microbes in the cloud layers above Venus's surface.

Earth

Earth is the only planet in the Solar System where life is known to exist. It is the largest and densest of the inner planets. Its liquid hydrosphere is unique among the terrestrial planets. Earth's atmosphere is radically different from other planets and contains **21%** free oxygen. It has one natural satellite, the **Moon**.

Mars

Mars is smaller than Earth, at **0.107** Earth masses. Known as the '**Red Planet**,' it's color is from the iron oxide (Rust) in its soil. Its surface is peppered with vast volcanoes and rift valleys, which suggest geological activity may have thrived up until as recently as **2** million years ago. Mars has two tiny natural satellites, **Deimos** and **Phobos**, which are thought to have been captured asteroids.

- Liquid water is thought to have existed on Mars in the past, therefore making it possible for life to exist. In July of **2008**, laboratory tests aboard NASA's **Phoenix Mars Lander** identified water in a soil sample.

Jupiter

Jupiter is **318** Earth masses, and **2.5** times the mass of all the other planets combined. It is composed largely of hydrogen and helium, and has strong internal heat that creates a number of semi-permanent features in its atmosphere, such as the **Great Red Spot**. Jupiter has **63** known satellites. **Ganymede**, which is the largest satellite in the Solar System, is larger than the planet Mercury.

- **Europa** (Moon of Jupiter) – Beneath Europa's thick ice layer contains liquid water. It is possible there are vents on the bottom of the ocean that warm the ice, making liquid beneath the layer.
- **Callisto** (Moon of Jupiter) – Same as Europa, possible underground ocean capable of

supporting microbes and simple plants, just like in Earth's hydrothermal vents.

Saturn

Saturn is similar to Jupiter, such as its atmospheric composition and magnetosphere, but is **60%** its volume. It is distinguished by its extensive ring system, which is made up of ice and rock particles. Saturn is **95** Earth masses, and is the least dense planet in the Solar System. It has **62** confirmed satellites, two of which, **Titan** and **Enceladus**, show signs of geological activity.

- **Titan** (Largest Moon of Saturn) – The only known moon with a significant atmosphere for supporting life. The **Cassini–Huygens** mission demonstrated data that showed the existence of liquid hydrocarbon lakes in the polar regions.
- **Enceladus** (Moon of Saturn) – Possible **'Under-Ice'** oceans heated by tidal effects, with geothermal activity.

Uranus

Uranus is **14** Earth masses, and is the lightest of the outer planets. Uranus orbits the Sun on its side, and its axial tilt is over ninety degrees to the ecliptic. It has a much colder core than the other gas giants, and radiates little heat. Uranus has **27** known satellites.

Neptune

Neptune is **17** Earth masses, but is slightly denser than Uranus. Neptune radiates more internal heat, but not as much as Jupiter or Saturn. Neptune has **13** known satellites. The largest, **Triton**, is geologically active, with geysers of liquid nitrogen

The Cosmos: (Extraterrestrial Life)

The word **Extraterrestrial**, defined as life that does not originate from Earth, is from the Latin words, **Extra** (Meaning 'Beyond' or 'Not of') and **Terrestris** (Meaning 'Of' or 'Belonging to Earth'). The idea of **Alien Life-forms** range from simple Bacteria-like organisms to Beings far more advanced than Humans.

Bacteria are believed to exist throughout the Universe. This thought relies on the size and consistent physical laws we are aware of through the Observable Universe. According to **Carl Sagan**, **Stephen Hawking**, and many others, it is improbable for life not to exist somewhere other than Earth. This argument is embodied in the **Copernican Principle** (Model of the Solar System centered on the Sun, with Earth and the other planets revolving around it). This principle holds there is nothing special about life on Earth.

The Church has never officially issued a position on Alien life, although some have speculated about the idea. In **1277**, **Étienne Tempier** the Bishop of Paris, declared that God could have created more than one world. It has been said **Cardinal Nicholas** of Kues speculated about Aliens on the Moon and Sun. In **2008**, an article published in the Vatican newspaper, Father **José Gabriel Funes**, director of the Vatican Observatory, said Intelligent Beings created by God could exist in Outer Space.

In **1961**, University of California, Santa Cruz astronomer and astrophysicist **Dr. Frank Drake** devised the **Drake Equation**. Drake used the equation to estimate there are approximately **10,000** planets in the Milky Way galaxy containing intelligent life with the possible capability of communicating with Earth.

As observed through the **Hubble Space Telescope**, there are at least **125** billion galaxies in the Observable Universe. It is projected at least **10**% of all Sun-Like stars have a system of planets. Even if just one out of a billion of these stars have planets supporting life, it is said that it would leave some **6,250,000,000** 'Life Supporting Planetary Systems' in the Observable Universe.

The possible existence of **Microbial Life** outside of Earth is a possibility that most scientist agree upon. In February **2005**, **NASA** scientists **Carol Stoker** and **Larry Lemke** reported they found evidence of present life on Mars. They based their claims on the methane signatures found in Mars's atmosphere, stating its resemblance to the methane production of some forms of primitive life on Earth. NASA officials soon denied their claims, while **Stoker** eventually backed off from her initial affirmations. Even though such findings are still in debate, the idea of life on Mars has grown amongst scientists. In an informal survey conducted by the European Space Agency, **75%** of the scientists reported to believe life once existed on Mars, while **25%** reported a belief that life currently exists there now.

In **2007**, scientists at the **European Southern Observatory** in La Silla, Chile, claimed to have found the first Earth like planet. The planet, known as **Gliese 581 c**, orbits its star **Gliese 581**, a Red Dwarf, which is **20.5** light-years from the Earth. It was originally thought that this planet could contain liquid water, but a computer analysis by **Werner von Bloh** and his team at Germany's Institute for Climate Impact Research, suggest carbon dioxide and methane are found in the atmosphere of **Gliese 581 c**, thus causing it to create a runaway greenhouse effect. This would in turn warm the planet well above the boiling point of water, thus reducing the hopes of finding life, nevertheless, it didn't stop scientists from looking elsewhere.

On **December 5th 2011**, **NASA**'s Kepler space telescope found a new planet, **Kepler-22b**, **600** light-years away from Earth. The planet joins a list of more than **500** planets found to orbit stars beyond our solar system. The reason why this planet is significant is because it is believed to be the most Earth-like planet found yet, according to the space agency. It circles a yellow Star similar to Earth's Sun.

The most promising thing about this planet is that it's in the so-called 'Goldilocks' zone around its host Star, the zone believed most habitable for life. Its surface temperature is estimated at an average of **72** degrees, which means liquid water, the ingredient necessary for life on Earth, may exist there as well.

Alan Boss of the Carnegie Institution for Science, wrote in an email to ABC News, saying, *"We know the star is Sun-like, and we know the orbit is Earth-like, but the size is super-Earth-like...In* *less than 20 years, we have gone from not knowing if any other planets exist in the Universe, to being able to look out at the night sky and realize that essentially any star we can see has at least one planet, and a good number of those are likely to be habitable."*

Geoff Marcy, a Professor of Astronomy at the University of California, Berkeley, and a pioneer of planet-hunting outside Earth's solar system, stated, *"This discovery shows that we Homo sapiens are straining our reach into the Universe to find planets that remind us of home…We are almost there."*

Numerous claims have been made for the existence of Extraterrestrial Life. While most scientists have dismissed the many **UFO** (Unidentified Flying Objects) sightings and Alien abduction claims, the evidence has been overwhelming.

On June **24**th **1947**, at about **3:00**pm, pilot **Kenneth Arnold** reported seeing **9** unidentified disk-shaped aircrafts flying near Mount Rainier, Washington. Arnold said the objects were shaped thin, flat, and disc-like, and moved as if they were a saucer skipping across water. Two to three days later, the term **'Flying Disc'** and **'Flying Saucer'** first appeared in newspapers. Arnold was interviewed by the **Chicago Times**, in which he was reported as saying that he didn't believe the strange contraptions were made on this planet, but hoped the devices were really the work of the U.S. Army.

Shortly afterwards, Arnold told the **TIMES** in a phone conversation, *"If our government knows anything about these devices, the people should be told at once. A lot of people out here are very much disturbed. Some think these things may be from another planet…Regardless of their origin, they apparently were traveling to some reachable destination…whoever controlled them obviously wasn't trying to hurt anyone…the discs were making turns so abruptly in rounding peaks that it would have been impossible for human pilots inside to survive the pressure."*

TIMES further added, *"He too thinks they are controlled from elsewhere, regardless of whether it's from Mars, Venus, or our own planet."*

This is just before the **Roswell UFO** incident. A month later in July **1947**, recovery of an object that crashed in Roswell,

New Mexico, has been alleged to have been an Extraterrestrial Spacecraft, with Alien occupants. Since, the incident has been the subject of intense controversy and conspiracy theories as to the true nature of this event.

Between **1948** and **1952**, the **US Air Force** investigated over **1,147** UFO sightings. While they were able to debunk many reports, their results showed **25%** remained unexplained.   In **1978**, the **United Nations** claimed between **1947** and **1978**, there were over **63,144** global reported UFO sightings. Since, that number has grown drastically. While it is extremely difficult to keep up with the exact number, today it is thought that it has grown to over **100,000,000** UFO sightings Worldwide.

CHAPTER FOUR
(Ancient Civilizations)

"A living civilization creates; a dying, builds museums."
- Martin H. Fischer -

Ancient Civilizations: (Introduction)

    The **United States of America** is roughly **230** years old. In **1776**, **Thomas Jefferson** wrote '**The Declaration of Independence**,' which declared the United States separate from England. Today, the United States is thought to be the World's Superpower, many have called this country a '**Modern Day Rome**.' Compared with the lifespan of other civilizations, it is merely an infant in years.

    Many dynasties before '**America**' have come and gone, leaving behind texts and artifacts to document their existences, some of those artifacts and monuments are so extraordinary that it has brought many in today's time to standstills when trying to explain how the people were aware of certain technology to build the things they did during an age many now look upon as primitive.

    Some '**Ancient Civilizations**' were conquered through wars or invasions, while others migrated to other regions because of their resources not being as resourceful as they once were. These ancient civilizations leave many more questions than they do answers, mainly due to their magnificent achievements with such things as monuments, artifacts and landscapes.

    To understand where you are headed, it is important to understand your past. Some ancient civilizations of Earth can reveal many secrets as to what may unfold in the future. It is important to understand **History** because of its reoccurrence in nature. Comprehending the ways of how history has repeated itself through the centuries is beneficial to anyone that wants to change or stay on course of the 'Common Way.' Decoding the past is a tool to understanding your future, it may hold the keys to the direction you are headed.

Ancient Civilizations: (Sumer)

Sumer, 'Land of the Civilized Lords' or 'Native Land,' was a civilization that existed in the historical region of Modern Day Iraq. The Sumerians referred to themselves as '**ùĝ saĝ gíg-ga**,' literally meaning 'The Black-Headed people.' The term 'Sumerian' is the common name given to the Ancient non-Semitic inhabitants of southern Mesopotamia Sumer, the **Semitic Akkadians**.

The **Sumerian Culture**, which has claims dating back as far to **6,000 BCE**, is the oldest known culture on Earth, and yet, even today we still use their same mathematical system and calendar. The first known settlement in **Southern Mesopotamia** was established at **Eridu** in **5300 BCE**, by farmers who brought with them the **Hadji Muhammed** culture.

The cities of Sumer were the first civilization to practice intensive, year-round agriculture, by perhaps **5000 BCE**, showing the use of core agricultural techniques. Examples of Sumerian technology include, the wheel, knives, drills, pottery, bows, spears, beds, cuneiform, tablets, necklaces ,bracelets, arithmetic and geometry, irrigation systems, Sumerian boats, bronze, leather, saws, chisels, hammers, braces, nails, pins, rings, hoes, axes, knives, arrowheads, swords, glue, daggers, bags, harnesses, armor, war chariots, scabbards, boots, sandals, harpoons, beer and a '**Lunisolar Calendar**,' which is a system of timekeeping that defines the beginning and length and divisions of the year. Sumer is also the site of early development of writing, progressing from a stage of proto-writing in the 4th **millennium BCE** to proper writing in the 3rd **millennium BCE**.

Sumerian civilization was divided into about a dozen independent **City-States**, which were divided by canals and boundary stones. Each was centered on a temple dedicated to the particular Patron God or Goddess of the city. The city was run by a priestly governor (**Ensi**) or by a king (**Lugal**) who was closely tied to the city's religious rites. The Sumerian City-States rose to power during the pre-historical **Ubaid** and **Uruk** periods, between **5300** and **2900 BCE**.

By the time of the start of the **Uruk Period** in **4100 BCE**, with populations of over **10,000** people, the volume of trade goods transported along the canals and rivers of Southern Mesopotamia made way for the rise of many large, stratified, temple-centered cities. The surplus of storable food created by this economy allowed the population to settle in one place instead of migrating elsewhere. This organization eventually led to the development of writing.

The **Dynastic Period** includes such legendary figures as **Enmerkar** and **Gilgamesh**, who are supposed to have reigned around **2700 BCE**. The earliest king authenticated in this period through archaeological evidence is **Enmebaragesi of Kish (26th Century BCE)**, whose name is also mentioned in the Legendary Gilgamesh Epic, which describes a 'Great Flood.' This leads to suggesting **Gilgamesh** may have actually been a historical **King of Uruk**. As the **Epic of Gilgamesh** shows, this period was linked with increased violence. Cities became walled and increased in size, as undefended villages in Southern Mesopotamia disappeared. **Gilgamesh** is credited with building the walls of **Uruk**, and it's Temple Eanna.

Sumerian Writing

Around **4000 BCE** the Sumerians developed a complex system of **Metrology**. This metrology advancement helped the creation of arithmetic, geometry, and algebra. From **2600 BCE** onward, they then began to use multiplication tables on clay tablets and dealt with geometrical exercises and division problems. The earliest traces of the Babylonian numerals date back to this period. The Sumerians were the first to use a place value numeral system, the first to find the area of a triangle and the volume of a cube.

The most important archaeological discoveries in Sumer are a large number of tablets written in **Cuneiform**. The

Sumerians' cuneiform writing system is the oldest example of writing on earth. Early Sumerian cuneiform was primarily used as a tool for record-keeping, it was not until the late **Early Dynastic Period** that religious writings first became prevalent to use as temple praise hymns, and as a form of 'Incantation' called the **Nam-šub**.

The Sumerian language is generally viewed as an isolate language in linguistics because it belongs to no known language family. There have been many unsuccessful attempts to connect Sumerian to other language groups. It is an agglutinative language, a form that units meaning, added together to create words. Most difficult are the earliest texts, much of which doesn't give the full grammatical structure of the language.

Sumerian Astronomy

The Sumerians were among the first astronomers known to exist, mapping the stars into sets of constellations, many of which survived in the zodiac and were also recognized by the **Ancient Greeks**. When the five planets were identified, they were associated with the Sun and Moon, and connected with the chief Gods of the **Hammurabi Pantheon**. A bilingual list in the British Museum arranges the sevenfold planetary group in the following order:

- The Moon (**Sin**)
- The Sun (**Shamash**)
- Jupiter (**Marduk**)
- Venus (**Ishtar**)
- Saturn (**Ninurta**)
- Mercury (**Nabu**)
- Mars (**Nergal**)

It is clear that the Sumerians were well aware of the five planets that are visible to the naked eye. An Azerbaijani-born American author by the name of **Zecharia Sitchin** hypothesized that they in turn not only knew about all the planets in our Solar System, but also planets we have yet to discover. Sitchin attributes the creation of the Ancient Sumerian culture to the **Anunnaki**, which he states was a race of Extraterrestrials from a planet beyond Neptune called **Nibiru**. Sitchin claims the Sumerians believed **Nibiru** is a remote '**12th Planet**.' He counts the **Sun**, **Moon**, and **Pluto** as planets, as well as suggesting that the **Asteroid Belt** between Mars and Jupiter is the shattered remains of an ancient planet called **Tiamat**, which he claims was destroyed by **Nibiru**, in one of its orbits through the solar system. **Sitchin** believes **Nibiru** to be in an elongated, elliptical orbit in the Earth's own Solar System, stating that Sumerian mythology reflects this view. According to Sitchin, **Nibiru** continues to orbit our Sun on a **3,600** year elongated orbit, stating that the Sumerians describe '**Planet X**' as being very far from Earth at times, roughly **30,000,000,000** miles away at its farthest point from Earth in orbit.

Sitchin further explains that **Tiamat** split in two when struck by one of **Nibiru's** moons, and then on a second pass **Nibiru** itself struck the broken fragments, and one half of **Tiamat** became the **Asteroid Belt**, while the second half was pushed into a new orbit and became today's planet **Earth**.

This should be extremely interesting to the 'Western World.' With the discovery of **Pluto** in **1930** by **Clyde Tombaugh**, and **Neptune** in 1846 by **Johann Galle**, it is hard to ignore that the Sumerians may have already known of its existence. Strong resemblances of our **Solar System**, with the planets, including **Pluto**, our **Moon**, **Tiamat** and **Nibiru** orbiting around our **Sun**, are depicted in Sumerian writing, as seen in some of the pictures below:

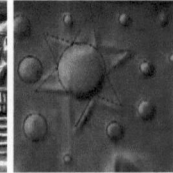

Sumerians believed the Universe consisted of a Flat Disk enclosed by a Tin Dome, they envisioned this Universe as a closed dome surrounded by a primordial saltwater sea. Underneath the Earth, which formed the base of the dome, existed an Underworld and a freshwater ocean called the **Apsu**. The God of the dome-shaped firmament was named **An**, the earth was named **Ki**. The underground world was originally believed to be an extension of **Ki**, but eventually developed into its own concept of **Kigal**. The primordial saltwater sea was named **Nammu**, and is believed to have later become known as **Tiamat** during the **Sumerian Renaissance**.

Sumerian Religion

The Sumerians originally practiced a polytheistic religion, with anthropomorphic deities representing cosmic and terrestrial forces in their world. The majority of Sumerian deities and demigods belonged to a classification called the **Anunna** (Offspring of **An**), whereas seven deities, including **Enlil** and **Inanna**, belonged to a group of '**Underworld Judges**' known as the **Anunnaki** (Offspring of **An** and **Ki**). During the Third Dynasty of **Ur**, the Sumerian pantheon included some **3600** deities. The main **Sumerian Deities** and **Demigods** are as follows:

- **An**: God of Heaven, '**Full God**'
- **Enlil**: God of air, patron deity of **Nippur**
- **Enki**: God of freshwater, male fertility, and knowledge, patron deity of **Eridu**
- **Inanna**: Goddess of sexual love, female fertility and warfare, matron deity of **Uruk**
- **Ki**: Goddess of the **Earth**
- **Nanna**: God of the moon, one of the patron deities of **Ur**
- **Ningal**: Wife of **Nanna**
- **Ninlil**: An air Goddess, wife of Enlil, one of the matron deities of **Nippur**
- **Ninurta**: God of war, agriculture, one of the Sumerian wind gods, patron deity of **Girsu**
- **Utu**: God of the Sun at the **E'barbara** temple of **Sippar**

Gods like **Enki** and **Inanna** were assigned their rank, power and knowledge from **An**, the Heaven Deity, or **Enlil**,

Head of the Sumerian Pantheon. The primordial union of An and Ki produced Enlil, who became leader of the Sumerian Pantheon. After the other Gods banished Enlil from **Dilmun** (The Home of the Gods) for raping **Ninlil**, she had a child, **Nanna** (God of the Moon). Nanna and **Ningal** gave birth to **Inanna** and to **Utu** (God of the Sun).

There was no organized set of Gods, each city-state had its own patrons, temples, and priest-kings. During the middle of the 3rd **millennium BCE**, Sumerian deities became more anthropocentric, which regarded humankind as the central or the most important element of existence, whereas the Gods became more like '**Nature Gods**' transformed into '**City Gods.**' According to Sumerian mythology, the Gods originally created humans for their servants, but freed them when they became too much to manage.

The Sumerians were eventually absorbed into the Akkadian (**Assyro-Babylonian**) population. Classical Sumer ends with the rise of the Akkadian Empire in the **23rd Century BCE**. Sumerian deities developed Akkadian counterparts, and some remained virtually the same until later Babylonian and Assyrian rule. The Sumerian God **An**, developed the Akkadian counterpart **Anu**, and the Sumerian God **Enki** became **Ea**.

Ancient Civilizations: (Egypt)

Ancient Egypt, which was formerly known as **Kemet** (Black Land), referring to the fertile black soils of the Nile flood plains or the 'Red Land' of the desert, was an Ancient Civilization of **Eastern North Africa**, concentrated along the lower reaches of the **Nile River** in what is now the modern country of Egypt.

By about **5500 BCE**, small tribes living in the Nile valley had come to develop into a series of cultures demonstrating a firm control of agriculture, with such things as their pottery, personal items, bracelets, and beads. The largest of these early cultures in **Upper Egypt**, the **Badari**, was known for its quality of ceramics, stone tools and its use of copper. In **Southern Egypt**, the **Naqada** culture began to expand along the Nile by about **4000 BCE**. Over a period of about **1,000** years, the Naqada culture developed from a few small farming communities into a powerful civilization whose leaders were completely in control of the people and the resources of the Nile valley.

Egyptian civilization merged around **3150 BCE** with the political unification of **Upper** and **Lower Egypt** under the first Pharaoh, **Narmer** (Sometimes called **Menes**). The history of Ancient Egypt occurred in a series of stable Kingdoms, the **Old Kingdom** of the **Early Bronze Age**, the **Middle Kingdom** of the **Middle Bronze Age** and the **New Kingdom** of the **Late Bronze Age**. **Egypt** reached the pinnacle of its power in the **New Kingdom**, during the eleventh pharaoh that took the name of **Ramesses**. It then entered a period of slow decline, in which it was conquered by a succession of foreigners. 'Periods' in Egypt are outlined below, the dates given are suggestions rather than fact, as much about this time is at debate:

Predynastic Period – (6000-3110 BCE)
(**Dynasty 0**) Egyptian society began to grow and advance rapidly toward refined civilization shortly after **3600 BCE**. Time of the first hieroglyphs, graphical narratives on palettes, and royal cemeteries. Notable Rulers: **Scorpion I, King Scorpion** or possibly **Narmer**, whom many consider the last king of this period.

Early Dynastic Period – (3110-2686 BCE)
(**Dynasty I & II**) The unification of **Upper** and **Lower Egypt**. During this time, it included civil war, and the center of power moved to **Memphis** (Capital). Notable Rulers: **Menes, Djer, Den, Hotepsekhemwy, Raneb, Nynetjer, Senedj**

Old Kingdom – (2686-2181 BCE)
(**Dynasty III-VI**) One of the most magnificent times for the development of Egyptian art. Known as the age of the 'Great Pyramids,' this was a time of internal security and prosperity. Notable Rulers: **Netjerikhet, Qahedjet,**

Sneferu, Khufu, Khafre, Menkaure, Djedkare Isesi, Unas, Teti, Pepi I, Pepi II

1st Intermediate Period – (2181-2055 BCE)

(Dynasty VII-X) Egypt divided politically between two competing power bases, one in **Heracleopolis** of Lower Egypt, and the other at Thebes in Upper Egypt. It is believed many statues and temples were stolen and destroyed as a result of political chaos, during this period. Notable Rulers: Little is known of the line of kings during this time. **Wakhare Khety I, Merykare I,**

Middle Kingdom – (2055-1650 BCE)

(Dynasty XI-XIV) **While** this was an era of chaos and disorder, the reunification of Egypt was established, along with the conquest of Nubia. The funerary cult of **Osiris** rose as the dominate religion in Egypt during this time. Notable Rulers: **Mentuhotep I, II, III, IV, Intef I, II, III, Amenemhet I, II, III, IV, Sesostris I, II, III, Queen Sobekneferu**

2nd Intermediate Period - (1650-1550 BCE)

(Dynasty XV-XVII) Egypt fell to disarray a second time. This period is best known for when the Hyksos (An Asiatic people who overtook the eastern Nile Delta) came to reign. They introduced new tools of warfare, such as the composite bow and the horse-drawn chariot. Notable Rulers: The **Hyksos** kings, **Sakir-Har, Khyan, Apophis, Khamudi**

New Kingdom – (1550-1064 BCE)

(Dynasty XVIII-XX) This period is best known for its military conquests in Canaan, and the eventually decline of the New Kingdom, with the eleventh pharaoh that took the name of Ramesses. Notable Rulers: **Amenhotep I, II, III, IV, Thutmose I, II, III, IV, Tutankhamen Seti I, II, Ramesses I, II, III, IV, V, VI, VII, VIII, IX, X, XI**

3rd Intermediate Period – (1070-664 BCE)

(Dynasty XXI-XXV) This period is characterized by the country's fracturing kingship. Egypt became divided with **Amun** rule in **Thebes** and **Pharaohs** in **Tanis**. While there were long periods of stability, there were also times of enduring instability and civil conflict. Notable Rulers: **Smendes, Psusennes I, II, Sheshonk I, Taharka.**

Late Period – (685-332 BCE)

(Dynasty XXVI-XXXI) This period marked the last of the native Egyptian rulers. There were many revolts and conquest in Egypt during this time, ending with the rule of **Alexander the Great.** The last of a once great Egyptian culture came to an end. Notable Rulers: **Psamtik, Necho, Apries, Amasis II, Cambyses II, Darius II, Nekhtnebf I, II**

Egyptian Writing

The Egyptian language is a northern **Afro-Asiatic** language closely related to the **Berber** and **Semitic** languages. It has the second longest history of any language after Sumerian. Ancient Egyptian was a synthetic language, but later it became more analytic, and into the writing form known as **Hieroglyphics.** Hieroglyphic writing dates as far back to **3200 BCE**, and is composed of some **500** symbols. A Hieroglyph can represent a word, a sound, or a silent determinative, and the same symbol can serve different purposes in different contexts. Hieroglyphs were a formal script, used on stone monuments and in tombs, and can be seen on individual works of art. Formal hieroglyphs may be read in rows or columns in either direction, though typically it is written from right to left.

Formal hieroglyphs were used in a ceremonial role until the **4th Century** towards the end of Ancient Egyptian's reign, although only a small handful of priests could still read them. As the old traditional religions were disbanded and new religions were establishments, knowledge of hieroglyphic writing was therefore mostly lost.

The **Rosetta Stone** was carved in **196 BCE**, and was responsible for enabling linguists to begin the process of hieroglyph decipherment. It is an Ancient Egyptian granodiorite stele inscribed with three languages (Greek, Demotic and Hieroglyphs), each saying the same thing. In **1799**, the Rosetta

Stone was rediscovered by a French soldier, **Pierre-Francois Bouchard**. In **1822**, after years of research by **Thomas Young** and **Jean-François Champollion**, Champollion eventually found the key to translating the Rosetta Stone, and the Egyptian hieroglyphs were then able to be deciphered. Being that the words are translated into the other languages, it made it easier for Champollion to decipher.

Egyptian Government Structure

The Pharaoh was the absolute monarch of the country, usually depicted wearing symbols of royalty and power. He wielded complete control of the land and its resources, was the supreme military commander, and head of the government. The **Vizier**, who acted as the Pharaoh's representative, was second in command of the administration. The country was divided into **42** administrative regions called **Nomes**, each governed by a **Nomarch**, who was accountable to the Vizier.

The economy was centrally organized and strictly controlled. The Ancient Egyptians did not use coinage until the **Late Period**, but they did use a type of money-barter system, with standard sacks of grain and the **Deben** (Ancient Egyptian weight unit), a weight of roughly **91** grams of copper or silver.

Egyptian society was highly stratified, and social status was vivid. Farmers made up the bulk of the population, but agricultural produce was owned directly by the state. Artists and craftsmen were of higher status than farmers, but yet were also under state control, working in the shops attached to the temples that were paid directly from the state treasury. The Ancient Egyptians sustained a rich cultural heritage with feasts and festivals accompanied by music and dance. The wealthy members of Ancient Egyptian society enjoyed hunting and boating as well.

The Ancient Egyptians placed a great value on hygiene and appearance. Most bathed in the Nile and used a form of pasty soap made from animal fat and chalk to bath themselves. Men shaved their entire bodies for cleanliness, used aromatic perfumes and ointments, and wore clothing made from simple linen sheets that were bleached white. Both men and women of the upper classes wore wigs, jewelry, and cosmetics.

Slavery was known in Ancient Egypt, but the extent and prevalence of its practice are unclear, and debatable. The Ancient Egyptians viewed men and women, including people from all social classes except slaves, as essentially equal under the law, and even the lowliest peasant was entitled to petition the Vizier and his court for redress.

Both men and women had the right to own property, marry and divorce and pursue legal disputes in court. Women such as **Hatshepsut** and **Cleopatra** even became **Pharaohs**, while others wielded power as **'Divine Wives of Amun.'** Despite these freedoms, Ancient Egyptian women did not often take official roles in the administration, serving only secondary roles in the temples. For the most part, women were not as likely to be as educated as men. Mothers were responsible for taking care of the children, while fathers provided the family's income.

Each home had a kitchen with an open roof. A grindstone for milling flour and a small oven for baking bread was also a common feature. Walls were painted white and were able to be covered with dyed linen wall hangings. Floors were covered with reed mats, while wooden stools, beds raised from the floor and individual tables were included as furniture.

Egyptian Architecture

Ancient Egypt achieved a relatively high standard of productivity and sophistication in technology, medicine and mathematics. They created their own alphabet and decimal system. The earliest attested examples of mathematical calculations that show a fully developed numeral system date to the **Predynastic Naqada Period**. Their complex use of math was greatly needed to build structures such as the **Sphinx** and the pyramids. In **1842, Karl Richard Lepsius** formed the first modern **'List of Pyramids'** in which he counted **67**. Since, many more have been discovered.

The **Pyramids of Giza**, believed to have been built around **2550 BCE** or as far as **3000 BCE**, is the oldest Egyptian Pyramid to date. Using only what they could be capable of from modern calculations, it is debated that it took an estimated **20,000** to **30,000** workers to build the pyramids, in a span over **80** years. The **Pyramids of Giza** consist of the **Great Pyramid of Giza**, the **Pyramid of Khafre** (A few hundred meters to the south-west), and the relatively modest-sized **Pyramid of Menkaure** (A few hundred meters further south-west).

All of Egypt's pyramids, except the small **Third Dynasty Pyramid** of **Zawyet el-Amwat**, are sited on the west bank of the Nile, and most are grouped together in a number of pyramid fields.

The pyramids are mostly thought to have been constructed to house the remains of the deceased pharaohs who ruled over Ancient Egypt. A portion of the Pharaoh's spirit, called the '**Ka**,' was believed to remain with his corpse. The embalmed body of the King was entombed underneath or within the pyramid to protect it. Proper care of the remains was necessary in order for the former Pharaoh to perform his new duties as 'King of the Dead.' It's theorized that the pyramid was also a storage for the various items he would need in the Afterlife.

In building the pyramids, the architects might have developed their techniques over time. They would select a site on a relatively flat area of bedrock (Not sand), which provided a stable foundation. After carefully surveying the site and laying down the first level of stones, they constructed the pyramids in horizontal levels, one on top of the other. It is not exactly known how they were made, and the debate is one of the most mysterious topics on Earth.

For the **Great Pyramid of Giza**, most of the stones for the interior seem to have been quarried to the south of the construction site. The smooth exterior of the pyramid was made of a fine grade of white limestone that was in turn quarried across the Nile. These exterior blocks had to be carefully cut, transported by river barge to Giza, and dragged up ramps to the intended construction site. Just a few exterior blocks remain in place at the bottom of the Great Pyramid. During the **Middle Ages** it is probable people may have taken the rest away for building projects in the city of Cairo.

It is also a belief that the Pyramids are a connection to the Gods.

Egyptian Religion

Even though religion affected every aspect of their culture, the Egyptians had no term for 'Religion.' Regardless, **Ancient Egyptian religion** was a complex system of polytheistic beliefs and rituals which were an integral part of Ancient Egyptian society. Their religion consisted of a wide variety of different beliefs and practices.

Formal religious practices centered on the pharaoh at the current time, although he was clearly a human being, the pharaoh was believed to be descended from the Gods. The Gods who populated this realm were linked to the Egyptian understanding of the Earth and the Universe. The pharaoh acted as the intermediary between his people and the Gods, and appeased the Gods through rituals and offerings so they could maintain order in the Universe. Individuals could interact with the Gods, alluring them for help through prayer or an act of magic. The myths about these Gods were meant to explain the origins and behavior of the forces they represented.

Another important aspect was the belief in the afterlife and funerary practices. The Egyptians went through great efforts to ensure the survival of their souls after death, by mummifying the body, providing tombs, grave goods, and offerings to preserve the bodies and spirits of the deceased.

The **'Ancient Egyptian Religion'** lasted for more than **3,000** years. The details of their religious beliefs changed over time as the importance of particular Gods rose and declined. At various different times certain Gods became preeminent over others, including the Sun God **'Ra,'** the creator God **'Amun,'** and the Mother Goddess '**Isis**.' Listed below are some of their most recognized **Egyptian deities** and **demigods**:

Name	God of	Appearance
Ra	Sun	Head of falcon and sun disk
Hathor	Music	Horns of cow and sun disk
Sekhmet	Destruction	Head of lion
Nut	Sky	Blue with golden stars
Geb	Earth	Color of plants and Nile mud
Osiris	Dead	Dressed in white with crook and flail
Seth	Desert	Animal head with long curved snout
Horus	Pharaoh	Head of hawk and crown of Egypt
Isis	Magic	Throne on head or holding baby
Thoth	Wisdom	Head of ibis
Anubis	Embalming	Head of jackal
Ma'at	Justice	Feather in her hair
Amun	Creation	Crowned with feathers
Bastet	Cats	Head of cat

The people of Ancient Egypt believed death on Earth was the start of a journey to the next world. The **Book of the Dead** is a guide to the deceased's journey in the afterlife. The first funerary texts were the **Pyramid Texts**, used in the Pyramid of **King Unas** of the **5th Dynasty**, around **2400 BCE**. These texts were written on the walls of the burial chambers within pyramids, and were exclusively used by the pharaoh. Parts of the Pyramid Texts later evolved into the Book of the Dead

The Book of the Dead is made up of a number of individual texts. Most sub-texts begin with the word '**Ro**,' which can mean mouth, speech, a chapter of a book, spell, utterance, or incantation. In the context of the Book of the Dead, it is typically translated as either '**Chapter**' or '**Spell**.' This reflects the similarity in Egyptian thought between ritual speech and magical power. There are **189** Chapters, and some **192** spells are believed to be known, though no single manuscript contains them all. They served a range of purposes. Some are intended to give the deceased mystical knowledge in the afterlife, or perhaps to identify them with the Gods. Others are to ensure that the different elements of the dead person's being were preserved and reunited, and to give the deceased control over the world around him or her. Such Spells as **26-30**, and sometimes **Spells 6** and **126** relate to the Heart, and were inscribed on scarabs.

    The Egyptians believed every human being was composed of physical and spiritual parts or facets. In addition to the body, each person had an **Ašwt** (Shadow), a *Ba* (Personality or Soul), a *Ka* (Life-Force), and a Name. The heart was considered the seat of thoughts and emotions. After death, the spiritual energy was released from the body and could move at will, but required the physical remains as a permanent home. The ultimate goal of the deceased is to rejoin their **Ka** and **Ba** and become one of the **'Blessed Dead'** living on as an **Akh**, or 'Effective One.' For this to happen, the deceased is to be judged worthy in a trial, in which the heart is weighed against a **'Feather of Truth.'** If one is deemed worthy, the deceased then continues their existence on Earth in spiritual form.

Ancient Civilizations: (Maya)

    The **Mayans** were a **Mesoamerican** civilization that existed in ancient **Maya**, which extended throughout the present-day southern Mexican states of Chiapas, Tabasco, and the Yucatán Peninsula states of **Quintana Roo**, **Campeche** and **Yucatán**. There is some dispute to when the Mayan civilization began. The most widely accepted view is that the first Mayan settlements were established around **1800 BCE** in the Soconusco region of the Pacific Coast, though discoveries of Mayan occupation at Cuello, Belize have been carbon dated to around **2600 BCE**. Writing, epigraphy, and the calendar did not originate with the Mayan, however, their civilization fully developed and perfected them.

During the **Classic Period** in **250–900 CE** (Common Era), the Mayan culture witnessed the peak of large-scale construction and urbanism. During this period the Mayans numbered in the millions, developing a city centered empire consisting of numerous independent city-states. The Mayans created a multitude of kingdoms and small empires, built monumental palaces and temples, engaged in lavish ceremonies, and developed an elaborate **Hieroglyphic Writing System**.

Mayan Writing

The first written inscription in **Mayan Hieroglyphics** dates to **250 BCE**. The Mayan hieroglyphs resemblances the **Ancient Egyptian** writing, it was a combination of phonetic symbols and logograms. It is most often classified as a **logographic** or **logosyllabic** writing system, in which syllabic signs play a significant role. In total, the script has more than **1000** different glyphs. At any one time, no more than around **500** glyphs were in use, some **200** of which had a phonetic or syllabic interpretation. It is believed the Mayan script is far more complete and complex than any other that has yet been found in the Americas. Much of the remainder of the Mayan hieroglyphics has been found on funeral pottery, most of which describes the Afterlife. Codex-style writing was usually done in black ink with red highlights, giving rise to the Aztec name for the Mayan territory as the 'Land of red and black.'

Mayan Architecture

The Mayans were master builders, yet they lacked many advanced technologies seemingly necessary for such constructions. The most notable monuments are the **Stepped Pyramids**. The palace at **Cancuén** is the largest in the Maya area, though the site interestingly lacks pyramids. Notable **Mayan Constructions** are listed below:

- **Ceremonial Platforms**: Limestone platforms, typically less than four meters in height, where public ceremonies and religious rites were performed.
- **Palaces**: Large and often highly decorated, usually sat close to the center of a city. Any exceedingly large royal palace might be referred to as an acropolis.
- **E-Groups**: Aligned according to specific astronomical events (primarily the Sun's solstices and equinoxes) and are thought to have been observatories.
- **Pyramids and Temples**: The most important religious temples sat atop the towering Mayan Pyramids, presumably as the closest place to the heavens.
- **Observatories**: The Mayan were advanced astronomers and mapped out the phases of celestial objects, including the Moon and Venus.
- **Ball Courts**: The courts for their ritual ball-game were constructed throughout the Mayan civilization.

Mayan Astronomy

The Mayans had independently developed the concept of '**Zero**' by **36 BCE**. Inscriptions show them working with sums up to the hundreds of millions and dates so large it would take several lines just to display it. They produced extremely accurate astronomical observations, their charts of the movements of the Moon and planets are equal or superior to those of any other civilization working from the 'Naked-eye observation.'

The Mayans configured constellations of Gods and places, saw the unfolding of accounts in their seasonal movements, and believed the connection of all possible worlds was in the night's sky. The night sky was considered much like a window, showing all supernatural doings.

The Mayan had measured the length of the **Solar Year** to a high degree of accuracy, far more accurate than the **Gregorian Calendar** used in Europe, which accumulates only a day's error in approximately **3257** years.

The Mayan believed in a cyclical nature of time. Their calendar, which is based around the **Mesoamerican Long Count Calendar**, begins on the date **August 11th 3114 BCE**, and ends on **December 21st 2012 CE**, roughly a **5000** year cycle. Among the many types of Mayan calendars which were maintained, the most important included a **260**-Day cycle, a **365**-Day cycle for the Solar Year, a cycle for **Lunation Periods** of the **Moon**, and a cycle for the **Synodic Period** of **Venus**.

There is some evidence to suggest the Mayan civilization may have been the only pre-telescopic civilization to demonstrate knowledge of the **Orion Nebula** as being fuzzy, not a stellar pin-point. The information that supports this comes from a folk tale that deals with the **Orion Constellation**'s area of the sky. Their traditional hearths (The floor of a fireplace) include in their middle a smudge of glowing fire that corresponds with the Orion Nebula. This is a significant clue to support the idea that the Mayan detected a diffuse area in the sky contrary to the pin points of stars, long before the telescope was invented.

Many pre-classic sites are oriented with the **Pleiades** and **Eta Draconis** (A star in the constellation Draco). The Mayans were very interested in 'Zenial Passages,' which is the time when the Sun passes directly overhead. These passages would occur twice a year equidistant from the solstice. To further represent this position of the Sun passing overhead, the Mayan had a God named **Diving God**.

The **Dresden Codex**, which contains the first forms of astronomical tables, is a pre-Columbian Mayan book in the **11th** or **12th Century** of the Yucatecan Maya in Chichén Itzá. It is believed to be a copy of an original text of some three or four hundred years earlier. This **Dresden Codex** is the oldest book written in the Americas known to historians. It appears the data in this codex is exclusively of an astronomical nature. Examination and analysis of this codex have revealed that **Venus** was the most important astronomical object to the Mayan culture, even more important to them than the **Sun**.

Mayan Religion

Much of the religious Mayan traditions are still not understood by scholars. What is known is that they believed the cosmos had three major planes, **Earth**, the **Underworld** beneath, and the **Heavens** above.

The Sun, '**Kinich Ahau**,' and an aged God, '**Itzamna**,' dominated the Mayan idea of the sky, another aged man, '**God L**,' was one of the major deities of the underworld. It has been believed that the multiple Gods signify nothing more than what they observed. Some scholars believe the Gods are said to represent a number, or an explanation of the effects observed by a combination of numbers from multiple calendars.

The rituals and ceremonies were closely associated with celestial and terrestrial cycles, which they observed and inscribed as separate calendars. The Mayan priest had the job of interpreting these cycles, examining the relation of the numbers to give outlook on past and future based prophecies, and to determine if the heavens were favorable for performing certain religious ceremonies. Philosophically, the Mayan believed knowing the past meant knowing the influences that create the present, which in turn, knowing the influences of the present can help one see the influences of the future.

It is believed the Mayan also practiced human sacrifice. In some Mayan rituals people were killed by having their arms and legs held while a priest cut the person's chest open, so that they could tear out the heart as an offering. This is depicted on ancient objects such as pictorial texts, known as codices.

Mayan Extinction

The Mayan civilization went into decline during the **8th** and **9th Centuries**, and was abandoned shortly thereafter. There is no universal accepted theory to explain this collapse, other than to notice that the cessation of monumental inscriptions and large-scale architectural constructions abruptly come to a stop. Some believe their decline was due to either overpopulation, foreign invasion, peasant revolt, the collapse of key trade routes, environmental disaster, epidemic disease or climate change.

The Spanish church and government officials destroyed Mayan texts and with them the knowledge of Mayan writing was lost. By chance, three pre-Columbian books have been preserved. These are known as the **Madrid Codex**, the **Dresden Codex** and the **Paris Codex**. A few pages survive from a fourth book, the **Grolier Codex**, whose authenticity is at times disputed, but mostly held as genuine. An excess of **10,000** texts were recovered, mostly inscribed on stone monuments, lintels, stelae (monuments fashioned by the Mayan) and ceramic pottery. The recovery and decipherment of the lost knowledge of Mayan writing has been a long and laborious process. Some elements were first deciphered in the late **19th** and early **20th Century**. By the end of the **20th Century**, scholars were able to read a majority of the Mayan texts, but recent field work continues to further bring light on its translations.

Ancient Civilizations: (Inca)

The Inca civilization was a pre-Columbian American tribe located in the **Cuzco** area (Modern-day Peru), from possibly as early as **300 BCE** to the **12th Century**. In **Quechua**, the term **Inka** (Ruler or Lord) was used to refer to the ruling class or the ruling family in the empire. The Spanish adopted the term **Inca** as an ethnic term referring to all subjects of the empire rather than the ruling class.

Under the leadership of **Manco Cápac**, they formed the small city-state of **Cuzco** (Quechua Qusqu'Qosqo), and in **1438**, they began a far-reaching expansion under the command of **Pachacuti-Cusi Yupanqui** who was the **Sapa Inca** (Paramount leader). During his reign, he and his son **Tupac Yupanqui** brought much of the Andes Mountains (Roughly modern Peru and Ecuador) under Inca control.

The Inca referred to their empire as **Tawantinsuyu**, which can be translated as **The Four Regions** or **The Four United Provinces**. There is some debate about the number of people inhabiting **Tawantinsuyu** at its peak, with estimates ranging from 4 to more than 37 million people.

The official language of the empire was **Quechua**, although hundreds of local languages and dialects of Quechua were also spoken. It is proposed the actual name of the spoken language of the Incan Empire was called **Qhapaq Runasimi**, and the Incan ruling elite spoke both **Puquina** and **Qhapaq Runasimi** (Quechua). Since the Inca Empire lacked a clear written language, the empire's main form of communication and recordings came from ceramics.

It is said those who obeyed the Inca moral code, **Ama Suwa** (Do not steal), **Ama Llulla** (Do not lie), **Ama Quella** (Do not be lazy), went on to live in the Sun's warmth while others spent their eternal days in the cold earth. The Inca also practiced cranial deformation. They achieved this by wrapping tight cloth straps around the heads of newborns in order to alter the shape of their soft skulls into a more conical form. This cranial reformation was made to distinguish social classes of the communities, with only the nobility having cranial reformation.

Incan Government Structure

The Inca Empire was a federalist system which consisted of a central government with the Inca at its head and four provinces, **Chinchay Suyu**, **Anti Suyu**, **Kunti Suyu** and **Qulla Suyu**. The four corners of these provinces met at the center, **Cusco**. Each province had a governor who oversaw local officials, who in turn supervised agriculturally productive river valleys, mines and cities. There was a separate command for both the military and religious institutions, which produced a system of a partial balance of power. The local officials were responsible for settling disputes and keeping track of family contribution through the **Inca Mit'a system**, which was a system of mandatory public service that consisted of a form of tribute to the Inca Empire, through labor.

The social structure of the Inca Empire varied from area to area, but still had the same basic structure. On top was the

Sapa Inca (Emperor), then came the Nobles (These were often the priests and relatives of past or current Emperors). Then were craftsmen and architects, they were very high on the social ladder because their skill was required by the Empire for certain buildings. Next was the working class, often farmers that were kept in their social groupings. Last were the slaves and peasants of the society.

Incan Architecture

Architecture was important to the Incas. The main example is the capital city of Cusco, the breathtaking site of **Machu Picchu**. The stone temples constructed by the Inca, used a mortar-less construction that fit together so well, even a knife cannot fit through the stonework.

Incan Religion

The Inca leadership encouraged the worship of **Inti**, the 'Sun God,' and imposed its sovereignty above other cults. The Incas considered their King, the **Sapa Inca**, to be the 'Child of the Sun.' Incan myths were an oral tradition until early Spanish colonists recorded them. The Inca also believed in reincarnation. A listing of the **Inca Deities** and **Demigods** are below:

- **Viracocha** (Also **Pachacamac**): Created all living things.
- **Apu Illapu**: Rain God, prayed to when they need rain.
- **Ayar Cachi**: Hot-tempered God, causes earthquakes.
- **Illapa**: Goddess of lightning and thunder.
- **Inti**: Sun God and patron deity of the Holy City of Cuzco.
- **Kuychi**: Rainbow God, connected with fertility.
- **Mama Kilya**: Wife of **Inti**, called Moon Mother.
- **Mama Occlo**: Wisdom to civilize the people, taught women to weave cloth, and build houses.
- **Manco Cápac**: Known for his courage and sent to earth to become first king of the Incas, taught people how to grow plants, make weapons, work together, share rescores, and worship the Gods.

- **Pachamama**: The Goddess of Earth and wife of **Viracocha**.
- **Qochamama**: Goddess of the sea.
- **Sachamama**: Mother Tree, goddess in the shape of a snake with two heads.
- **Yakumama**: Mother Water, represented as a snake, when she came to earth she transformed into a great river.

Incan Extinction

During their explorations, the Spanish arrived at the borders of the **Inca Empire** in **1528**. Later, in the **1532** Battle of Cajamarca, **169** Spanish soldiers under **Francisco Pizarro** and their native allies ambushed and captured the Emperor of the Inca Empire, **Sapa Inca Atahualpa**. It was the first step in a long campaign that took decades of fighting to claim the mightiest empire in the Americas.

Almost all of the gold and silver work of the empire was melted down by the **Conquistadors**, from Spain. It is believed the Spaniards used the **Inca Mit'a** System (Mandatory public Service) to literally work the people to death. After the fall of the Inca Empire many aspects of Inca culture were systematically destroyed.

CHAPTER FIVE
(Ancient Unknowns)

"The only thing that scares me more than space aliens is the idea that there aren't any space aliens. We can't be the best that creation has to offer. I pray we're not all there is. If so, we're in big trouble."
- Ellen DeGeneres -

Ancient Unknowns: (Introduction)

Many theorists and authors have made compelling cases for the theory of intelligent extraterrestrial beings called **Ancient Astronauts** or **Ancient Aliens**, visiting Earth to help humans progress as a species, through culture, technology, government and religion. A common claim in their hypothesis is that the deities from most, if not all religions are actually extraterrestrials, proclaiming the many mysterious and unexplainable structures around the world are evidence of their divine status.

Supporters of Ancient Astronaut theories believe humans are either descendants or creations of extraterrestrial beings from thousands of years ago. It is said that much of our human knowledge, religion, and culture came from extraterrestrial visitors in ancient times, and those Ancient Astronauts acted as a 'Mother Culture.' Ancient Astronaut proponents also believe that these travelers also built or aided humans in building many of the structures on Earth, such as the **Pyramids** in Egypt, the **Moai Stone Heads** of Easter Island, or **Stonehenge** in **Wiltshire, England**.

Advocates argue that the evidence to support Ancient Astronauts comes from gaps in historical and archaeological records. They claim the absence or incomplete explanations of historical data point to the existence of Ancient Astronauts. They claim archaeological artifacts are anachronistic or beyond the presumed technical capabilities of the historical cultures at the time, stating that modern day efforts can't even duplicate the same results, therefore, they side with such achievements to extraterrestrial technologies.

Francis Crick, the co-discoverer of the **Double Helix** structure of **DNA**, strongly believed in what he called 'Panspermia,' the concept that Earth was 'Seeded' with life, probably in the form of blue-green algae by intelligent extraterrestrial species, for the purpose of ensuring life's continuity. He believed this could have been done on any number of planets of Earth's class and climate, possibly using unmanned shuttles.

Erich von Däniken, author of '**Chariots of the Gods?**,' is a leading proponent of this theory. In the late **1960**s and early **1970**s, he gained a large audience through his book and sequels. **Von Däniken** states that certain artifacts and monuments required a more sophisticated ability in technological construction than what was available to the Ancient cultures at the time. He maintains these artifacts were constructed either directly by extraterrestrial visitors or by the humans that learned the knowledge from them.

Ancient Unknowns: (Ancient Bagdad Electric Batteries)

The **Baghdad Battery**, sometimes referred to as the **Parthian Battery**, is the common name for a number of artifacts created in Mesopotamia, between **250 BCE** and **224 CE**. Discovering the Baghdad Battery has opened up a field of theories that support civilizations such as Ancient Egypt, having the use of electricity long before **Thomas Edison** created the 'Light Bulb' in **1879**.

In **1940**, **Wilhelm König** director of the National Museum of Iraq, published a paper suggesting they may have been **Galvanic Cells**, perhaps used for electroplating gold onto silver objects. If this is so, then the artifacts would predate **Alessandro Volta**'s invention of the electrochemical cell in **1800**, by more than a thousand years.

The artifacts consist of terracotta pots approximately 5 inches tall, with a one and a half inch mouth, containing a copper cylinder made of a rolled up copper sheet, which then houses a single iron rod. At the top, the iron rod is isolated from the copper by bitumen plugs or stoppers, and both the rod and cylinder fit comfortably inside the opening of the jar, which bulges outward towards the middle. The copper cylinder is not watertight, so if the jar was filled with a liquid, this would surround the iron rod.

Some scholars believe lemon juice, grape juice, or vinegar was used as an acidic electrolyte solution to generate an electric current from the difference between the electrochemical potentials of the copper and iron electrodes. Copper and iron form an electrochemical couple, so that in the presence of any electrolyte, an electric potential will then be produced.

Wilhelm König observed a number of very fine silver objects from Ancient Iraq which were plated with very thin layers of gold, and speculated they were using these cells as electroplated batteries. This theory was tested when **Willard Gray**, an engineer at the **General Electric High Voltage Laboratory** in Pittsfield, Massachusetts, reconstructed one of these batteries and filled it with grape juice to demonstrate current production.

Ancient Unknowns: (Great Pyramid of Giza)

The **Great Pyramid of Giza** (Called the **Pyramid of Khufu** and the **Pyramid of Cheops**) is the oldest and largest of the three pyramids in the **Giza Necropolis** bordering what is now **El Giza, Egypt**. Egyptologists believe the pyramid was built as a tomb for fourth dynasty Egyptian Pharaoh **Khufu**, over approximately a **20** year period, concluding around **2560 BCE**. The Great Pyramid was the tallest man-made structure in the world for over **3,800** years, a record for the longest period of time ever held.

The Great Pyramid of Giza is the only pyramid in Egypt known to contain both ascending and descending passages. There are three known chambers inside the Great Pyramid. The **Lowest Chamber** is cut into the bedrock. The **Queen's Chamber** and **King's Chamber** are higher up within the Pyramid structure.

It is estimated that **5,500,000** tons of limestone, **500,000** tons of mortar, and **8,000** tons of granite (Imported **500** miles away from **Aswan**) were used to build the Great Pyramid. Originally, it was covered by casing stones that formed a smooth outer surface, what is seen today is the underlying structure. Some of the casing stones that once covered the structure can still be seen around the base. Many of the casing stones and inner chamber blocks of the Great Pyramid were fit together with extremely high precision. Based on measurements taken on the north eastern casing stones, the opening of the joints are only **1/50th** of an inch.

At the time of completion, the Great Pyramid was originally **480.6 ft** tall, but with the absence of its **Pyramidion** (The uppermost piece or capstone), its present height is **455.4 ft**. Each base side is **755.9 ft** long. The mass of the pyramid is estimated at **5,955,000 tons**. The base is horizontal and flat to within **0.82 inches**. As suggested by Egyptologist **W. M. Flinders Petrie**'s survey, the dimension's first completed design is estimated to have been **280** cubits high by **440** cubits long at each of the four sides of its base. The perimeter to height of **1760/280** cubits is a ratio that equates to **2π**. Many Egyptologists believe these proportions were the result of deliberate design.

Dr. Miroslav Verner, a Czech Egyptologist wrote, *"We can conclude that although the Ancient Egyptians could not precisely define the value of π, in practice they used it."*

Petrie, author of **'Pyramids and Temples of Gizeh**,' concluded, *"But these relations of areas and of circular ratio are so systematic that we should grant that they were in the builder's design."* Others have argued the Ancient Egyptians had no concept of **pi** and would not have thought to use it in their monuments.

There have been varying theories about the Great Pyramid's construction techniques. One of the more mainstream theories is that it was built by moving huge stones from a quarry, while dragging and lifting them into place. The disagreements center on the thought by which the stones were conveyed and placed, and how possible the method was. **Roger Hopkins** and **Mark Lehner** believe the stones were placed by flipping them with levers. They experimented with this technique during a **'NOVA'** pyramid building experiment. They found that they could flip stones up to about **3/4** of a ton with **4** to **5** men. While they were successful in flipping stones of at least **2½** tons with more men, they still found this was too slow to explain how the pyramids were built in such a short a time. In this case, building the Great Pyramid in **20** years would involve moving and installing almost **800** tons of stone a day. Since the Great Pyramid consists of an estimated **2.3** million blocks, completing the building in **20** years would involve placing an average of more than **12** of these blocks each hour…day and night.

Ancient Unknowns: (Stonehenge)

Stonehenge is a prehistoric monument located in the **English** county of **Wiltshire**. It is composed of earthworks surrounding a circular setting of large standing stones. It is at the center of the most dense complex of **Neolithic** and **Bronze Age** monuments in England, including several hundred burial mounds.

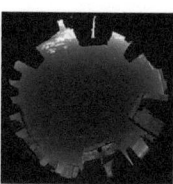

Archaeologists believe the Stone Monument was erected around **2500 BCE**. More recent theories have suggested that the first stones were not erected until **2400** to **2200 BCE**, while another suggests that bluestones (a loose term to cover the foreign stones at Stonehenge) may have been erected at the site as early as **3000 BCE**. Archaeological evidence found by the **Stonehenge Riverside Project** in **2008** indicates Stonehenge could possibly have served as a burial ground from its earliest beginnings. The dating of cremated remains found on the site indicate that deposits contain human bone material from as early as **3000 BCE**, when it is believed the initial ditch and bank were first dug, though archaeologists have found four or possibly five large **Mesolithic Postholes** (One may have been a natural tree throw), which date to around **8000 BCE**.

Many aspects of Stonehenge remain subject to debate. Stonehenge was produced by a culture that left no written records. There is no direct evidence for the construction techniques used by the Stonehenge builders. Over the years, various authors have suggested supernatural or anachronistic methods were used, declaring that the stones were impossible to move otherwise.

Proposed functions for the site have mostly centered on its usage as an astronomical observatory, or as a religious site. Professor **Geoffery Wainwright**, president of the Society of Antiquaries of London, and Professor **Timothy Darvill** of Bournemouth University have suggested Stonehenge was a place of healing, a prehistoric Lourdes. They claim that this accounts for the high number of burials in the area, and for the evidence of trauma deformity in some of the graves, but they do concede that the site was multifunctional and perhaps used for ancestor worship as well.

Even though the mystery behind Stonehenge remains, its design includes a celestial observatory function, which might have allowed predictions of an eclipse, solstice, equinox and other celestial events important to a contemporary religion.

Ancient Unknowns: (Moai of Easter Island)

Easter Island is a **Polynesian** island in the southeastern Pacific Ocean, at the southeastern most point of the Polynesian Triangle. It is famous for its **887** extant monumental statues, called **Moai**, created by the early **Rapanui** people. It is claimed to be the most remote inhabited island in the world. Estimated dates of initial settlement of Easter Island range from **300** to **1200 CE**, roughly coinciding with the arrival of the first settlers in **Hawaii**.

The name 'Easter Island' was given by the island's first recorded European visitor, Dutch explorer **Jacob Roggeveen**, who encountered it on Easter Sunday **1722**. The current Polynesian name of the island, **Rapa Nui** or 'Big Rapa' was termed after the slave raids of the early **1860s**. **Rapa Nui** refers to the island's topographic resemblance to the island of **Rapa** in the Bass Islands of the Austral Islands group. A Norwegian ethnographer and adventurer, **Thor Heyerdahl** claims that **Rapa** was the original name of Easter Island.

The history of Easter Island is rich and controversial. According to oral traditions by missionaries in the **1860s**, the island originally had a strong class system, with an **Ariki**, 'High Chief,' wielding great power over nine other clans and their respective chiefs. The High Chief was the eldest descendent through firstborn lines of the island's legendary founder, **Hotu Matu'a**.

The most noticeable element in the culture was the production of massive statues in which represented deified ancestors. It was believed that the living had a symbiotic connection with the dead, where the dead provided everything the living needed, and in turn the living through offerings provided the dead with a better place in the spirit world.

Its inhabitants have endured famines, epidemics, civil war, slave raids, colonialism, and near deforestation, populating and declining rapidly more than once. European accounts from **1722** and **1770** mention standing statues, but **Captain James Cook**, a British explorer, noted in **1774** that several Moai were lying face down, possibly having been toppled in war.

Ancient Unknowns: (Pumapunku)

Pumapunku is part of a large temple complex or monument group that is part of the **Tiwanaku Site**, near Tiwanaku, Bolivia. In **Aymara**, its name means '**The Door of the Cougar**.' Determining the age of the Pumapunku complex has been a focus of researchers since the discovery of the Tiwanaku site, but it is commandingly speculated to have been built anywhere from **440** to **600 CE**.

The Pumapunku complex consists of an **Unwalled Western Court**, a **Central Unwalled Esplanade**, a **Terraced Platform Mound** that is faced with megalithic stone, and a **Walled Eastern Court**. The largest of these stone blocks is **25.62 ft** long, **16.96 ft** wide, averages **3.5 ft** thick, and is estimated to weigh about **131** metric tons, which is roughly around **288,800** pounds. Archaeologists argue the transport of these stones was accomplished by a large labor force in **Ancient Tiwanaku**. Several theories have been proposed as to how this labor force transported the stones, although these theories remain speculative, due to the weight of the stones. Some of the more common proposals involve the use of llama skin ropes and the use of ramps and inclined planes.

In assembling the walls of Pumapunku, forming load-bearing joints without the use of mortar, each stone was finely cut to interlock with the surrounding stones so the blocks would fit together like a puzzle. One common engineering technique involves cutting the top of the lower stone at a certain angle, and placing another stone that was cut at the same angle, on top of it. The precision with which these angles have been utilized to create even joints is indicative of a highly sophisticated knowledge of stone-cutting, as well as a thorough understanding of geometry.

Much of the stonework is performed by accurately cutting rectilinear blocks of such consistency that they could be interchanged for one another while maintaining a level surface. Some believe the technologies were so far advanced for the people at the time, even today it would be hard to duplicate with all our modern day equipment. The blocks were so evenly cut, and many of the joints are so precise that not even a razor blade will fit between the stones.

Ancient Unknowns: (Machu Picchu)

Machu Picchu is a pre-Columbian **15th Century** Inca site, located **7,970** ft above sea level. Often referred to as the '**Lost City of the Incas**,' it is situated on a mountain ridge above the **Urubamba Valley** in Peru, which is **50** miles northwest of **Cusco**, the Inca capital. Most archaeologists believe that Machu Picchu was built as an estate for the Inca emperor **Pachacuti** (**1438–1472**). It was abandoned **100** years later, in **1572**, as a result of the Spanish Conquest. It is possible most of its inhabitants died from smallpox that was brought from travelers before the Spanish conquistadors arrived.

Machu Picchu was unknown to the outside world before being brought to international attention in **1911** by the

American historian **Hiram Bingham**. It was built in the classical Inca style, with polished dry-stone walls. Its three primary buildings are the **Intihuatana**, the **Temple of the Sun**, and the **Room of the Three Windows**. These are located in what is known by archaeologists as the **Sacred District** of Machu Picchu.

The space is composed of **140** structures or features, including temples, parks, and houses with thatched roofs. There are numerous water fountains and more than one hundred flights of stone steps, often completely carved from a single block of granite.

The Incas never used the wheel in any practical manner. Their use in tools demonstrates the principle was known to them, although it was not applied in their engineering. Some Inca buildings were constructed using mortar, but by Inca standards this was a quick, shoddy construction, and therefore was not used in the building of important structures. A mortar free construction was more earthquake resistant than using mortar.

The stones of the dry stone walls built by the Incas can move slightly and resettle without the walls collapsing. Inca walls had numerous design details that helped protect the structure from falling in earthquakes. The site was never known to the Spanish during their conquest, thus it remains relatively intact, free of man-made destruction.

The **Intihuatana Stone** is one of many ritual stones in South America. These stones are arranged to point directly at the Sun during the winter solstice. The Inca believed the stone held the Sun in its place along its annual path in the sky. At midday on **November 11**[th] and **January 30**[th] the Sun stands almost above the pillar, casting no shadow at all. On **June 21**[st] the stone is casting the longest shadow on its southern side, and on **December 21**[st] a much shorter shadow is casted on its northern side. Researchers believe this structure was built as an astronomic clock or calendar.

Ancient Unknowns: (Nazca Lines)

The **Nazca Lines**, located in the Nazca Desert in Southern Peru, are a series of ancient geoglyphs. The high arid plateau stretches more than **50** miles between the towns of **Nazca** and **Palpa** on the **Pampas de Jumana**. After people traveled over the area by plane in the **1930**s and saw the Nazca Lines from the air, Anthropologists then started studying them, focusing on trying to understand how they were created. Mainstream scholars believe the Nazca Lines were created by the Nazca culture between **400** and **650 CE**.

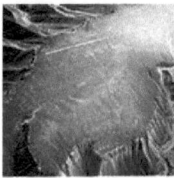

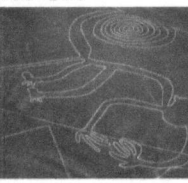

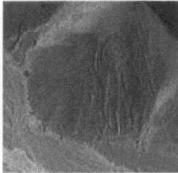

The hundreds of individual figures range in complexity from simple lines to drawings of **Hummingbirds**, **Spiders**, **Fish**, **Sharks**, **Orcas**, **Llamas**, and **Lizards**. More than **70** are zoomorphic designs of animals such as **Birds**, **Fish**, **Jaguars**, **Monkeys** or **Human Figures**. Other designs include phytomorphic (Having or represented with the attributes of a plant) shapes such as **Trees** and **Flowers**. The largest figures are over **660** ft across.

The lines are shallow designs made in the ground by removing the ubiquitous reddish pebbles, uncovering the whitish ground beneath. When the gravel is removed, it leaves a shallow trough ranging from **3.9** inches to **5.9** inches deep. In total, the earthwork is huge and complex, the area encompassing the lines is nearly **190** square miles, and the largest figures can span nearly **890** ft. The windless and extremely dry climate of the Nazca region, a temperature of around **77** °F all year round, has helped to preserve the lines.

Scholars differ in interpreting the purpose of the designs, but in general they ascribe it to religious significance. The geometric ones could indicate the flow of water or be connected to rituals to summon water. The Spiders, Birds, and

Flowers could be fertility symbols. Other possible explanations include an Irrigation Scheme or Giant Astronomical Calendars.

Theories range as to why these lines were made. One theory is that the Nazca people created them to be seen by their Gods from a sky viewpoint. In **1985**, archaeologist **Johan Reinhard** theorized that the lines and figures were part of a religious practice involving the worship of deities associated with the availability of water, which directly related to the success and productivity of crops. He interpreted the lines as sacred paths leading to places where these deities could then be worshiped.

Jim Woodman believes the Nazca Lines could not have been made without some form of manned flight to properly see the figures. Based on his study, he suggests a hot air balloon was the only possible means of flight, according to their available technology. Woodman made a hot air balloon using materials and techniques he thought may have been available to the Nazca people. Most scholars have rejected Woodman's thesis, because of the lack of any evidence of such balloons.

Many believers in Ancient Astronauts cite the Nazca lines as evidence because the figures are mostly only visibly viewed from the air. Swiss author **Erich von Däniken** suggests the Nazca Lines, along with many other complex constructions throughout the world, represent higher technological knowledge. Von Däniken believes the Nazca Lines are runways of an 'Ancient Airfield' that was used by extraterrestrials, who were mistaken by the natives to be Gods. Alleged physical evidence for his hypothesis includes the discovery of artifacts such as the '**Saqqara Bird**' in Egypt and Colombia-Ecuador, which are similar to modern planes and Gliders, and although archaeologists have interpreted these stylized representations of birds and insects, Ancient Astronaut enthusiast believe these are representations of some form of Aircraft. Furthermore, the picture of the **Giant Man** on the side of a large mountain, with his arm in the air waving to what seems to be someone in the sky, is an extremely strong piece of evidence, giving further support to Von Däniken's theory.

Ancient Unknowns: (Coral Castle)

    Coral Castle is a stone structured castle north of the city of **Homestead, Florida**, created by **Edward Leedskalnin**, a Latvian American eccentric. Considered to have been built single handedly by Leedskalnin using magnetism and/or supernatural abilities, the structure includes numerous megalithic stones (Mostly limestone formed from coral), each weighing **several tons**.

    According to the Coral Castle's own promotional material, Edward Leedskalnin left for America after he was jilted by his **16** year old fiancée **Agnes Scuffs**, just one day before their wedding in Latvia. Leedskalnin, who was a small man, barely over **5** feet and **100lbs**, spent over **28** years building **Coral Castle**, and refusing to allow anyone to view him while he worked. He did much of his work at night by lantern light. The Castle has numerous lookouts along the walls that were designed to help protect his privacy.

    Leedskalnin originally built the castle, which he named **Rock Gate Park**, in Florida City, Florida around **1923**. The castle remained in Florida City until he was badly beaten one night by hooligans looking to rob him. **Leedskalnin** then decided to move in order to protect his privacy, and in **1936** decided to take the Castle with him. He spent three years moving the Coral Castle structures **10** miles north from Florida City to its current location in Homestead, Florida.

    There are signs carved into rocks at the front gate. One sign reads 'Ring Bell Twice,' and a second sign inside the property reads 'Adm. 10c Drop Below.' Ed, as he liked to be called, would then come down from his living quarters in the second story of the Castle Tower (Close to the gate) and conduct the tour. Leedskalnin never told anyone who asked him how he built the Castle, he would merely reply, *"It's not difficult if you know how."*

The grounds of Coral Castle consist of nearly **1,100** short tons of stones in the form of walls, carvings, furniture and a castle tower. The stones are set on top of each other using their weight to keep them together, and fastened without mortar. The craftsmanship is so skillfully detailed and the stones are connected with such precision that no light passes through the joints. The **8** ft tall vertical stones that make up the perimeter wall have a uniform height.

There are many notable features in the Castle. Among them are a two-story castle tower that served as Leedskalnin's living quarters, an accurate sundial, a Polaris telescope, an obelisk, a barbecue, a water well, a fountain, celestial stars and planets, and numerous pieces of carvings that served as furniture. The furniture pieces include a heart-shaped table, a table in the shape of Florida, chairs resembling crescent moons, a bathtub, beds and a throne.

Most of the objects are made from single pieces of stone that weigh an average of **15** short tons. The largest stone weighs **30** short tons and the tallest are two monoliths standing **25** ft. The gate is carved so well, it fits within a quarter of an inch of the walls. It was so well-balanced, a child could open it with the push of a finger. The mystery of the gate's perfectly balanced axis and the ease with which it revolved lasted for decades until it stopped working in **1986**. It took six men and a **50** short-ton to lift it. Once the gate was removed, engineers discovered how Leedskalnin had centered and balanced it. He had drilled a hole from top to bottom and inserted a metal shaft. The rock rested on an old truck bearing, the rusting out of this bearing is what resulted in the gate's failure to revolve. Workers set the gate back into place in **1986**. In **2005**, it failed and needed to be repaired again, however it does not rotate with the same ease as it originally functioned.

When asked why he had built the castle, Leedskalnin would vaguely answer, it was for his, *"Sweet Sixteen."* This is widely believed to be a reference to **Agnes Scuffs**. In

Leedskalnin's only known publication '**A Book in Every Home**,' he implies his 'Sweet Sixteen' was more an ideal than a reality. According to a Latvian account, the woman existed, but her name was actually **Hermīne Lūsis.**

Leedskalnin continued to work on the castle up until his death in **1951**. When he became ill in December, he put a sign on the front gate door that read, *"Going to the Hospital."* He took a bus to a Miami hospital, and died three days later.

There are various theories as to how Leedskalnin constructed the castle using some unknown form of science. Some claim Ed Leedskalnin used and left behind the blueprints of nature, a '**Secret Knowledge of the Ancients**.' The only tool Leedskalnin spoke of using was a 'Perpetual Motion holder.' A few teenagers claimed to have witnessed his work, reporting he had caused the blocks of coral to move like hydrogen balloons.

Photographs show Leedskalnin working, appearing to use traditional methods, although some point out that the tripods appear to rise only about **20** ft, while the largest stones are **25** ft long and stand vertical. The tripods made from wooden telephone poles could not support the larger stones, stones of **Several Tons**. There are not enough pulleys to lessen the weight of the stones for a **100lbs** man to be able to apply enough force to lift the stones.

The Coral Castle site states, *"If anyone ever questioned Ed about how he moved the blocks of coral, Ed would only reply that he understood the laws of weight and leverage well."* He also claimed he had 'Discovered the secrets of the Pyramids.' Even with the passing of decades and the many hurricanes that have passed through the area, the stones have not shifted. Edward Leedskalnin's accomplishment is truly a remarkable.

Ancient Unknowns: (Bosnian Pyramids)

In **2005**, **Dr. Sam Osmanagich** discovered what he claims to be pyramids in **Bosnia**, dating back to what could be **12,000** to **15,000 BCE**. The **Bosnian Pyramids** is a term for a cluster of natural geological formations sometimes known as flatirons near the **Bosnia** and **Herzegovina** town of **Visoko**, northwest of **Sarajevo**. The hill named **Visočica** became the focus of international attention in **October 2005** following a media campaign promoting the idea that they were human made and the largest and possibly oldest Pyramids on Earth.

The **699** ft **Visočica Hill** is roughly pyramid-shaped. The idea that it constitutes an ancient artificial edifice was publicized by **Osmanagich**. His subsequent excavations at the site have uncovered what he claims are a paved entrance plateau and tunnels, as well as stone blocks and ancient mortar which he has suggested once covered the entire structure. He named the Visočica Hill, the **'Pyramid of the Sun,'** and two nearby hills, the **'Pyramid of the Moon,'** and the **'Pyramid of the Dragon.'** Another two, **'Pyramid of the Earth'** and **'Pyramid of Love,'** have been mentioned in reports.

Osmanagich claims to have found tunnels in the hillside which he interprets as ventilation shafts. He believes his discoveries around Visoko will have further implications on world prehistory. By comparing the varying heights of the tallest pyramids in Mexico and Egypt with Visočica Hill, he believes the pyramids were all built by the same people. He has also further theorized that the Visočica Hill could be the 'Mother of all Pyramids,' a claim he says would be corroborated by the existence of **Sacred Geometry** and further numerological study of messages left in the pyramid for future generations.

Osmanagich estimates the **Pyramid of the Sun** stands **722** ft high, while others suggest this structure to be **230** to **328** ft high, depending on the report. If it is **722** ft, it would be one third taller than the **Great Pyramid** of Giza, making it the largest pyramidal structure on Earth.

In **2007** a report by Egyptologist **Nabil Mohamed Abdel Swelim** was publicized by the Archaeological Park, stating the

Pyramid of the Sun was the world's largest pyramid. After two visits to Visoko he concluded, *"Arguments in favor or in disfavor have no effect on the fact that the pyramid concept and the properties are there for everyone to see."* In **2010** he released a report in which he clarified that he does not claim it is a man-made pyramid, but that he uses the term for any natural or artificial formation which is a geometric pyramid, though he does not exclude the possibility that it is man-made.

Some scientists have criticized **Osmanagich**'s work, suggesting scientific investigations of the site have shown the pyramids are really natural formations that show no signs of human building. This is still very much up for debate. At the present time, the current project is not yet completed and hopes to be fully excavated in a few years.

Ancient Unknowns: (Ancient Astronauts Rounding Theory)

'Ancient Astronaut' theorist contend some of these ancient achievements and monuments could not have been built with the technical abilities and tools of the people of their time, and further argue that many could not be duplicated if tried today. With many of the feats, such as the **Great Pyramid** and **Pumapunku**, they suggest that the size of the stones, the precision with which they were cut and laid, the distances many were transported, and the massiveness of their work, leaves the question open as to who really constructed these sites.

In their book **'Intelligent Life in the Universe**,' published in **1966**, astrophysicists **Carl Sagan** and **I.S. Shklovski** devoted a chapter to the possibility that extraterrestrial contact may have occurred during recorded history. Sagan and Shklovski argued that extraterrestrial visitation to Earth was plausible, and that pre-scientific narratives can potentially offer a reliable means of describing contact with outsiders. They cited tales of **Oannes**, a fishlike being, and attributed it with teaching agriculture, mathematics and the arts to early Sumerians. Due to the detail of the story, it led to more scrutiny of a possible act of **Paleocontact** (Extraterrestrials influencing human culture).

In Hindu mythology, the Gods and their Avatars travel from place to place in flying vehicles, variously called 'Flying Chariots' or 'Flying Cars.' There are many mentions of these flying machines in the **Ramayana**, which dates to the 5th or 4th **Century BCE.**

In the **Old Testament, Chapter 1** of the **Book of Ezekiel**, it recounts a vision in which **Ezekiel** sees an, *"Immense cloud,"* that contains fire and emits lightning, *"Brilliant light."* It continues, *"The center of the fire looked like glowing metal, and in the fire was what looked like four living creatures."* These creatures are described as winged and humanoid, they, *"Sped back and forth like flashes of lightning,"* and, *"Fire moved back and forth among the creatures."* The passage continues on to describe four shiny objects, each appearing, *"Like a wheel intersecting a wheel."* These objects could fly, and moved with the creatures. It is described, *"When the living creatures moved, the wheels beside them moved, and when the living creatures rose from the ground, the wheels also rose."* Many Ancient Astronaut enthusiasts suggest Ezekiel may have seen a spaceship.

The building of the pyramids has also been mentioned as knowledge that may have been brought to Earth by extraterrestrials. Some believe there are also pyramids on Mars. If this is true, then the knowledge of the structures far exceeds our earthly atmosphere. That does not mean such knowledge is not attainable now by humans, and without alien assistance. Whether aliens made or aided in the buildings of the pyramids, they were constructed and exist; a fact that proves it is possible to build them again.

In **'The Law of One: Book I The Ra Material,'** published in **1984**, a group of three people, channeled a **Social Memory Complex** known as **'Ra.'** The group consisted of **Don Elkins**, who asked questions to a hypnotized **Carla L. Rueckert**, while **Jim McCarty** would transcribe the answers from **Ra**, being received through **Rueckert**. The Book is formatted with a **'Questioner'** and **'Ra'** outline, with **Ra** playing the part as the **'Answerer.'** After a series of questions, Don Elkins then asked **Ra** to explain the building of the Pyramids. In the sessions, when Ra mentions

'**Mind/body/spirit**,' it is another term for modern human being, soul, or a life-force. Excerpts from the conversation are as follows:

> **Questioner** (Don Elkins): *Were you responsible for the building of the pyramid, and what was the purpose of the pyramid?*
>
> **Ra:** *I am Ra. The larger pyramids were built by our ability using the forces of One. The stones are alive. It has not been so understood by the **mind/body/spirit** distortions of your culture. The purposes of the pyramids were two, firstly, to have a properly-oriented place of initiation for those who wished to become purified or initiated channels for the Law of One. Two, we wished then to carefully guide the initiates in developing a healing of the people whom they sought to aid and the planet itself. Pyramid after pyramid charged by the crystal and initiate were designed to balance the incoming energy of the One Creation with the many and multiple distortions of the planetary mind/body/spirit. In this effort we were able to continue work that brothers within the Confederation had effected through building of other crystal-bearing structures and thus complete a ring, if you will, of these about the Earth's, as this instrument would have us vibrate it, surface.*
>
> **Questioner** (Don Elkins): *How were the blocks moved?*
>
> **Ra:** *I am Ra. You must picture the activity within all that is created. The energy is, though finite, quite large compared to the understanding/distortion of your peoples. This is an obvious point well known to your peoples, but little considered. This energy is*

intelligent. It is hierarchical. Much as your mind/body/spirit complex dwells within an hierarchy of vehicles and retains, therefore, the shell, or shape, or field, and the intelligence of each ascendingly intelligent or balanced body, so does each atom of such a material as rock. When one can speak to that intelligence, the finite energy of the physical, or chemical, rock/body is put into contact with that infinite power which is resident in the more well-tuned bodies, be they human or rock. With this connection made, a request may be given. The intelligence of infinite rock-ness communicates to its physical vehicle and that splitting and moving which is desired is then carried out through the displacement of the energy field of rockness from finity to a dimension which we may conveniently call, simply, infinity. In this way, that which is required is accomplished due to a cooperation of the infinite understanding of the Creator indwelling in the living rock. This is, of course, the mechanism by which many things are accomplished which are not subject to your present means of physical analysis of action at a distance.

Questioner (Don Elkins): *My question then would be, are there individuals incarnate upon the planet today who would have the inner disciplines to, using your instructions, construct and initiate in a pyramid they built? Is this within the limits of what any one on the planet today can do? Or is there no one available for this?*

Ra: I am Ra. *There are people, as you call them, who are able to take this calling at this nexus. However, we wish to point out once again that the time of the pyramids, as you would call it, is past. It is indeed a timeless structure. However, the streamings from*

> *the universe were, at the time we attempted to aid this planet, those which required a certain understanding of purity. This understanding has, as the streamings revolve and all things evolve, changed to a more enlightened view of purity. Thus, there are those among your people at this time whose purity is already one with intelligent infinity. Without the use of structures, healer/patient can gain healing.*

This is striking, and can be the answer to how **Edward Leedskalnin** built Coral Castle, he did indeed know the secrets or lost knowledge of the Egyptians. As stated by Ra, this is something that is available to all, it is old knowledge. The most important thing to have in mind is to connect to the rock or earthly material you wish to move, but you need to do so with more than a careless action. It is described as being one with the object, to not look upon it as 'Simply material,' but to recognize the life in it, and to communicate with it.

This makes sense when you realize no intelligent being likes to do something while being forced into it without communication. Communication is the key to coherence, harmony, understanding, peace, love and last but not least, building the pyramids. It is a level of understanding most today have not recognized that they have. Think of how many people you know that disregard the beauty around them, the magnificence of things, and have no care or thoughtfulness to their day. How could people like that build a pyramid? They can't. They are only communicating with themselves, and not in harmony with the things around them.

Through harmony, you have a stronger sense of being connected to what is around you. They almost go together. Communication leads to harmony, and vice versa. The more harmony, the more you feel a communication to all that is around you. To feel this communication is important if one is to build such structures as a pyramid. Building a pyramid isn't about moving large rocks, it's about communicating with the vibrating energy that rock is innate to.

One must recognize, while the Earth is so many things, it is also a magnet, and using its magnetism can help levitate the rocks, and enable them to being light enough to move. If you take two magnets and place them near each other, one side facing negative and other facing positive, they will then come together, pulling into one another. Whereas, if you flip one of the magnets over, leaving positive to face positive, or negative to face negative, the magnets will push away from each other. Through an acute measure of communication and magnetism, **Leedskalnin** moved thousands of tons of granite stone, using the positive and negative side of the magnets, and built Coral Castle in the same manner and thoughtfulness as the Egyptians built the pyramids.

CHAPTER SIX
(Religion)

"When you knock, ask to see God - none of the servants."
- Henry David Thoreau -

Religion: (Introduction)

Religion is defined as *'The body of persons adhering to a particular set or institutionalized system of beliefs, attitudes and practices, in recognition or worship of a superhuman controlling power.'*

It is something all of us participate in. Whether we know it or not, whether you are a part of a church or mosque, claim to be spiritual, think of God occasionally, or deny God exist, we are all religious. Even those that claim they are unreligious, in turn are adhering to a set of beliefs that recognize a superhuman being. Even denying God exist, is in fact recognizing God. For God to be placed in your thoughts to not exist, you in turn recognize the thought of God, therefore you are recognizing God, and however you view God, is how you recognize such an 'Entity.'

Whether you find yourself in an organized system of going to church, praying **5** times a day, or daily reading religious text some people call holy, it still holds the same structure as someone who claims to have a loosely belief in God (In the sense of those who think they don't have a structure), they are simply acting out the structure of their non-structure. Even **Atheists** are very much as religious as **Christians** or **Muslims**, because choosing not to recognize God, is again, recognizing God. You cannot, not recognize God.

In a sense you have no choice but to be religious, it almost comes with the territory. Where some people may fail or go wrong, lies in some of the ways of their religious practices, it has been the greatest divider amongst people.

Religion: (Beliefs in God)

It is important to understand your view or belief in **God**. Your outlook on God, in turn affects your outlook on Creation, which affects your outlook on You. There are numerous different ways to believe or not to believe in this **'Being'** or **'Beings.'** While there are many, listings of some of the different ideals of the way people believe in the **'Creator,'** are as follows:

Monism:

Monism is the belief that there is only one form of **'Ultimate Substance,'** and reality is one unitary organic whole, with no independent parts. The Universe is one, rather than dualistic or pluralistic. In some diverse religious traditions, Monism may hold that there is one God who has many manifestations.

Monotheism:

Monotheism is the belief in the existence of a **Single God**. While **Monotheism** professes the existence of only one **God**, monotheistic religions may incorporate concepts of the **Divine**, for example, the **Christian Trinity**, in which God is a triune spirit of three eternal persons, God (Father), **Son** and the **Holy Ghost**. The concept of monotheism in Islam and Judaism rejects this distinction.

Monolatrism:

Monolatrism is the recognition of many Gods, but with the consistent worship of one God. Monolatrism differs from **Monotheism**, which acknowledges the existence of one God, and **Henotheism**, which consistently worships one God but without denying other Gods are of equal validity.

Polytheism:

Polytheism is the belief of multiple Gods and Goddesses. It is documented in historical religions of **Classical Antiquity**, **Greek Polytheism** and **Roman Polytheism**. It persists in modern traditions today such as **Hinduism, Buddhism, Shintoism, Chinese Folk** religion.

Gnosticism:
Gnosticism is a spiritual practice common to early **Christianity, Hellenistic Judaism** and **Greco-Roman Mystery** religions. They saw the material world as created through an intermediary being (Demiurge) rather than directly by God, and that **Gnosis** (Esoteric or intuitive knowledge) is the way to salvation from the material world.

Henotheism:
The belief and worship of a single God while accepting the possible existence of other Gods. **Max Müller**, a German Philologist and Orientalist, brought the term into common usage.

Deism:
Deism is the standpoint that reason and observation of the natural world, without the need for organized religion, can determine the creation of Universe and its Creator. God does not intervene with the laws of the Universe. The **Founding Fathers** of the **United States** were deeply inspired by enlightenment philosophies, and is generally believed that many of them were deists.

Theism:
Theism is the belief that at least one God exists. It conceives of God as personal, present and active in the governance and organization of the world and the Universe.

Pantheism:
Pantheism is the view that the Universe and God are identical. Pantheists thus do not believe in a personal, anthropomorphic or creator God. Pantheism signifies the idea that God is best seen as a method of relating to the Universe.

Panentheism:
Pantheism is a belief system which suggests that God personally exists. **Panentheism** is differentiated from Pantheism, which holds that God is not a distinct being but is synonymous with the Universe. In **Pantheism**, God is the whole, while in **Panentheism** the whole is in God. In

Panentheism, God lies within and beyond the outside of our Universe.

Agnosticism:
Agnosticism is the view that the true value of certain claims such as the existence or non-existence of God is unknown or unknowable. An agnostic is someone who neither believes nor disbelieves there is a God, whereas an atheist disbelieves there is a God. Agnosticism usually view human reason as incapable of providing sufficient rational to justify whether God does or does not exist.

Atheism:
Atheism is the rejection of the belief in the existence of deities. In a narrower sense, atheism specifically takes the position that there is no God. Atheists tend to be skeptical of supernatural claims, citing a lack of empirical evidence.

Religion: (Evolution of Religion)

The origins of religion date back to the **Middle Paleolithic** Era, from **300,000** to **30,000** years ago. This era is when the **Homo** species started to show signs of rituals and religious worship. The use of burial rituals is evidence of religious activity, which there is inconclusive evidence that Homo Neanderthals may have done, as modern humans do now.

Humanity's closest living relatives are chimpanzees. **Barbara King** suggests that while non-human primates are not religious, they do exhibit traits that would have been necessary for the evolution of religion. These traits include high intelligence, communication, a sense of social normality, realization of 'Self,' and a concept of continuity. **Marc Bekoff**, Professor Emeritus of Ecology and Evolutionary Biology at the University of Colorado Boulder, argues that many species grieve death and loss, though elephants are the only other species known to have any recognizable ritual surrounding death.

Most scientists agree religion is an outgrowth of brain architecture that evolved early in human evolution, but the exact mechanisms which drove the evolution of the religious mind is up for debate. The two main theories explain either religion evolved from natural selection, or is an evolutionary byproduct of other mental adaptations.

Stephen Jay Gould, an American Paleontologist, believed religion was an exaptation (A feature functioning not through natural selection, or not functioning for what it was originally adapted for) and evolved as a byproduct of psychological mechanisms. Such mechanisms included are 'Agent Detection,' the ability to infer the presence of organisms that might do harm, 'Etiology,' which is the ability to come up with causal narratives for natural events, and the 'Theory of Mind.' These adaptations enable humans to imagine purposeful agents behind many observations that could not be explained otherwise.

Some scholars suggest religion is genetically hardwired into the human condition. The '**God Gene Hypothesis**' states that some human beings bear a gene which gives a predisposition to interpret incidents as religious revelation. The '**VMAT2**' gene is one gene claimed to be of this nature. The evolution of religion can also be explained by the nature of human comprehension and the belief in the supernatural. When natural causes are not available to comprehend an experience or sight, the brain can then assume it is the causes of the supernatural, therefore it relies strictly on beliefs. Beliefs like 'Believing in God' cannot be falsified by experiment or disproved.

Wentzel van Huyssteen suggests the translation of the non-visible through symbolism aided early human ancestors to hold beliefs in abstract terms. Art and symbolism establishes a capability for abstract thought and imagination helpful to hypothesis religious ideas. Symbolism is a universal occurrence in religion. Middle Stone Age sites in Africa show evidence of some of the earliest symbolic behavior. From at least **100,000** years ago, there is evidence of the use of pigments such as Red Ochre. The color 'Red' has been argued universally among human cultures to represent blood, sex, life and death.

Organized religion traces its roots **11,000** years ago to the **Neolithic Revolution**, which is believed to have begun in the **'Near East,'** but may have occurred independently in several other locations around the world. The Neolithic Revolution included the acceleration process in foraging communities to states and empires, through more specialized forms of religion that reflected the new social and political environment.

Religion essentially emerged as a means of providing social and economic stability. A religious belief gains credibility and becomes part of the social consensus when it becomes shared by a group through ideas and language.

Religion: (Hinduism)

Many view **Hinduism** as the 'Oldest living religion,' with roots reaching back into prehistory **India**, although it is more often defined as a religious 'Tradition' or 'Practice.' Regarding traditional Western religious theology, Hinduism is difficult to define as a religion because of its openness and complete tolerance to differences in belief. **Hinduism** has no single founder, and is viewed as the most complex of all of the historical world religions, consisting of an extremely diverse tradition.

Numerically, Hinduism is one of the largest faiths in the world, and is the leading religious practice of the Indian subcontinent. While the exact date of the founding of **Hinduism** is not known, the earliest evidence for a 'Prehistoric Religion' in India date back to the **Harappan Period**, between **5500** to **2600 BCE**, when the **Vedic Religion** (A historical predecessor of Hinduism) was predominant. Hinduism became more recognizable when the **Vedas** (The oldest scriptures of Hinduism) were composed, roughly between **1700** to **1100 BCE**, also recognized as the early **Vedic Period**. While **Hinduism** has no central doctrine of authority, the primary beginning concepts grew out of the **Vedas**. The Vedas are made up of four compositions, the **Rig Veda**, **Sama Veda**, **Yajur Veda** and

Atharva Veda, which all are thought to be **Apauruṣeya**, 'Not human compositions.'

Hinduism is known to its followers as **Sanātana Dharma** (The original name of what is now called Hinduism). To its followers, it is the traditional way of life, but because of the wide range of philosophies incorporated within it, to fully understand the concept of Hinduism can be difficult. In Hindu, God is multifaceted and complex, and depending on the individual and practice, its philosophy can span from **Monism, Monotheism, Polytheism, Gnosticism, Henotheistic, Pantheism, Panentheism,** as well as **Agnosticism** and **Atheism** beliefs, although any such term is a simplification.

The many Hindu philosophies include a wide field of laws and remedies of 'Daily Morality,' although it grants a great level of freedom of worship. Classical Hindu thought accepts **puruṣārtha** (That which is sought by man; human purpose or one's goal). The following objectives of human life, known as the **puruṣārthas**, are listed below:

- **Dharma**: Righteousness
- **Artha**: Livelihood, wealth
- **Kāma**: Sensual pleasure
- **Mokṣa**: Nirvana, freedom from Samsara.

Hindu Beliefs & Practices

Hinduism follows **Samsara** (the belief in reincarnation), determined by **karma**, and the belief that salvation is the freedom from this cycle of birth and death. **Hinduism** normally involves seeking 'Awareness of God,' and has developed numerous practices designed to help think of divinity. Some Hindu traditions regard certain rituals as essential for salvation, although a variety of interpretations on this co-exist. Some of the more prominent themes in Hindu beliefs are listed below:

Dharma:

The concept of a 'Power' that lies behind the nature of all things, and keeps everything in balance. Dharma acts as the law, order and harmony, and is the moral principle of the

Universe that first sprang from Brahman (The One Supreme, Universal Spirit).

Samsāra:

The cycle of **action, reaction, birth, death** and **rebirth** as a continuum. It is thought that after several reincarnations, an **ātman** (Individual self or Eternal Soul) eventually seeks unity with the Supreme Spirit (Brahman). Escaping the world of Samsara through **Moksha** is thought to ensure lasting peace and harmony.

Karma:

The law of 'Cause and Effect." The **'Linga Sharira,'** an invisible double of the human body, retains impressions from one lifetime to the next, whether physical or mental, creating a unique path for each individual.

Moksha:

Meaning 'Release' or 'Let go,' is the liberation from **Samsara** (Cycle of repeated death and rebirth). The key to obtaining **Moksha** is **Atma-Jnana** (Self-Realization). The ultimate goal of life, referred to in **Moksha**, is mainly understood as the realization of one's union with God.

Yoga:

A spiritual and ascetic Hindu practice, including breath control, meditation, and the adoption of specific bodily postures, practiced for health, relaxation and union with God. A Hindu usually practices one or more forms of Yoga. In whatever way a Hindu defines his or her goal of life, there are several methods taught by sages for reaching that goal. According to his or her understanding and preference, one may prefer a certain practice of yoga over the other, however, one form of yoga does not exclude others. Many schools of yoga believe the different practices of yoga naturally aid and blend into the other yogas. There are four different types of Yogas for the attainment of **Moksha**. Practices and paths that one can follow include:

- **Bhakti Yoga:** (Love and Devotion) - Serving the **Supreme**. Bhakti Yoga is the spiritual practice of fostering love to a personal God through movements.

The **Bhagavad Gita** and **Bhagavata Purana** scriptures are important in explaining the Bhakti.
- **Karma Yoga:** (Right Action) - Working for the **Supreme**. **Karma Yoga** is the discipline of thinking, by which one comes to the realization to act accordingly, and achieve perfection in action, without consideration of personal desires.
- **Rāja Yoga:** (Meditation) - Meditating on the **Supreme**. **Rāja Yoga** is the practice of mediation, through the primarily concern of the mind. Controlling all thought-waves, helps one to achieve liberation.
- **Jyâna Yoga:** (Wisdom) - Realizing the **Supreme**. **Jyâna Yoga** entails properly understanding the difference between the body and the soul. It is the Yoga of knowledge, will and intellect, by use of their mind to inquire into their own nature. Jyâna yoga teaches there are four Jyâna Yoga paths:
    - **Viveka / Discrimination:** Ability to distinguish between what is real and unreal.
    - **Vairagya / Detachment:** Practice includes removing oneself from the world around you, everything that is temporary.
    - **Shad-Sampat / The 6 Virtues:**
        - **Sama:** Tranquility, control of the Mind
        - **Dama:** Control of the Senses
        - **Uparati:** Renunciation
        - **Titiksha:** Endurance
        - **Shraddha:** Faith
        - **Samadhana:** Perfect concentration
    - **Mumukshutva:** Intense longing for liberation.

Hindu Concept of God

According to Hindu scriptures, living beings are not apart from God, but are a representation of God. God lives in each and everyone in the form of an **ātman** (Individual self or

Eternal Soul), thus each living creature is its own unique manifestation of God. The **Advaita** school of Hinduism (Pantheistic in its outlook) teaches that the goal in Life is to realize one's ātman is identical to **Brahman** (Supreme Soul).

In ancient times it was believed there were **330** million living beings, thus, Hindus in turn believed there to be **330** million Gods or Deities. Everything represents God, the trees, birds, plants, rocks, ocean, etc. In **1961**, **Joe David Brown** said in **Time-Life**, *"Though the popular figure of 330 million is not the result of an actual count but intended to suggest infinity, the Hindu pantheon in fact contains literally hundreds of different deities."*

Hindus believe each God is a manifestation of a single **Universal Spirit** called **Brahman**, or Brahman itself. They believe Brahman is responsible for the creation of the world and preserves it. While **Hinduism** associates with the idea of many Gods, it does not endorse the worship of one particular God. Listed below are some of the major Gods in the Hinduism tradition:

- **Brahman**: The Godhead. The Divine Ground of all being, and origin of the Universe.
- **Brahma**: (Not to be confused with Brahman) The Creator. Not commonly worshipped. Part of the Hindu Trinity (**Trimurti**).
- **Vishnu**: The peace-loving deity of the Hindu Trinity. He is known as the Preserver or Sustainer of life, and has been incarnated nine times with one more still to come.
- **Shiva**: Perhaps the most powerful and complex of Hindu deities. He is known as the Destroyer or Transformer, and is one of the godheads in the Hindu Trinity.
- **Saraswati**: (The wife of **Brahma**) The Goddess of knowledge, art and music, representing the free flow of wisdom and consciousness. She is the mother of the **Vedas**. She is the daughter of **Shiva** and Goddess **Durga**.
- **Lakshmi**: (The wife of **Vishnu**) **Lakshmi**, meaning 'Good Luck,' is the Goddess of wealth and prosperity.

Lakshmi is depicted as a beautiful woman with golden complexion and four hands.
- **Parvati**: (The reincarnation of Shiva's first wife) The Divine Mother. She has many forms, such as **Durga** and **Kali**, and is often shown together with Saraswati and Lakshmi as the **Tridevi** (Triple Goddess).
- **Ganesh**: Son of **Shiva & Parvati**, **Ganesh** is the God of success and destroyer of evils and obstacles. **Ganesh** is arguably the most popular God in Hindu. He is also worshipped as the God of intellect, knowledge, wisdom and wealth.
- **Durga**: The Mother Goddess, is a fiercer form of **Parvati**. She represents the fiery powers of the gods. She is the protector of the righteous and destroyer of evil.
- **Rama**: Known as the **7th** avatar (incarnation) of Vishnu. Rama is an all-time favorite among Hindu deities, and is widely believed to be an actual historical figure, whose exploits formed the great Hindu epic of **Ramayana**.
- **Hanuman**: Believed to be an avatar of Lord **Shiva**, known as an ape-like God known for assisting Rama. **Hanuman** is worshipped as a symbol of devotion, perseverance and physical strength.
- **Murugan**: The God of war, Son of **Shiva & Parvati**.
- **Kali**: The Goddess of time and death, and is the ferocious form of the mother goddess **Durga**. Kali perhaps has the fiercest features amongst all the deities, and is shown standing with one foot on the chest of her husband, **Shiva**.
- **Krishna**: Thought to have been born in **3228 BCE**, is the **8th** and complete avatar (incarnation) of Vishnu. He is a central figure in Hinduism, and influenced Indian thought, life and culture in numerous ways. **Krishna** is believed to have authored the **Bhagavad Gita** (Hindu scripture part of the Sanskrit epic **Mahabharata**).
- **Surya**: The God of the Sun

While a few Hindu sects do not believe in worshiping God through icons, most Hindus perform their worship through **murtis** (icons), an image which expresses a Divine Spirit. The icon serves as a link between the worshiper and the particular God.

Hindu Denominations

While many practicing Hindus do not claim to belong to any specific denomination, the differences in the denominations are primarily due to which God is being worshiped, and the traditions that surround it. Listed below are four of the major denominations in Hinduism:

- **Vaishnavism:** The majority of Hindus are **Vaishnavas**, and worship Vishnu as the Supreme God.
- **Shaivism:** The oldest sect of Hinduism, and worship Shiva as the Supreme God.
- **Shaktism:** Worship Shakti or Devi (The Hindu Divine Mother) as the Absolute, Ultimate Godhead.
- **Smartism:** A liberal view of the Vedic Hindu religion, which accepts all the major Hindu deities as forms of the one Brahman.

There are other denominations in Hindu, although the **Smarta** view is the '**Western**' conception of what Hinduism has been defined by. Other major movements brought the beginning of a new period of Hindu thought, **Jainism** and **Buddhism**. Gautama **Buddha** (founder of **Buddhism**) taught that to achieve **Nirvana**, one did not have to accept the **Vedas**.

Religion: (Buddhism)

Buddhism is a religion and philosophy encompassing a variety of traditions, beliefs and practices, largely based on teachings attributed to **Siddhartha Gautama**, commonly known as the **Buddha**, 'Awakened One.' Buddha is recognized by Buddhists as an enlightened teacher who shared his insights to help people end ignorance of dependent origination, thus evading the cycle of suffering and rebirth.

Foundations of the Buddhist tradition and practice are based on the **'Three Jewels'** which are the **Buddha**, the **Dharma** (Teachings), and the **Sangha** (Community). Taking 'Refuge in the triple gem,' has traditionally been declared as to what distinguishes a Buddhist from a non-Buddhist. Some practices may include following support of the 'Monastic Community,' renouncing conventional living, the development of mindfulness, practice of meditation, study of scriptures, devotional practices and ceremonies.

The Buddha

According to the **Theravada Tipitaka** scriptures, the Buddha was born in Lumbini in modern-day Nepal, around the year **563 BCE**, and raised in Kapilavastu. This narrative states that shortly after the birth of **Siddhartha Gautama**, a wise man named **Asita** visited the young prince's father, **King Śuddhodana**, and prophesied **Siddhartha** would either become a great king or renounce the material world to become a holy man, depending on if he saw what life was like outside the palace walls. Śuddhodana was determined to see his son become a king, so he hid from him the sick, aged and suffering, by preventing him from leaving the palace grounds, keeping him confirmed behind the walls.

When **Siddhartha** reached the age of **16**, his father reputedly arranged for him to marry a cousin of the same age, named **Yaśodharā**. According to the traditional account, she gave birth to a son, named **Rahula**. Siddhartha is then said to have spent **29** years as a prince in Kapilavastu. His father ensured that Siddhartha was provided with everything he could want or need, but the future Buddha felt material wealth was not life's ultimate goal.

At age **29**, despite his father's efforts, Siddhartha ventured beyond the palace several times. In a series of encounters, known in Buddhist literature as the 'Four Sights,' he learned of the suffering of ordinary people, encountering an **Old Man**, a **Sick Man**, a **Corpse**, and finally an **Ascetic Holy Man**, whom was apparently content and at peace with the world around him. These experiences encouraged Siddhartha to abandon royal life and take up a spiritual quest.

Siddhartha then went to Rajagaha and began his ascetic life by begging for alms in the street. After studying with famous religious teachers of the day, and mastering the meditative attainments they taught, he found they did not provide a permanent end to suffering, so he continued on his quest. He then entered into extreme asceticism, which was a religious pursuit common among the **Shramanas**. A Shramana is one who renounces the world and leads an ascetic life for the purpose of spiritual development and liberation.

Siddhartha underwent prolonged fasting, breath-holding, and exposure to pain. He almost starved himself to death in the process. He then realized he had taken this kind of practice to its limit, and had not put an end to suffering, so in a pivotal moment he accepted milk and rice from a village girl and changed his approach. He devoted himself to **Anapanasati** meditation, through which he discovered what Buddhists call the 'Middle Way,' a path of moderation between the extremes of self-indulgence and self-mortification.

Siddhartha famously seated himself under a Pipal tree, now known as the **Bodhi Tree**, in Bodh Gaya, India, and vowed never to arise until he had found truth. **Kaundinya** (The first disciple and arahant of Buddha) and four other companions left, believing he had abandoned his search and become undisciplined. After a reputed **49** days of meditation, at the age of **35**, Siddhartha is said to have attained '**Enlightenment**.'

At the time of his awakening he realized complete insight into the cause of suffering, and the steps necessary to eliminate it. These discoveries became known as the '**Four Noble Truths**,' which are at the heart of Buddhist teaching.

After his 'Awakening' as **Buddha**, he then attracted a band of followers and established a monastic order. Buddha spent the remaining **45** years of his life traveling the northeastern part of the Indian subcontinent, teaching the path of awakening that he had discovered.

According to the **Mahaparinibbana Sutta** of the **Pali** canon, at the age of **80**, the Buddha announced he would soon reach '**Parinirvana**,' the final deathless state, and abandon his earthly body. The Buddha then ate his last meal, which was an offering from a blacksmith named **Cunda**. Falling violently ill, Buddha then instructed his attendant **Ānanda** to convince Cunda that the meal he had eaten had nothing to do with his passing, and his meal would be a source of the greatest merit as it provided the 'Last Meal' for Buddha. At his death, the Buddha told his disciples to follow no leader. The Buddha's final words are reported to have been, "*All composite things pass away. Strive for your own liberation with diligence.*"

His body was cremated and the relics were placed in monuments or Stupas. Scholars have varied when putting a date to Buddha's life. The more popular opinion is that his passing came in **483 BCE**, but more recent suggestions have been from between **486** to **483 BCE**, or even as late as **400 BCE**.

Most accept that he lived, but do not consistently accept all details in his biography. In writing her biography of Buddha, **Karen Armstrong** noted, "*It is obviously difficult to write a biography of the Buddha that will meet modern criteria, because we have very little information that can be considered historically sound...but we can be reasonably confident* **Siddhartha Gautama** *did indeed exist and that his disciples preserved the memory of his life and teachings as well as they could.*"

Teachings of the Buddha

Buddha is known for many teachings, but constantly expressed the understanding of 'Suffering.' When asked about the existence of God, he replied that he did not concern himself with such a question, but the nature of suffering and how to decrease it, during this life, was the essence of his teachings. He taught that the mind creates suffering as a natural process. The **Dukkha**, which is a Buddhist term translated as 'Suffering,' is centered in the **Four Noble Truths**. Through mastery of the '**Four Noble Truths**,' a state of 'Supreme Liberation' or **Nirvāna** is possible. The Buddha described Nirvāna as the perfect peace of mind that's free from ignorance, greed, hatred, and other afflictive states. Nirvāna is also regarded as the 'End of the world,' where no personal identity or boundaries of the mind remain. A summary of the **Four Noble Truths** are as follows:

- **The Truth of Dukkha:** The '**First Noble Truth**' is that 'suffering' exist, the lack of satisfaction. Buddha recognized there is both happiness and sorrow, but believed happiness is not permanent. He taught that unless we gain insight into the real truth of happiness, the dissatisfaction of suffering will persist.
- **The Truth of the origin of Dukkha:** The '**Second Noble Truth**' is that desire leads to suffering; the conditioned ignorance of one's '**Cravings**.' The cravings are based around three conditions, which are craving for pleasures (**Kama-tanha**), craving to be (**Bhava-tanha**), and cravings not to be (**Vibhava-tanha**).
- **The Truth of the cessation of Dukkha:** The '**Third Noble Truth**' is the end of suffering. This truth focuses on the causes of suffering, and the removal of it, so they never occur again. This stage is often referred to as 'Nirvana.'
- **The Truth of the path leading to the cessation of Dukkha:** The '**Forth Noble Truth**' is the 'Path' to end of suffering. This is called the **Noble Eightfold Path**, and is practical method for overcoming **Dukkha**, which is considered the essence of Buddhist practice. The Eightfold Path consists of: Right **Understanding**, Right **Thought**, Right **Speech**, Right **Action**, Right **Livelihood**, Right **Effort**, Right **Mindfulness**, and Right **Concentration**.

Buddha is thought to be the most psychological of the spiritual teachers. He taught all things that come to be, have an end, and nothing in the realm of experience can really be said to be 'I' or 'Mine.' He also encouraged his followers to question and think for themselves, believing that any teachings should not be accepted unless they are from their own experience. He declared, *"Believe nothing until you have experienced it and found it to be true. Accept my words only after you have examined them for yourselves; do not accept them simply because of the reverence you have for me."*

Rebirth

Buddhism rejects the concepts of a 'Permanent Self,' or an unchanging Eternal Soul. According to Buddhism there is no such thing as a self-independent from the rest of the Universe. Rebirth must be understood as the continuation of a dynamic, ever-changing process of 'Dependent arising,' determined by the laws of 'Cause and Effect' through Karma. Each rebirth is said to take place within one of five realms according to **Theravadins**, or six realms according to other branches in Buddhism. The realms in which rebirth can occur are as follows:

- **Naraka Beings**: Those who live in one of many **Narakas** (Hells).
- **Preta**: Sometimes sharing space with humans, but invisible to most people.
- **Animals**: Shares space with humans, but are considered another type of life.
- **Human Beings**: This is one of the realms of rebirth in which attaining Nirvana is possible.
- **Asuras**: Variously forms of low deities, demons, titans, and antigods.
- **Devas** including **Brahmas**: Gods, high deities, spirits, angels.

Rebirths in some of the 'Higher Heavens' known as the **Śuddhāvāsa Worlds** (Pure Abodes), can only be attained by skilled Buddhist practitioners known as **Anāgāmis** (Non-Returners). Rebirths in the **Arupa-dhatu** (Formless Realms) can be attained only by those who can meditate on the **Arūpajhānas**, which is the highest object of meditation.

According to **Tibetan Buddhism**, there is an intermediate state, '**Bardo**,' between one's life and the next. The **Orthodox Theravada** position rejects this, however, there are passages in the **Samyutta Nikaya** of the **Pali Canon** (Tradition Theravada Texts), which seem to support the idea Buddha taught of an intermediate stage between lives.

Religion: (Judaism)

The origins of **Judaism** are held in the history of the **Israelites**, a Hebrew speaking people of the Ancient Near East who inhabited the land of **Canaan** (Modern day Israel, western Jordan, southern Lebanon and Palestinian territories), during the Monarchic Period from **11th** to **7th Centuries BCE**. The foundation of the Israelite nation surrounds their mythological exit from Egypt under the guidance of **Moses**. Jewish tradition places this in **14th Century BCE**.

Rabbinic tradition holds at that time it was forbidden to write and publish the **Oral Law**, as any writing would be incomplete and subject to misinterpretation and abuse to God. Through exile and persecution, this tradition was dispersed when it became apparent that writing was the only way to ensure that the Oral Law could be preserved.

After many years of effort by a great number of **Tannaim** (A group of Rabbinic Sages), the Oral Tradition was written down around **200 CE** by Rabbi **Judah haNasi**. He took up the compilation of a nominally written version of the Oral Law, the **Mishnah**, which became the **Hebrew Bible**. The text of the **Hebrew Bible** (Jewish Bible) was put into its existing form during this time. It takes its name from the fact that the **Jewish Bible** is composed mostly in **Biblical Hebrew**, with a few passages in **Biblical Aramaic** (Almost half the **Book of Daniel**, parts of the **Book of Ezra**, as well as a few other passages).

The Jewish Bible consists of **39** books, broken into three parts, the **Torah** (Teachings), the **Nevi'im** (Prophets), and the

Kethuvim (Writings). The most important and prevalent of these parts, is the **Torah** (Hebrew for Instruction or Teach). The Torah is the first of the three parts of the **Tanakh**, the founding religious document of Judaism. Much of the contents of the **Tanakh** were compiled in **450 BCE**, by the **'Men of the Great Assembly,'** and have since remained unchanged.

Tanakh is a Hebrew abbreviation alluding to its three parts, the Torah, the **Nevi'im** (Prophets), and the **Ketuvim** (Writings). Together, these books comprise the Hebrew Bible, known in Christianity as **'The Old Testament,'** which is the first part of the Christian Bible.

The **Torah** is the entirety of Judaism's founding legal and ethical religious texts. It is made up of the **Five Books of Moses**, which are: **Genesis, Exodus, Leviticus, Numbers** and **Deuteronomy**. According to Jewish Tradition, Moses is believed to have written all of the books in the Torah, except the last eight verses of **Deuteronomy**, which in turn, describes his death. **Genesis** which describes the creation of the Earth and the 'Beginning of Times,' was revealed to Moses by God at **Mount Sinai**. Dates for this event have varied with Biblical Scholars from **1500 BCE** to **1200 BCE**.

Torah

The Hebrew names of the **Five Books** of the Torah, which Christians in turn call the **'Pentateuch,'** are known by their incipit, taken from the initial words of the first verse of each book. For example, the Hebrew name of the first book, **'Bereshit,'** is the first word of **Genesis 1:1**. The Five Books and their initial words are as follows:

- Genesis: **Bereshit** (תישארב, meaning 'In the Beginning')
- Exodus: **Shemot** (תומש, meaning 'Names')
- Leviticus: **Vayikra** (ארקיו, meaning 'And He called')
- Numbers **Bamidbar** (רבדמב, meaning 'In the desert')
- Deuteronomy: **Devarim** (םירבד, meaning 'Things' or 'Words')

The **Book of Exodus**, begins **Moses**'s journey. Moses was a son of **Amram** (Member of the **Levite Tribe** of Israel, descended from Jacob), and his wife **Jochebed**. Moses was born in a time when his people, the Children of Israel, were increasing in number and the Egyptian Pharaoh was worried they might help Egypt's enemies, therefore he ordered the killing of the Israel newborns. Moses's mother hid him in a small boat, in which she placed in the Nile River. The Child was in turn found by the Pharaoh's daughter, and adopted by the Egyptian royal family. Moses later grows up to kill an Egyptian slave, in which he flees across the **Red Sea** to **Midian**, where he has his encounter with the God of Israel, in the form of the '**Burning Bush**' at **Mount Sinai**.

In the narrative, an angel of **Yahweh** is described as appearing in the bush, and God is then described as calling out from the bush to Moses, who had been grazing the flock of **Jethro** (his father-in-law). When Moses starts to approach, God tells Moses to first take off his sandals, due to the place being holy ground. When challenged on his identity, God replies he is the, *'God of Abraham, Isaac, and Jacob,'* and that he is Yahweh. Yahweh is a Hebrew word meaning 'He who is he' or 'I am that I am.'

The text describes Yahweh as noticing the Israelites were being oppressed by the Egyptians, therefore he was sending Moses to the Pharaoh in order to bring the Israelites out of Egypt. Yahweh tells Moses what is to take place, and then performs a variety of wonders in order to reinforce his word, as well as instructing Moses to take the staff in his hands to perform miracles with it.

Despite the signs, Moses is said to have been reluctant to take on the role, arguing he lacked eloquence, and that someone else should be sent instead. Yahweh reacts angrily, rebuking Moses for presuming to lecture the one who made the mouth on who was qualified to speak and not to speak, yet Yahweh concedes and allows **Aaron**, Moses's brother, to assist Moses since he is eloquent. Aaron is described as being Moses's mouth piece.

Moses and Aaron went to Pharaoh and told him the Lord God of Israel wanted Pharaoh to let the Israelites celebrate a feast in the wilderness. Pharaoh replied that he did not know their God and would not permit them to go celebrate. Eventually, they gained a second hearing with Pharaoh and changed Moses's walking staff into a serpent, but Pharaoh's magicians did the same with their rods.

This is when God began to send the '**10 Plagues on Egypt**.' The **First Plague**, Moses and Aaron met Pharaoh at the Nile riverbank, and Moses had Aaron turn the river to blood, but Pharaoh's magicians could do the same. The **Second Plague**, Moses met Pharaoh again, and had Aaron bring frogs from the Nile to overrun Egypt, but Pharaoh's magicians were able to do the same thing. Pharaoh asked Moses to remove the frogs and promised to let the Israelites go to their feast in the wilderness. Once Moses removed the frogs, Pharaoh decided against letting the Israelites leave to their feast.

The **Third** and **Fourth Plagues** were of gnats and flies. The **Fifth Plague** was diseases on the Egyptians' cattle, oxen, goats, sheep, camels, and horses. The **Sixth Plague** was boils on the skins of Egyptians. The **Seventh Plague** was fiery hail and thunder. The **Eighth Plague** was locusts. The **Ninth Plague** was total darkness.

The **Tenth** and **Final Plague** was the slaying of the first-born Egyptian male babies. These events are commemorated as **Passover**, referring to how the plague 'Passed over' the houses of the Israelites who marked their doors with lamb's blood, while striking the Egyptians. This in turn caused the Egyptians to order the Hebrews to leave Egypt. After the **Ten Plagues**, Moses leads the exodus of the Israelites out of Egypt, but not before the Pharaoh had changed his mind.

In pursuit of the Israelites, the large Egyptian army shut the Israelites in between themselves and the **Red Sea**. With the Israelites trapped, Moses then took his staff and called upon God to give him the power to cross the water. God then divided the water so the Israelites could safely cross on dry ground. When the Egyptian army attempted to follow, God made the water return and drowned them.

Eventually, after **45** days of traveling, Moses leads his people to a find shelter at **Mount Sinai**, where Moses previously had first talked to the Burning Bush. Moses was summoned by God again, and stayed on the mountain for **40** days and nights, a period in which he received the **Ten Commandments**. The Commandments are thought to be laws from God. Moses then descended from the mountain to deliver the Commandments to the people, but upon his arrival he saw that the people were involved in the sin of the Golden Calf. In a range of anger, Moses smashed the Commandment Tablets, and ordered his own tribe (The Levites) to go through the camp and kill everyone, including family and friends, upon which totaled a killing of **3,000** people. God later commanded Moses to inscribe two other tablets to replace the ones Moses broke. Moses went to the mountain again for another **40** days and nights, and when he returned, the Commandments were finally given. In Jewish Tradition, Moses is referred to as 'The Lawgiver' for this single feat of delivering the Ten Commandments.

In Jewish tradition, the first Book of the **Torah**, referred to as **Genesis**, which describes the creation of the Earth and the 'Beginning of Times,' is believed to have been revealed to Moses by God at **Mount Sinai**, as well. Dates for this event have varied with biblical scholars from **1500** to **1200 BCE**.

The word '**Genesis**' signifies '**Generation**' or '**Origin**.' It is an appropriate title for the first book of the Bible, which contains the record of the origin of the Universe, the human race, family life, nations, sin and redemption. The first **11** chapters of **Genesis**, which is also referred to as **Bereshit**, begins with describing the world's beginning, from the history of **Adam** (First Man) to the descent of **Abraham** (The First of the Patriarchs). The story of 'Creation' in biblical terms is said to have happened over the course of **6** days, with God choosing to rest on the 7th.

"*In the beginning God created the heaven and the earth,*" as stated in **Genesis 1:1**. It continues to explain that the Earth was once void of life, so then the spirit of God breathed life into its world. The course in how this was performed is as follows:

- **First Day**: God separated Light from Darkness.
- **Second Day**: God separated the Waters, creating Sky.
- **Third Day**: God created Land and Sea, caused vegetation to sprout from the land.
- **Fourth Day**: God separate Days and Years, creating the Sun, the Moon, and the Stars.
- **Fifth Day**: God had the waters bring forth Living Creatures.
- **Sixth Day**: God had the Earth bring forth living creatures, and made Man in God's image.
- **Seventh Day**: God rested from work and blessed the **Seventh Day**, declaring it holy.

In the **Hebrew Bible** it is said that God formed man from the dust, blew the breath of life into his nostrils, and made him a living being, calling him Adam. From Adam, a bone was then taken from one of his ribs while he slept, and made woman, **Eve**. The **Torah** teaches that Man was without sin, until being convinced by Eve to eat the fruit in the Garden of Eden. God warned them neither to eat nor to touch the fruit, on pain of death, therefore God banished man from the Garden of Eden, to till the soil.

God eventually found disfavor with his creations, and decided to punish them for their wickedness. Summoning **Noah**, a descendant to **Seth** (Brother of **Cain** and **Abel**, and the third son to **Adam** and **Eve**), God instructs him to build an Ark, which will hold his family and one of each male and female animal, to repopulate the Earth after he sends a Great Flood. After the devastation, God promises not to destroy the world a second time with water. In **Genesis 12–50**, God gives to the Patriarchs, **Abraham, Isaac, Jacob** and his son **Joseph** (Prophets chosen by God to carry out 'His' plan for the redemption of his Chosen People), a promise of the land of **Canaan**. Genesis closes with these **'Chosen People'** in Egypt.

The remaining books of the Torah, **Exodus**, **Leviticus**, **Numbers** and **Deuteronomy**, give accounts of laws and the conquests of the Israelites for the next **40** years, until which they finally enter the **'Promise Land.'** In Deuteronomy, the last book of the Torah, Moses is not allowed to go to the Promise Land with his people, but is allowed to see it only from a mountain. It is not known what happened to Moses on the mountain, but he was never seen again. Knowing he was nearing the end of his life, Moses appointed **Joshua** his successor, bequeathing to him the mantle of leadership. Soon afterwards, Israel began the conquest of Canaan.

Nevi'im

Nevi'im (Prophets) is the second of the three major sections in the Hebrew Bible, which consist of books **Joshua**, **Judges**, **Samuel**, **Kings**, **Isaiah**, **Jeremiah**, **Ezekiel**, and **Minor Prophets**.

In Judaism, **Samuel** and **Kings** are each counted as one book. In addition, twelve relatively short prophetic books are counted as one in a single collection called *Trei Asar*or, 'The Twelve Minor Prophets.' The Jewish tradition thus counts a total of eight books in *Nevi'im* out of a total of **24** books in the entire Tanakh. *Nevi'im* is traditionally divided into two parts:
- **Former Prophets** or *Nevi'im Rishonim*, containing the narrative books of Joshua through Kings.
- **Latter Prophets** or *Nevi'im Aharonim*, mostly contains prophecies in the form of poetry.

Ketuvim

Ketuvim or **Kәṯûḇîm** is the third and final section of the **Hebrew Bible**. The *Ketuvim* are believed to have been written under the **Ruach HaKodesh**, one level less authority than that of prophecy. Found among the writings within the Hebrew scriptures, **I** and **II Chronicles** form one book, as does **Ezra** and **Nehemiah**, coming together as **'Ezra-Nehemiah.'** Collectively, **11** books are included in the **Ketuvim**, which are

Psalms, Proverbs, Job, Song of Songs, Ruth, Lamentations, Ecclesiastes, Esther, Daniel, Ezra-Nehemiah, and I & II Chronicles.

Besides the three poetic books (**Psalms, Proverbs, Song of Songs**) and the five scrolls (**Job, Ruth, Lamentations, Ecclesiastes, Esther**), the remaining books in Ketuvim are **Daniel, Ezra-Nehemiah** and **Chronicles**. There is no formal grouping for these books in the Jewish tradition, although they nevertheless share a number of distinguishing characteristics:

- The narratives openly describe relatively late events.
- The **Talmudic** tradition ascribes late authorship to all of them.
- **Daniel** and **Ezra** are the only books in **Tanakh** with significant portions in **Aramaic**.

The **Ketuvim** is the last of the three portions of the Tanakh accepted as Biblical Canon. While the Torah may have been considered canon by Israel as early as the **5th Century BCE**, the **Nevi'im** are thought to have been canonized by the **2nd Century BCE**, while the **Ketuvim** was not a fixed canon until **2nd Century CE**.

Jewish Denominations

There are many **denominations** of **Judaism**. While they all believe the Hebrew Bible to be the Holy texts, they have slight differences in how they are perceived. A listing of some of the major Jewish denominations and their differences are below:

Orthodox Judaism:
> Orthodox Jews strictly follow the Torah, and believe in the binding nature of Jewish law. They are generally not open to change, and do not recognize the validity of any other denominations.

Kabbalah (Jewish Mysticism):
> Kabbalah is a mystical form of Judaism that is believed to date back to the time of the **Second Temple**, in **70 CE**.

It focuses on the transcendence and immanence of God. After many years of protected oral tradition, it became systematized, and spread during the Middle Ages.

Reform Judaism:
Reform is a very relaxed version of Judaism. It emphasizes personal ethical responsibility over traditional laws, and usually views the Torah as an important moral guide, and absolute law.

Reconstructionist Judaism:
Reconstructionist is often philosophically more liberal than reform, but in practice it is more traditional.

Conservative Judaism:
Conservatives keep to many traditions, but believe in updated versions of some of the Jewish laws to have more liberal views. Thus, some believe conservative movement and the reform movement are growing in similar ways.

Religion: (Christianity)

Christianity is a monotheistic religion, based on the life and teachings of **Jesus Christ**, whom was regarded as a teacher and healer. While there are **27** books in the New Testament, the four canonical Gospels (**Matthew, Mark, Luke,** and **John**) of the **New Testament** are the most essential to Jesus's Life. Christians believe the Bible was written by human authors under the inspiration of the Holy Spirit.

In terms of theology, Christianity has struggled with the relationship between '**Old**' and '**New**' Testaments from its very beginnings. The God portrayed in the **Old Testament**, and the God in the **New Testament**, have two distinct different personalities. Christians believe Jesus brought in the 'New' and cleared man of their sins. **Christianity** teaches that Christ is the **Son of God**, and he is the Messiah prophesied in the Hebrew Bible, which is the **Old Testament** in Christianity.

In Ancient Greek, 'Christ' means 'Anointed one.' Christians commonly refer to Jesus as Christ or Messiah.

Adherents of the Christian faith call themselves Christians. Christians traditionally believe Jesus was born of a virgin, had no children, was unmarried, a virgin, performed miracles, crucified, died for the sins of humanity, rose from the dead and ascended into heaven from which he will return.

Some biblical scholars maintain that the works describing Jesus were initially passed through oral tradition, and weren't written down until several decades after his crucifixion. The oral stories were first transcribed into Greek, and then later translated into other languages.

Three of the four canonical Gospels, **Matthew**, **Mark** and **Luke** are known as the **Synoptic Gospels**. These three Gospels display a high amount of similarity in content, language and narrative arrangement. The presentation in the fourth canonical Gospel, the **Gospel of John** differs from these in that it is more thematic rather than a narrative format. Scholars generally agree it is impossible to find any direct literary relationship between the **Synoptic Gospels** and the **Gospel of John**. Most biblical scholars agree the **Gospel of Mark** was written several decades after Jesus's crucifixion, about the time of the destruction of the Jewish Temple by the Romans in **70 CE**. The other Gospels, **Mathew**, **Luke** and **John** are believed to have been written between **70** and **100 CE**. The four canonical Gospels are the principal sources of information regarding Jesus, while other parts of the New Testament, such as the **Pauline Epistles**, which were likely written decades before them, also share some details.

Some scholars believe apocryphal texts such as the **Gospel of Thomas** and the **Gospel of the Hebrews** are also applicable. It is believed the Gospel of Thomas, a collection of **114** sayings of Jesus, predates the four canonical Gospels, and may have been composed around the **Mid1st Century**.

The mainstream viewpoint among most scholars is that the gospels were written by non-eyewitnesses who worked with second hand sources that modified their accounts to fit their religious agendas. A minority of scholars, such as **John A.T. Robinson**, have suggested that the writers of the gospels of

Matthew, **Mark** and **John** were either 'Disciples' or close to those who were eyewitness to Jesus's ministry and death.

The Gospels devote about one third of their text to just seven days, namely the last week of the life of Jesus in Jerusalem.

Jesus Christ / Jesus of Nazareth (Start of Common Era)

Jesus of **Nazareth**, was born in Bethlehem, of Jewish parents **Mary** and **Joseph**, through what Christians believe of the immaculate conception of God (The Holy Ghost). In **Luke 1:31** of the **New Testament**, the angel **Gabriel** tells Mary to name her child **Jesus**, and in **Matthew 1:21**, an angel tells Joseph, *"You shall call his name Jesus, for he will save his people from their sins."* In both their Gospel accounts, **Luke** and **Matthew** associate the birth of Jesus with the reign of **Herod the Great**, who is generally believed to have died around the time of **4 BCE**. The most common calendar people use today for numbering years is the **Gregorian Calendar.** It is based on the decision of a **Monk Dionysius** in the **6th Century**, to count the years from a point of reference (Jesus's birth), which was placed sometime between **2 BCE** and **1 CE**. Most biblical scholars generally assume a date of birth between **6 to 4 BCE**, while other scholars assume Jesus was born sometime between **7 to 2 BCE**. Christians feast in celebration of his birth on **December 25th** for Christmas, even though there is no historical evidence for the exact day or month of the birth of Jesus.

Matthew, the only one of the four canonical Gospels to mention the **Magi** (3 Wise Men), states that they came from the east to worship the Christ, *"Born King of the Jews,"* and to present 3 gifts, gold, frankincense and myrrh. The account does not tell how many they were, although the widespread assumption that they were three could be due to the three gifts.

There is a large gap of Jesus's life that is missing from the texts. **Luke 2:41–52** includes an event in his childhood where he was lost, and his parents later found him teaching in the temple. This is the only event found in the Gospels from Jesus's infancy to his baptism.

Jesus was baptized by **John the Baptist**. John had foretold of the arrival of someone, *"Mightier than I,"* as in **Luke 3:16**. In **Matthew 3:14**, upon meeting Jesus, John says to him, *"I need to be baptized by you."* Instead, Jesus persuades John to baptize him instead. After Jesus emerges from the water, the sky opens and a voice from Heaven states, *"This is my beloved Son with whom I am well pleased."* The Holy Spirit then descends upon Jesus as a dove. Shortly afterwards, Jesus's followers were merged with the disciples of John the Baptist after John was beheaded.

Jesus then goes to the desert for **40** days to fast, while Satan appears to him and tempts him in various ways. After asking Jesus to prove that he was the Son of God, by asking him to do such things as turning stone to bread, he tempted him by offering Jesus worldly rewards in exchange for his worship. Jesus in turns rejects every temptation, and when Satan leaves, angels then appear and minister to Jesus.

Jesus then starts his ministry at, *"About **30** years of age,"* as noted in **Luke 3:23**. The Gospels place the beginning of Jesus's ministry in the countryside of **Judaea**, near the **River Jordan**. In this period Jesus preaches around Galilee. In **Matthew 4:18-20**, he encounters his first two **Apostles**, Simon who is also known as **Peter**, and **Andrew**. From there, they began to travel with him, while Jesus further preached, healed and performed miracles throughout Jerusalem, eventually forming the core of the early Church. The three Synoptic Gospels refer to just one 'Passover' during his ministry, while the **Gospel of John** refers to three, suggesting a period of about three years.

Teachings of Jesus

The teachings and works of Jesus include a number of sermons throughout the narrative of the Gospels. Jesus does not claim his teaching to be of his own, as in **John 7:16**, *"My teaching is not mine, but his that sent me,"* and again re-asserting this message in **John 14:10**, *"The words that I say unto you I speak not from myself, but the Father abiding in me doeth his works."*

Some of the teachings of Jesus took place in a synagogue, while much of his work was held during conversations. Many of the miracles he performed teach the importance of faith, as in the **Cleansing Ten Lepers** and the **Daughter of Jairus**, both were beneficiaries of being healed due to their faith. The **Gospel of Matthew** has a structured set of sermons, referred to as the **Five Discourses**, which offer many of the key teachings of Jesus. Each of the five discourses has similar passages in the **Gospel of Mark** and the **Gospel of Luke**. The **Five Discourses** in **Matthew** begin with the Sermon on the Mount, which captures many of the moral teachings of Jesus. The **Five Discourses** are as follows:

- **The Sermon on the Mount**: The first discourse in **Matthew 5-7** is one of the most quoted parts of the New Testament. It displays the highest ideals of the teachings of Jesus on mercy, spirituality, compassion , and his principles on love and humility. The first discourse includes the **Beatitudes** and the **Lord's Prayer**.
- **The Missionary Discourse**: The second discourse in **Matthew 10** offers instructions to the **Twelve Apostles**. Jesus tells them how to travel from city to city, carry no belongings and to preach only to Israelites.
- **The Parabolic Discourse**: The third discourse in **Matthew 13:1-53** provides several parables for the Kingdom of Heaven. Jesus addresses the disciples and multitudes of people who have gathered to hear him.
- **The Discourse on the Church**: In **Matthew 18**, the general theme in the fourth discourse is the anticipation of a future community of followers, and the roles his Apostles should play.
- **The Discourse on End Times**: The fifth and final discourse in **Matthew 24** was given on the **Mount of Olives**. Here, Jesus provides his longest response in the

'New Testament,' from a question by one of his disciples about the 'End of the age.'

The 'Beatitudes,' which are thought by some scholars to be some of Jesus's most important teachings, were given on the **Sermon on the Mount**. There are a version of these beatitudes in **Matthew** and **Luke**. The beatitudes describe the character of the people of the Kingdom of God, expressed as '**Blessings**.' The **8 Beatitudes** in **Matthew** are listed below:
- The poor in spirit: For theirs is the kingdom of heaven. (**Matthew 5:3**)
- They that mourn: For they shall be comforted. (**Matthew 5:4**)
- The meek: For they shall inherit the earth. (**Matthew 5:5**)
- They which do hunger and thirst after righteousness: For they shall be filled. (**Matthew 5:6**)
- The merciful: For they shall obtain mercy. (**Matthew 5:7**)
- The pure in heart: For they shall see God. (**Matthew 5:8**)
- The peacemakers: For they shall be called the children of God. (**Matthew 5:9**)
- They which are persecuted for righteousness' sake: For theirs is the kingdom of heaven. (**Matthew 5:10**)

The Crucifixion

The **Last Supper** is the final meal Jesus shares with his **12 Apostles** before his **Crucifixion**. The **Gospel of John** gives the only account of Jesus washing the feet of his disciples before the meal. During the meal, Jesus predicts one of his Apostles will betray him. Despite each Apostle's declaration that he would not betray him, Jesus reiterates the betrayer is one of those who were present. In the Gospels **Matthew** and **John**, **Judas** is singled out as the traitor. Jesus then predicts **Peter** will deny any knowledge of knowing him, telling Peter that he will disown him three times before the rooster crows the next morning.

Just after the Last Supper, while accompanied by Peter, **John** and **James the Greater**, in the **Garden of Gethsemane**, Jesus is betrayed by his apostle Judas, and arrested by the Romans. Just after Peter denies Jesus three times as predicted, Jesus is then captured and led to the cavalry. On the orders from **Pontius Pilate**, the **Roman Prefect** of Judaea, Jesus was then crucified on the charge of sedition against the Roman Empire. He was crucified between two convicted thieves, one of whom rebuked him and the other whom defended him. While on the cross, above Jesus's head, was the inscription '**King of the Jews**,' as soldiers and onlookers mocked him about the title.

Each gospel has its own account of Jesus's last words, comprising the 'Seven last sayings on the cross.' In **Luke 23:34** he states, "*Father, forgive them, for they know not what they do.*" Following Jesus's death, the body was removed from the cross, wrapped in a clean cloth and buried in a tomb, with guards to protect the body from it possibly being stolen.

Three days after his crucifixion, **Mary Magdalene** is stated in all four Gospels as the first to arrive to the tomb and find the body of Jesus is missing. **Mary**, mother of Jesus is accounted for in three of the Gospels as accompanying Mary Magdalene to the Tomb, thus they informed the Disciples about the 'Resurrection.'

After the discovery of the empty tomb, Jesus made a series of up to **12** appearances said to have been seen by up to **500** people, first to Mary Magdalene and later to his Disciples. In his final post resurrection appearance, Jesus ascends to Heaven where Christians believe he remains with God and the Holy Spirit. The Gospels include brief mentions of the ascension of Jesus. In **Luke 24:51** it states that Jesus, "*Was carried up into Heaven.*" The **Church of Jesus Christ** of **Latter-Day Saints**, teaches that **Apostle John**, which is the only apostle not to have later been killed or commit suicide, was immortalized and will live to see the **Second Coming of Christ**.

Astronomers and scientists have used diverse computational methods to estimate the date of the crucifixion. **Isaac Newton** used a method relied on the relative visibility of the crescent of the new moon, in which he suggested the date as **Friday, April 23rd 34 CE**, while Astronomer **Bradley E. Schaefer** later computed the date as **Friday, April 3rd 33 CE**. These dates have been up for debate for many of years, and continue to be a contested subject. In **1991, John Pratt** stated that Newton's method was sound, but included a minor error. Pratt suggested the year **33 CE**, using a completely different approach of a lunar eclipse model.

How Christianity Spread

In the New Testament, '**The Acts of the Apostles**,' contain 'Post-Ascension' appearances by Jesus. In **Acts 9:10-18**, Jesus instructs **Ananias** in Damascus, to heal Paul. Most Jews view Paul as the founder of Christianity, who is responsible for the break with Judaism.

Christianity began as a Jewish sect in the **Mid-1st Century**, originating in the eastern **Mediterranean Coast** of the **Middle East** (Modern **Israel** and **Palestine**). Even though it is thought that Paul established a church, it took centuries for a complete break to manifest. Some biblical scholars believe in a twin birth of Christianity and Judaism, rather than a separation of the former from the latter. **Daniel Boyarin** writes, "*For at least the first three centuries of their common lives, Judaism in all of its forms and Christianity in all of its forms were part of one complex religious family, twins in a womb, contending with each other for identity and precedence, but sharing with each other the same spiritual food, as well.*" There are many reasons for this eventual split, however, what set Christians apart from Jews is their faith in Christ as the resurrected Messiah. Once the split occurred, Christianity grew in size and influence, and rapidly spread to Syria, Mesopotamia, Asia Minor and Egypt, and into the Roman Empire.

Christianity suffered a setback in the **80s CE**, when Roman Emperor **Domitian** explicitly outlawed the religion as a 'Jewish superstition.' His efforts may have backfired, the persecution of **Christians** seemed to increase the number of **Christian** converts, eventually leading to the adoption of Christianity by the Roman Emperor **Constantine**.

Constantine became the emperor of **Rome** in **306 CE**, and was the most powerful person in his part of the world at the time. During this era, Romans worshiped the **Sun** as their **Godhead**. His conversion to Christianity was greatly critical for the advancement of its practices. According to historian **Eusebius Pamphilus**, Constantine was convinced he needed divine assistance. While Constantine was praying for such assistance, God sent him a vision of a cross of light at midday, bearing the inscription, "***In hoc signo vinces***," which means 'In this sign you will be victorious.' That night he dreamt of his earlier vision, and God in turn told him to use the sign he had been given as a safeguard in all of his battles. Thus, Constantine converted to Christianity and ordered the symbol to represent his army. Constantine was victorious in his battle, and he continued to wear the 'Symbol' for Christ against every power he faced afterwards. After his vision, he completely abandoned Paganism and declared Christianity legal, putting his full force in advancing the cause of the **Church of Christ**.

Constantine granted followers of Christianity safe from persecution, and provided Christian leaders with many gifts. He also made **Sunday** an official Roman holiday so that more people could attend church, and in turn made churches exempt from paying taxes. He funded Christian leaders and the construction of churches, some of which he dedicated to his mother. Constantine tolerated Paganism for a while, keeping Pagan Gods on coins and retaining his pagan high priest title, '**Pontifex Maximus**,' in order to maintain popularity with his subjects. In many cases he persuaded people to follow the laws by combining Pagan worship with Christianity. According to the bible Jesus was born in the springtime, but Constantine made **December 25th**, which was originally the birthday of the '**Pagan**

Unconquered Sun God,' the official holiday and birthday for **Jesus**. This merging coincidently transformed a winter pagan holiday. It is likely he also instituted celebrating **Easter** and **Lent**, based on Pagan holidays as well.

The **Roman Crusades** were also extremely instrumental in the growth of Christianity. The Crusades were a series of religious military campaigns, sanctioned by the Pope, to restore Christian control to Jerusalem and the Holy Land from Muslim rule. The crusaders were mainly Roman Catholics who came from all over Western Europe to fight against Muslims. Orthodox Christians also took part in fighting against Islamic forces in some Crusades. They had some temporary successes, but the Crusaders were eventually forced out of the Holy Land. Later campaigns were waged against Pagan Slavs, Pagan Balts, Mongols, and Christian heretics. Another goal of the **Crusades** was to return the Christian churches to the state of early Christianity. **Jehovah's Witnesses** argue that mainstream Christianity has departed from its original views and practices, due in part to such Pagan influences.

Christian Denominations

Following the 'Age of Discovery,' through missionary work and colonization, Christianity has spread throughout the World. As of the early **21st Century**, Christianity is the world's largest religion, representing about a quarter to a third of the world's population, with over **2.2** billion supporters. Among all Christians, around **37.0%** live in the Americas, **26.0%** live in Europe, **23.0%** live in Africa, **13.0%** live in Asia, with less than **1.0%** living in the Middle East.

There are over an estimated **3400** denominations of Christianity in the world today. The three largest groups are the **Roman Catholic Church**, the **Eastern Orthodox Churches**, and the various denominations of **Protestantism**. Ironically, most of the branches seemed to have spilt apart from one another. Christians differ in their views on the extent to which individual salvation is pre-ordained by God. The **Catholic Church** teaches that salvation does not occur without faithfulness on the part of Christians, converts must ordinarily be baptized and live in accordance with the principles of love. 'Reformed Theology' places emphasis on grace, by teaching that individuals are completely incapable of self-redemption, but that sanctifying grace is a must. Most denominations teach that Jesus will return to judge all humans and grant eternal life to his followers.

While there are many important different interpretations and opinions of the Bible, Christians share a set of beliefs they hold as essential to their faith. One major interpretation is the 'Holy Trinity.' Most Christian denominations believe in the Trinity, which refers to God comprising three distinct, co-existing beings, the **Father**, the **Son** (Jesus Christ), and the **Holy Spirit**.

In the words of the **Athanasian Creed**, an early statement of Christian belief, *"The Father is God, the Son is God, and the Holy Spirit is God, and yet there are not three Gods but one God."* According to this, God is not divided in the sense that each has a third of the whole, but instead each is considered to be fully God. Each third is distinct, but cannot be divided from one another in being or in operation. Regardless of their apparent differences, the three are each eternal and omnipotent. Some denominations disagree with its exact interpretation, though all Christians believe Jesus came to fulfill the prophecy from the **Old Testament**, thus rewriting the laws of the 'Old way.'

Religion: (Islam)

Islam is a monotheistic religion articulated by the **Qur'an** (Muslim Holy Text) and by the teachings of **Muhammad**, considered by Muslims to be the last prophet of God. An adherent of Islam is called a Muslim. Some scholars believe the origin of Modern Islam can be traced back to 7th **Century** Saudi Arabia.

Muslims believe the purpose of existence is to worship God, and that the creation of everything in the Universe is brought into being by God's sheer command, *"Be, and so it is."* God is thought to be beyond all comprehension and Muslims are not expected to visualize God. God is described and referred to by certain names or attributes, the most common being **Al-Rahmān**, meaning 'The Compassionate,' and **Al-Rahīm**, meaning 'The Merciful.'

Muslims also believe Islam is the complete and universal version of a primordial faith that was revealed at many times and places before, through Adam, Abraham, Noah, Moses and as well as Jesus, whom they all consider prophets. Unlike Christianity, Muslims believe that prophets are human and not divine, though some are able to perform miracles. Muslims maintain that the Qur'an, which was written by Muhammad, to be the unaltered and the final revelation of God.

The Qur'an also has many texts from the Hebrew Torah, the Psalms of David, and the Gospels of Jesus Christ. It not only accepts these books as divinely inspired, but the Qur'an even encourages us to test its disagreements. For instance, the Qur'an clearly denies Jesus Christ's crucifixion, as in **Sura 4:157-158**, while all Four of the Christian Gospel account clearly describe Jesus Christ as being crucified and resurrected. In Islam, Jesus is considered to be a **Messenger of God** and the Messiah who was sent to guide the **Children of Israel**. According to the Qur'an, Jesus was given the ability to perform miracles, and born to Mary as the result of virginal conception. In Islamic traditions it is also believed Jesus will return to Earth near the '**Day of Judgment**' to restore justice and defeat the Antichrist.

Jesus is seen in Islam as a precursor to Muhammad, and is thought to have foretold the latter's coming. Muslims believe God finally sent Muhammad (Seal of the Prophets) to convey the divine message to the whole world, to sum up and to finalize the word of God.

Religious concepts and practices include following Islamic law and the **Five Pillars of Islam** (Which are the basic concepts and obligatory acts of worship). The Five Pillars of Islam are the foundation of Muslim life. A basic description is as follows:

- **Shahadah:** Faith in the Oneness of God and the finality prophethood of Muhammad.
- **Salat:** Establishment of the daily prayers.
- **Sawm:** Concern for and almsgiving to the needy.
- **Zakāt:** Self-purification through fasting.
- **Hajj:** Pilgrimage to Mecca for those who are able.

Muhammad ibn ʾAbdullah (570–632)

Muhammad ibn ʾAbdullah was born in **Mecca**, in 570 CE. According to the tradition, Muhammad's father **Abdullah** died almost six months before he was born, and lost his mother **Amina** to illness when he was **6**. He became fully orphaned, and under the care of his uncle **Abu Talib**, the new leader of Banu Hashim. When Muhammad was either **9** or **12**, he met a Christian monk or hermit named **Bahira** who is said to have foreseen Muhammed's career as a prophet of God.

Due to his upright character as a merchant or a shepherd, he acquired the nickname 'Al-Amin,' meaning faithful and trustworthy. His reputation attracted a proposal from **Khadijah**, a **40** year old widow. Muhammad consented to the marriage at **25**, which by all accounts was a happy one.

At some point Muhammad adopted the practice of meditating alone for several weeks every year in a cave on **Mount Hira** near Mecca. Islamic tradition holds that during one of his visits to Mount Hira, in **610 CE**, the angel **Gabriel** appeared to him and commanded for Muhammad to recite the following verses from **Sura 96:1-5**, *"Proclaim! In the name of thy Lord and Cherisher, Who created man, out of a clot of congealed blood: Proclaim! And thy Lord is Most Bountiful, He Who taught the pen, taught man that which he knew not."*

According to some traditions, upon receiving his first revelations Muhammad was deeply distressed. After returning home, Muhammad was consoled and reassured by Khadijah and her Christian cousin, **Waraqah ibn Nawfal**. **Shi'a** tradition (A denomination in **Islam**), maintains that Muhammad was neither surprised nor frightened at the appearance of Gabriel but instead welcomed him as if he was expected. The initial revelation was followed by a pause of three years during which Muhammad further gave himself to prayers and spiritual practice. When the revelations resumed he was reassured and commanded to begin preaching, *"Thy Guardian-Lord hath not forsaken thee, nor is He displeased,"* as stated in the Qur'an, **Sura 93**.

One of Muhammad's mission involves preaching monotheism, as instructed to him by the Divine, to not worship idols or associate other deities with God. Around **613 CE**, Muhammad began his public preaching. Most Meccans ignored him and mocked him, while a few others became his followers. According to **Ibn Sad**, hostility in Mecca started when Muhammad delivered verses that condemned idol worship and the Meccan forefathers who engaged in polytheism.

After the death of Muhammad's wife Khadijah and his uncle Abu Talib in **619 CE**, he was forced out of Mecca, and into Medina, due to not having the protection he once had from the clan of his uncle. From here, he recruited men for his army, some who had also been banished, and entered into a bloodily 10 year war with the Mecca regime.

Islamic tradition share that in **620 CE**, Muhammad experienced the **Isra and Mi'raj**, a miraculous one night journey said to have occurred with the angel **Gabriel**. In the first part of the journey, the 'Isra,' he is said to have travelled from Mecca on a winged horse to, *"The farthest mosque,"* which Muslims usually identify with the **Al-Aqsa Mosque** in Jerusalem. In the second part, the '**Mi'raj**,' Muhammad is said to have toured **Heaven** and **Hell**, and spoken with earlier prophets, such as **Abraham**, **Moses** and **Jesus**. When he was in Heaven, he reported seeing an angel with, *"**70,000** heads, each head having **70,000** mouths, each mouth having **70,000** tongues, each tongue speaking **70,000** languages; and everyone involved in singing God's praises."* This would mean the angel spoke **24 quintillion** languages for the praise of Allah. This description is also a very similar word for word description of an angel seen by Moses in the '**Revelation of Moses**.'

Finally, after years of fighting with Mecca, in **630 CE** Muhammad marched into Mecca with an enormous force, said to number more than **10,000** men. With minimal casualties, Muhammad took control of Mecca. He declared an amnesty for past offences, except for ten men and women who had previously mocked and ridiculed him in songs and verses, although some of these people were later pardoned. Most Meccans converted to Islam and Muhammad subsequently destroyed all the statues of Arabian Gods.

Able to carry out his first true pilgrimage, Muhammad then taught his followers the rites of the annual Great Pilgrimage (**Hajj**). After completing the pilgrimage, he then delivered a famous speech known as **The Farewell Sermon.** In this sermon, Muhammad advised his followers not to follow certain Pre-Islamic customs such as adding intercalary months to align the **Lunar Calendar** with the **Solar Calendar.** Muhammad abolished all old blood feuds and disputes based on the former tribal system.

Commenting on the vulnerability of women in his society, Muhammed asked his male followers to, *"Be good to women, for they are powerless captives in your households. You took them in God's trust, and legitimated your sexual relations with the Word of God, so come to your senses people, and hear my words."* Ironically, he also told them they were entitled to discipline their wives but should do so with kindness. According to **Sunni** tradition, the following verse from **Qur'an 5:3**, *"Today I have perfected your religion, and completed my favors for you and chosen Islam as a religion for you,"* was delivered during this event.

A few months after the Farewell Pilgrimage, Muhammad fell ill in Medina, suffering for several days with a fever until he died **June 8th 632 CE**. With his head resting on the lap of one of his wives, **Aisha** (Whom was married to Muhammad when she was **six**, though thought to have been for the purposes of strengthen his ties with **Abu Bakr**), it is reported by her that his last words were, *"Rather, God on High and Paradise."* He is buried where he died, which was in Aisha's house and is now housed within the **Mosque of the Prophet** in the city of Medina. Next to Muhammad's tomb, there is another empty tomb that Muslims believe awaits Jesus.

Aftermath of Muhammad's Death

In the last years of his life, Muhammad united the **Tribes of Arabia** into a single Arab Muslim religious polity. With Muhammad's death, disagreement then broke out over who would succeed him as leader of the Muslim community. **Umar ibn al-Khattab**, a prominent companion of Muhammad, nominated **Abu Bakr**, Muhammad's friend and collaborator. Others added their support, and Abu Bakr was made the first **Caliph**. This was in turn disputed by some of Muhammad's companions, who held that **Ali ibn Abi Talib**, his cousin and son-in-law, had already been designated by Muhammad as the successor. Muhammad is said to have had thirteen wives or concubines, with **9** of his wives surviving him after death. **Aisha**, who became known as Muhammad's favorite wife in **Sunni** tradition, survived him by many decades and was instrumental in bringing together the scattered sayings of Muhammad, which would later form the **Hadith** literature for the **Sunni** branch of Islam.

Muslim Denominations

Islam is the second largest religion and one of the fastest growing religions in the world. A comprehensive **2009** demographic study of **232** countries and territories reported that **23**% of the global population or **1.57** billion people are of Islamic Faith. Approximately **62**% of the world's Muslims live in **Asia**, with over **683** million adherents in Indonesia, Pakistan, India, and Bangladesh. Of the denominations, most Muslims belong to one of two denominations.
- **Sunni** – (80-90% of Muslims) Sunni Muslims believe the first four caliphs were the rightful successors to Muhammad. Sunnis believe that a caliph should be chosen by the whole community. Since God did not specify any particular leaders to succeed him, those leaders had to be elected.

- **Shia** – (10-20% of Muslims) Shia Mulims believe that Ali ibn Abi Talib was the first Imam (leader). Shias believe that a caliph is appointed by divine will. To Shias, an Imam rules by right of divine appointment and holds 'Absolute spiritual authority' among Muslims.

Day of Resurrection

Belief in the 'Day of Resurrection' is crucial for Muslims. This day is believed to be preordained by God, but unknown to man. On **Yawm al-Qiyāmah** (Day of Resurrection/ Day of Judgment), Muslims believe all mankind will be judged on their good and bad deeds. Good deeds, such as charity and prayer, will be rewarded with entry to heaven. Muslims view heaven as a place of joy and bliss, with Qur'anic references describing its features and the physical pleasures to come. The Qur'an in turn lists several sins that can condemn a person to hell, such as disbelief and dishonesty, however, the Qur'an does make it clear God will forgive the sins of those who repent if he or she so wills.

Religion: (The Effects)

The **Dead Sea Scrolls** are a collection of **972** biblical texts found between **1947** and **1956**, at Khirbet Qumran on the northwest shore of the Dead Sea. They are of great importance to both biblical scholars and historians. Written in Hebrew, Aramaic and Greek, these texts are alleged to be the oldest known surviving copies of biblical and extra-biblical documents, generally dating between **200 BCE** and **70 CE**. An Ancient Jewish sect called the **Essenes** are thought to be responsible for writing these scrolls, but some suggest the documents were inscribed by priests in Jerusalem known as **Zadokites** (A sect of Jews formed around the time of the **Hasmonean** revolt in **200 BCE**), or other unknown Jewish groups. Regardless of its origins, the texts are closely identical to the **Torah** and the canonized **Bible**, which suggest that the Dead Sea Scrolls could have possibly inspired parts, if not all the texts in those books.

Along with the similarities, there are many differences which leads one to believe if these text did inspire the Bible and the Torah, could those writings have possibly been tampered with. For the most part, these texts have not been released in its entirety to the public, therefore much about the material is unknown.

This is important because new information on our past is constantly presenting itself, giving new insight into old histories, and withholding this type of information does not benefit anyone. These texts have not been released in its entirety mostly due to fear of religious backlash, wishing to keep things in order for as long as possible. These texts, along with many others, give insight into a history many have been trying to put together like a puzzle. It is important for these texts as well as many others to be made public, because people are only seeing a few pieces of the puzzle, judging the whole picture from the pieces they have. If they had more pieces they might be able to see a broader picture, and have a clearer understanding of themselves and the world around them.

In the grand scheme of things, when comparing the ages of some the major religions, you will find that **Judaism** is just a teenager, **Christianity** is a young child, and **Islam** is a baby. You cannot refute this. Taken into consideration, when comparing the three based on its timeline, this is the only observation one can have. This does not mean one is correct because it is older or more recent. One before the other does not make it more or less valid. They are just tools, all religions are tools that can either be helpful or overlooked. It is your choice to use or disregard them, unfortunately too many times when religion has been embraced it has been misused or misunderstood.

For the most part, people tend to view the texts in which their religion is based as holy or divine, the **Torah**, the **Holy Bible**, the **Holy Qur'an**, not taking into account that they are missing one important fact in their reading. The Torah and the Bible state the impurities of man repeatedly within its pages, the Qur'an does the same. The Prophet Muhammad, the author of the Qur'an, makes no secret that he is of sin. All religious texts were written through the hands of man, and if you are to take this thought into account, 'Man is of sin,' then there is a big contradiction to the religious text. They are not 'Holy,' this of course is if you side on the belief that man is impure.

Being that the Bible and Qur'an were written through the hands of man, regardless if it were the words of a Holy God, the purity is in turn diluted with the impurity of man writing the words. For if any drop of impureness blends into something that is pure, it taints it, it smears it, it is not pure, it makes it unholy. The messages in the text, when spoken of man being of sin, are clues and hints to make you understand do not take this literally, they are there to make you realize the faults of man that could either purposely or accidently mislead you, just to make their point. One must also take this into account, explaining the ideas of God can be extremely difficult to put into human words.

Another observation is that most of the prophets, in which people worship today, did not practice the religious faith that came after them. Buddha was not a Buddhist, he was Hindu. Buddhism came after him. Jesus, being a Jew, did not practice Christian customs, he practiced Jewish customs because he was Jewish. What he spoke, were of Buddhist values. What came after him was Christianity.

Since its origins, the population and numbers of different religions have grown drastically. There are more than 20 major religions that exist in the world today. As of **2011**, a listing below is an account of its members:

Religion	Founded	Sacred Texts	Members
Tribal Religions	Prehistory	Oral tradition	232 mil
Judaism	2000 BCE	Torah	14.5 mil
Hinduism	1500 BCE	Bhagavad-Gita	950 mil
Wicca	800 BCE	None	0.5 mil
Zoroastrianism	600 BCE	Avesta	2.7 mil
Jainism	570 BCE	Siddhanta	4.3 mil
Taoism	550 BCE	Tao-te-Ching	2.7 mil
Buddhism	523 BCE	Tripitaka	350–1,600 mil

Confucianism	520 BCE	Lun Yu	6.3 mil
Chinese Folk Religion	270 BCE	None	390 mil
Christianity	30 CE	Bible	2,039 mil
Shinto	500 CE	Kojiki	2.7 mil
Islam	622 CE	Qur'an	1,570 mil
Sikhism	1500 CE	Guru Granth Sahib	23.8 mil
Baha'i Faith	1863 CE	al-Kitab al-Aqdas	7.4 mil
Other Religions	Various	Various	1.1 mil
New Religions	Various	Various	103 mil
Spiritualism	No date	None	12.6 mil
Atheists	No date	None	150 mil
No Religion	No date	None	775 mil

Looking at this chart, it is easy to recognize how there can be such strong division amongst the people in the world today. Religion has molded our society in such a segregated way that it has drawn away from its true intentions. If you truly embrace the message, you will see it is the same, Islam, Christianity, Judaism, Buddhism, Hinduism and almost every other religion we have on planet Earth, the message breaks itself down to the same thing.

What is it that divides us religiously? The **Messenger**. The messenger is who divides us, however, it is not the messenger themself who does this, it is the people who follow the message of that particular messenger. For centuries people have killed, tortured, and burned villages, not because of the message, but because they are fighting over who translated the message, they are in turn fighting over the messenger. People have often found themselves worshiping the prophet that brought the message, instead of the message, even though the prophet reveals over and over again that the message is the most important. In fact, all prophets, whether it is Jesus, Moses, Muhammad or Buddha, have expressed that they themselves should not be worshiped, so it is ironic to have religions in their name.

More importantly you should wonder, what type of God would want you to kill, torture and commit genocide in its name? Possibly, a jealous one. What kind of God would want you praying to 'It' to solve all your problems? Possibly, a needy one. God is not jealous, nor needy. God is accepting. No matter the outcome, it has accepted the course of your journey, but to the contrary, would rather you solve all your own problems, especially since you have all the tools to do so. God would not let you come here without all the proper measures for you to live out the best possible life you could have, so in actuality there is no need to ask God for anything.

When you find yourself depending on God to make your decisions, this is when you are giving over the power of your own fate. That is the last thing God would ask, for you to give away the control of your own outcome. It is much more satisfying, more appreciative and way more gratifying when you realize you are the 'Maker' of your own fate, this is something that God knows for you.

It is simple as not relying on another human being to be the aider in your dilemmas. Think of all the times you have accomplished something by yourself, whether it was a project you worked on for school, or a Job you are hoping to get. In both cases, when one goes the length to achieve such measures by their own will, it is so much more fulfilling of an experience than to know someone else has done it for you.

Religion takes away all your power and leaves it in the hands of another. Religion is just a tool, it is something you use, it is not something that becomes you. The second you join or claim a religion, you have then segregated yourself from a part of the world, when God holds no separation.

Beyond all the customs and rituals that surround most religions, at the base floor, the message is essentially the same, therefore there is essentially one religion. The message all religions try to present is love one another, treat those how you wish to be treated, live your life to the fullest and find appreciation for the world that was given to you by the 'Creator.' How hard can it be to do this? Why do people make this so complex? It doesn't matter what religion you find yourself a part of, you don't need to be religious, you don't even have to believe in God to know these are the core values to finding a peaceful coexistence. The message is simple, it always has been, and always will be.

CHAPTER SEVEN
(Human Evolution)

"A round man cannot be expected to fit into a square hole right away. He must have time to modify his shape."
- Mark Twain -

Human Evolution: (Introduction)

  Scientist and theorist have been trying to find the 'One' correct answer to how **Human Beings** have come into existence. People have gone to many extremes and measures to come across these results, through science, trance channeling, and ancient findings. Being that there are no records historians and psyches all collectively view as accurate, scientists have had a more 'Common Acceptance' of their findings, with the mainstream public.

  Homo Sapiens can evolve through **Breeding, Genetic Manipulation** or **Natural Selection.** Breeding and genetic manipulation has been used for many different scientific experiments through the centuries. One clear example of breeding is dogs. Dogs have been bred over and over again, to make new breeds from its original makers. Natural selection is most effective when a species has to adapt to the new environment, therefore forming traits that better enable them to adapt to the specific pressures of their current environment, this usually happens over the course of hundreds of thousands of years.

  Ernst Mayr, a German American Evolutionary Biologist, noted that, *"A species need not evolve. Some species remain identical for hundreds of thousands or millions of years. And the evolution of humans has had long periods of little change, such as the **Homo Erectus** which did not change very much for **1.5** million years."* This is a compelling statement to make, because it leads to further wondering about the arrival of the **Homo Sapiens**, due to its supposed timeline. Could it be another form of evolution of human beings came about through **Migration**, from other worlds?

Most scientists feel that understanding ancestry roots of humans is important for its future evolution. To further understand the possibilities of **Human Evolution**, it may be best to fully understand your options and what they entail.

Human Evolution: (Evolution Theory)

When it comes to the progression of the 'Human Body,' the most widespread modern belief is the **'Theory of Evolution**,' a theory made popular by **Charles Darwin**. **Human Evolution** is the phenotypic history of the emergence of **Homo Sapiens** into its own distinct species of hominids, deriving from chimpanzees or the **Australopithecus, 4** million years ago.

The word **'Homo**,' the name of the biological genus to which humans belong, is Latin for 'Human.' In Latin, 'Homo' derives from the Indo-European root **'Dhghem'** or 'Earth.' The adjective **'Sapiens'** is Latin for wise or intelligent.

The genus **Homo** had diverged about **2.3** to **2.4** million years ago in Africa. Today, all humans belong to one population of **Homo Sapiens**, undivided by species barrier. Recent origin hypothesis suggest Homo Sapiens arose in Africa and migrated out of the continent around **50,000** to **100,000** years ago, replacing populations of **Homo Erectus** in Asia and **Neanderthals** in Europe.

When comparing single nucleotide polymorphisms, human **DNA** is approximately **98.4%** identical to chimpanzees. Scientists have estimated humans branched off from their common ancestor with chimpanzees about **5** to **7** million years ago. **Homo Sapiens** are the only extant species of its genus, Homo. A time line of the Homo species is provided below:

Homo Habilis: 2.3 million – **1.4** million **BCE**
    Height: **3.3–4.9 ft**, located in **Africa**
Homo Gautengensis: 2.0 million – **600,000 BCE**
    Height: **3.3 ft**, located in **South Africa**

Homo Rudolfensis: **1.9** million **BCE**
   Height: **Unknown**, located in **Kenya**
Homo Ergaster: **1.9** million – **1.4** million **BCE**
   Height: **6.2 ft**, Located in **Eastern** and **Southern Africa**
Homo Georgicus: 1.8 million **BCE**
   Height: **Unknown**, located in **Georgia**
Homo Erectus: 1.5 million – **200,000 BCE**
   Height: **5.9 ft**, located in **Africa, Eurasia**
Homo Antecessor: Lived **1.2** million – **800,000 BCE**
   Height: **5.7 ft**, located in **Spain**
Homo Cepranensis: Lived **900,000** – **800,000 BCE**
   Height: **Unknown**, located in **Italy**
Homo Heidelbergensis: 600,000 – **350,000 BCE**
   Height: **5.9 ft**, located in **Europe, Africa, China**
Homo Neanderthalensis: 400,000 – **30,000** BCE
   Height: **5.2 ft**, located in **Europe, Western Asia**
Homo Rrhodesiensis: 300,000 – **120,000 BCE**
   Height: **Unknown**, located in **Zambia**
Homo Sapiens: 200,000 BCE – **Present**
   Height: **4.6–6.2 ft**, located **Worldwide**
Homo Sapiens Idaltu: 160,000 – **150,000** BCE
   Height: **Unknown**, located in **Ethiopia**
Homo Floresiensis: 100,000 – **12,000 BCE**
   Height: **3.3 ft**, located in **Indonesia**

   Homo Neanderthalensis lived from **400,000** to about **30,000** years ago. Nearly all modern non-African humans have 1% to 4% of their DNA derived from Neanderthal DNA. Each phase of homo started at a higher level than the previous one, but further development slowed once the 'Bump' in initial progress occurred. For the most part, the homo species were culturally conservative in comparisons to other mammals, but after **50,000 BCE** modern human culture started to change at a greater speed.
   Human behavior has progressed through the years from cave drawings, to specialization of tools, hunting techniques, use of jewelry, organization of living space, rituals, burials,

migration to more habitual living conditions and trade networks. Debate continues as to whether a sudden 'Big Bang' in human consciousness led to modern humans, or whether the evolution was gradual over time.

Understanding how man may have evolved from apes can be comprehended in extraordinary ways. The evolution progress of all creatures seems to advance physically and mentally to perform adequately for its present time, from its predecessors.

The many fossils found to have been a part of the homo body structure seem to progress itself into an upright walking motion over time, but understanding how the homo species could evolve from apes and start to have conscious thinking is of a greater evolution. Most people think apes have much lower capabilities of being civilized in the same fashion humans think they are now. What could bring forth this growth in consciousness, which would in turn find the need to evolve its body structure? It is to wonder, did the physical growth bring forth consciousness, or did consciousness bring forth physical growth? If conscious did bring forth this growth, how could consciousness come into play?

A theory of the growth in an ape's consciousness can be attributed to some of the drugs humans use today. **Mushrooms** containing **Psilocybin**, traditionally used for spiritual purposes with a history of use spanning creation, were one of the drugs that seemed to define the **'Hippie Era.'** In **1957**, published in a **Life** article, an American banker, R. **Gordon Wasson** introduced the drug to popular culture by describing his experiences ingesting psilocybin-containing mushrooms, during a traditional ceremony in Mexico.

The effects of **Psilocybin Mushrooms** have ranged from **Out of Body Experiences, Hallucinations,** seeing **One's Self,** and extreme **Revelations** of **Knowledge.** The intensity and duration of the effects are highly depended on the cultivar of mushrooms, dosage, individual physiology, and setting. The mind-altering effects of psilocybin typically last anywhere from **3** to **8** hours.

Psilocybin is produced by over **200** species of fungi, the most notable being those of the genus **Psilocybe**, such as **Psilocybe Cubensis**, **Psilocybe Semilanceata**, and **Psilocybe Cyanescens**. While **Psilocybin Mushrooms** are found in many areas of nature, it has also been known to be found on cow manure.

Comedian **Bill Hicks** once performed a routine on the evolution of 'Ape to Man,' using the philosophy behind such mushrooms. Explaining how a monkey was one day walking around in the jungle and steps in some form of manure, Hicks then acts out as he were the monkey, seeing the mushrooms in the manure, and thinking they're good to eat. After eating the mushrooms, Hicks continues acting out as the monkey, feeling lightheaded and queasy from what he just ate and the effects of the psilocybin in the mushrooms. Sitting himself down by a stool, rubbing his head and making chimpanzee noises, he then started to act out as if he were having visual effects and zoned out into watching extraordinary things. As the monkey (Hicks) then comes out of his experience and hallucinations, he then slowly stops making chimpanzee noises, and starts to hum the theme song from the movie '**2001 Space Odyssey**,' giving the impression as if he had some type of awakening. He then looks out into the audience and says, "*I think I want to go to the Moon.*"

The idea of monkeys eating mushrooms and having psychedelic experiences or hallucinations has to seem logical, especially since it gives human such effects. Humans today receive all kinds of hallucinations and revelations from these drugs, ranging in intensity and effects, some describing things as calm and feeling a sense of enlightenment, to visions some have during the '**Near Death Experience**.' If monkeys indeed digested these chemicals, than surely their brains were affected in a drastic way as well. If these types of drugs can make humans look within themselves and find spiritual awareness, then why can't it affect monkeys to find spiritual growth or awareness as well?

Today, as humans evolve physically, the bodies are living longer, the arms are getting stronger, the legs of sprinters are getting faster, breaking world record after world record, only because of the thought that says, 'We can do better.' The thoughts motive changes in the bodies. Could it also be true that the thoughts of an ape motived changes in its own body as well? Just as humans get a sense of feeling more than being 'Human' when digesting such chemicals, could an ape's thoughts of wanting to be more than just an ape have been affected by these components as well?

Human Evolution: (Planet Migration Theory)

Professor Chandra Wickramasinghe of **Cardiff University** has explained that many things support the view of human life beginning from outside our planet. As published in the **Cambridge University International Journal of Astrobiology**, Wickramasinghe says, *"Yes, we are all strangers. We are descendants of various cosmic."* Wickramasinghe believes life was sent from planet to planet over billions of years, suggesting that a comet hit the planet's life, therefore pushing the material into space. *"We are part of a connected chain that extends over a large volume of the cosmos,"* he explains. Until now, Wickramasinghe cannot explain how life actually began and where it is from.

Trance Channelers such as **Carla L. Rueckert** and **Barbara Marciniak** have provided a more in depth rationale to human existence. Through their trance sessions, they have brought forth new models on human origins. Most channelers who are able to tune into another place and time to receive such information, explain they are in turn no way divine or special. They are simply willing to do so. Many humans have always had the capacity to do this.

In **'The Law of One: Book I The Ra Material,' Don Elkins** asked the **Social Memory Complex** known as **'Ra,'** who was being channeled through Carla Rueckert, to explain the origins of **Human Beings**. Excerpts from the conversation are as follows:

Questioner (Don Elkins): *Are there any people such as you find on Earth on any of the other planets in our solar system?*

Ra: *I am Ra. Do you request space/time present information or space/time continuum information?*

Questioner (Don Elkins): *Both.*

Ra: *I am Ra. At one time/space, in what is your past, there was a population of third-density beings upon a planet which dwelt within your solar system. There are various names by which this planet has been named. The vibratory sound complex most usually used by your peoples is **Maldek**. These entities, destroying their planetary sphere, thus were forced to find room for themselves upon this third density which is the only one in your solar system at their time/space present which was hospitable and capable of offering the lessons necessary to decrease their mind/body/spirit distortions with respect to the Law of One.*

Questioner (Don Elkins): *How did they come here?*

Ra: *I am Ra. They came through the process of harvest and were incarnated through the processes of incarnation from your higher spheres within this density.*

Questioner (Don Elkins): *How long ago did this happen?*

Ra: *I am Ra. This occurred approximately **500,000** of your years ago.*

Questioner (Don Elkins): *Is all of the Earth's human population then originally from **Maldek**?*

Ra: *I am Ra. This is a new line of questioning, and deserves a place of its own. The ones who were harvested to your sphere from the sphere known before its dissolution as other names, but to your peoples as **Maldek**, incarnated, many within your Earth's* *surface rather than upon it. The population of your planet contains many various groups harvested from other second-dimension and cycled third-dimension spheres. You are not all one race or background of beginning. The experience you share is unique to this time/space continuum.*

Questioner (Don Elkins): *Where did the people who are like us who were the first ones here, where did they come from? From where did they evolve?*

Ra: *I am Ra. You speak of third-density experience. The first of those to come here were brought from another planet in your solar system called by you the* **Red Planet***,* **Mars***. This planet's environment became inhospitable to third-density beings. The first entities, therefore, were of this race, as you may call it, manipulated somewhat by those who were guardians at that time.*

Questioner (Don Elkins): *What race is that, and how did they get from Mars to here?*

Ra: *I am Ra. The race is a combination of the mind/body/spirit complexes of those of your so-called Red Planet and a careful series of genetical adjustments made by the guardians of that time. These entities arrived, or were preserved, for the experience upon your sphere by a type of birthing which is non-reproductive, but consists of preparing genetic material for the incarnation of the mind/body/spirit complexes of those entities from the Red Planet.*

Questioner (Don Elkins): *I assume from what you are saying that the guardians transferred the race here after the race had died from the physical as we know it on Mars. Is that correct?*

Ra: *I am Ra. This is correct.*

Questioner (Don Elkins): *How long ago did this transfer occur from the Red Planet to Earth?*
Ra: *I am Ra. In your time this transfer occurred approximately 75,000 years ago.*

Questioner (Don Elkins): *Then our human race is formed of a few who originally came from Maldek and quite a few who came from Mars. Are there entities here from other places?*
Ra: *I am Ra. There are entities experiencing your time/space continuum who have originated from many, many places, as you would call them, in the creation, for when there is a cycle change, those who must repeat then find a planetary sphere appropriate for this repetition. It is somewhat unusual for a planetary mind/body/spirit complex to contain those from many, many various loci, but this explains much, for, you see, you are experiencing the third-dimension occurrence with a large number of those who must repeat the cycle. The orientation, thus, has been difficult to unify even with the aid of many of your teach/learners.*

Barbara Marciniak, who is known for her books on the **Pleiadians**, adds to the Human Migration theory from her accounts of channeling 'Higher Sources.' The Pleiadians are from the star system **Pleiades**, a small cluster of seven stars located in the Constellation of 'Taurus the Bull,' **500** light-years away from planet Earth. With a telescope, you can see about **100** stars, without a telescope you can see about seven. The names of these seven stars in the Pleiades system are as follows, **Taygeta**, **Maya**, **Coela**, **Atlas**, **Merope**, **Electra** and **Alcoyne**.

The **Pleiadians** are a very ancient race of humanoids that is believed to visit Earth often and whom share a common ancestry with humans. The **Lyrans** from **Lyra** are our supposed common ancestors. The **Pleiadians** claim Earth is **626** billion years old, and have kept a record of the complete history of

Earth's human evolution from the very beginning to present time.

Around **225,000 BCE**, the Pleiadians found a small sun system with a planet on one of their scouting missions away from the Pleiades. On Earth, they discovered **three** groups of uncivilized people. The larger of these groups were light skinned and of **Lyran** descent. The **Lyrans** had landed on Earth around **228,000 BCE** and were forced to stay behind and enter into an incarnational cycle, because of their ill treatment of the original brown skinned natives. At this time the Pleiadians decided to stay and create societies on Earth, to help with the progression in the next step in human evolution.

The Pleiadians are humans' next level of evolution. Many are highly evolved, more so than most of the human species. They are on a **Fifth Dimensional Frequency** which is one of, '**Love** and **Creativity**.' The Pleiadians do not claim to be God, yet they bring wisdom, as many others have brought throughout the ages from higher realms.

With many fascinating legends and stories of their existence, the Pleiadians have been known of for thousands of years. In certain Cherokee folklore, much of which has been encoded, kept secret or hidden, it is said that their people originated from the Pleiades a long time ago, and came to Earth as Starseeds, to bring **Light** and **Knowledge**.

While this hypothesis may seem farfetched to many, to others, humans migrating from other planets beyond the Solar System fits perfectly. The **United States of America** is a great example of the many different shades, breeds and build of Human Beings that exist within a country. Walk down the street of **Broadway Avenue** in **New York City**, you will not see one type of human race, there will be many, people from different backgrounds, with many different shapes, structures and sizes, it is a mixing pot of culture, a lot of everything.

While there are hundreds of different nationalities, they all derived from a handful of human breeds. The **African, European, Asian, Arab** and **American Native** seem to be the most vivid among today's societies.

The **Asian Culture** for instance has different demographics of the **Chinese**, **Japanese** and **Korean**, being a few to name, yet although they are of Asian descent, they all have different cultures and histories of their own, but still rather much resemble each other in appearance. The slant of the eyes may be the most notable to some, while others may recognize the build and hair texture as their most comparing features. Regardless, once making this observation, it should be recognized the region in which the people originally resided before migrating to other places on the planet.

The peoples of the **African** countries have the same case. While many are from **Nigeria**, **Ethiopia** or **Ghana**, they all have features similar, dark skinned, wide noses, lips, body structure, they all have slight differences, but are designated to the same group.

Europeans (Caucasians), before migrating to other parts of the world, such as the **Americas**, are just the same. The fair skin, narrow noses, facial build and eye color are a few examples to show their similarities. Whether from **Spain**, **England** or **France**, they all have slight differences, but yet share the same structure.

This could also be said for **Arabs** or the **North** and **South American Natives** as well. While other cultures such as the people of the **Philippians** or the **Caribbean Islands** may be a mixture of these different demographics, over the course of time it could cause the original components of that breed of human to mix into a new breed. This can be seen today with the many different people in the United States, many different cultures and races that when one group mixes with another, they seem to take on resemblances of the features that help breed them.

Of the major demographics, how did people come to look so different? The theory of man first originating in Africa, then spreading out to other parts of the planet for their bodies to form accordingly to their climate is a strong case, but in the span that this is said to have occurred, genetically it is not enough time for the features on their bodies to look so different.

Human skin color ranges from almost black to almost white, with a pinkish tinge due to the blood vessels underneath. In human beings, **Melanin** is the primary determinant of skin color. Melanin is produced by cells called **Melanocytes**, and is triggered by an enzyme called **Tyrosinase**, which creates the color of skin, eyes, and hair.

The variation in natural skin color is thought to be mainly due to genetics. According to scientific studies, natural skin color diversity is highest in **Sub-Saharan African** populations, with skin reflectance values ranging from **19** to **46**, compared with **Europeans** at **62** to **69**, and **East Asian** populations at **50** to **59**. A person's natural skin color is impacted from its exposure to the Sun.

It is believed that between **70,000** to **100,000** years ago, modern humans began to migrate away from African regions and onto the northern hemisphere, where they were exposed to less intense sunlight. If this is accurate, than this means in the terms of evolution, it took at least **70,000** years for the skin color and features of the current Homo Sapiens to slightly evolve to show the difference they have now. If you take **Ernst Mayr**'s suggestion that a species remains identical for hundreds of thousands or millions of years, then **100,000** years may not have been enough time for the Sun and the climate to change the way modern day humans differ today.

Could it be that the species of man originated from outside its Solar System? To imagine the climate of the Earth could over time cause these distinct differences in people can be hard to digest, but to imagine the human species came from other planets, where those atmospheres are possibly drastically different from one another, just to spread across different sections of the Earth, could be a way to explain the differences. Surely someone from **Lyra** might have a slightly different structure than someone from the **Red Planet**, Mars. Taking into account the possibility of different climates and locations these planets are in, it would make for a more compelling case to why one might have fair skin, slanted eyes, or wide noses.

Human Evolution: (Alien Creation Theory)

Most scientists have agreed there is one major problem with the evolution of man, a 'Missing Link' that connects the current human species to Neanderthals. There is compelling evidence from sequencing **Mitochondrial DNA** that indicates no significant gene flow occurred between **Neanderthals** and **Homo Sapiens**, therefore the two must be separate species that may have shared a common ancestor. In **1997**, **Mark Stoneking** explained, *"These results* (Based on Mitochondrial DNA extracted from Neanderthal bone*) indicate that Neanderthals did not contribute Mitochondrial DNA to modern humans...Neanderthals are not our ancestors."* A following investigation of a second source of Neanderthal DNA also supported these findings.

Lloyd Pye published a book called, '**Everything You Know is Wrong**,' in which he challenges the evolution of **Darwinism** (Humans evolving from apes), and states that human beings do not have a natural scheme on Earth. He explains that **Darwinism** supports **Macroevolution**, which is species evolving into species, but humans have changing body-parts, which is called **Microevolution**. He explains, **Darwinism** is the extrapolation of microevolution (If you can have changing body parts, you can have changes in the whole body), but though it seems logical, there is no trace of that being true anywhere in the historical record. **Pye** continues to explain the theory that **Australopithecus** evolved into early homos **4** million years ago is wrong, and the **Australopithecus** are the ancestors to today's living hominoids, being **Big Foot, Sasquatch**, and the **Abominable Snowman**.

Primates have **48** chromosomes, while humans have a total of **46** chromosomes, in pairs of **23**. The mitochondrial DNA, which goes back **150,000** years, is regarded as the smallest chromosome and is the first significant part of the human genome to be sequenced. The human genome looks very much like a primate genome, except the second and third chromosomes are fused together into one. This gives you all the chromosome material of the primate, now taking up the space in the combining **46** chromosomes. It is **46** chromosomes with **48** chromosomes of genomic material still in there. One must wonder, how could nature fuse these two chromosomes in **150,000** years of time?

Pye believes the writings by the **Sumerians** are the most logical depiction of how humans came to be. He goes on to explain that human DNA was created by an extraterrestrial species called the **Annuanki**, using the creature of Earth, now known as the **Australopithecus**, and made the **Atom** move, to make humans in their own image and their own likeness, as we look like them. He suggests the Annuanki gave humans their bodies, as the **Bible** states in **Genesis 1:26**, *"God said, let us make man in our image, after our likeness."*

Zecharia Sitchin's series of books, **'The Earth Chronicles,'** beginning with, **'The 12th Planet,'** centers on Sitchin's theory that the Sumerians were created by a group of Anunnaki. He suggest that **50** Anunnaki from planet **Nibiru**, came to Earth approximately **400,000** years ago with the intent of mining raw materials, particularly gold, to transport back to their planet Nibiru. Sitchin wrote the Anunnaki grew tired of mining, due to their small numbers, and mutinied over their displeasure with their working conditions, therefore **Enki** (A God in Sumerian mythology) ordered them to relive themselves by genetic engineering slaves to replace them in the gold mines, by crossing extraterrestrial genes with those of the **Homo Erectus**, which after many trials and errors they eventually created the **Homo Sapiens**.

According to Sitchin, ancient inscriptions in Sumer report the human civilization was set up under the guidance of these 'Gods,' and kingship was installed to provide intermediaries between mankind and the Anunnaki, creating the **'Divine Right of Kings'** doctrine. Sitchin states the Anunnaki, who he believes to be **Nephilim** in **Genesis**, were active in human affairs until global catastrophes caused the destruction and abrupt end to their culture, around **12,000** years ago, near the last **Ice Age**. Seeing that some humans survived but all they had built was destroyed, the Anunnaki left Earth, giving humans the opportunity and capability to govern themselves.

Sitchin suggest in the case of '**Adam**'s alien genes,' the **223** unique genes found by the **Human Genome Sequencing Consortium** are without the needed predecessors on the genomic evolutionary tree. Some researchers have debated the conclusion from the Human Genome Sequencing Consortium cannot be drawn, due to a lack of a comprehensive gene database for comparison.

Sitchin believes his research coincides with many biblical texts, claiming the biblical texts such as Genesis originally come from Sumerian writings. Sitchin believes a fallout from nuclear weapons used during a war between groups of the extraterrestrials is the '**Evil Wind**' described in the '**Lament for Ur**' (A Sumerian lament/poem composed around the time of the fall of Ur), in which destroyed **Ur** around **2000 BCE**.

The reason for 'Aliens creating Human Beings' being a sound argument is from the simple notion of knowing what human beings have been capable of. Think for a moment, the knowledge, wisdom and technology humans have obtained in just **100** years alone, throughout the **20th Century**. In **1903** the **Wright Brothers** invented the first airplane. It traveled **7** miles per hour and stayed in the air for **12** seconds. Now there are jets that can do laps around the sound barrier. We have grown to have nuclear energy, the Internet, cell phones, USBs and telescopes that let us see millions of light-years away and last but certainly not least…cloning.

Just **15** years ago, in **1996**, a sheep named **Dolly** was cloned by **Ian Wilmut, Keith Campbell** and colleagues at the **Roslin Institute** near Edinburgh in Scotland. The cell used as the donor for the cloning of Dolly was taken from a mammary gland, therefore proving that a cell taken from a specific part of the body could indeed recreate a whole individual. Why is this important? It is important because to understand that scientists are able to clone sheep, than surely they are able to clone a human being. Whether they have achieved this or not is up for debate, but the mere fact that it is possible is now undeniable. Surely it has been an amazing progression to be able to do these things.

Take the timeline from the first intelligent civilization, this being Sumer, dating back to at least **4500 BCE**, to what some believe possibly **10,000** years ago, and this excluding the new findings of pyramids discovered in Bosnia which could be as old as **12,000** to **15,000 BCE**, and use this as a comparison for progression with human knowledge. If we take the **10,000** years of intelligent life that we know and see how we have progressed from making tools and writing on cave walls to now cloning sheep, and compare that to the possible timeline of an alien species beyond this Earth, it begins to become clearer of how it is possible for Human Beings to be a race that was created, and not evolved.

If the existence of aliens is correct, which there are many documented findings here on Earth, artifacts, statues and sightings that build on the possibility of this to be true, and if aliens are advanced enough to come here into the atmosphere of Earth, whether on spacecrafts or other means of transportation, then their knowledge would seem to date beyond more than **10,000** years. Surely their civilizations have been around much longer than the timeline we have for ourselves as humans, if in turn we are just realizing what we are capable of. Alien species must be more in tuned to their abilities, and much more evolved than most creatures here on Earth, especially since to the best of our knowledge humans haven't traveled further than walking on the Moon.

If aliens are advanced enough to come here, and their knowledge is beyond the **10,000** years we know for our own intelligent means of communication, than for certain they are not only advanced enough to clone a sheep, but possibly advanced enough to create a whole new living being. Surely they could be advanced enough to take the 'Missing link' of Neanderthals and manipulate the DNA in a way that it brings about the upright structure we all know as Homo Sapiens.

Some could find fear with this being true, our 'Creators' being an alien species, some might not be able to handle feeling as though their bodies were created in 'In a Lab.' If so, this fear should be no more than a passing thought. The fear of Extraterrestrials possibly being your creator only extends to just your body, a body that even if they had their hands in creating, they have no control over.

Human Evolution: (Theory of Us All)

Unfortunately for most scientists, after coming up with an understanding of how humans came to be, they tend to let their information lead them to one conclusion, one answer. Whether it is the evolution process, the migration theory or if humans were genetically engineered, they do not leave the window open for all three or possibly more resolutions, when there could really be many reasons to why and how humans evolved on Earth.

Why can't all three theories be correct? Could it be that our bodies have been processed in more than one way? Could some humans have evolved from apes and others migrated here from other planets? Yes, especially if beings from another planet had in fact populated Earth, they too would be evolutions of something. Possibly they were genetically engineered, and if so, maybe that is why they knew how to create a human body. Could it be that some of these beings who could have migrated here, stayed behind with the beings they help engineer?

In modern standards these are revolutionary ideas, but just the thought of you being here is revolutionary. Why can't all of this be true, why can't we be evolutions of them all, especially since the one thing that is true is 'You' aren't any of these things at all.

You are not the descendants of apes, you are not of a race from another planet, and you are not a body that has been engineered. While many of us think we are Human Beings, instead, you are simply just being…Human.

CHAPTER EIGHT
(What You Really Are)

"You are not a human being in search of a spiritual experience. You are a spiritual being immersed in a human experience."
- Teilhard de Chardin -

What You Really Are: (Introduction)

What are you, really? What is the thing that makes you, You? People often look into the mirror and see their reflection as what makes them who they are. The features of the face, the structures and curves, most people tend to identify themselves as what they look like. There is a very interesting alternative to this. People only know what they look like, from their reflection.

People know what they look like because they see themselves through other things like mirrors, still water, photographs and videos. People can't actually physically see themselves. The placement of the eyes makes it so that the only parts of the body you are able to vividly see, is from the chest on down. You can't actually look at your own face. You know what you look like through the aid of other materials. , therefore, if there were never mirrors, still water, photographs or videos, you would not know what you look like, but what you look like can't be who you truly are.

The skin is just a layer. The face is just a makeup of bone structure behind that layer. Many have changed what they look like through plastic surgery, some feeling better about themselves after doing so, but this is another illusion. The person you truly are, the thing that makes you 'Yourself' can't be reconstructed with the process of a change in body structure.

You must wonder, so who are you, and what are you, really?

What You Really Are: (The Reconstructing Body)

Many people have put emphasis on the importance of calling the body, a 'Temple.' This theory needs explaining if one chooses to look at the body this way. The idea that the body should be viewed as a temple is and is not correct.

The body is a temple, in the sense that you should take care of it, for it is like your car, it is your means of transportation here in the 'Physical Realm' and it should be taken care of like a vehicle. Get a check-up, go for an emissions test, you should treat your body like you do your car. If not taken care of properly, you may find yourself with a decaying engine and it could go out on you on the middle of the highway (Life). Take care of your body, even if it is just flesh, it's the only one you have for this current experience.

The body is also not your temple, in the sense of tattoos or even plastic surgery for that matter. It is just a body, nothing more than that. Sometimes people have been judged, ridiculed or condemned for the body markings or placing things on and through their skin, but it is in comparisons of having a paint job, or fixing and adding a new part to your vehicle. It is just a body.

You are the driver (Mind) in this experience of life, and the body is the vehicle. If you are to depend on this vehicle, it is important to take care of it in order for it to provide the functions the driver wishes upon. Just like vehicles, the body has so many different forms, Fords, Chevys, Chryslers, Mercedes, BMWs, there are so many different models, cars, trucks or jeeps to choose from, some with special features and from different years. There are so many different ways to get to where you want to go, and all of them have their disadvantages and advantages, for there is no positive without a negative.

The body should be looked at objectively and appreciated for what it is, and what its purposes are. Its purpose is for you to use as a physical structure to carry out your thoughts in physical form.

Unknowingly to most, our bodies actually feel uncomfortable to us. Being placed and maneuvering in a body is an adjustment. For instance, some may find themselves with what they call a nervous twitch, but twitching at times when they aren't actually nervous. Maybe someone moves a shoulder over and over again, blinks a lot or has a stutter. Surely some people have these symptoms and others sum it up to being nervous or paranoid, when really there are many who don't feel nervous or paranoid in these moments. It is because the body is uncomfortable.

Imagine living inside your car for your whole life, after a while you're going to feel a little boxed in, you're going to feel like you want to reach out and stretch. For the most part, you may get accustom to this over time, but once you have a moment of freedom to get outside that car, getting back in it will be an instant reminder of how uncomfortable it actually is.

According to **Ra**, the **Social Memory Complex** channeled in the books '**The Law of One**,' the purpose of us having physical bodies that grow weak with age is to move us towards compassion and caring as we watch each other's bodies deteriorate. **Ra** stated that once we learn this quality of **Love**, we then move on to the higher densities (Planes of Existence or **Mind/Body/Soul** Levels), where the incarnations are significantly longer.

What You Really Are: (The Mind)

The question still remains, if you are not a human being in the sense of your body, than what must you be? To further understand this, first, get pass this notion that you are the make-up of your 'Family history.' You are not of the namesake of your family tree, you are not the descendant of your ancestors and forefathers, and you are not of their bloodlines. You are simply not these things. These are things that are the letterheads or titles on your vehicle, almost like a brand name, but you are not a brand name, you are not even your name.

The name you have now was given to you by your parents, probably from days and weeks and months of thought of what they felt might suit you, but whatever name they have picked out for you, this is not who you are. Surely your parents aren't passing over a name to you that they know you once took, in hopes of believing this name is who you are. No name could ever be who you are. You represent more than a name.

Names are things we come up with here on Earth, to separate and distinguish ourselves from others. As humans, we have isolated ourselves with names, in death, we are part of the 'One,' in which giving names is not a practice that is needed to identify you. Whatever your name is now, this is not who you are. The creator does not ultimately identify you by the name your parents gave you. The thought is mildly amusing to begin to think that your parents can name you any better than God chooses. Your parents do not hold that right, to name you something you will be called for your eternal life. If a name were to be how you are to identify yourself to the Universe, 'You' should then hold that right, no one else. A name is something that is given to you for temporary means.

Take your own lifespan and compare it to the possible **15** billion years of age many believe the Universe is, to think all of a sudden you just popped into existence, was giving a name by your parents, and this is who you now are to the Universe, doesn't make sense. Why? Because you are not a stranger to the Universe.

If you are not your body and you are not your name, then what are you? Energy. What you are is 'Pure Energy,' occupying the body people know as your *'Given Name.'* What you are is an Enlightened Being, what you ALL are, are Enlightened Beings occupying many upon many of different species and forms of nature and life, as vehicles. Truly you are no more different than the trees that surround you.

To better understand this concept, it is important to comprehend the difference between the brain and the mind, they are two totally different things. As stated earlier in a previous chapter the brain is like the hard drive to a computer, but in comparison to the Mind, your mind is like the Internet. Take away the computer, the Internet and its functions and knowhow is all still there, always was, always will be. It takes the computer, to see the Internet. Truly, the Internet isn't something that was created, it was always there, it took the computer to be able to see that the Internet exists. You can't touch the internet, you can't touch the mind. You can touch the computer, you can touch the brain. The internet is endless, so is the mind.

How does this relate to you? It relates to you, because to understand who you are, you must withdraw from the thoughts of body parts. For instance, let's start with the leg. Take away one's leg, surely the person is still who that person is, the person's identity doesn't exist in their leg. Take away the arm, the same can be said. As we take away other body parts, eventually taking away the head and then the brain, it then leaves one to wonder so what part is actually you?

What you are, and who you are, is **Energy**, **Thought**, **Consciousness**. You ARE your MIND. You are this beautiful thing which talks to you ever so silently that you don't even notice how it dictates your day. You are your Thoughts.

The Holy Trinity, in which Christianity preaches **Mind**, **Body** and the **Soul**, can be said to have given one too many properties to this sum, because it is not particularly **Mind, Body,** and **Soul**, it's more like, **Body** and **Mind-Soul**. Your 'Mind' and your 'Soul' are more so the same thing. When a soul or 'Conscious Energy' decides to take part in the physical, it searches for a bodily form. During the process of physical creation or conception, the Mind locks itself with its chosen vehicle, to begin its conscious experience.

To better understand what these bodies are to our Consciousness or soul, you can think of yourself as an '**Avatar**.' This was depicted extremely well in the movie **Avatar** by James Cameron, where the main character was enlisted in a program to infiltrate the **Na'vi** (A fictional indigenous species that live on the planet Pandora), as being seen as one of them. He did this by using an unconscious **Na'vi** body, and giving it 'Consciousness,' activating it with his thoughts as they were being transferred through a type of channeling chamber in which he was placed in during his times as being a '**Na'vi**.' The only difference between this movie and you is that you are not giving consciousness to a Na'vi's body, you are giving consciousness to a human body.

This should give calming notion to anyone finding it difficult to think they may need to adhere to another or any physical species that could have created humans. You have no master. The only master you have is yourself.

What You Really Are: (You're Higher Self)

Higher Consciousness is a concept of a spiritual transcendence of human consciousness. Within **Monotheism**, it also refers to the awareness or knowledge of the 'Ultimate,' sometimes known as God. Higher Consciousness is usually associated with exceptional control over one's mind and will. In a spiritual context, it may also be associated with **Transcendence, Spiritual Enlightenment, Channeling, Astral Projection** and **Out of Body Experiences.**

Meher Baba, an Indian spiritual teacher, explained that higher levels of consciousness emanate from love for God, expressing a notion that the higher the conscious thought, the closer to God one becomes. What we don't recognize is that we can, and do experience this type of consciousness every single day.

'**God**' is of pure enlightenment, its only manifestation is to love, give, accept and extend. In turn, we are capable of extending the same '**Light**' that God shares, through our own daily habits. A kind gesture we may do for someone, telling them they look nice in an article of clothing, whether it is giving a homeless man a meal, helping someone move, or loaning someone money, we get self-fulfillment and joy to know we have helped someone. This light comes from your **Higher Self**. Why? Because **You** are here to extend yourself. You are here to help make the world a positive place for '**Others**' and more importantly, yourself. When one finds gratification in helping someone, in turn it is channeling the higher vibrations of the true you.

There is another presence of you, here and always, it is what many call the **'Spirit'** or the soul. The soul is the part of you that knows it is divine in nature and all existence. The soul, which in turn is your **Higher Self** (You), is watching your every single move, has seen every single imagery continuity of your life, witnessed how you've lived all your lives before, knows every memory you've ever forgotten, is aware of your darkest secrets, deepest fears, most undeniable guilt and above all, it loves you unconditionally, because essentially, it is you, and you are it.

Pindar, an Ancient Greek lyric poet, explains that the soul sleeps while the limbs are active, but when one is sleeping, the Soul is active and reveals in many of dreams, *"An award of joy or sorrow drawing near."* The Soul reveals many awards in our dreams, but while the Soul is active when we sleep, it in turn does not rest when we awake, it is being forgotten that it is here. Why? You are the 'Active Driver' playing the part of Consciousness, you are taking ahold of the course of your day. Even though your Soul remains in the background, this does not mean it is resting. Your Soul is watching your every move. Watching, not resting. It is attentive, it is a listener, and it is a revealer. Throughout your day, it whistles clues or little reminders for you to be aware of your surroundings. Its sole purpose while we are awake is to remind us that we are **'Conscious**,' and have many different decisions and choices we can make.

Your Soul is playing this game with you, and knows it better than you, so it guides you, like a coach or owner of a team, that watches his players play the game. The **Commissioner** of the League, **God**, stands further in the background, operating all facets of business and marketing in order for the game to exist. This thought is close to **'Deism**,' a concept in which God does not alter the Universe by intervening in it; but nevertheless, God is in control of it.

You and your Soul are in conjunction with one another, and your purpose is initially the same, to progress. Like many coaches, your Soul has done this before, played the game before, led a team on the field before, won championships, lost championships, so it knows exactly how you should play the game, but it's the coach, so it can't play it for you. You have to take the shot, run the ball, or throw the pitch. The soul can give you hints as to what plays might work best, but it is you who has to do the legwork, and it is you who ultimately makes the last decision. Why? Because the ball is in your hands.

With this understood, do not be confused as to thinking your Soul is separate from you, your Soul is you. Your Soul could never be apart from you. It is not something you can lose, ever. The popular sayings people use such as, '*Sold my soul,*' or, '*Trying to buy back my soul,*' could never logically happen. No one else can occupy your Soul, your true self. It is yours, it is you, and just as much as it is 'You,' it is just as much a part of God.

Your Soul is connected to the 'Source' of which is all, therefore it is like a bridge from You, to God. The information it retains and gives you is based upon your own experiences and past lives, as well as from the Source (God). While you play the part of the **Conscious**, your Soul is in the background watching, and assisting you when you truly need it.

The soul, in turn is not apart, but a part in between **You** and **God**, which could be thought of as the **Superconscious**. It is the **Conscious** that is always learning, it is the **Subconscious** and **Superconscious** that always knows.

Plato, drawing on the words of his teacher **Socrates**, considered the soul the essence of a person, being that which decides how we behave. He thought this to be an incorporeal, eternal occupant of our being. As bodies die the soul is continually reborn in subsequent bodies. This is a brilliant observation. The soul is eternal, it is the body that is temporary, and the soul has occupied many of them.

The soul, playing the part of the coach or owner, has made trades, cut bodies from the team, and signed new bodies to help its ball club. The only connection you have with your body is right now. Your body is just a body, but your Soul is who you truly are, thought, the Mind. The body is not what you will take with you, it is an outlet for your Soul to use temporarily. Energy, you are Energy, You and your Soul are one, yet playing different parts to your experience.

It has also been speculated that your Soul, holds some type of mass. In **1907, Dr. Duncan MacDougall** explained the weight of the soul in the **'Journal of the American Society for Psychical Research.'** He had made weight measurements of patients as they died, claiming there was weight loss of varying amounts at the time of death. His results have never been reproduced, and are generally regarded either as meaningless or considered to have little if any scientific merit. The **2003** film **21 Grams** takes its title from the approximate weight loss measured in one of MacDougall's tests. If this is to be true, then what kind of weight could your Soul possibly hold? Life, your Soul holds the weight of life.

The soul is an entity, which holds the weight of your Higher Self, you're truest 'You.' Without the soul, you could not have life here, you wouldn't know life here, you would not be Conscious of it, and your body would not respond to your wishes. You are your Soul.

What You Really Are: (The Eyes)

There is a uniqueness to every one of us, a uniqueness that travels with us throughout each lifetime, and stays with us as 'Souls.' It is not a physical feature, yet, it is noticed in the eyes. It is not the color, nor the shape, but more so the expression in the eyes, it's **Aura**. This aura is always located in the eyes because it is where we most often look when we are communicating with another person or being. It is located in this area so that we can subtlety find each other when we are here, in the physical.

This 'Aura' has been with you throughout every journey you personally take. It is like placing your name or ownership on each body you choose to take. This aura does not change, while you will experience many different bodies, you only have one aura, and it is different from everyone or thing in the Universe.

Many times people have felt like they have known someone they just met, whether it was a positive or negative feeling, sometimes people instantly feel some type of connection with people they are just introduced to, even though they have never before seen the bodily form they are encountering, but it is only the bodily form they have not seen before. They have encountered the aura around the eyes many upon many of lifetimes.

We must be careful not to judge this aura, because the aura is pure goodness. If a person feels negative about someone while meeting them, it is not because of the aura itself, but it is because their aura may remind them of an experience they may have shared, however, that was a previous experience in another lifetime. It is not the aura that is tainted, the aura can never be tainted; it is the actions from the individual that presently taints them in each physical existence, therefore, every new person you encounter should be embraced on a clean slate, no matter how their aura makes you feel.

The aura is hard to detect without intentionally taking notice, but it can be presented with concentration. If you look into someone's eyes for an extended period of time, eventually all around them will dim and fade, so the outline of their face is more prevalent. As you continue to gaze, their face will dim as well, making it so their eyes is all that is clearly noticed. Eventually the physical presence in their eyes will retract, and the Aura around them will extract. The Aura around the eyes will seem to lay itself just overtop the eyes, across their nose, and present itself in a subtle, indefinable, shadowy, glowing fashion. It may slightly resemble what one might see when watching a **3D** movie without having the 3D glasses on.

Your Aura is your uniqueness, and how you identify yourself to the Universe. It is a way to say, "Hello, it's me again."

CHAPTER NINE
(The World of Questions)

"I cannot imagine how the clockwork of the universe can exist without a clockmaker."

- Voltaire -

The World of Questions: (Introduction)

This is a magical place we are surrounded by. The **Universe**, the **Planets**, **Earth**, the **Mountains**, **Oceans**, **Trees**, **Hills**, it is simply…marvelous, beyond all wonders of human thought. Man has wondered for years how something so spectacular could be created. How could something so grand be achieved, how could something come into the '**Physical**' from out of nowhere?

The sheer fact that you can actually reach out and '**Touch**' something is the greatest creation that has ever been made. You can hike a mountain, climb a tree, swim in the waters and build spacecrafts to travel to outer space, you can '**Physically**' act out your '**Thoughts**.'

The '**Physical Realm**' we reside in is imposing by all magnificence of the word. It gives us feelings, we see and touch, while our own bodies react to the laws of this physical realm as well. We feel pain, whether it is cancer, breaking a bone in the body, or heartache from a bad breakup, we feel physical and emotion pain. On the other end of the coin, we feel joy, happiness and excitement, riding roller coasters, the pleasures of sex or winning a competition, we all feel physical and emotional joy. We '**Feel**' it!

The physical realm otherwise known as the '**World of Questions**,' has left us with just this, a world filled with unanswered questions. Questions of, 'How could this come to be?'

Many cultures have stories describing the origin of the Universe. The **Sumerians, Egyptians, Mayans** and many other civilizations of the world have many artifacts and writings that show they had their own theories of how the world was created.

The Chinese story of **Pangu** or the Indian **Brahmanda Purana**, which explains how the world being born from a **World Egg**, is one creation type. As with the Ancient Egyptian God **Atum** story, the **Tibetan Buddhism** concept of **Adi-Buddha**, the Ancient Greek story of **Gaia** and the **Genesis** narrative, the creation idea is caused by a single entity emanating or producing something from itself. The Maori story of **Rangi and Papa** is another type of creation story, where the world is created from the union of male and female deities. In other creation types, the Universe is created by crafting it from materials, such as from **Tiamat** in the Babylonian Epic **Enuma Elish**, or from **Izanagi and Izanami** in Japanese mythology. The list continues, with other creation types as the Universe emanating from energies and fundamental principles, such as **Brahman and Prakrti**, or the **Yin and Yang** of the Tao.

Since the dawn of human consciousness, man has tried to figure out how creation was actually created. What type of time went into putting this together? What kinds of tools or materials were used for this to come into formation? How long has it been here, and how long is it going to remain? The Universe and the physical plane we exist in right now, how was it created? What created it?

These are questions many philosophers and scientist have tried to solve. Some philosophers tend to lean on the side of the spectrum where the world was created from a consciousness higher than themselves, while scientist break down the creation of the Universe into mathematics and materials. Their theories could seem drastically different from one another, but they are much closer to each other than they realize.

The World of Questions: (Creation from Thought)

The Universe is just one current frame of life that plays forever, but how was it created? The '**Big Bang**' theory is the main cosmological model of the early development of the Universe. The theory holds that the universe was once in an extremely hot and dense state that expanded rapidly. After its rapid expansion, the young Universe cooled to its present continuously expanding state.

According to scientific evidence and observations, this happened nearly **15** billion years ago, while some philosophers have presented a theory of the Universe always being here, and always will. These are two totally different theories, two drastically different thoughts about how the Universe came to be, so which is the right answer? They both are. They both are correct, but inaccurate with their understanding. The Universe was indeed created, and indeed has always been here.

To further explain, the Universe, a place that holds over a **100** billion galaxies with over **100** billion solar systems in each galaxy, was created by something so complex, so powerful, so magnificent, so abstract that it could only come from '**Thought**.' There is no device that made the Universe, no gadget, no secret potion, these are means that could not concoct something of this magnitude. The only thing that can create this world, the physical world...is the '**Collective Conscious**.'

While humans have tremendously advanced themselves through the years with technology, knowledge, nuclear energy and so on, there is nothing greater, nothing more powerful than the '**Collective Mind**,' for it can do anything, and imagine anything it wishes upon...even a Universe.

The Big Bang theory is correct. The means behind it is rather simple, because that spark, that burst of rapid progress we know as '**Time** and **Space**,' started with a humble thought, a thought of, *"Let there be Light."* With that thought, an action expressed in the Bible and most religious texts throughout the world, the Universe presented itself. One might think this is the start of all creation, but this is not so.

Thinking the Universe was created from a 'Big Bang' would lead most to thinking that it hasn't always been here, but it has. How? Why? Because the consciousness in which we are all a part of has always created this experience. This level of understanding is something that will become far more understood once certain parts of the human brain is activated, or once one is in the **'World of Answers,'** which can be looked upon as the 'Afterlife.' The thought process and knowledge in the 'World of Answers' is not always easily understood with the limitations of the human mind, but to further clarify why the Universe has always been here, it is because it is the **Yin** to the **Yang**, one does not exist without the other. In a sense, the physical realm balances the realm of the unphysical.

The Universe is a thought, and while we think a thought is a relatively new idea at the time of thinking it, in turn, thoughts have always existed. The Universe is a material thought, which has always been thought of, therefore it has always been.

The World of Questions: (Atoms)

For years scientists have dedicated themselves to understanding the make-up of the 'Human Body,' just to find the human body resembles much of what is around them. If you keep breaking down the things that make up the body and the things around you, the 'Physical Matter,' it all gets down to **Atoms**.

Atoms can only be observed individually using special instruments such as a scanning tunneling microscope. The name **Atom** comes from the Greek word 'Atomos,' which means indivisible, something that cannot be divided further. In the **17th** and **18th Centuries**, chemists provided a physical basis for this idea by showing that certain substances could not be further be broken down by chemical methods. In **1805**, a Natural Philosopher **John Dalton** used the concept of Atoms to explain why elements always react in ratios of small whole numbers. Dalton is considered the originator of modern atomic theory. He proposed that each element consists of atoms of a single, unique type, and these atoms can join together to form chemical compounds.

The thought of the Atom not being able to be divided further was found untrue in **1886**, when **Eugen Goldstein** discovered the **Electron** inside the make-up of the Atom. Now, it is known that the Atom consist of three basic particles, **Protons** (Positive electrical charge), **Electrons** (Negative electrical charge), and **Neutrons** (No electrical charge). The Electron has no known components or substructure, and is generally thought as an 'Elementary Particle,' with a size approximately **1/1836** of the proton, and contributes less than **0.06**% to an Atom's total mass. Protons and Neutrons are bundled together in the center of the Atom, called the Nucleus (Center of the Atom). The Electrons of an Atom are bound to the Nucleus by the electromagnetic force, and moves around the Nucleus, each in its own orbit much like the way the planets revolve around the Sun. It seems, ironically so, you are made up of little Solar Systems.

Over **99.94**% of an Atom's mass is concentrated in the Nucleus, with Protons and Neutrons having roughly the same mass. The Atom lacks a well-defined outer boundary, so their dimensions are usually described in terms of an atomic radius. Atomic dimensions are thousands of times smaller than the wavelengths of light (**400–700 nm**) so they cannot be viewed using an optical microscope. To visualize the size of the Atom, a typical human hair is about **1** million carbon atoms in width, while a drop of water contains about **2 Sextillion** (2×10^{21}) atoms of oxygen, and twice the number of hydrogen Atoms, so to imagine how small an Electron would be compared to an Atom is almost unthinkable.

To begin to think that you can see an Atom, is misleading, because Atoms are moving at speeds so fast, when you try to look directly at it, you can't. It moves to the side of your peripheral, this enabling the thought of 'It not really being there' to have a deeper concept. The idea of what you are looking at is not actually there at all, can leave one to wondering what, if anything is actually there in the first place. This notion has more significance when understanding that the 'World of Questions' was literally developed from imagination.

To sum this up, the same things that make-up you and the things around you, whether it be a table, a tree, a building, an ocean, or a planet, are made up of the same component. Not only is your human body the beautiful complex piece of machinery that it is, made up of nothing but Atoms, but everything is made up of Atoms. You (The body), and a table, are made up of the same thing. The reason you are different from a table, is because you 'Think' you are. It is as simple as that.

To further understand the body, once breaking it down to the root, you find that Atoms do not touch each other, leaving space in between the next, so much space in fact that you could actually fit hundreds of Atoms in between those spaces before it touches the next closest Atom. In actuality, the make-up of our bodies isn't a solid structure. Thus in theory, you should be able to put your hand right through the table, or even walk through a wall without destroying it.

If so, then how come this isn't necessarily happening whenever we try to do so? The illusion is strong, and there are many different facets that are aligned to make this loose structure seem to have a solid format. It is necessary, if not, we would slip right through each other, sliding in and out of things without any order to it, however, this does not mean bending the laws of physics can't be done in a structured method.

Unlocking the potential to do something as extreme as to walk through a wall, or build a pyramid is all in the **Superconscious** of the mind, and it hasn't gone anywhere, it's here. It's not hiding, or hibernating, more or less just waiting, to be remembered, or used at any moment it is humbly chosen to be accessed. Just as in the same aspect the Universe has always been created, the knowledge of being able to walk through objects has always been there as well. It is not new information. It is not something you will learn. It is something you will chose to remember.

The World of Questions: (Paintings, Symbols & Numbers)

There is no art greater than the painting we call 'Life.' It is precise and accurate, even though as explained with Atoms and how they never touch each other, somehow, someway this world we have does not look like a bunch of random dots jittering around. It is the most beautiful piece of art ever created, it is magnificent, however, it is nothing more than a painting, a painting that constantly moves.

If you will imagine, **Pablo Picasso**, the great painter from Spain, envision just after finishing one of his paintings, he leaves to attend to another painting, because he knows the one he recently finished is complete and ready for display. He has no more worries about it, he doesn't feel a need to touch it up, or make changes, because he knows it is perfect, just the way it is. He has faith in it, he knows it will be able to stand on its own.

Now, imagine all of a sudden the painting he finished creating, came to life. Imagine the painting started to move and interact with itself, the colors looking at each other wondering why it is different, looking at the diverse structures and wondering why things are curved the way they are, or why some things are placed where they reside in the painting. Surely that painting would have questions about how it came into existence. It is going to want to know, 'Why does it have color,' or, 'Where did the color come from,' it would want to know, 'Why were the brushstrokes used in its manner,' or, 'Where is the Creator of the painting now?' It would want to ask the Creator, but Picasso is off making new artwork, so the painting is left to figure it out all on its own.

This realm we reside in now, the 'World of Questions' is a painting from the Creator, and just like Picasso, the Creator has many, this is just one of the Creators paintings, and like Picasso, the Creator has faith in its artwork that it can stand alone, it is perfect. Unlike a painting in which would come to life from Picasso, this Creator does not detach itself from its artwork to go to another. It can't detach itself from its artwork. It is bonded to its artwork, because it is its artwork.

While the Creator is doing other things, it is extensively studying its own artwork, watching its every move. For comparison, you can think of the video game '**The Sims**,' where characters are created by the user, and they interact with each other and react to their situations and problems, very much like life itself. This is exactly what the Creator is doing, watching the video game. One huge difference is the Creator does not take preference over its characters. Unlike some video game users that may favor certain characters, or if they are playing a sports game they may constantly use a particular team, the Creator watches everything unfold evenly, just as it is calculated to do.

Like a video game, or more preferably the 'Internet,' the 'World of Questions' is made up of numbers, not numbers in the sense that we know and use today in the physical realm, the calculation of numbers used to make-up this realm is far too advanced for current math. These numbers are more like symbols, symbols play a part in our physical make-up.

This place we know as the physical realm is like a website. The **numbers/symbols** are used as what web-designers call 'Coding.' For those that know anything about building websites, it is easier to relate to this example. Once the code is written, you can then upload this code to the Internet to display the images of your website. The coding has to be exact and precise, if not, the images would come out imperfect. The images would not be placed where they are, and would very much be chaotic. Furthermore, without the coding, it would not be able to be seen.

The coding needs to be uploaded so that the website is viewable. This is very much like how the 'World of Questions' is able to be seen and exist. The physical realm exists through an upload of **numbers/symbols**, but what kinds of numbers/symbols?

The World of Questions: (Sacred Geometry)

Sacred Geometry is the blueprint of creation and the genesis of all form, known as the mathematical order to the intrinsic nature of the Universe. The concept of God creating the Universe through a geometric plan has ancient origins. It is an **Ancient Science**, which explains the precise way that the energy of 'Creation' organizes and unifies itself through its energy patterns. Every natural pattern of growth or movement conforms to one or more geometric shapes.

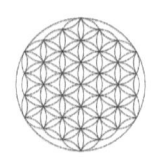

While there are many significant shapes and designs associated with Sacred Geometry, the most prominent symbol is considered to be the **Flower of Life**. The **Flower of Life** represents deep meaning to many people throughout history. It is a geometrical figure that is believed to encompass ancient and spiritual value depicting the essential forms of creation, space and time. It is a visual expression of the connections life weaves through all sentient beings. It consists of a multiple of perfectly-spaced, overlapping circles, arranged to form a flower-like pattern, with a six-fold symmetry. Each circle is the same diameter with its center at the circumference of the surrounding six circles.

Those who study the Flower of Life believe it provides deep spiritual meaning and forms of **Enlightenment**, and contains an **Akashic Record** of basic information of all living things. This design is found all throughout nature, as well as temples, art, and the manuscripts of civilizations from all over the world.

Drunvalo Melchizedek, speaking in a presentation on the **Flower of Life**, said, *"These are not words I'm making up, these are the actual words that were used in ancient times to describe this. I think they called it the Flower of Life because it looks like a flower and because it (represents) the laws and proportions for everything alive and even not alive, everything that's manifested."*

There are many shapes found within the Flower of Life's design, each is believed to possess essential meaning all to itself. In forming the Flower of Life, it begins with a '**Seed of Life**,' which also has shapes within in its own design. A description of some of the important symbols involved in the process of forming the 'Seed of Life' and the 'Flower of Life' are listed below:

Circle (Sphere)

The first step in forming the **Seed of Life** is to begin with a **Circle**. It is believed that the 'Creator' formed this shape, and then spun it on its axes, so in this way it would form a **Sphere**. The Creator's consciousness exists within this sphere, with the only thing physically existing is the membrane of the sphere itself. This 'First step' is thought to be the creation of 'God's boundaries.'

Vesica Piscis

The **Vesica Piscis** represents the 'Second Stage' in creating the **'Seed of Life.'** It was formed by God creating a second Sphere and joining them together at their circumferences. Creating the 'Second Sphere' is what is known as the **'First Day.'** The Creator's conscious began inside the 'First Sphere' and then journeyed outside its surface to create the 'Second Sphere.' God created light through the 'Second Sphere' as some scholars point to **Genesis 1:2-3**, *"And the Spirit of God moved upon the face of the waters. Then God said, 'Let there be light', and there was light."* The Vesica Piscis represents the fusion of opposites and a gateway through the world's polarities. It is believed to be the basis for the **Ichthys** fish, a Christian symbol representing Jesus Christ. Jesus is known as the 'Son,' which is represents the Vesica Piscis.

Tripod of Life

The **Tripod of Life** is also known as '**Borromean Rings.**' It is formed by adding a 3rd circle to the **Vesica Piscis**. The three Circles intersect at their circumferences. In the Christian religion, the **Tripod of Life** represents the **Holy Trinity** (**Mind, Body, and Soul**, or the **Father, Son**, and **Holy Spirit**).

Seed of Life

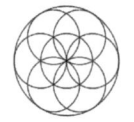

The **Seed of Life** is a symbol believed to depict the **Seven Days** of creation. The **Vesica Piscis** was created on the **First Day**, the **Tripod of Life** constructed on the **Second Day**, followed by one sphere for each day until all Seven Spheres formed the **Seed of Life** on the **Sixth Day** of Creation. The **Seventh Day** is the 'Day of Rest' known as the **'Sabbath.'**

Tube Torus

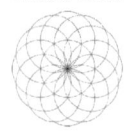

By intensifying the **Seed of Life**, it then forms the **Tube Torus**. The **Tube Torus** is considered a basic structure in the study of Vortex forms. It is believed it consists of a code of vortex energy that describes light and language in an **Akashic Record**.

Egg of Life

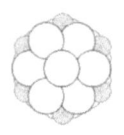

The **'Egg of Life'** consists of seven circles taken from of the **Flower of Life** design. It is said to be the shape of a multi-cellular embryo in its first hours of creation. Shapes derived from the **Egg of Life** are the **Cube**, **Tetrahedron** and the **Star Tetrahedron** (Much like the Jewish Star of David).

Fruit of Life

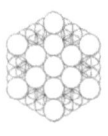

The **'Fruit of Life'** consists of **13** circles taken from the **Flower of Life**. It is said to be the blueprint of the **Universe**, and contains the basis of everything in existence. When each Node (Center of a circle) is connected to the other nodes using a single line, a total of **78** lines are created, forming a **Metatron**'s Cube, which brings forth the **Platonic Solids**, which are the Tetrahedron, Cube, **Octahedron**, **Dodecahedron** and the **Icosahedron**.

Scientists have revealed to see the same geometric and mathematical patterns relating to natural principles. All forms of nature are related to geometry, for example, the **Chambered Nautilus, Snowflakes, Honeybees, Pinecones, Flower Petals,**

Diamond Crystals, **Trees**, the strands of our **DNA**, the **Cornea** of our **Eye**, the **Star** our planet spins around, the **Galaxy** our Solar System spirals within and even the **Air** we breathe are all forms of life that emerge out of timeless geometric codes. Below are several pictures in which Sacred Geometry is applied in nature:

The ancients understood that these formations were codes of our own inner realm and the subtle structure of awareness, therefore studying sacred geometry was essential to the education of the soul. Viewing these forms allowed them a glimpse at the inner workings of the Universal Mind.

Why is this all relevant? It is relevant, because these are the shapes and patterns, the **number/symbols** that have been downloaded to the 'Physical Website' in order to show us what we see now. Sacred Geometry is the 'Coding.'

The World of Questions Created: (Complex Hologram)

The 'World of Questions,' a place that seems solid, is actually more lucid than water, it is merely like a drainer, in the sense that it can be ran through. Quite frankly, the 'Physical Realm' is like a **Complex Hologram**. Holograms are visuals that stand in **3D** right before your eyes, in which you can walk right through the image that is presented, and that image would not be distorted. This place, the 'World of Questions' is nothing more than a hologram, but it is complex, it has structure, it seems solid. Even though nothing touches each other, we believe it to have solid structure. The hologram is so closely knit that even after understanding there is no solid structure, you seem to have trouble trying to place your finger through the wall. Why is this?

If what you are looking at isn't really there, and is a figment of your imagination, created from thought, than why aren't you able to place your hand through a door? Your imagination also thinks it's solid. The things you are seeing, the things you are touching are nothing more than images, images your thoughts have given solid matter to.

The hologram is just something you think you're seeing, what's really behind it is a bunch of **numbers/symbols** that have been uploaded to a server, a server that displays the criteria for you to see these holographic images. The day you put your finger through a wall, is the day you choose to put your finger through a wall. When the thought of knowing you can, not only exceeds the level of thinking you can't, but drowns it out so that the thought of 'Can't' is no more, then is when you will be able to achieve the things you've made yourself think is impossible.

The 'World of Questions' reveals clues to you every day that it is waiting for you to see your potential. Scientific studies of the atom have shown that nothing truly touches each other, therefore the only thing that can give us a solid foundation for us to think the things we are seeing are of solid material, is the belief. We think it's solid, therefore it is.

The World of Questions: (Colors)

Understanding 'Color' leads you to having a better comprehension of your presence, and the reflection you can possibly leave on the world today. Just as all things not truly being solid, can it be said that all things do not have the color you perceive them to be as well?

Blue, it is such an amazing color, a color we see on a daily basis whenever looking up into the gorgeous outline of our sky. It is magnificent, at certain parts during the day the blue grows from a light blue, to a deep dark blue at night. Why? Why the color blue, and how come the blue changes throughout the day? How come it doesn't look pitch black at night, and how come the sky doesn't have a gray tone during the day? Why blue?

The color of our sky, displaying all the shades of the color blue that it does, isn't really blue at all. The color of our sky looks blue, because of the reflection from the light of the Sun hitting our ocean's body waters, and shining back into our sky. Even at night, the reason why it isn't completely black, like the darkness of the Universe, is because of the Moon. At night it is the Moon's turn to color the sky with the reflection from its light hitting the ocean waters. This is why the sky may sometime seem to be a darker blue at night through the month, because the moon has less light to reflect as it is rotating around the Earth. When it is a full moon, the night's sky is not as dark as its deepest blue, because of its light's reflection.

What is the color of water? Nothing. Water is clear, if water seems to have color it is because it is either mixed or polluted with some form of other chemical, or is sitting over something that would give it a tinted look of that object. In turn, the ocean's body waters are a reflection of its surroundings. Understanding the colorlessness of our sky and water can best give way to a deeper understanding that colors themselves aren't the colors you imagine them to be at all. For everything is just a reflection, of a reflection.

Example, have you ever had a moment, when you perceived a piece of clothing to be a certain color, maybe a jacket, a pair of shoes or t-shirt, it could be your own piece of clothing or someone else's. This article of clothing, maybe it was worn in a dark place, whether at night, inside of a nightclub, movie theater, or in dim settings around the house. The color may look navy blue to you, however, once this article of clothing is worn outside in the bright sunny day, it looks black, or a slightly different color that you didn't recognize it having before. Maybe you thought it was green, and now it looks light-blue, or maybe you thought it was orange, and it's really red. This new color you now see, you equate it as being the color that it actually is. You disregard what you thought it was before, and chalk it up to your eyes playing tricks on you, due to the dimness of the environment you first wore or saw the color. It is the reflection that causes this. The reflection of light or lack of light is what gives things color.

This breaks itself down to there being only **2** types of color. The name of these colors won't be found on any names of the crayons in a Crayola Crayon box, it won't even be found on a list of names for colors. The names of these colors are **'Light'** and **'Darkness.'** It is not black and white. Black and white are reflections from the colors of Light and Darkness. Light and Darkness are the only **2** colors that truly exist, and the things that make colors look like what they seem to be, are reflections of the Light hitting the Darkness.

One can further grasp this concept when thinking how colors are just displays of the reflections that equal to the amount of light it is radiating from, reflecting the color that it is equivalent to in light. Just as all things are not solid, it can be said that all things do not have the color you perceive them to be as well, it is just the light within itself that you see, possibly exhibiting the color it is corresponding to. Understanding color in turns leads you to having a better comprehension of your own presence, and the reflection you can possibly display, the type of 'Color' you can paint the World.

The World of Questions: (Running in One Place)

Movement, we are all at constant movement. Whether it is going to work, walking in the park, playing sports, or taking a stroll through the neighborhood, we are all constantly walking, running, hiking, or sitting in a car, plane or some kind of vehicle used for transportation, going somewhere. Even something as simple as getting up from the couch, to go to the refrigerator to get something to eat, you are moving, and in doing so, objects around you, are passing by you.

We have this conception that every forward step we take, we are making forward motions. A track runner for instance, sees the track that he or she is sprinting on and as they run forward, it seems as though they are running towards the finish line. The finish line seems as though it is something they are running to, something that they are approaching, when in actuality, the 'finish line' is something that is coming towards them.

You are in one place, one area. You are not really moving at all. It is your Consciousness that makes you think you are making forward motions, backward motions or lateral motions, when really your Consciousness is bringing what you see, towards you. Simply, you are being in one place. In comparisons, it's like walking on a tread mill, with the scenery to your sides moving pass you, and the scenery in front of you, coming towards you, but yet you are still on the tread mill, in one place. This depiction has been presented in movies, where the main character would be standing in one place, and everything around them moves towards and passed them, while they remain still.

How, and why is this so? How, in a place that seems as though you are walking towards something, can it be that it is making its way towards you? Understanding that you are not just Consciousness but where your Consciousness relies can help aid someone to further understand this concept.

Your **Conscience** is in one place. Where is the one place your Conscience is in? Everywhere. Your Conscience is everywhere, therefore, if your Conscience is everywhere, it means it is only in one place. Why? Everywhere is one place, and Everywhere and Everything is of you, therefore you are not in it, it is of you, and around you. You are simply planted in one place, with the Universe coming towards you.

Whether you are climbing a mountain or running in a marathon, you are telling yourself that you are doing these things, so your thoughts make your body react to it as if it is actually doing these things. Running long distances will in turn make you tired, swimming for hours could leave you out of breath, and a simple trip to the grocery store could be tiring, but if you aren't actually moving, then why would you get tired from doing these things? Because you think you are actually doing these things. You thinking you are moving is in turn making you imagine you are putting forth an effort to do so.

It should now seem amusing when thinking of asking someone for directions. Where are you going? Where are they actually leading you? To places that already exist in the Conscience. There is not a new direction you can take, everywhere you go or haven't gone is already programmed in the Superconscious. When approaching a destination, whether new or not, you do not 'Travel' there, you 'Think' your way there.

Imagine if you will, that you are playing a one player video game, the kind where the visual of the game is seen out of the eyes of the first character. This game, it is the type of game that is based on adventure and mystery, where you look and search for things in the game, there are obstacles, and other characters in the game you will come across, some of them will aid you, some of them will try to stop you from finishing the game. There are many facets to the game, and while on your adventure it may all seem new, it isn't. Everything your character is experiencing, everywhere it is going in the game is already in the game. It's not like the game all of a sudden added new features to it. Whether you choose to make your character go left or right is your choice, and the decisions or options that come from that are already chosen to take place in the game. This game you are imagining yourself playing, imagine that you are at home, sitting on the couch, playing the game on the television, and the television is resting on a desk. As you are playing this game, you recognize the scenery in the game, the visuals that are coming towards the screen and coming towards the character, are coming towards you because you choose to go in that direction. Now, while playing the game, image you can actually put yourself in the game, and be the character you were controlling from sitting on the couch. Image, you are now in your television, being this character, moving around, thinking that you are going places, but are actually making the imagery come towards you. Surely, while you are in the game, the television has remained in the same spot, resting on the same location of the desk.

The game you are playing, it's called the 'World of Questions.' Welcome to your video game.

The World of Questions: (Hallucinogenic)

Psychedelics can slide you down a deep rabbit hole, and depending on the intake, it can take you down the rabbit hole and into 'Alice and Wonderland,' and depending on the substance, it can take you even further and into the **'World of Answers.'**

Psilocybin Mushrooms, otherwise known as '**Magic Mushrooms**' or '**Shrooms**,' contain the psychoactive compounds **Psilocybin** also known as **Psilocybine**, which is a prodrug for the classical hallucinogen compound **Psilocin**, or **4-HO-DMT** (4-hydroxyl-dimethyltryptamine). Once ingested, psilocybin is rapidly metabolized to psilocin, which then acts as a partial agonist at the **5-HT$_{2A}$** and **5-HT$_{1A}$** serotonin receptors in the brain.

Among the native peoples of Mesoamerica, the hallucinogenic species of **Psilocybe** have a history of use for religious communion, shamanism and healing. There is archaeological evidence for the use of psyilocybin-containing mushrooms in Ancient times. Mushroom shaped statuettes found at archaeological sites seem to indicate that ritual use of hallucinogenic mushrooms is quite ancient, as found with mushroom stones and motifs in the Mayan temple ruins, in Guatemala. Hallucinogenic psilocybe were known to the **Aztecs** as **Teonanácatl** (Divine Mushroom). Aztecs (Ethnic groups of central Mexico, who dominated large parts of Mesoamerica) and **Mazatecs** (Indigenous people of Sierra Mazateca in Northern Oaxaca, Mexico), when translated into English, referred to psilocybin mushrooms as genius mushrooms, divinatory mushrooms and wondrous mushrooms.

The first mention of hallucinogenic mushrooms in Western medicinal literature appeared in the **London Medical and Physical Journal** in **1799**. A man had accidentally picked psilocybe semilanceata in London's Green Park, and served them for breakfast to his family. The doctor who treated them later described how the youngest child, "*Was attacked with fits of immoderate laughter, nor could the threats of his father or mother refrain him.*"

When Psilocybin is ingested, it is broken down to produce Psilocin, which is the cause for the hallucinogenic effects. Typically lasting anywhere from **3** to **8** hours, the mind-altering effects can seem to last much longer or shorter depending on the dosage, and the psilocybin's ability to alter time perception. Noticeable changes to the audio, visual and physical senses may become apparent. The shifts in perception visually could also include enhancement and contrasting of colors, strange light phenomena, increased visual acuity, surfaces that seem to ripple, objects that warp, morph, or change of solid colors, a sense of melting or blending into the environment, and complete clarity of sound. Music can often take on a profound sense of cadence and depth. Some may experience synesthesia, where they perceive a visualization of colors upon hearing a particular sound.

Psilocybin Mushrooms are non-addictive. As with other psychedelics, the experience is strongly dependent upon your setting. A negative setting or environment could likely induce a bad experience or 'Trip,' whereas a comfortable and familiar environment would allow for a pleasant experience. Most users find it preferable to ingest the mushrooms with friends, either people they're familiar with, those also joining in or people who had the same experience. Even with its extraordinary effects, while psilocybin mushrooms has been demonstrated in constructive ways to help some see a different importance or value in life, it only scratches the surface when it comes to the psychedelic.

Dimethyltryptamine (DMT) is a naturally occurring psychedelic compound found in several plants, and trace amounts in humans and other mammals. DMT produces a deep metaphysical experience similar to **psilocybin mushrooms**, but extremely more intense. Structurally, DMT is analogous to the neurotransmitter serotonin (5-HT), the hormonemelatonin, and other psychedelic tryptamines, such as **5-MeO-DMT**, bufotenin, and psilocin (The active metabolite of psilocybin).

When DMT is inhaled or consumed, it can produce powerful hallucinations and its subjective effects can range from milder psychedelic states to extremely intense experiences. Inhaling this substance usually gives the user an experience of about **3 to 10** minutes, but with after-effects ranging around half an hour. After consumption, it may include a total loss of connection to conventional reality that may be so extreme that it becomes indescribable. Some have reported visitation from external intelligences attempting to impart information, loss of time and space, visual and auditory illusions, and erotic imagery and sensations.

Terence McKenna, an American philosopher, has written books and lectured on the entities he sometimes described as, *"Self-Transforming Machine Elves,"* as well as other forms. Most encounters seem to defy verbal or visual description, but McKenna believed DMT to be a tool that could be used for communication with other worldly-entities.

In some cultures DMT is ingested as **Ayahuasca**. Taken orally, with an appropriate **MAOI**, DMT produces a 'Psychedelic Journey' that usually lasts over 3 hours. Ayahuasca, an Amazonian Amerindian brew used for divinatory and healing purposes, has extremely old origins, having a traditional use that predates written records. Many studies have been reported on its use in Shamanism, and especially in healing rituals. It is part of both the ancient religions and the healing customs of people who live throughout the Amazon area, from Brazil to the upper areas of Columbia, Equator and Peru.

In a study conducted in the **1990s** at the **University of New Mexico**, Psychiatrist **Rick Strassman** advanced the hypothesis that a massive release of DMT from the pineal gland prior to death or near death was the cause of the **Near Death Experience** (**NDE**). Several of the volunteers used for his research reported NDE-like audio or visual hallucinations, while other research subjects reported contact with 'Other Beings' in highly advanced technological environments. Strassman has speculated that DMT is found in the pineal gland (Located in the center of the brain), basing his reasoning on the statement that all the enzymatic material needed to produce DMT is found in the pineal gland, and at a greater concentration than in any other part of the body.

Understanding the pineal gland enables one to comprehend why dimethyltryptamine may be located in this area. The chemicals are believed to activate your pineal gland (Third Eye), and once triggered, it then opens up its doorways into the '**Afterlife**' or the '**World of Answers**.'

While Strassman suggested that small amounts of dimethyltryptamine is released in the brain whenever someone is sleeping, therefore causing our dreams, the most amount of dimethyltryptamine is released from this area of the pineal gland when one is born and when one dies. This is a startling theory, because if the pineal gland is what many believe it to be, then entering into this 'Physical World,' or leaving from it and back into the 'Afterlife,' is logical that the largest amount of dimethyltryptamine is released during these times.

For some, having experiences with psilocybin mushrooms or any forms of dimethyltryptamine has been life-changing experiences, although most tend not to understand exactly what it is that they are witnessing or taking a part of. Even though the experience can reveal many revelations about one's self, some may not comprehend exactly what these chemicals are doing.

Drugs like cocaine, heroin and ecstasy are known to the users as what people would call 'Body highs,' and while the chemicals found in psilocybin mushrooms and dimethyltryptamine, affect the feelings of the body, its main effects are usually based on the 'Mind.' It takes you inside the 'Thoughts of your Consciousness.' Each time experiencing with these substances, it takes you closer to what you really are, and where you come from. It opens doors from the 'World of Questions' and into the realm from which you came. It must be understood the chemicals that come from certain drugs, such as cocaine, heroin, methamphetamine, marijuana, dimethyltryptamine and others, are all found in your body. Your body is only reacting to these drugs because the chemicals are already in you, what these drugs are doing is activating these chemicals in your body. If these chemicals were not in your body, these drugs would not have any effect on you.

It is believed that dimethyltryptamine is the most potent psychedelic of them all, but it could in turn be thought of as having the opposite effect. While one may think they are getting 'High,' or hallucinating, the psychedelic experience they may think they are having could in turn be breaking them away from the **'True Hallucinogenic,'** and into the surface of what is really real.

The World of Questions: (Oxygen)

The most potent psychedelic of them all, the most potent hallucinogenic we have ever inhaled is something that **100** percent of us are guilty of, and it is something that we cannot keep ourselves from either. We are doing it constantly, on a regular basis throughout our day. Ultimately, it is something that we can't do without, that is if we are to remain here, now.

The **'True Hallucinogenic,'** and the most potent hallucinogenic of them all, is 'Oxygen.' A substance that we all take for granted, a substance that we don't even pay attention to, or consciously tell ourselves that we are inhaling, oxygen is the most potent hallucinogenic or psychedelic that we have ever consumed. Why? Because it allows us to constantly get high off the greatest trip there is...Life. Oxygen is what keeps us imagining we are here, breathing in and out the fumes, to give us the illusion that what we see is really there in this 'Make-Believe Land' of Questions. It keeps our Conscience in the Video Game. No more oxygen, no more hallucination.

Often people have tried to find ways to get high, or intoxicate themselves away from this reality, but in turn, what you are actually doing is forgetting that you are already on the greatest high there could ever be. To actually touch, feel, hear, taste, experience and breathe, is the greatest trip there is. The mere fact that you are reading this right now is a 'High,' but we constantly consume our bodies with things like cocaine, heroin, methamphetamine, mushrooms, Ayahuasca and marijuana, hoping it can take us to different zones or realms, these things pollute your oxygen, they sway you away from your trip while you are here, and pull you from the state of your 'Current High.'

This is not a bad nor good thing, it just is what it is. It should be clear of what you are doing when you use such substances. Some of those drugs have been used for medical advancement, patients, meditation, or used as gateways to opening up the pineal gland to activate the 'Third Eye.'

Depending on how far you go when consuming certain substances, you realize you aren't actually getting high at all, what you are doing, is coming down from your trip, 'Life.' The oxygen we inhale is our constant inhaler. It keeps you high, even when you think you are not.

People often wonder about imaginary things, places, situations, but what could honestly be more amazing than the story we have given ourselves? We have histories of **civilizations**, the wonders of the **Universe**, the **technology** we are discovering, places you can travel to, the many different **experiences** you can have, different **people** you can meet. What type of 'High' could be more fascinating than the one you live in?

This world is amazing, think about it. To be able to touch, something physical, is literally amazing. What could possibly make you think you can do this? What can possibly keep you from realizing that the atoms in your body do not touch each other? What can stop you from realizing this is just a hologram, and you can actually walk through objects? How come you think you're actually moving around, walking, running, active, but remaining in one place? Why is the color so crisp and vivid here, what could make you think things actually have color? How come you don't see what this place is made up of, nothing but numbers and symbols like a website design?

What could possibly make you unaware that all this is happening?

Oxygen...it keeps you 'High' on 'Life.'

The World of Questions: (Particle inside You)

There is a rather large misconception of the Universe. For however big the Universe may inconceivably seem, it is also inconceivably small, small enough that the Universe is actually just a '**Particle**.' It is a particle among many other particles, with more Universes than there are Stars in our own one Universe. To imagine how many Universes there could possibly be, a figure of almost endless should suffice.

Ironically these Universes, these particles sit alongside each other, like the atoms that make up our bodies, not touching each other, but next to each other, given each other its own space. The concept of a multiverse may be good illustration for this explanation, but it should be understood that for however many Universes there may be, and for how large they may seem, it is the size of a grain of sand.

The Universe is so small that it actually exists inside of you. This is not a poetic phrase, this is not a catchy slogan, this is where the Universe resides, inside you. You do not exist in the Universe, the Universe exists inside you, inside all of us. How can this be? How can something so massive, so large, so unthinkably big, exist in something so small as You? How? You are not your body. You are **Consciousness** occupying your body. The Universe does not exist inside your body, it exists inside your Consciousness. Your thoughts are the only reason the Universe is here, because you believe it to be so.

The Universe is a thought. It is a particle of thought. Thoughts do not exist outside of you, thoughts are from you.

CHAPTER TEN
(The World of Answers)

"Heaven is not the end: It's only the beginning!"
- David Brandt Berg -

The World of Answers: (Introduction)

The '**World of Answers**,' otherwise known as the **Afterlife**, or **Heaven** is far grander than any Heaven, any human brain could ever conceive there to be.

From the dawn of man, we have looked up into the sky and wondered of something greater than ourselves, whether it was the **Sun**, **Stars** or **Aliens** that man has mistook for **God**, we have always thought there is as a place we came from. This '**Place**' in which we came from is not a physical place, it is not a Star, it is not the Sun, nor a Universe that your eyes can see. Your eyes are too close to your face to see it, too close to your senses to detect it.

It hasn't gone anywhere, in retrospect, you haven't gone anywhere. You have just blended from the '**World of Answers**' and into a physical realm. The place in which we all come from, and the place in which we all return, is '**Pure Consciousness**.'

The only Heaven that exists is the '**Consciousness of Knowing Everything**.' This is where we come from. This is what we call '**Home**.' All of us. There is nowhere else for us to go. There is no Hell, there is no alternative realm you could slide to, there is only '**Home**,' although, '**Home**' is far more complex than what humans think Heaven or Home to be. It is a world among many worlds, levels among many of levels, and realms among many of realms.

'Home' is every and anything. While understanding how the 'World of Questions' was created, many may wonder how the place in which we came from was created as well. Simply, when you are there, the definition of this would be '**It**

just Is.' However, 'It just Is' is not enough for most humans to understand what this means.

While extremely difficult to place in human words or terms, there are certain facets to 'It just Is' that can be explained on a minute level, when compared to all that it is. Human language in any form does not involve enough uses that describe 'Home' for what it truly is. While the 'World of Questions' was created from thought and imagination, the 'World of Answers' is beyond imagination. Simply, it is why imagination exists.

The World of Answers: (Dreams)

We venture into the **'World of Answers'** every single night of our life. Every single time we go to sleep, we scratch the surface to this realm through our dreams. There have been countless upon countless of theories to what our dreams mean, and what their purposes are, so many in fact that it would be like trying to find a needle in a haystack to find the one correct meaning to our dreams. The answer to what our dreams mean is a simple one.

Out of all the theories that can explain our dreams, which one is the correct observation? All of them. Our dreams and anything we conspire from it is actually what it will mean to us while we are here, and whatever they mean to us, is its purpose.

For example, if one has a dream where they are walking down a street, and as they continue to walk, along the way they see images of their life in every single building window they walk pass, someone could easily depict this dream to mean multiple things. For instance, one could think the mere feeling of them walking towards something and watching flashes of their life as they progress to mean it is time to leave something behind. Someone else could get a totally different revelation from the same dream. Someone else could easily find that it could be reminding them that you are approaching a place in which you shouldn't forget who you are and the obstacles that led you there. It is entirely up to you, how to decipher this dream.

Your dreams are like moving art, and to an artist, their artwork, whether it be a painting or a song, it tends to mean something significant to them, it tends to have a message, it tends to speak life. Our dreams are just one of our **Collective Mind**'s creative pieces of art.

Just as well, they are also little clues, our dreams are hints, showing us a deeper concept than what we see here, now. It is showing us not to forget all that we are capable of while you are here, and this place we live in, is also a figment of our imagination.

There are those that say they do not dream. Whether this is true or if it is something they do not remember, this concept is up for debate, only because it is up for the person themselves to tap into this state, nevertheless, the idea of not having dreams isn't uncommon.

Osho, a guru from Madhya Pradesh, India, was once asked about his dreams, and he replied, *"One dreams because there are unfilled moments, repressed desires, things you wanted to do but could not, because of the society, because of the culture, because of the religion...more a man becomes repressed, civilized, it starts repressing its nature and projecting a certain personality which is respectable, then there are dreams. Dreams are simply to help you, what you could not do in your awaken world, you can do in your sleep...I never leave anything incomplete. I do only what I want to do...I don't care about respectability, I don't care about what others think of me. I simply live my life, and because I live so intensely and totally, that there is no residual that can create the dreams. Dreams are your unlived life...I have never sacrificed anything, I have never done anything against myself, whatever I want to say, I say. Whatever I want to do, I do. I have never followed anybody, I have never taken anybody's advice. I have lived a very innocent, primitive, simple life, that's why there are no dreams."*

While this seems like a heavy understanding to digest for those that do dream, you can't ignore the way the math adds up when reevaluating our dreams. Dreams can be fun, dreams can be lessons, dreams can remind us of our decisions here that we need to make, and tap us into our past lives, however, if one is already living out all those possibilities here, as far as the enjoyment in their dreams, then it may not be a need to dream, because you are already living out your dreams here.

In a sense, your dreams remind you not to forget to dream. Live your dream, do not dream your dream.

The World of Answers: (Déjà Vu)

Déjà Vu, the experience of feeling like you already experienced a particular moment or event once before, is in turn something we are constantly experiencing, but only at times do we recognize that it is happening. For the most part we tend to recall this feeling at certain occurrences in our life, when truly, Déjà Vu is a continuing process. Every facet, every angle and direction in your life has already been foretold, you are merely making the choices you see fit for this experience as you go along.

When people experience Déjà Vu, usually they recognize it and then and brush it off as a coincidence or a fluke, but how can something be a fluke, if it happens to them ever so often in their life? Déjà Vu is not a fluke, it is not a mishap in your thinking, it is not a coincidence or something strange. While it may yet seem weird, the reason it is weird is because it is familiar.

Déjà Vu is like a marker in your life, not a chapter, not a page, but somewhat like placements you may use when leaving a trail, kind of like a point in your life you can use to say, 'You were here.' Its meaning does have an importance to it. Ultimately, like any choice you make, the importance lies with you to determine how much value it actually holds.

Déjà Vu can mean a couple of things, it can remind you that you are on the path in which you ultimately wish to go, or it can bring you to a point of decision. Sometimes it is unclear which of the two it actually is, due to the taste of temptation. Temptation shouldn't be looked at as good or bad, but something you need to be aware of. All temptation doesn't lead us into negative situations. There are many times when temptation has aided one's experience. For instance, temptation can cause someone to want to lose weight because they were tempted to fit into a certain article of clothing, it can cause someone to do better in school because they were tempted to receive a scholarship, it can cause for someone to become a better musician because they were tempted from a certain melody. Temptation is not a bad thing, it just is what it is, though you should be aware that it does have effects, causes and consequences.

Déjà Vu is something that reminds you to be aware. It is silently screaming to you, "Hey, don't forget action has a reaction." It's not telling you should or should not do something, it's showing you that you can do, or not do something. Whether you think this means you are on the right path, or you need to drastically change something, the decision is up to you, whichever one of the two you find works best for you at the moment. This is in turn the most precious part that Déjà Vu plays, it leaves it up to you, it does not act or make a decision for you. Your life is up to you to constantly change, and this is what Déjà Vu tries to remind you of. It is not telling you to change something, it doesn't tell you when to turn, or tell you if you are going the wrong way, it shows you that there is choice to taking another way, and that you can if chosen to.

The World of Answers: (The Moment of Transition)

Death is defined as, *'The action or fact of dying, the end of the life of a person or organism.'* There's only one problem with this definition. This definition does not exist. There is no such thing as dying, there is no such thing as the end, there is only the 'Continue.' The word death should be redefined as, 'A transition from one to the next.'

A transition is something that is happening constantly. People are having deaths all the time during their life, whether it is leaving behind old habits, transitioning into new areas of their experience, moving from one place to the next, meeting new friends or cutting ties with people that aren't in your best interest, the idea of death is happening at every moment of the day. The moment you begin to contemplate a feeling or an emotion, you are about to commit a death to a previous idea. Death is not a negative thing, a lot of times death leads to new growth and new opportunities. Death is a transition, and that is all it is, but a transition into what is the question.

When a person has exhausted all of their oxygen, whether it be from age, disease or untimely demise, the transition of 'Death' can be confusing at first, and may take a moment for one to understand what is truly happening. This is mostly due to the shock that nothing has ended. When people pass from the physical realm, their thoughts continue to move and operate as they are, therefore when people start to realize that another process is taking place, a process they aren't familiar with, they are somewhat at a standstill. Expecting one thing and getting another can lead many people to stop in their tracks and think for a moment, "What is happening?" This is exactly like death, when the transition starts, people are mostly at a pause, thinking, "What is going on?"

Depending on the individual, it could take just a second or an extended period of time to realize what is actually taking place, and that is continuing on from this physical dimension into one that has no physical means. It could lead people to think they are dreaming, therefore they may resist the process at first, but rest assured if this happens, it is temporary, we all get on the right track. It is almost like a magnet, sooner or later you will gravitate towards your next step. This usually depends on how much the person has accepted the transition.

At the point of 'Impact,' when the moment the last breath is exhaled from your lungs, things come to a slow pause, where it may seem like everyone around you grows still, but you are the only one with thought, therefore this world seems stuck. From this point, most tend to get a glimpse of their body by viewing it from just slightly above, as this revelation takes place, things around may start to slowly move again. As things start to gradually move, the people around your body will have no recognition that you are actually still present, not as the body, but as Consciousness. You will have thus been shifted into spirit form (Pure Energy).

You will feel weightless, almost one with everything, and there will be a feeling that you have blended in with all that is around you. Eventually, a 'Light' will present itself, sometimes surprising you from behind or in front of you, but it will casually present itself to you, moving closer towards you as you move closer towards it. This light is the 'Source,' it is the way, do not be afraid, for it is your wormhole towards your next transition, and the only door you can possibly take out of here. It will suck you in, regardless of your efforts, but it is something to be embraced.

You will then be transported through a tunnel, depending on the person, the imagery of this tunnel may vary, but it is the passage way we all will go. Along the way, at some point, you may start to be reminded of 'Everything,' and the most important thing, that this is your experience, chosen by you, and designed by you, for you. Depending on the person, you may hear words like, *"You are the Creator,"* being spoken to you, almost as if it is reminding you, in a manner that seems as though it doesn't want you to forget.

Most will feel a sense that they do not miss being here, in the 'World of Questions.' Your friends, family members and loved ones you left behind will be missed in a totally different fashion that we know of now. You will not feel the pain of missing anyone, for you will instantly know that no matter what happens, they too will totally be alright, and the understanding of knowing this is such a calm and peaceful feeling that you do not miss or worry about them or anyone. The level of comprehension is so great in the 'World of Answers,' that the revelation of peace which forever awaits you and everyone, is and will always be enough to ease whatever moments of heartache we have of missing our loved ones.

This transition of death is only that, a transition. You do not stay here, you do not dwell at this moment, there is much to do, and death is just the process to get you there.

The World of Answers: (Death & the Panoramic Life Review)

The **Near Death Experience** (**NDE**) has been well documented by many people. In fact, the number of people who reveal that they have had such an experience is growing, not because there are more people who are having them, but because people aren't as afraid to tell others about their experiences as they once may have been in the past. While the stories and revelations one receives may be different from someone else, they all somehow seem to recant the same message and outlines.

From his book, '**Parting Visions**,' Dr. Melvin Morse explains, "*I have never interviewed anyone who had a near-death experience who told me that they came back to make more money or to spend more time at their jobs away from their families... Instead, they become convinced that they need to be more loving and kind. They react to their experience by living life to its fullest. They believe their lives have a purpose, even if that purpose is obscure to them. Invariably it involves concepts such as love of family or service to others. They seem to know that the love they create while living will be reflected and radiated back to them when they die.*"

One of the more reoccurring events which seem to take place, during the Near Death Experience, is the '**Panoramic Life Review**.' For the most part, many religions, rituals and ancient civilizations have stressed 'The Moment of Judgment' or 'Moment of Truth' in the eyes God. Throughout the pages in the bible and other holy books, it seems to stress that what we do here will one day be what we are faced with at the end of our time. While some religions have somehow derailed the path of us understanding who we are, they have somehow managed to touch the surface on this subject, but not without trying to force a level of fear to promote believing in their cause.

Many don't miss the chance to mention the consequences of being left out of the good intentions of the 'Creator' if you haven't achieved all that you were set to do here, or if you haven't praised God enough, or lived a righteous life. This is not true, the Creator of your experience, is you, your highest amongst Highest Self, so you will always have your best intentions at the forefront of your decisions, whether there are some things you need to work on, or if it is indeed time to move onto the next stage. The only thing that judges you, is You. In a sense the term, 'Only God can judge you,' is accurate, because you are a part of the All, 'God.'

The process may vary for some, but for the most part it is the same outcome. Some have explained the Panoramic Life Review process as there being a voice that hovers over them, while others have expressed a **Spirit Guide** being there to assist them, or God itself, but they all say they feel the presence of the Creator whether it being noticeable or faintly in the background, the common trait is being in the presences of the 'All Knowing.'

The Panoramic Life Review is a process we cannot escape, and we cannot put it to the side and leave it for later. It will come. At some point, you will be taken to a place where it will resemble being in a television department store, with what will seem like endless upon endless of televisions, lined up in a row, all flipping through the channels of your life. This visual may vary for some, but the concept is the same procedure we all will encounter.

The process will get less chaotic, eventually you will focus on one of the views (Screens) and you will then start to see your life flash right before your eyes, scene after scene, in order, seeing how they relate to other parts in your life, all at once. Some scenes will go faster than others, while other scenes will stay for a longer period, marinating on the situation. You will remember how you felt about yourself in these moments of your life. Your feelings aren't the only feelings you will remember.

After your life has flashed before your eyes, remembering all that has affected you, you either will simultaneously, or repeat those flashes of your life all over again, reliving the same moments, except this time you will step into the shoes of the other person and people in your life, so that you will not just see, but also 'Feel' how you have affected them as well. You will know how they felt about you. Everyone whom you have ever touched, everyone whom you have ever lied to, harmed, said something nasty to, cheated out of money, scammed, made feel good, cried or inspired, any and everything you have ever done to someone else, you will feel the reception of your actions. You will feel it in a way as if it were your own, and it will be as real as any emotion and feeling you know to be true.

You will judge yourself, truthfully and harshly, because there is no hiding, there is no running away, the only thing you can do is stand there and face the music that you have played for yourself. Do not worry, this is not a torturous process, actually, it's something you quite look forward to.

Some may witness this for themselves without any communication from any other source, while others may experience hearing a voice, or Spirit Guide asking them what they thought of themselves in certain situations, or actions. You may be asked things like, "Were you the best friend you could be to this person," or, "Do you think you were the best son you could be," or, "Do you think you could have been a better Wife?" It will ask you what you thought about certain issues, and if you think you handled it correctly. It will ask you so many things, including do you think you experienced this life to the fullest? You are viewing yourself in the mirror, and there is no way, no chance in lying.

This is a just stage that opens the gateway to your next process. Here, you will have an upfront look at the issues you may need to work on, or maybe something you might want to experience differently. You could possibly choose to be done with this level of physical existence and continue advancing, or you could find that you need more work on this stage, or just want to come back again for the experience.

This is ultimately like attending your graduation, to see if you are going to get your diploma or not. You wouldn't attend the graduation if you knew you weren't getting a diploma, so this process comes with many rewards. The wisdom you receive from your Life's experience is what you carry on with you to the next process. The Panoramic Life Review is just a graduation, it is not the celebration. The celebration comes after the graduation.

The World of Answers: (Healing Process)

After the transition of Death and your Panoramic Life Review, another process takes place before you make your decision to return to another physical realm or retake a part in the operations of the 'World of Answers.' This next process is called the '**Healing Process**.' This is an optional process, but a process that most go through. The only reason this is optional is because one may not feel the need to serve in this process long, but for the most part many do make a transition through this stage.

Your Healing Process ultimately comes along instantly as you are crossing over and during your Panoramic Life Review, but once that portion is complete, the Healing Process comes into further effect. This process serves as a 'Cleansing' or 'Rejuvenation' point. This in particular is hard to explain, because while your Soul is not damaged and could never be damaged, and is not, nor ever will be in jeopardy of being harmed or lost, it sometimes requires a type of cleansing/rejuvenation effort. It is an energetic process. You will not be in a hospital, or recovery center, but you will be monitored up until the point you know you have been fully cleansed from the residue of the 'World of Questions' before you further go on in the 'World of Answers.'

The Healing Process has many of facets, but its main focus is to cleanse you from the residue of the 'World of Questions.' This does not mean to make you forget, you will have recall of the things that took place in your life, and other lives before it. The Healing Process is necessary because little do you know, but being in the 'World of Questions' is traumatizing.

This is an over exaggeration, but it is to get across the idea that 'Being in your body' is a peculiar feeling, it is extremely awkward to us. While we yearn for the experience of the physical realm, when you are re-becoming one with 'Everything,' you tend to realize how comfortable that feeling is.

Furthermore, while everything you just went through has been compiled over a course of time, you now have all this wisdom wrapped up in one moment, and being that you are now digesting that you have all this wrapped up in one unit, it is heavy. Some of your experiences have been thrilling, exciting, but yet overwhelming and tiring, so you may require some healing.

Some processes are instant, while others can serve in this stage for a while, but it is ultimately up to the 'Individual Energy' itself to realize when this process has reached its serving point. This is for everyone. There is no Hell, there is no ultimatum, there is only healing, even for the wickedest of us. In, '**The Law of One: Book I The Ra Material,**' **Don Elkins** asked the **Social Memory Complex** known as '**Ra**,' questions concerning the Afterlife, and eventually asked about Adolf Hitler, a Germany dictator known for the holocaust and genocide of millions Jews during World War II. Excerpts from the conversation are as follows:

> **Questioner** (Don Elkins): *Can you tell us what happened to* ***Adolf*** **(Hitler)**?
>
> **Ra**: *I am Ra. The **mind/body/spirit** complex known as Adolf is at this time in a healing process in the middle astral planes of your spherical force field. This entity was greatly confused and, although aware of the circumstance of change in vibratory level associated with the cessation of the chemical body complex, nevertheless, needed a great deal of care.*

This stage is not a secluded process where only a few are welcome. You may wonder, or ask yourself why would someone like Adolf Hitler be allowed to be a part of the Healing Process? What you should really ask yourself, is why not? He may need it more than most.

After your Panoramic Life Review, you will have judged yourself more truthful than you ever thought you could, and when realizing how much a part of 'Everything' you really are, you feel a heightened sense of the role you played in the totality of the experience. People with 'Blood on their hands' will feel the guilt, sorrow and sadness of everyone that was ever affected by their actions, not just the person they may have directly harmed or betrayed, but the people that were also affected by the actions done to that particular person.

Most do not stay in this Healing Process for a long duration, but again it is up to the individual. The next stage after this process is a choice that is left up to you. Some energies return back to a physical body, re-entering the 'World of Questions,' or go off to another level of a World of Existence, or choose to stay for an extended period of time in the 'World of Answers,' to re-checkout the scenery.

The World of Answers: (Inside the World of Answers)

The 'World of Answers' is a place that is extremely difficult to put into human words. Many have tried, but many admit they fall short on giving a valid description. Whether they are relaying something they saw from a Near Death Experience or Astral Projection, they seem to always end by saying, "It was unexplainable." Yes, it is unexplainable, to truly understand the 'World of Answers,' first, you have to be in the 'World of Answers.' Being in the 'World of Questions,' trying to fully understand something that you only get a glimpse into, is not understanding it, that's only realizing it's there.

Trying to describe what is going on inside the 'World of Answers' is like standing on the outside of a sports stadium. You see the people passing by you going in, and you hear them inside cheering and having fun, and every so often someone from the stadium may come out and tell you the score of the game, and what's going on, but you still don't know how to describe exactly what's taking place inside. They may even take you in for a quick breeze inside the stadium, but on the bottom level, and they only take you to the hotdog stand. You're looking over at the merchandise table, but they tell you, "Don't worry about that, we're at the hot dog stand right now." Maybe you're in the stadium for a quick second, at the hotdog stand, you still don't see the game. They may even let you take a peek at the monitors on the walls that are showing the game, which is going on just behind those walls and beyond the hotdog stand, but still, you are missing what's going on inside, and seeing one quick play on the monitor doesn't let you know who's actually winning the game. It's just one quick play, and by the time you had your quick walk through on the bottom level of the stadium, at the hotdog stand, you're right back outside the stadium, thinking, "That was weird." This is like trying to explain the 'World of Answers.' It is difficult, but that doesn't mean there is no need to try.

First, everything is alive...Everything. In comparison, if you were in a bedroom, with a bed, television, phone and a dresser, they would in turn all be 'Awake' with life. At points, it may seem to vibrate in the manner of a heartbeat, slowly fading back and forth towards you.

Second, it is always 'On.' Always. Meaning, everything that is alive, gives off a feeling that it isn't going anywhere for a long, long time. In comparison, if it were a light switch, that light switch would not have an off button. It is on, constantly.

Third...it's a party going on inside, and they are celebrating, but on such a different level of imagination our human minds can't conceive, 'What it means to party.'

It is the ultimate gathering inside, one in which you can go almost anywhere, at any given moment, and communicate with any being you wish to communicate. In the sense of Heaven, the idea that you see your friends and loved ones is true, but much different in the terms of a human aspect. You will not have human bodies, but in turn will recognize those that have taken upon human bodies on a physical realm.

Communication with them will be extremely different as well, there will be no need for explaining, or trying to understand something that the two of you may have shared, it will be known, understood, forgiven and accepted at the moment of seeing each other. You will know each other's thoughts, and converse telepathically, but much more telepathic than we think the word telepathic means.

There is no course of trying to find the answers, or to try to figure out something when you are in this realm, every answer you ever wanted or ever wished upon is here, and available at the same time. For example, if you were standing with a group of 5 people, and one person is talking to you, and after that person finishes, then the next person takes their turn in talking to you, and after that person finishes the next person takes their turn with talking to you, and so on, this seems very coordinated. In the 'World of Answers' there is no taking its turn, all 5 people will be speaking to you at once, while in the 'World of Questions,' this would seem extremely chaotic, when you are in the 'World of Answers' it is a normal process that is easily taken in. Even though it may seem chaotic, it is very structured and ordered in its randomness. It is only chaotic to the 'World of Questions' or the human mind. The 'World of Answers' does not have the same conflicts or rules, therefore it is not limited to the conversations you can have at once, nor the knowledge you can attain or have access to.

You will not lose this sense of who you are. You will recognize that you are still you, 'In thought,' but you have in turn become more of who you truly are. You will have joined, or merged with the wisdom you have gained from other lifetimes, in which all have played a part in your 'Ultimate Personality.' There is a characteristic in which you will not own, and that is the feeling of 'Want.' This feeling of 'Want' is not of your own, and it does not exist in the 'World of Answers.' It only exists in the 'World of Questions.' Questions want answers, but answers already know the answers, therefore the answer just accepts the question. This is the realm in which you come from, 'Answers,' and this is more of your emotional make-up, 'Acceptance,' therefore, a lot of the jealously, or animosity you may have felt for people when you are in the 'World of Questions,' you do not share this characteristic in the 'World of Answers.'

While this realm of 'Answers' is massive beyond any imagination of the word, and endless beyond all comprehension of the word, you are still able to go to almost any point you think of. The imagination will allow you to go where it desires. There is no solid structure. Its physical features are vibrations of sound. While it does have some form of foundation, calling it solid, in the sense of human terms would be a great misunderstanding. There is structure, and it has form, but you can easily go right through it, and come out somewhere totally different. Imagine, a building you walk towards. In the 'World of Questions,' as you approach this building you would either stop or bump right into the solid formation, however, in the 'World of Answers,' you can continue walking towards this configuration, and as you walk into it, it would morph into whatever dimension or degree you so choose. You wouldn't walk through it, you would make way for something entirely new to form from it.

The 'World of Answers' is Pure Consciousness, it is Everything, and All Things. It is the 'Land of God,' and there is no end in sight. There is nothing but structures and palaces and space, upon structures and palaces and space, levels upon levels and space, worlds upon worlds and space, but at the same time you are One with Everything, so no matter where you are in it, you are connected to every part of it.

It is not something you break free from, it is not something you escape from, it is something you take a leave of absence from, when going to the 'World of Questions.' This is your home, your country, your nation, and you take pride in it, as most tend to do with the physical neighborhood or land they are from. Many people talk about giving back to the community, and when you are in the 'World of Answers,' you in turn do just this, give back. While this place is magnificent and beautiful, filled with wisdom upon wisdom, with many having the best of times, it does not mean it is all play and no work.

There is a lot of work, but do not be deterred, work only feels like labor in the 'World of Question.' The idea of work in the 'World of Answers' can be thought of with a common quote that many use when describing their jobs, "*When you do what you love, it doesn't feel like work.*"

While there are many levels inside this realm, as the Universe, it grows, it expands, and for the most part that is its objective, to grow, to progress, so it isn't finished. It needs workers to help make this happen.

The World of Answers: (Spirit Workers)

First, before processing what it is that the 'Energies,' or what many call 'Souls' or 'Spirits,' are doing for us from the 'World of Answers,' it is important for us to understand that we, ourselves, are those same Energies. We are the souls that we call upon to help aid us through our troubles here in the 'World of Questions.' As of now, we are occupying a physical bodily form, a form we feel extremely bonded to, but the truth of the matter is that we are these same entities, souls or spirits many of us have claimed to see, or speak to.

Our **Spirit Workers**, souls from the 'World of Answers' who help aid us here, have been with us since before the conception of our birth. Some of them have done this experience with us before, while others we may later get the chance to share an experience with, or maybe help aid them in their process as well, as one of their own Spirit Workers.

They are assigned to us for the duration of the current experience for many reasons. One could be that their frequency level matches yours, this is a good advantage to have if you may be embarking on an experience that may entail a lot of solitude, or embarking on a journey where you may feel singled out or odd amongst other physical presences. Another reason for their assignment to you could also be that they are the right frequency for the experience, maybe they have participated in a type of existence you are embarking on and can assist you spiritually with its vibrations. Other times, we have asked certain Spirit

Workers to be our guides. Some Spirit Workers could have been our best friend on another life, could have been our parent, child or lover, while some Spirit Workers could be considered our **Soulmates**. Yes, sometimes our soulmates do not make the journey with us. To put it plainly, what a Spirit Worker is, they are our friends, and they love us unconditionally.

Whichever relation you have with your Spirit Workers, they are always taking notes on you. They have never let their eyes off of you, they are constantly watching, and know more about you than you know about yourself, at the time. They know every angle, every decision you make, all the possibilities you possess, and all the things you are thinking about. Yes, they are eavesdropping.

In a sense, you and them, are like scientist, experimenting and taking in the knowledge from your findings of having a 'Life Experience.' You share a team with them, but you and your Spirit Workers have different assignments to this process.

To better understand your current relationship to these Spirit Workers, it may be best to compare yourself to a boxer, with a crew of trainers. When we come to the 'World of Questions,' we do so with a team of souls behind us, supporting us from the 'World of Answers.' These Spirit Workers are your trainers, some of them have boxed themselves (Lived a physical life), some of them are like corner cut-men, some doctors, some have been your sparing partners before you were born (Getting you ready), others are there for motivational support as hype-men, others train you, and some are focused on your body being as efficient as it can be to do battle in the ring. They all play different positions to your experience, but yet, they all have one common focus, to make sure you are prepared and have everything you need, before you get in the 'Ring of Life.' This crew of trainers can't fight for you, but when you win, they win, and they want to win. They go through the ups and the downs with you, because you represent not only yourself, but them as well. This experience is as much a part of theirs, as it is yours, but your 'Team' can only send out one boxer to the ring. It just so happens that the soul your team sees fit to do the job, is you.

Unfortunately, sometimes when a boxer is in the ring, even though their corner is shouting for them to watch out for punches and to attack a certain part of their opponent's body, that fighter is so wrapped up with their opponent that the messages and forewarnings from their corner often go unheard. Their corner is constantly giving them advice, but the fighter has to fight the fight, so the boxer may ignore a lot of these suggestions as distraction, when their corner is simply telling them what is best. When you sleep, this can be compared to when boxers go to their corners in between rounds, taking a breather to talk to their corner (Spirit Workers), before they go back into the next round. While the boxer (You) is in their dreams, they are receiving advice from their trainers, nodding their head in agreement during the time-out, but as soon as they step foot back into the ring, their concentration is right back on the fight again, and a lot of what their corner just told them goes right to the back of their mind.

While your Spirit Workers focus is based around the duration of your stay here, they in turn have many different objectives. One of those objectives is to see you through your experience, another objective is to help the betterment of this world, the 'World of Questions,' so while they are constantly looking over you, they are also looking over your surroundings.

Their work is nonstop, for there is no sleep in their realm of answers, there is no need for it, so while we are resting and rejuvenating our bodies through the night, they never stop working on you, or your bodies. They are not just our friends, they are psychologist and technicians, they are doing all kinds of work, not just through your thoughts, but with your own 'Soul' as well. Yes, they are operating and making advancements on your Soul, which in turn aids the progression of the body.

They are constantly at work, even at this very moment they are healing you, aiding you, listening to you and talking to you. They do not speak English, they do not speak German, or Chinese, Spanish or Arabic. If you ever do hear them speaking in these languages, it is because they are transferring the thoughts of that language to you. They aren't actually speaking that language. They aren't actually speaking. The way they speak to you is through thoughts and images, and they NEVER, EVER, tell you what to do. They only show you your options, just a bit clearer than you may have previously seen for yourself.

When fortunate to realize their presence, their personality can sometimes seem extremely familiar, other times, you may even recognize that it has taken upon your own image. At times they are very humorous, and though you get the sense that there is much else that they could be doing, they seem to never get impatient. The humor they display comes from a side of them 'Knowing' what you 'Think' you don't know. It is almost like they have a secret to tell you, and 'YOU' are the only one that can figure it out, but it is assuming to them how many times you've come close to getting the answer.

Furthermore, as the comparison to a Boxer with a crew of trainers, your journey is also their journey, therefore, they want you to succeed. They want you to be happy, you being happy makes them happy. They do not get sad, and never too overjoyed, for the most part they are levelheaded, but they are attached to your feelings. You being depressed, sad or in grief does not benefit them. They have a job to do, and it is to silently aid you as your bodyguards.

The World of Answers: (Soulmates)

The Term **'Soulmate'** is believed to have originated in Rabbinic literature, but it is indeed as old as Consciousness itself. According to **Edgar Cayce**, God created androgynous souls, equally male and female. He suggested that God split the souls into separate genders, possibly because they incurred karma while being 'Separate from God' here on the Earth. Cayce explains that through a number of reincarnations, each half seeks the other, and when all karmic debt is selected, the two will fuse back together and return to the ultimate.

This being said, our 'Soulmate' shares an extremely important part in our progression. Soulmates play a more significant part in your existence than someone you marry or fall in love with lifetime after lifetime. Our soulmate does not value our sexual companionship as the most important thing to share, the most important thing for you to share is progression, and you do this in a number of ways.

Too often do we tend to label the person we are currently dating, as the 'One.' Think of how many times we have dated someone and gotten that thought. Think of how many times you have said that again, and again, and again. People spend their lives thinking their soulmate is the person they are currently dating or married to, just to think it is the next person that comes along and fills those shoes. What about the last person you were in a relationship with? Just because both of you had an argument and now have split paths because you can't stand to be around each other, does this mean that they are now not your soulmate? Do not let this discourage you, but the person you are walking away from, to possibly never to see again, could indeed be your soulmate.

Our soulmate plays a much larger part in our evolution than the greatest love of our life. In turn, your soulmate could be your fourth grade teacher, and something they say or do, inspires you in a manner that it changes your life in such a way that without them it wouldn't have been the same. Sometimes our soulmate is a family member, or even a complete stranger, someone we will go our whole lifetime without speaking to. Just their mere existence, seeing them the times that you have has inspired you in such a way that it made a drastic difference on your life. Sometimes we may go through this experience of life without them here with us, instead they will be watching us, like a Spirit Guide, or Spirit Worker from the 'World of Answers.' At other times, your soulmate could be the person you come to find yourself disliking the most while you are here, your most hated enemy. Why? How can this be? Without them, you may not have become the person you are. That is their main objective, for you to experience the most high that you can, and to progress.

This is why your soulmate can be a lost love, or an ex-girlfriend/boyfriend that you haven't spoken to in years, even decades. Your broken heart from a particular experience may have been the best thing for you. Most people never think about these things, how they are driven by their downfalls, or failures, or heartbreak, most people never realize how much that attributes to their success. Your soulmate is here for your success, and if being apart from one another is the best thing for the both of you on a particular experience, then that is how the journey must play itself out for the betterment of your progression.

For the most part, when they are here, most people never realize who their soulmate is. Recognizing who your soulmate is can possibly cause confliction with your forward progression, it can lead you to becoming overly consumed in maintaining that relationship during a lifetime. You are not suppose to force maintaining anything, let alone a relationship, especially with your soulmate. When it is time to part, it is time to part. They have already given you your greatest gift, you just think the greatest gift is 'Them.' This is not so. The greatest gift is the inspiration they have given you. If it just so happens that their gift involves staying in your life as a partner in marriage or a relationship, then those experiences will come about. Your soulmate plays numerous identities, not just the 'Love of your Life.'

It has also been thought some people may actually have more than one soulmate. This is not so much the case, but it can sure feel like it. You must remember your soulmate is not the only energy you are connected to. You are connected to many, hundreds, thousands and millions of different energies here. Some of those energies you have shared many upon many of lifetime experiences with. Sometimes when we meet someone new, we have an instant connection with them, it feels so smooth, so easy, almost like they could be our soulmate, when really it is one of our closest friends from another life. Those relationships are extremely valuable as well. Do not let them go because you are so determined to find your soulmate.

For the most part, your soulmate is not the person you will end up marrying or falling in love with during each lifetime here, but your soulmate will be the energy you will end up with happily ever after. Our soulmate can also be compared to the Yin and Yang, therefore lies the notion 'You cannot have one without the other.'

The soulmate of the 'World of Answers' can be considered the 'World of Questions.'

The World of Answers: (Akashic Records)

For most artist, their artwork is extremely dear to them. The hours they put into perfecting their craft, whether they are a musician, painter, dancer, writer or producer, they tend to dedicate a lot of time to one performance, one show, one poem, one novel or just one painting. They may have many pieces of art, but still, the hours spent to present one particular piece of art far exceeds the time it takes to display it, therefore, it would be devastating to have all the work, time and effort for that piece of art, to either be lost, stolen or destroyed. They would have to do it all over again from scratch.

Compare this to your lifetimes. The wisdom you accumulate through each experience, it would be severely upsetting if it all went to waste, to lose memory of all your experiences, your families, people who you fell in love with, the best of times and even the worst of times. It would almost seem like losing a piece of who you are, if you ever forgot these memories, however, you don't lose a piece of who you are, ever. Some of you have experienced many, upon many of lifetimes, accumulating wisdom, upon wisdom. Where can you place all this information?

Inside the 'World of Answers' is something some have referred to as the '**Akashic Records**.' It is a vibrational record of every 'Soul,' and its voyage. It is known as '**The Totality of All Information**,' or the '**Hidden Library**.' Akasha is a Sanskrit word, which originated over **5000** years ago, meaning 'Eye,' or 'Aether,' which means the material that fills the region of the Universe above the terrestrial sphere. In Hinduism, Akasha means, 'The basis and essence of all things.'

These records not only contain all knowledge of human experience and the history of the cosmos, but it contains the records to all that there ever previously was. The Akashic Records is somewhat like **'God's Library,'** and God has put everything in there, every book, every video, every piece of audio that was ever been recorded throughout existence. It resembles something of a **'Universal Supercomputer,'** or **'God's Internet.'** Just like the Internet, it keeps every bit of information that has ever been placed on it, and it is constantly being updated. It is connected to Everything that exist, therefore the second something happens it is being updated as it is occurring.

Your own life, and all other lives you have lived are recorded through a special frequency of energy that is completely unique and different in its vibration from anyone and anything else. Your 'Soul' has its own special barcode that is scanned into the **'Hall of Records,'** making it so that once it is accessed, it not only gives you the answers to all that you desire, but it also gives you your own personal download of information.

The records hold the blueprint to each individual soul, it is like the 'Thumbprint' of a person, the individual divine essence, the root of you, the base. This thumbprint of who you are has been with you since the moment of your inception as an individual soul, and will continue to be the root of you throughout the end of time. It is the primary substance of you, it is who you really are. It is a thumbprint before the energy of your thoughts start to take it over. Our feelings give it a push, and use it as the foundation to the personalities we take up on each lifetime.

The Akashic Records keeps data on this thumbprint of all your experiences, how you act, react, your relationship with friends, family, things you liked and disliked. It keeps all this information in a catalogue assigned specifically for you, and will continue to hold this information forever.

It contains the answers to plagues, cancers, diseases and wars, it gives the meanings behind creation, life, love, peace, happiness, and the details of your own missions and purpose for being here. It is the 'All,' but it is also extremely personal. It is personal because it is essential to knowing who you are. It is important to be personal, it is important to retain every bit of information of your past, present, and possibilities of the future, because that is the only way we can know who we truly are. While accessing the Akashic Records, both the events and responses are received. Future events are foretold, but it is just a probable response. The foretelling of future events are based on past events, therefore it is something that can always be changed.

While in the Akashic Records, it is like having a super-mega-ultra-enhanced cinematic experience, except you are actually in it and not watching it. For the most part, the information is not in writing, but in symbols, images and feeling.

In her book, '**How to Read the Akashic Records**,' **Linda Howe** explained that the make-up or build of the Akashic Records consist of is **Love**, **Wisdom**, and **Power**. Power in the sense of the word that it is a '**Life-Force**,' and it is extremely strong, more powerful than anything in the physical realm. She continues to explain that the Akashic atmosphere is operated by **3** principles. **Fear not. Judge not. Resist not.** When these **3** get together, it creates an environment for the Akasha Reader that is extremely supportive, honorable and full of love and acceptance.

The Akashic Records can be reached through dreams, astral projection, meditation, shamanism, hypnosis, or through thought. In, '**The Law of One: Book I The Ra Material**,' **Don Elkins** asked the **Social Memory Complex** known as '**Ra**,' a series of questions that lead to him being told about the Akashic Records. Excerpts from the conversation are as follows:

> **Questioner** (Don Elkins): *Where did the information come from that Edgar Cayce channeled?*

> **Ra:** *I am Ra. We have explained before that the intelligent infinity is brought into intelligent energy from eighth density or octave. The one sound vibratory complex called Edgar used this gateway to view the present, which is not the continuum you experience but the potential social memory complex of this planetary sphere. The term your peoples have used for this is the "**Akashic Record**" or the "**Hall of Records**."*

Edgar Cayce stated that after each lifetime, a person is held to account for their own personal Akashic record of what they have or have not done in a karmic sense. Cayce also believes the Akashic records are particularly concerned with 'Intent,' why we did what we did.

A good example to this would be a comparison that was explained by **Kevin J. Todeschi**, A.R.E.'s Executive Director and CEO. He gave a story of how Cayce did readings on two different women that very much had the same past life experiences. The first woman had a hard time making friends. She was known as being loose with men, and other women didn't want to be around her because of it. Men even joked this was true, saying that if you want a good time, she would be a real good date. According to this woman, none of this was true. After Cayce read from her Akashic Records, he had learned that in her most recent past life she had been a prostitute, and she used her body to get what she wanted. Her intent, is what carried over in the next life, therefore some people are somehow picking up on that previous deed in her past life, even though she wasn't doing anything in the present to bring this about. A few years later another woman came to Cayce, and received a reading. She was a very loving woman, and people wanted to be around her because she exuded love. Cayce said in her past life she was also prostitute, but had given the only thing she had, out of love, to give companionship to lonely men. Her intent was love, so this carried over and was reinforced in the present, while the first woman's past intent which was greed, also got reinforced in the present.

Thus, Todeschi went on to say Cayce explained that while many may feel it is the deed in which they will be judged by, it is always the intent of the deed that is more important. In fact, Edgar Cayce says people get credit for the 'Try,' more so than the deed itself.

Throughout history, it is believed the Akashic Records has been mentioned in many religious or mystical texts. It has been claimed the **Vedas** (An Ancient Indian holy texts) of Hindus, and the language of Sanskrit were extracted from Akasha. In Ancient Egypt, it has been said those who could read from the Akasha were held in high standing, and would advise the Pharaohs on daily activities, future events and dream interpretation. Buddhist believe a reason people knew Buddha had reached enlightenment is because he was able to remember all of the details of all of his past lives, by accessing them from the Akashic Records. There are also references in the Bible which some point out to be other names for the Akashic Records. For instance, in **Psalm 69:28** it mentions the **'Book of Life,'** and in **Revelation 21:27** it reads, *"Nothing impure will ever enter it, nor will anyone who does what is shameful or deceitful, but only those whose names are written in the Lamb's* **Book of life**.*"*

Through scientific discoveries, some scientists believe the Akashic Records are real and exist as a zero-point energy field, which is the lowest possible energy a quantum mechanical physical system can have. Truly, the Akashic Records exists 'Everywhere,' because it is connected like wiring, to every point of everything that exist. It can be accessed from anywhere, by anyone.

In accessing the records, one must be receptive. The information does not come through force. At times you will be granted the knowing of 'Everything.' At other times you may receive certain information you feel does not pertain to you, but it does, it is all pieces to a puzzle, however, decoding the information takes acute awareness, and in-depth knowledge. The information contained in the Akashic Records is astronomical and will confuse the mind if the reader is not exactly sure what they are receiving.

The information is freely there for everyone, just as the **'World Wide Web.'** All of us have access to this information because we are each connected to the Everything. Just like the internet, there are certain sites where you must to place in a password, this can be compared to certain levels of the **Akashic Records**. Based on your understanding at the time, it will reveal to you what you can handle. Ultimately the information as a whole is there for you to access.

The World of Answers: (Where does it Exist)

Where does the 'World of Answers,' a place we call 'Heaven,' really exist? This place is so magnificently enormous, you would think it must exist somewhere, but where? If this place is so gigantic, much larger than the many particles of Universes, you would assume it exists somewhere far away, in a vast section.

It is hard not to imagine 'Heaven' being above us. In all depictions of those having spiritual encounters, talking to God or a Higher Being, they are all doing so by looking upward, most of the times into the sky. Why? Could it be from the thought of thinking something at a higher Conscience level is above them? Why not look below? Could it be this idea of Hell being below us that we don't look to the ground? Why not to the left or the right, or behind us?

The 'World of Answers' does not exist above, below, to the right or left of us, it exist in the same area as everything here. It does not exist on top or below the 'World of Questions,' it exists in it, around it, through it, and throughout it. It is merely naked from our eyes, but it is here, all around us, intertwining with this realm. It exists above us, but it also exists below us, to the right and left of us, but more importantly, it exists through us.

You do not travel billions of light-years to go to Heaven, you don't even take a step. At the moment of crossing over through astral projection or death, you aren't shooting off to another far off place, you aren't going anywhere. What you are doing, is blending into it. The 'World of Answers' and the 'World of Questions' do not exist on top of each other, or around each other, they exist within one another, but with the 'World of Questions' continually trying to understand what it is. It is almost unaware of itself, thus it wants to learn about itself, and seeks understanding, it seeks Light (Answers) from the 'World of Answers.'

For example, when taking a photograph, there are two sides that come from a photograph, the '**Negative**' and the '**Positive**.' For the sake of this comparison, imagine the 'World of Questions' as the positive side of the photograph, and the 'World of Answers' as the negative side. The negative side of the photograph is always there, it in turn creates the positive side of the picture. It not only creates the positive side of the picture, but it can also reproduce the positive side of the picture, whenever it wants. Sometimes the positive side of the picture comes out tainted or smeared, having some type of defect to it, but the negative of the picture is always there, and is able to reproduce that picture again to make a better print. It is the foundation for that particular image to show itself on the positive side. It is the foundation to everything. The positive of the picture exists within the negative of the photograph, but the negative can't be revealed without the positive.

They need one another. The 'World of Answers' needs the 'World of Questions,' just as much as the 'World of Questions' needs the 'World of Answers,' in order for the picture to come into fruition. They exist within one another, like the Yin to the Yang, and they need each other for one to understand what the other is.

CHAPTER ELEVEN
(God)

"People see God every day, they just don't recognize him."
                                          - Pearl Bailey -

God: (Introduction)

     '**God**,' otherwise known as the '**Ultimate**' or the '**Divine Being**,' has been referred to with many different names when called upon by humans. The list can go on, we have called God, the '**Creator**' or the '**Originator**.' The '**Supreme**' and '**Most High**' are also very popular, as well as '**The Way**' or the '**Light**.' God is the '**Uncaused-Cause**' and the '**First-Cause**.' Some religions have even given God personal names, such as '**Yahweh**' or '**Allah**.'

     After a while, no matter what you feel to call this '**Energy**,' it should seem that we are giving this '**Being**' nicknames, especially if we refer to this Being as the '**One**.' Surely, if this Being is the 'One,' than everything you think to call this Being would just be a nickname.

     Humans tend to refer to this '**Divine Presence**' as '**Him**' or '**Her**.' '**It**' seems more accurate. Surely, God cannot be a 'Him' nor a 'Her.' Maybe a '**Both**.'

     God is a 'Creator,' it is an '**Artist**,' a '**Performer**,' God performs and creates, creates and performs, performs and creates and so on. God, is the most publicized Artist the world as ever known, it continues to make art, draw, sculpt, record sounds, it cannot stop. God is '**Continuous**,' and God is the '**Only**' thing there is.

     There exists nothing else in the world, but God. God, the '**Everything**' is only '**One Thing**,' therefore the connection of '**God**' and '**You**' exist. Everything is not separate, Everything is One thing.

God: (How God came into Existence)

Many have wondered how all this came to be. When backtracking to the beginning of everything, you must get to an **'Uncaused-Cause,'** something that comes from nothing. For example, the technology created today, for the most part we can say it came from human development. You would then wonder, so what made humans? Whether humans were created by aliens, came from another planet, or evolved through time, it is easy for us to comprehend that something created or helped the evolution of human beings. If we think about the entities that made human beings, then what made those entities? We can go on finding causes for what made the after-cause, until we get down to the Uncaused-Cause, God.

There is nowhere else to go but to end up at the Uncaused-Cause, something that wasn't created. How? How can there possibly be something from nothing? How can there be a God, if nothing made God? How is it possible for something to simply exist?

To understand the existence of God is to understand the existence of **Sound**. First, you must recognize that there is no such thing as silence. You can be in the quietest of places, no radio, no one else around, TV off, no air condition blowing, and you will still hear noise. If you have never noticed this before, place yourself in a quit area, and take the time to pay attention to the light humming sound in your ears. At times it can feel like a light tea whistle, with a strange buzzing vibration to it, almost like vibrational static. Once recognized, this noise grows louder, and can become clearer over the years.

If you are noticing this for the first time, it has always been there, and always will. You can't escape it, you can't run or hide from it, it will hover over us forever, Sound. There could be nothing here, and still there will be Sound. Why, and how does this relate to God?

The Uncaused-Cause…is a Sound. Nothing made God, God has always been, because at the root of God, it is a Sound. Some equate this sound to the **Om** (**Aum**), as defined in

Hinduism. Hindus believe that when creation began, the **'Divine All-Encompassing Consciousness'** took the form of the first original vibration manifesting as the sound 'Om.' The Om is usually uttered as a mantra, and more frankly is believed to be the spoken essence of the Universe and/or God.

In simpler terms the Om represents the Everything. This makes sense when comprehending the sound and pronunciation of the Om. The Om, a beautiful sound, is a sound in which we use every day in the simplest of ways as when you are thinking, or trying to say something to someone, with the expression, 'Ummm.' Constantly, we are channeling God, searching our database for the 'Answers.' We use the sound continuously and do not realize it.

On a broader level, think of every sound you've ever heard, every drum beat, every horn, piano, word, sound of the cars driving by and honking, children laughing, playing, crying, think of every sound you have ever heard, and lay them on top of each other. Lay every sound you can think of, the sound of someone typing on a keyboard, the sound of a door slamming, the sound of wind, the ocean, animals, think of everything you can think of and place them all together. Eventually it starts to play into a chaotic noise that begins to sound like static, but when continued to be layered with sound after sound, the static of everything as one will grow to a sound that resembles the pronation of the Om (This being at pitch level much higher than human vocal cords).

How does sound relate to God, and the Light that God is? How can sound, be at the root of the creation to everything there is? To understand this in human terms, a great example would come from a television show shown on the History Channel. In a series called **'Stan Lee's Superhumans,'** a show designed to show living human beings that display some of the same powers and supernatural abilities as some of the comic book characters in the **Marvel Universe**, it hit the idea of God right on the head without even know it. It is no secret blind people use other senses to adapt to this physical realm. A character named **'Daredevil'** from Marvel Comics is known for being able to see even without the ability of sight. He is blind, but moves around as if he had use of his eyesight. Is this just comic book fiction? On one of the episodes, a man by the name of **Juan Ruiz** introduced himself to the host of the show by riding up on a bicycle, though he has no use of his eyesight. Just like the character Daredevil, Ruiz is blind. When the host asked him how he could ride a bike even though he is blind, Ruiz's response was that he could see the vibrations from the sound hitting the things around him, therefore it outlines the objects in light, which in turn makes it able for him to see.

Sound…makes **Vibration**…and vibration makes **Light**. Light enables us to see and feel all that we do, and can be associated as the physical component of God.

God: (Forgetting Everything)

You cannot understand the meaning of God, unless you fully know 'Everything. This is God, 'Everything.' For you to imagine what God is, imagine that you know everything.

What would it be like to know everything? What would it be like to know every point in History? What would it be like to know the blueprint for every obstacle you've already figured out, to have all the knowledge that one can hold, to know everything there ever was, and will be? Many think this would be flattering, to know 'Everything.'

God, a being that knows Everything, every turn, every decision, every point in the past and future, every experience one could make, nothing new to learn, no new journey to take, no new memory it could have, it is All and Everything, and knows any of all that there ever could be. How much longer before this begins to sound boring? Knowing Everything, is boring.

When you know everything, you can't do one thing new, you can't have a new experience, you can't learn new knowledge, you can't go in a new direction, quite simply, you're stuck. You're stuck to knowing everything. You can't find a new discovery, you can't stumble onto new information, you can't improve on anything, because you know everything. You can't grow, because there is no room for growth. This is not fun. This is not exciting.

God, a being that knows everything, also knows the ultimate price of boredom. A Creator at its purest form cannot keep creating when it knows everything. How can you continue to create when you know everything? You can't. For there is not one thing that could surprise such a being, not one thing could give God a new experience or the feeling of something new. It knows everything, so it is stuck, to not growing, to being stagnate, this is the worst place for any artist, stagnate, to have writer's block. For any being that calls itself a Creator, this is not where it wants to be, not being able to create something new.

How can God continue creating when there's nothing new to create? There's nothing God can do to experience something new, if it already knows Everything…unless…God forgets…Unless God forgets it knows everything.

The only way for God to experience something new is for God to forget it knows Everything, and to give itself 'Amnesia.' There is no other way for anyone or anything who has already experienced everything and knows all things, to continue experiencing the brilliance of creation unless they forget they have already created everything.

This is such a delicate thing to gamble with, to risk never remembering who you are again. This is just too risky of a process to forget you know everything, especially since you are the creator of all things. This is too much to jeopardize as a whole, and more risky to jeopardize in the realm of Consciousness, so what does God do? How does the Creator, who wants to continue creating, have its 'Cake and eat it too?'

Forgetting you know Everything, and there just being 'One' of you, wouldn't be any fun either. This wouldn't be exciting, to figure out things by yourself, to have no one to talk to, run your ideas across, share your experiences with. It's like the saying, *"Success is nothing without someone to share it with,"* so what do you do, when there is 'One' of you, and you know 'Everything?' There's no way for you to share your newfound joy, or keep creating as many things as you want…unless…you break yourself apart, into two. Let's make it a little more exciting, and break yourself down into many. Let's make it even more entertaining and break yourself down into countless of pieces, countless of energies, that way God can experience itself in countless of ways. This is extraordinary, but as well too risky, to break Itself down to countless of different energies and forget they are all connected, and a part of each other, as God.

How can God play a hand at poker and enjoy itself by giving itself the chance of not always winning the pot, but never truly actually lose the game? The only way to do this is to give God a place to play, a place to learn, a place to hold itself back from knowing everything. It would be too critical a move to gamble never being able to realize itself again, so where can it go? Where can it take this type of gamble, where can God play this game with itself? The 'World of Questions.'

God, an **'All Powerful'** and **'All Knowing'** energy, has played an extremely risky trick on itself, to forget it is the Creator. In doing so it has covered its tracks immensely. It would be devastating for God to forever forget it's actually God, so the chance of playing a game with itself where it does not know thyself, turns out to be a Game within a Game, because God made it so that there is no way possible for it to forever forget exactly what 'It' is, only because 'It' still knows that it is.

Referencing back to the **'Moment of Transition'** process with death, you may be reminded 'You are the Creator,' this is the beginning process God gives itself to remember what it is, in the 'World of Answers.' Every living thing that exists in the 'World of Questions' has its own personal path it is to venture, but we are all reminded that this experience is of our own creation, once we return home. Once this is recognized, it then goes into a deeper level of remembrance, a level that reminds you how your experience is connected to many other experiences, and how those experiences are in line with the experience of the 'Everything,' and how the 'Everything' is really 'You.' The levels God takes to remind 'Itself' what it is, is never ending and all fulfilling.

In the 'World of Answers,' God could never truly forget it is God, because the 'World of Answers' will instantly give God those answers. On the other hand, the 'World of Questions' was made for God to forget even the most important things, so it can give itself a place where it can rediscover itself, again and again, which, to discover the truth of oneself is the greatest experience one can have.

God, created from Sound, and knows Everything, breaks itself down into what we know as, 'Souls' or 'Spirits,' and makes the Physical Realm, known as the 'World of Questions,' comes here, forgets it knows Everything, and experiences itself through all the different things it has broken itself down to be. Thus, it can now gamble without ever truly losing, because the 'World of Answers,' which is God's home, will always remind itself that it is God, when 'It' returns.

God: (What is Love)

For many, the word '**Love**' is the most difficult word to give a definition to. Think of the many times you have heard someone say, 'Love can't be defined.' This is correct, but only due to the extent of knowing that God, in its entirety is unexplainable to a human's capability. God, which consists of 'All Love,' it would seem nearly impossible to give a definition to its greatest attribute, that being 'Love.'

Ironically, defining love is the one of the main reasons we are here, and it is such a simple word to define, the definition has been right underneath our noses since the beginning of time. Understanding the '**Free Will**' that God has given each soul, is the passage way to comprehending love.

'Free Will' is a gesture that comes from love. It is a choice most scriptures and texts express that God has given human beings, but not without placing the definition of Free Will inside of a box. Free Will does not have consequences tied to the end of its definition, for there is no Hell you will go to because of the mistakes you think you have made here. If so, that wouldn't be Free Will, that would be a consequence. God is all love, God does not send you to Hell for bad judgment, God understands the forgetful process you have endured and knows there is much to remind itself.

How could God not love every part of itself? All God wants is the experience, and in order for God to have the experience, God had to accept what it will freely be, whatever the experience will entail. God accepted the outcome, even before you decided to enter into your own path. God accepted whatever it is that you chose or will choose for yourself. God accepted and will always and forever accept. Why? Because God is all love.

God is not a police station, where someone may do something wrong in society and the judge will give them a life prison sentence. God is more like a parent that knows way more than their child, and when the child does wrong, the parent shows them ways to better themselves, and says no matter what, 'I love you unconditionally.' With them, you can always come home. They will not send you to jail and throw away the key, and neither will God. With God, you can always come home, because God accepts you!

Acceptance is a show of love. When you accept something for what it is, this is a sign of love, God is all accepting, therefore God is all love. The definition of love...is acceptance.

Someone stole money from you, accept it, the money wasn't truly yours anyway. Someone looks at you coldly, accept it, how much harm can someone's ugly stare hurt you more than it does them? You had a bad day at work? Accept the fact that it was actually beautiful to be able to have a bad day at work. You could be experiencing complete nothingness. This place, the physical realm is here for you to accept, for you to love, for you to experience.

Someone calls you a slur, accept them. Be the 'Love' you want for yourself. That is the only way love recognizes itself, when it is being the love it wants for itself. You want to be loved, than you accept everything for what it is. This does not mean do nothing to make this place a more positive environment for you to cohabitate, it means to love this place, and to discontinue being or reacting in the ugliness you may complain about seeing.

You do not want to be condemned, then you do not condemn. You do not want to feel judged, then you do not judge. You do not want to be betrayed or cheated upon, then do not behave in such a manner. You want to feel gratitude from others, than show gratitude to others. You want to be accepted, then show acceptance. For even the most evil of men, God has forgiven, the most cruelest individual or society is just as loved and accepted as someone that lives their life serving others.

Describing her **'Near Death Experience,' Mary Jo Rapini**, explained, *"I looked up and I saw this light, it wasn't a normal light, it was different, it was luminescent, and it grew. I kept looking at it like, 'What is that?' Then it grew large and I went into it. I went into this tunnel, and I came into this room that was just beautiful. He called me by name, and he told me, 'Mary Jo, you can't stay.' And I wanted to stay. I protested. I said, 'I can't stay? Why not?' And I started talking about all the reasons, I was a good wife, I was a good mother, I did 24-hour care with cancer patients. And he said, 'Let me ask you one thing, have you ever loved another the way you've been loved here?' And I said, 'No, it's impossible. I'm a human.' And then he just kind of chuckled. He gave me the illusion of a sweet protective chuckle. It wasn't human, but it was able to relate to me in a very human way that made me feel loved. And it wasn't laughing at me, but it was a chuckle, like it had a playful edge. And it said, 'You can do better."*

To know love, is to know no boundaries, and God has no boundaries. This could be confusing to some. Some people may wonder, with all the killing, rape, robbery and betrayal have led to the devastations of millions, you could possibly wonder how could God forgive everyone, for everything, even the ugliest of our actions. They may wonder, or think God may then not even care for the world.

This thought is such a difficult concept to understand, but they are correct. They are correct, only because God is 'All Accepting,' and God does not care in the sense of judgment, but cares so much that God would actually give you the 'Free Will' to live out your life as you see such.

God loves you as God loves itself, for however and all the ways it chooses to play this game. It's waiting for you to love yourself and others, as much as God accepts you. That in turn is the main goal here, to figure out that we don't have to wait to go to the 'World of Answers' to treat each other with the love and compassion of the 'One.' We can be the 'One,' here.

God: (How You relate to God)

First, it may be more important to understand your relationship to God, before understanding what God is or how 'It' came to be. Understanding how you relate to God is like understanding your single thought for existence. As quoted by, **René Descartes**, *"I think, therefore I am."* The only thing holding people from knowing they are God, is because they think they are not. You are just as much a part of God, as the thoughts that run through your mind. Remember, this is the game God is playing with itself, to think that it is not.

Our connection, or how we as 'Souls' relate to God, can be explained with a few comparisons. For starters, the Collective Consciousness is and by all means 'One' and 'Everything.' God extends itself throughout the Collective Conscious to experience itself in countless of ways. You are of this Collective Conscious. You aren't just in it, you are It.

The way 'Souls' are set up to God, first, imagine a sheet or paper, which represents God, the 'All,' the 'Everything.' Now, imagine bubbles slightly poking out from this sheet. Those bubbles represent the souls of God. Each soul has their own space, but yet it is still connected to the sheet. It is not just connected to the sheet, but it is of the sheet, and it is the sheet.

Another good comparison would be to take a piece of loose leaf paper and cover your hand so that it only leaves your fingers showing. For this comparison, the sheet of paper now represents the 'World of Questions.' The fingers represent the people, as individuals. One finger may totally feel separate from the next finger, because the sheet of paper (The World of Questions) hides that it is actually connected to the hand (God). That finger's knowledge is also limited to what it sees, which are the 4 other fingers. They each look different from the other, some taller, others shorter, some wider, others thinner, but yet they still look similar. This can be confusing, however, once you remove the sheet, you will then see how the fingers are all connected to the hand. Not only is it connected to the hand, but you then see that each finger is essentially working for one common goal, the hand (God).

One last example of how you relate to the 'Infinite' is that coming into the 'World of Questions' is like a drop of water breaking away from its group. You are a 'Drop' of water that is experiencing itself among other 'Drops of Water.' You are made up of the same things that make-up all the other drops of water, and yet you feel separate here in the 'World of Questions.' As soon as you go through the transition of death, the drop of water you represent is then poured back into the 'Ocean' from which it came from. You are a Drop of Water that merges with the Ocean Body of God.

CHAPTER TWELVE
(The Game)

"The Universe is an intelligence test."

- Timothy Leary -

The Game: (Introduction)

What is this beautiful thing we call 'Life?' What is the big point of all this, and what are we actually doing here?

What we are doing here, is playing a 'Game.' We are playing a game on a **'Chessboard.'** This 'Life' is a 'Game' that God (You, Us) is playing with itself, and it's the most brilliant Game anyone could ever think of. It has rules, it has consequences, something God can't give itself in the 'World of Answers.' It has boundaries, it has limits, again something God can't give itself in the 'World of Answers.'

The Game is designed by one of the greatest computer programmers that has ever existed…You. You have designed this system, and you are not playing with a **1980's** version Atari. You have placed yourself in **High Advanced Programming**, and the **Collective Consciousness** is anything but ordinary.

The Game would be boring starting off completely from scratch, with a blank backboard, so you give yourself scenery, and LOOK at it! It is magical, mountains you can climb and ski down, waves you can surf and swim in, sand you can run on or play in, rainforest you can hike and explore, this place is a Video Gamer's dream! The oceans, hills, trees and stars you look up to, this was designed just for you.

Then it has people, people with so many different personalities, some Rooks, some Bishops or Horses, and others Kings, Queens and even Pawns, and they all affect the game differently. People who know the rules of Chess know a pawn is as significant as your most important piece, even the smallest move you make is a major leap, and once you start playing your pieces, you understand that every move you make is essential for your growth.

Most people that play video games also love to give themselves immediate obstacles, or mysteries they can figure out, something that initially gets them going. You have given yourself things like Pyramids to leave you with wonder, Stars above that leave you thinking how we came into existences. Everything a Video Gamer would want is here.

It's a game, this is all it is, life is nothing but a large playing field. The 'World of Questions' is our **Playground**. It is a **School**, and even a **Prison**. The game is designed for us to experience ourselves, it is meant for us to have fun (Playground,) it is meant for us to learn (School), and it is meant for us to experience limitations (Prison). Your body can be thought of as the prison, being in the physical plain is a prison in itself of sorts, because it confines you to its boundaries, and there is no prison, but the prison you place yourself in.

These boundaries are things we are blessed to experience, because there is no boundary where we come from, and how we react to these boundaries here in the world we have giving ourselves, results into **Wisdom**, which in turn makes us better understand who we are and how we deal with struggle. In turn, knowing we can actually face struggle and maneuver pass this is exciting, it is exciting to **Enlighten Beings**, which you are.

You have given yourself such an amazing playing field, exciting scenery, obstacles, and a history to help you remember 'Who You Are.' You've left yourself all kinds of secrets and hints to remind yourself that this World is your Chessboard.

The Game: **(Why Play)**

As souls, we are here experiencing the consequences of our own actions through karmic energy, from one lifetime to the next, until we become fully aware of our own 'God Self,' our own 'Light' in the physical plane. We come into each lifetime to re-evaluate the **Wisdom** that we have gathered on previous lifetimes, and to clarify if it is true in the present lifetime. Simply, you are engaging in the physical realm what you know to be true, while experiencing your wisdom from the opposite side of the spectrum.

You may ask yourself, 'Why play the game?' If one is so divine to know Everything, why play a game in which it has to relearn itself all over again? In simple terms, the answer is because it is fun, in deeper terms, the answer...because it is the only thing for us to do, to experience.

By nature, God is a 'Creative Being,' that keeps creating and creating, in which its creations are no different. Creating is experiencing, you cannot have an experience without creation, and at the root of everything we are, we yearn to create, experience and experiment.

The reason to play the game is because there is no other choice but to play the game. The only other thing for us to do is to watch others play the game, in the 'World of Questions.' While some of us may choose to do just this (Choose not to play), somehow this does not come without aiding those that are playing the game, even though eventually we all play the game, and continue to play the game. The only other thing for us to do, as souls, is to experience the 'World of Questions,' or another form of 'World of Questions,' another realm of existence, and play by the rules we give ourselves during that particular experience. Some experiences differ in boundaries, while some tend to have reoccurring limitations.

One may wonder, 'Why would we give ourselves limitations?' The reason to give ourselves limitations is because it's fun. It's fun to go through the process of rediscovering there really are no limits. It's fun to rediscover the **Mind** and the **Collective Consciousness**, it's fun to go through the experience and walk through the doors not knowing where it may lead you.

In human terms, the game you have entered into is the biggest '**Mind Trick**' you have ever played on yourself. The Mind Trick is to forget you are God, to forget you are a part of Everything, to forget you already know Everything, and to see how you react to starting from scratch. Truly it is the greatest trick, the greatest practical joke anyone or anything could ever pull off, and only 'You' could do this to yourself.

The Game is to rediscover who you really are, and to realize all that you are capable of in the Game. Some people may walk in this realm, the 'World of Questions,' moping around, feeling sorry for themselves, settling for the pieces of the puzzle life hands them, instead of going out and trying to find the extra pieces to the puzzle and put it together for what they can come to see for themselves. You are suppose to look for the other pieces to the puzzle, you are suppose to experience, to learn, to love, to interact.

One of the most important parts of the game for you to realize, is to understand that no one, or nothing forced you here. You willingly came and decided to participate in this game. People have resorted to all kinds of measures to get themselves out of this game, just to realize that it was all a game in the first place, so they realize they forgot to have fun, and in turn come right back into the Game. Some people go through their whole life sulking, depressed, feeling like there is no sense in trying, but why put yourself in the Game if you're not going to play the Game?

The second we understand this experience was not forced upon us, is the moment we can begin to feel differently about being here. No person likes to do things against their will, and no Enlightened Being would either. This process of 'Life' is not a punishment, it is a gift, a gift that all of us have given ourselves. No being, thing, or energy, pushed you over the edge while you were blindfolded. You willingly, dove into the 'World of Questions' with our eyes wide open.

Furthermore, while this 'Life' is an experience, it is more essentially an 'Experiment.' We are experimenting with ourselves during this experience. Everything we do here does not vanish, it is kept in a 'Memory Bank' that holds all the wisdom of your lives. Once you realize this experiment is a Game, the Game then becomes easy, it becomes less stressful. Why? Because you then understand that you are actually just playing a Game, and realizing you are in the Game is a greater advantage than it is to those who have no idea they are on a playing field, with the other team running up the points on the scoreboard.

The Game: (Wisdom & Problems)

There is a deeper purpose to us being here than it just being for a physical experience. We want it to be about something more than just an experience, so we have given it an objective. Do not let this deeper objective scare you, because we have given ourselves endless possibilities to get it right. The only logical objective to the Game is 'Growth,' and the key ingredient to growth, is 'Wisdom.' Through wisdom, there is growth.

To understand where the wisdom lies, it is necessary to know that it does not come from a problem or problems, nor does it come from the answer. The wisdom comes from the entire involvement of going through the problem and answer.

The wisdom is the experience. For example, if one was presented with a math problem of **2 + 3**, the wisdom would not be what it is equaled to, which is **5**. The wisdom is the entire equation of **2 + 3 = 5**. If someone was to just give you the answer of **5**, and you not know why or what led it to **5**, the answer would be meaningless, fFurthermore, **4 + 1** equals **5**, and so does **5 + 0**, so the answer of **5** would be irrelevant without the problem. The answer without the proper question defeats the purpose of having the correct answer. You need to understand why the numbers **2** and **3** came up in the problem, not just **2** and **3**, but why it was **2** and then **3**, and not **3** and then **2**. You need to know the background story to why it is these numbers, and in its particular order, and you need a problem to understand the wisdom. Where does the problem lie? In the experience.

Everyone has something to battle with while they are here, quite frankly, this is the point, to give yourself an obstacle. Along the way, many other obstacles that weren't initially a part of your main obstacle can become prevalent.

Depression is a common emotion, whether it is losing their job, over money, a bad relationships, losing something material, depression seems to be a force all of us are battling or have battled at one point of time in our lives. If even for a moment, sometimes we let our problems take over the importance of the rest of the world. We give into letting a problem be the most vivid thing in our life, forgetting we have people that love us, forgetting that even though we may've lost a job, at least you may have a place to sleep, something to eat, maybe extra money to give yourself a cushion until finding a new job, and friends that somehow pull through in your time of need and offer some type of assistance. We forget that if you didn't have those extra things, being fired from a job would be the least of your worries, but we forget being just here is the best problem solver of all.

This experience, wouldn't be what it is without giving ourselves obstacles, and like any video gamer, no one likes something too easy. Most video gamers are determined to reach the highest level and conquer the ultimate stage, but if it is too easy, it's not as enjoyable, it's not as meaningful, it's not as thrilling. When you work hard for something or overcome an obstacle to come out from a previous stage to be in a better position than you were in, it is the ultimate feeling of self-satisfaction to know 'You did it,' and no one gave it to you but you.

Many have this feeling that they are a 'Human Being,' and what's mostly fun for Human Beings is material things, such as fast cars, clothes, jewelry, video games, mostly superficial things, all things that sum up to something that doesn't really matter. As explained earlier, you are not really human beings, you are all **Enlightened Beings**, occupying human bodies.

You are the Mind, the body you have is what you have picked out for your **Vehicle**. You are a **Chess player**, you are not a **Checker player**. You are all Thinkers, Creators. Checkers is for human beings, Chess Players like to give themselves problems and situations they can experience. Some problems, they quickly move through, others they sit and think about before making their next move, knowing each decision, each step, each move on the board affects the outcome of the whole game.

The problems in our life are there for a reason, because we love to give ourselves a good Chess game. Understanding that this is nothing but a '**Board of Life**,' makes it easier and more entertaining to digest our problems. In a sense, it could make you welcome the obstacle. Without problems, how can you understand triumph, how can you understand what it is not to struggle? Without struggling, how can you perfect something without figuring out all the ways to get it wrong?

We are Chess Players (Enlightened Beings), and our problems come from the moves we make on the board. We give all our problems to ourselves, no one else truly makes them for you, they come from how you play your pieces on the Chessboard, with your problems just a figment of your imagination. Once understanding this, it makes it a little easier to move through your problems on the chessboard, to take chances, to take risk.

Our problems have been something we have gotten too wrapped up in, and in turn haven't appreciated them for what they are here for. Our problems are entertainment, entertainment for Enlightened Beings. They are meant to give us something to do, something to figure out. Whether it's being late on the rent, getting a job, struggles as an artist, situations with your friends or family members, every little thing you may get irritated over or get annoyed by is here for a reason, to give us something to do, to give us entertainment, and to give us something to work through.

We are here to experience the grandest parts of ourselves, and you cannot experience the grandest parts of yourself without experiencing everything.

The Game: (Reincarnation Process)

We yearn for the chance of this experience, 'Life.' It is fascinating to us, all aspects of it. Some of us have an easy time with this, while others need a little bit more time to make the adjustment, but however so, it is still something we are all willing to venture into, with a purpose to learn, enjoy and to inspire.

Some of us have experienced lives on different planets in different **Star Systems**, therefore some of us may tend to feel out of place, or a stranger amongst those that are our closest friends and family. No matter how hard they try to adjust or blend in, Earth just seems foreign. The reason for this is simple, for some, experiencing Earth is a first. This does not necessarily mean they are 'New Souls,' but may be new to this plain of existence, or planet.

Many of us have done this so many times that the choices of what physical presence we come into is more selective, while others jump right back into the experience at any given chance, no matter what form or species they may take. Those that take any physical option that is given to them mostly haven't lived as many lives in the physical as some other souls. Some souls will wait out an opportunity that they feel best fits them, though eventually, everyone experiences it all. This can be explained when understanding the consciousness of animals and insects, all the way to people who are born into poverty or wealth, or even Extraterrestrials from other planets. All these are things that have Consciousness, planets, stars and Universes, all these things have Life, but yet go through processes in how they choose to experience Life.

Our next incarnation mostly depends on our previous incarnation, therefore some can be more selective while others have no problem experiencing the life of a worm. Many may wonder, 'Why would anyone want to experience the life of a worm?' It must be understood, when thinking this way you are thinking with a human mind. All souls experience everything, and want to experience everything, and you do not understand a worm by dissecting a worm, you understand a worm by experiencing the life of a worm.

To clarify, most humans do not retract, the purpose is to grow, so if you are human now, more than likely you will either be human again, or another species that is either equivalent or of a higher level of consciousness.

Some of us may have lived the lives of prisoners and the homeless, but our choices aren't always based on what body or form we can come into, but more so the experience we can have. For instance, one may think being born into a family of millionaires gives them the best possible opportunity or advantage for growth, but this is not so. Sometimes the best advantage for growth is to place yourself in the poorest household you can find. Maybe the mother of that particular household is one of the most insightful, hardworking and caring people in the world. How could this not be an advantage? How could it not help your growth, to have someone who is extremely caring, hardworking and insightful? These things can inspire a child to dream further than the boundaries from lack of money.

Contrary to popular belief, our parents did not bring us into the world, we brought ourselves into the world. They did not create or choose us, we chose them. We not only chose our parents, but we chose our friends, lovers, situations, and opportunities, with choices upon choices to make. These decisions aren't necessarily based on wanting to see a particular soul, friend or family member, but it is based on the experience. Our parents and friends are chosen depending on the type of experience we choose to take. It just so happens that a lot of our experiences are shared with souls we already know. In some sense, we make deals with them to come into this realm together.

We do not come into this experience by ourselves, we always make the venture with another or several, hundreds or thousands of other energies. In the grander scale of things, we all know each other. Truly, there is no stranger amongst us. We are playing a 'Game,' with our 'One Self,' with all our friends playing games with themselves, on the same chessboard, we all have created.

The Game: (The Laws of Forgetting)

The 'World of Questions' offers many 'Rules' or 'Regulations' in which we enjoy, but one rule in particular Enlightened Beings look forward to experiencing is the process of forgetfulness. This seems to be the fairest way for us to play the Game. If we enter into the Game knowing Everything, knowing all our opponents plays, all its weaknesses, all the right angles to score, all the right moves to make, the game would not only get too easy, but it would get boring. It would very much resemble the phrase, 'Taking candy from a baby,' so we forget.

We forget we know Everything. We forget we're even playing a game. We give this game as much equal opportunity that it can have, because this is the only way 'All-Knowing Enlightened Beings' such as yourself, can make it fair. If we realize we are the King on the Chessboard, and are actually able to break the laws of the Chessboard and place Itself wherever it wants to on the board, it could inhibit us from using other pieces, therefore missing the importance of them entirely. We forget we're on a Chessboard, we forget we are the 'All Moving King,' and we begin by placing ourselves in the shoes of a foolish pawn.

Some of us have already lived the life comparable to a Pawn, or Rook, Knight, Bishop, Horse, Queen or King, over and over again. Remember every move we've made on prior boards could get confusing when concentrating on the game you are playing right now, so you go into a deeper level of amnesia, you forget that once you actually already played the game.

When most people recall their life, they can only go back to memories as early as 3 to 5 years of age. The early years, from the day someone is born, doesn't necessarily seem like a blur, it in turn seems like it didn't happen at all. It could feel as though you just popped out of nowhere. The only proof you have for this not being true are pictures and stories of your parents telling you that you were here, so you know you didn't pop out of nowhere.

There is a reason for this, it is because it is the age of your innocence and you are still very much connected to the 'World of Answers.' You do not ever lose this connection, but most people forget the connection exist, therefore you begin to lose your innocence as you grow in the physical, and begin judgment of your experience. When you are born, you are fully accepting of the experience. As you grow, your parents and other people push their own values upon you, and as you get older you begin to judge and look upon your life with some of those same values and morals. People, unknowingly so, have been aiding you into losing your innocence.

Many times have children said something that didn't totally resonate or make sense to something current, with their parents thinking they may be confused. They are not confused in the least, they are comparing what they know from a previous experience. Children are far more connected to their past lives than adults, and as they grow, they start to forget their previous life or lives, as we do with our own life's memories here.

Sometimes when we recall our childhood memories, we get this newfound feeling of being able to remember such a beautiful moment in our life, other times, memories easily go ignored because of it possibly being from a traumatic incidence, or sometimes it could be beyond our level of comprehension at the time, so it goes forgotten. Truly, our past lives are just like some of the childhood memories you may have forgotten in this lifetime.

Sometimes our past lives might not make any sense to us now, it might not relate or resonate to the life you are experiencing at the moment, so the possibility of it coming into play would be confusing, and mostly ignored as random thoughts. Other times, our memories have been suppressed, due to traumatic experience.

There are many examples of those who have come forth from repressing the memories of being sexually abused or harmed when they were younger. Studies have shown sometimes the individual places the experiences in a location of the brain they wish not to think about anymore. This could be a strong case for why we don't remember our past lives. Some of them may have been of traumatic experiences, in which we might wish to forget during our current process, for the betterment of our current process. Maybe in a past life, you were a slave, or a murderer, or did something you would like to forget. Knowing it right now, during this experience could be too much for you to handle. What if a teacher who dearly and truly loved to inspire children, found out in their past life they may have harmed a child or stole from their job, this could possibly have a conflicting effect on their current efforts.

In other cases, sometimes our past lives merely go on being forgotten. Think of how many times someone has reminded you of something you did in the past, or a funny thing you said that made the people around you laugh. How many times has someone reminded you of something 'Cool' you may have done in the past, and you forgot? Truly, there has been many, upon many of memories we all have forgotten in this lifetime. Surely there are many, upon many of fascinating lives we have forgotten we've lived as well, especially if we have lived them over and over again.

The Game: (Destiny)

The choices you make, are yours and yours alone. 'Fate' and 'Destiny' is no more in control of your life than you are, though there are certain things you are destined to be faced with. Ironically so, the things you have given yourself to be faced with, there are in turn a multiple of fates that will come from those decisions.

Think of your life as if all the roads have already been foretold, you're just choosing the roads you want to take. It is pretty similar to reading a **'Gamebook,'** which is more commonly referred to as a **'Choose your own Adventure,'** book. A Gamebook, which became popular in the **1980**'s, allows the reader to participate in the story by making choices which affect the course of the narrative, in various paths through the use of numbered pages.

Basically, once you got to a certain page, you are faced with a decision of what you want the character to do next. Let's say this particular character can either drive down the street, or he/she can walk into a store. The option would be to turn to page **5** if you wanted the character to drive, and to turn to page **17** if you wanted the character to walk into the store, after making your decision, you would then turn to the desired page to continue reading and see how the story unfolds from that point on. The story would seem to go into two different directions, sometimes reconnecting to certain parts of the book, but with more decisions comes different experiences. This is very much like your life. Sometimes Déjà Vu can reveal itself to be some of these page markers.

Before coming here to the 'Physical,' we exactly know the trails, the paths, the decisions we are going to be faced with, but we leave it in our hands to make those choices while here. There is no wrong turn, because there is no right or wrong, but we do have an ultimate agenda in mind, this is why we give ourselves hints along the way, such as Déjà Vu, or dreams, just in case we get off course from our main focus.

There is actually no better way to go about such an option, to have all your roads already foretold, and you are in search of the ones you most desire for your experience. Your fate is in your own hands, the paths that you can take were all created for you, with so many different turns, twists, issues, dilemmas and problems. The next stage in your life is a simple choice of which page you wish to turn to.

The Game: (Parallel Universes)

The '**Parallel Universe**' or '**Alternate Reality**' is an extremely fascinating place, because it is a place you are doing everything that you aren't doing here, meaning, you are existing and experiencing everything at once.

The correct **Quantum Mechanical** definition of the Parallel Universes is, 'Universes that are separated from each other by a single quantum event.' It is a world where the laws of nature may bend from the 'Current Reality' you are in now. Examples are, exceeding the speed of light, lighter mass, more or less landscapes, people you don't know now, and people you know now that would in turn be strangers. The options are almost limitless.

The Alternate Reality has been depicted in countless of movies, for example, in the movie called '**The One**,' actor **Jet Li** is playing a character that is ironically being hunted down by an alternate version of himself, from another dimension. In a brief clip, it shows an image of '**President Bush**,' the President of the United States of America, speaking to congress. When the movie takes a turn and shows **Li** in another realm, during the same timeline the clip instead displayed a '**President Gore**' talking to congress. In our current Earth timeline, **Al Gore** lost the **2000** Presidential Election on account of a voting conflict. Even though this outcome was not shown in depth in the movie, this scenario has actually already played itself out.

The Election played out in an unlimited amount of ways. Instead of Bush winning the election with the majority of the **Electoral Vote**, and losing the **Popular Vote**, Gore in turn won on account of having more electoral votes and not having the popular vote. It has also played out with both men being from different parties, instead of Bush being a **Republican**, he was a **Democrat**, and the same with Gore. This has also played out with each losing their party's primary, so that the runner up in the **2000** Republican election, **John McCain** actually ran for president that year against **Bill Bradley**, the runner up to the **2000** Democratic election. In different Alternate Realities, both have won, and so on, and so on. This has happened over and over again, to the point that 'You' are actually the President of the United States of America. This scenario has to happen, it has to play itself out, because it is a part of you, the 'Everything.' After your experience here, it gives you an alternate roadmap as to how your experience could've been.

It is a realm, which more or less allows us to judge your current experience 'Now.' It is a realm as real as the one you are living in, but a world that begins to exist all on its own, parted from the choices you didn't make here. 'You' are channeled to this Earth timeline experience, but your 'Superconscious' holds all energy, and thought, not only for you to have as something to compare your travels to 'Now,' but because it is information that needs to be played out in order for the Superconscious to have all wisdom of all experiences. Your thoughts create energy, and that energy does not disappear, it lives on in a section for it to blossom.

You may wonder where this world exists, or if you can travel there with a spaceship or transport through a wormhole, but to get there you need to break many more laws than space travel. This dimension does not exist far away, it exist right here, overlapping and intertwining with the physical world we have now. It is a realm that exists in thought, just as this realm is of thought that has been made physical, the Alternate Realm is of thought that has been made physical, but they somehow exists in one another. This can be the cause to many people who have felt out of place at a particular moment in time, or have conversations that seem similar, with the feeling that you've already told someone something, but in turn didn't. You are receiving images or feelings from these scenarios, the Alternate Reality.

Ultimately, all the Alternative Realities center around the Reality you are living now. The one you are experiencing now is the '**Focal Point**,' it is the one you determine or base what the other realities may have meant to you. This is also an extremely beneficial gift, because it will allow you to see and decide what you may want to experience on your next life's 'Focal Point.'

Some may think they might want to always experience being 'Ruler of the World,' so to speak, but, this is the furthest thing from what you want to do. You can't continue learning anything by being 'Ruler of the World' all the time. In turn, more than likely you have already done this. Your goal is to experience the 'All,' and to progress. You do this in so many different ways, not by continuing to be 'Ruler of the World.' You are an 'Enlightened Being' that does not value life on being

'Ruler of the World.' You are a being that values life on experiences, and the wisdom generated from those experiences.

The Game: (Levels of the Physical)

The concept of different planes of existence, stages or levels may be found in many religious, philosophies and esoteric teachings, including **Shamanism**, **Theosophy**, **Anthroposophy**, **Gnosticism**, and **Kabbalah**. The idea of a whole series of dimensions and worlds in which we are to process through is not new, in fact it is something that is as old as the Game itself.

The Universe, in which we reside, consists of a multitude of levels and subtle planes that interpenetrate themselves through what we know as reality. Once a level is completed, a new plane or level culminates itself into the physical Universe and gives structure to your surroundings. What this basically means is that you have many stages of Life to go through before you reach the end of the Game.

This does not mean, one life, one complete stage. Most of the time, it takes many lives to experience each stage, certainly the beginning ones, mostly due to the short lifespans we may have with particular stages. Think of the lifespans of animals, compared to humans, and humans compared to Extraterrestrials, surely Extraterrestrial lifespans are much longer than that of the current human body. The longer the lifespan, the more chances and information one can attain.

This is not to say humans can't cross into the next stage with just one life, this is only to say that most humans have the length of a lifespan that has not enabled them to experience everything around them and all there is to fully understand who they are at this stage. Most leave the stage confused and misled, needing to come back.

When you are confused and misled and still in search of who you are, this does not mean you completed the stage. This means there are things you still must do to finish the level. If you haven't created, inspired or become aware, how can you possibly complete the stage? The reason we come back to the same stage is to repeat certain lessons we didn't quite fully grasp the first time around.

Each stage is different, but can have facets of the stage before it, but mostly if chosen to. Take telepathy for example, you should think that advancing up the ladder of Consciousness will in time lead us to experience telepathy. Once this comes about, of course this does not mean you can't speak. It means you have chosen to communicate in a different, more coherent and honest means of communication. You will have the ability of speech, but using telepathy is a more efficient tool.

Another comparison is to think of the different stages in Life, like the video game **'Super Mario Brothers,'** when the game's main character '**Mario,**' would advance through levels of the game. Each level is different, but shows facets of the level before it. With each stage, Mario grows stronger, and there are more treasures and secrets and adventures that came about with each level. It is the same with our physical planes of existence. With each stage, we equip ourselves with better ammunition for our venture.

In '**The Law of One,**' the **Social Memory Complex** known as '**Ra,**' explains a group of densities and levels that each 'Density' will attain. When asked what a Density was, **Ra** proceeded to explain. Excerpts from the conversation are as follows:

> **Ra:** *I am Ra. The term density is a, what you call, mathematical one. The closest analogy is that of music, whereby after seven notes on your western type of scale, if you will, the eighth note begins a new octave. Within your great octave of existence which we share with you, there are seven octaves or densities. Within each density there are seven sub-densities. Within each sub-density, are seven sub-sub-densities. Within each sub-sub-density, seven sub-sub-sub-densities and so on infinitely."*

In translation, 'You,' a 'Soul,' experiences being a **Density**. You are the **Density** that you are experiencing. In the book, **Ra** goes on to explain the levels of densities. A brief description of the **Density Levels** we experience through what Ra claims to be a multibillion-year cycle, are as follows:

First Density
> The First Density is the **Four Elements**, **Earth** (minerals), **air** (wind), **fire**, and **water**. Fire and wind act on the minerals and water, causing evolution to consciousness.

Second Density
> Animals and plants. This stage of evolution on Earth took **4.6** billion years.

Third Density
> Humanity's current stage, the density of **Self-Awareness** and **Self-Consciousness**. Rational thinking and intuitive thinking are the two fundamental necessities. Through applying both these abilities, we're to figure out that we're one with each other. Ra says the cycle for the Third Density is **75,000** years.

Fourth Density
> Plane of compassion. Achieved through understanding sorrow for the **Third Density**. Harmony is created through group consensus, because people know what others are thinking. A 'Social memory complex,' is formed, where all experiences of each entity are available to the whole. The typical time for one incarnation in the Fourth Density is **90,000** years, with the entire cycle of this density for all incarnations **30** million Earth years.

Fifth Density
> **Wisdom** and **Instant Manifestation**. Lessons of compassion learned in the **Fourth Density** lead to **Wisdom** in the **Fifth Density**. Entities are now able dissolve one manifestation and create another at will.

Sixth Density

Experience the **Self** as **Light**. **Ra** is a **Sixth Density** entity. This cycle is **2.5** million years. **Sixth Level** or above **Densities** can serve as the Higher Selves for lower-dimensional entities, in which at times, we refer to them as **Ghost**, **Souls**, or **Spirit Guides**.

Seventh Density

This is the **Culmination**. The **Seventh Density** is a **Completed Being**, it knows itself again, and readies itself to enter the **Eighth Density**.

Eighth Density

The **Eight Density** is the return to **Infinity**, return to the **Source**. According to **Ra**, there is a mystery with the **Eight Density** that cannot be put into words. Just as in the musical scale, the Eighth Density is also the First Density of the next octave.

Ra further explains, "*Since each entity has free will, the timelines given above are flexible. No entities can be forced to move up the density ladder until they are ready and have chosen to do so.*"

The most interesting thing to point out is the 'Eight Density,' where it states that it is the First Density in the next octave. This means once you complete your stages, and you will because you have no choice but to, and once you then eventually return to the **Source (God**, the **Creator)**, the only thing left for you to do...is to do it all over again. In comparisons to '**Super Mario Brothers**,' when Mario advances through stage after stage, spending life after life, trying to make it to the last board, once Mario gets to the end, once he finally defeats the dragon, once he saves the princess and finally wins the game...he celebrates...and then the game starts all over. The game starts from the beginning again, with certain changes made on each level. The game looks familiar, it looks very much like something you've played before, but nevertheless it's different, much like a Parallel Universe or an Alternative Reality.

Could it be that this isn't our first time on a '**Third Density**' level? Could it be that we are experiencing this moment, right now, somewhere else, and making a different decision? Yes...it is very possible.

This is the process we have given ourselves throughout our physical existence. We go through all stages, all directions to rediscover all that we already know, just to forget and relearn it all over again in a different way. Why? Because it is the only thing there is for us to do, to continue playing the Game.

The Game: (**Levels of the Soul**)

To understand the reasons for the many changes occurring with our Earth and our 'Conscious Levels,' it is important to know that it is not necessarily due to anything we have done or are doing here in the 'Physical Realm.' The reason for the changes here in the 'World of Questions' is because it is changing in the 'World of Answers.' In comparison, think of a clock, and inside this clock there are many wheels working and turning, catching each other by their gears (rotating machine parts with cut teeth, or cogs). The 'World of Questions' exists on what one might think of as a 'Gear' on a wheel, and as it is turning in the 'World of Answers,' it is approaching a different position. This is the cause for the changes in our 'Physical World,' we are approaching another 'Level of Existence' here, because it is changing its location in the 'World of Answers.'

The more we grow and understand our world here, the more we comprehend and resemble our world there. In other words, the 'World of Questions' is becoming more and more like the 'World of Answers.' Why? How come? It wants 'Know,' the 'World of Questions' yearns to have the same understanding as the 'World of Answers.' We can see this with technology, the advancements society has taken is a reflection of the knowledge that already exists in the 'World of Answers.' Simply, one realm is becoming like the other. Quite frankly, this is what it is designed to do, to learn from the other, this is progression, evolution, creation, growth.

The 'World of Questions' isn't the only thing that is growing, and the reasons for it growing is directed at none other than 'You.' We have tied this experience to the growth of our soul's potential. The time you spend in each 'Physical' life, not only determines when you advance to the next physical realm, but it also aids the growth of your Soul. When you are transitioning into another level of physical existence or another plane of reality, you are also progressing to another stage of your Soul. In simpler words, as you grow physically so does your Soul.

To imagine experiencing another physical plane or body is a little simpler than imagining what it will be like experiencing another level of the soul. For one, you are experiencing a physical plane right now, having forgotten all that you know as a soul, therefore understanding the level of the soul may be difficult to understand while in a physical realm. This is also part of the process you have given yourself, each plane of existence is designed for you to figure out how your Soul relates to that particular level before advancing, therefore, one becomes like the other.

Your Soul is on a mission to advance and grow, but advance and grow into what? The spiritual teacher **Meher Baba**, of India, explains there are six planes of Consciousness we are to experience before one can achieve God-Realization on the seventh plane. **Baba** states, *"Each definite stage of advancement represents a state of consciousness, and advancement from one state of consciousness to another proceeds side by side with crossing the inner planes. Thus six intermediate planes and states of consciousness have to be experienced before reaching the seventh plane which is the end of the journey and where there is final realization of the God-state."*

What exactly is your Soul doing, and what part is God playing in this process? What your Soul is, is a part in a **'Spiritual Machine.'** The part your Soul is playing to this extraordinary machine, is the Universe. While there are many Universes that consist in this 'Spiritual Machine,' your Soul is just one of these Universes. This does not mean one soul, one Universe, this means that your Soul is actually the designed Universe it is in, as well as many other souls that occupy this Universe, therefore everything in the Universe being 'One.'

'You' are the Universe. The world and everything in the world is 'You.' The things broken down within it, the Stars, planets, galaxies, etc., are as small as the bacteria that run inside your body. Most people tend to look at their body as 'One thing.' It has extensions, as far as legs, arms, head, but the whole body is one thing. This is exactly like the Universe.

Furthermore, the Universe also represents a God. Yes, a God, not the God. The God, made itself into many upon many Gods, with those Gods breaking themselves down into what we know as souls. The first God, is Light, and the only break down, or duplication of itself is into the **'Many Gods,'** therefore, God making itself into its own image. The Many Gods broke itself down into souls so that it can grow into fully becoming God again, like the God it was parted from. This does not mean you are separate from God, but in turn are of God, and a God, currently operating as a 'Soul.'

The objective of your Soul is to grow into its next phase to fully understanding itself. Once an understanding has been comprehended on a stage of existence, the soul advances to the next stage, but it does so with souls merging as it advances, becoming more 'One' over the course of its expansion.

To understand this, it may be best to compare yourself to a large bubble, representing God. You, in turn would be a small bubble, representing a soul, with other souls representing their own small bubble. Right now, these bubbles are separate from each other, but as the stages progress, some bubbles merge with other bubbles, leaving less bubbles, and instead larger bubbles of souls then are present. The 'Large Bubble,' God, is still large and complete, waiting for the bubbles to continue to merge and eventually become complete just like 'It.'

The Sephirot

A further understanding of how your Soul plays a part to a larger scheme could be explained using a method devised by **Kabbalah**. Kabbalah is a set of scriptures that exist outside the traditional Jewish texts. While it is used by some religious denominations, it is not a religion or denomination in and of itself, but thought of more as a practice. It is a set of esoteric teachings that seeks to define the purpose of existence, nature of the Universe, and understanding of the human soul. The **Sephirot**, also known as the '**Tree of Life**,' is referred to as the 'Cosmology' of the Kabbalah. A **Sephirah** is a channel of 'Divine Energy.' These channels are called the '**Ten Sephirot**,' which represents the basic concepts of the inner wisdom of the Torah, known as Kabbalah. Kabbalah teaches that in the process of creation, an intermediate stage from God's infinite light came to form what we know as finite reality (The Physical).

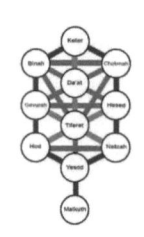

Each sephirah is a various stage of the creative process God generated from its own infinite being, with the progression of realms that concluded in the making of our own physical Universe. It is considered revelations of God's Will, ten different ways the Creator reveals itself through the 'Emanations,' or different levels of its Consciousness, which in turn creates the existence of the soul. As a coexisting group, the Sephirot establishes the interacting components of a single metaphysical structure, whose genetic imprint (God) is identified at all stages, and within all aspects of Creation.

The **Sephirot** are often counted as ten, although altogether there are eleven sephirahs in Kabbalistic literature. This is because the Sephirot of '**Keter**' and '**Da'at**' are actually thought of as one, representing different dimensions of a single force. **Keter** (Crown), known is the **Superconscious** of the soul (The Divine Will), manifests itself in **Consciousness** and transforms into the **Da'at** (Knowledge). therefore, **Keter** and **Da'at** are two sides of the same coin, existing in one another, an 'Unconscious' side and a 'Conscious' side. When referring to the Ten Sefirot, one usually counts **Keter** and does not count **Da'at**, or visa-versa, counting **Da'at** and not **Keter**, therefore, there is actually only ten **sephirah**, but all together eleven names.

There is a specific order for the Sephirot, from center, right, left, center, right left, etc. Beginning with **Keter** the order continues to **Chochmah, Binah, Da'at**, which is the First Triplet, known for the 'Mind.' The Second Triplet, **Chesed, Gevurah, Tiferet**, represents the 'Heart.' **Netzach, Hod, Yesod** is the Third Triplet, which stands for 'Behavior.' The final stage, **Malchut** can be viewed as either an extension of the last subgrouping, or as an independent entity receiving all the energies that precede it. **Malkuth** represents the physical world upon which we live and exist, while **Keter** represents the highest attainable understanding of God that can be understood.

Each sephirah has a hidden motivational force that corresponds with the psycho-spiritual state of the soul. None of the sephirahs are in turn separate from the other, but instead help the other to form a more complete view of the whole. Below, all **11** sephirahs are named and explained, but to reiterate, **Keter** and **Daat** are Superconscious and Conscious dimensions of one principle, conserving **10** forces. The names of each sephirah or 'Channel' are as follows in descending order:

1) **Keter** – Crown
   Keter is the 'Crown,' the first sephirah. It is the Divine Will Light. Link between the finite world we physically inhabit, and the infinite world of '**Ein Sof**.' In the stages of creation, Keter is where material reality began to come into existence.
2) **Chochmah** – Wisdom
   Chochmah is the second sephirah, meaning 'Wisdom.' It represents the beginning of thought, and contains creative inspiration. First infinite flash of an idea before it takes on limitations, creation from nothingness.
3) **Binah** – Understanding
   Binah is the third sephirah, which means 'Understanding.' It handles powers of reasoning, intellect, gives birth to emotions.
* **Daat** – Knowledge
   The Daat represents 'Knowledge,' and is the central state of unity of the entire **10** Sephirot (The **Tree of Life**).
4) **Chesed** – Kindness / Mercy

Chesed, the fourth sephirah, stands for 'Kindness.' Represents love, giving, and mercy. It is the beginning of emotional energy, grace of giving and inspiring vision. Chesed is linked with biblical **Abraham**, the Patriarch.

5) **Gevurah** – Severity / Judgment

   Gevurah is the fifth sephirah, which means 'Severity.' It represents power of discipline, restriction, strength, judgment, intention and awe of God. Gevurah is often associated with **Isaac**, Abraham's son.

6) **Tiferet** – Beauty

   Tiferet is the sixth sephirah, and represents 'Beauty' and 'Balance.' It balances and is the mediator of Gevurah (Mercy) and Chesed (Judgment). Tiferet is related to biblical **Jacob**, who fathered the 'Twelve Tribes of Israel.'

7) **Netzach** – Eternity

   Netzach is the seventh sephirah, meaning 'Eternity.' It represents limitless energy, great quantity, endurance, and victory. It is also the '**Quantity** of the flow of **Divine Abundance**.' Netzach is identified with **Moses**.

8) **Hod** – Splendor

   Hod is the eighth sephirah, meaning 'Splendor,' which also stands for, withdrawal, surrender and sincerity. It is a very specific flow, contained energy, which is clearly defined, and is the '**Quality** of the **Divine Abundance**.' Hod is tied to **Aaron**, the first high priest in the Old Testament.

9) **Yesod** – Foundation

   Yesod is the ninth sephirah, meaning 'Foundation,' which represents wholly remembering and coherent knowledge. The influence of astrology begins at this level. It serves as the mediator of Netzach and Hod. **Yesod** is associated with biblical **Joseph**, Jacob's son.

10) **Malchut** – Kingship

    Malchut is the tenth and final sephirah, meaning 'Kingdom.' It represents the 'Physical World,' and is associated with God's presence as it is revealed.

5 Levels of the Soul

In **Kabbalah**, it teaches different levels of the soul that relate to different levels of planes of existence it will inhibit. In ascending order, **Nefesh, Ruach, Neshamah, Chaya,** and **Yechida** are levels of the soul. These **Five Levels** of soul can be compared to various states of Consciousness, or 'God Self-Revelation.'

These five levels of the soul correspond to the **Four Worlds**, with the fifth World, '**Ein Sof**,' in turn being the same as the 5th soul level of '**Yechida**,' which is the Godhead. In ascending order, the Four Worlds are, **Asiyah, Yezirah, Beriah, Azilut,** and **Eyn Sof**. The Four Worlds are not places such as planets, but rather different planes of existence, or 'Stages of removal' from the Creator. The Four Worlds enable the soul to ascend towards the '**Divine**' through a method of upward progress for a return with the Creator. Each World is spiritual, and increasingly grosser and further removed from awareness of the Creator, until where in **Asiyah**, the 'Final World,' which is our physical Universe, it is possible to deny God. Kabbalah explains that the current Physical World is the final and lowest of all Worlds, which means those inhibiting this World are experiencing the first levels of the soul, which is '**Nefesh**.'

In all Worlds, the **10 Sephirot** are the Divine channels which every level is created from nothing. While a particular sephirah dominates each World, all ten sephirahs emanate in every World. Consciousness flows in both directions at the same time, therefore one cannot be without including all.

As taught in Kabbalah, below is a brief description of each level of the soul, and the World in which that particular soul inhibits, in ascending order:

Nefesh - 1st Level of the Soul – (The Animal Soul):

The Nefesh is the lowest level of the soul, where Consciousness (Life-Force) attaches itself to the physical body, and has awareness of the physical world, **Asiyah** (The world of Action). Nefesh represents the rational mind involved with the physical world through our senses, hear, smell, taste, sight and touch, the sense that we are alive but

nothing more. This is the level of the soul Kabbalah teaches that we are currently on.
- **Associated World – Asiyah** (Action) – Asiyah represent the material Universe in which we live. On this level, creation is restricted to its physical realm and the lowest of all Worlds, 'Physical man and the Earth.' In this World, it is not the soul, but the person which dies and goes to the grave with the body. The **'Lower Face'** of Asiyyah is **Physical Man**, while the **'Upper Face'** of Asiyyah is the **Conscious**, which holds the opportunity of each soul's advancement to the higher worlds.
  - The sephirah **Malchuth** is associated with this level.

Ruach - 2nd Level of the Soul – (The Emotional Soul, 'Spirit'):
Ruach represents a stage of Consciousness that's primary focus of intellect in the world of 'Yezirah,' is contemplation in order to arouse emotion. The soul expands its awareness, in turn encompassing its own reflection. **Ruach** is less dense than **Nefesh**, giving way to a now floating sense of awareness. Awe of God is aroused by contemplating the divine energy that formed the world of Yetzirah.
- **Associated World – Yezirah** (Formation): On this level, creation is related to form. Yezirah is a world in which we touch the interface between our thoughts and the world around us, instead of actually touching the world, as is in the case with **Asiyyah**.
  - Sephirahs **Yesod** to **Chesed** from the entire **Sephirot** predominate this level.

Neshamah - 3rd Level of the Soul – (Divine Intellectual Soul):
The Neshamah transforms from Ruach into a more firmly controlled sphere of influence. In the Neshamah, we have a higher level of understanding. For instant, in the physical world of **Asiyyah**, while experiencing the **Nefesh** level of a soul, one may see a particular event first, and then come with a level of understanding. While in Neshamah, a level of comprehension has been built so that once the event

happens, it is instantly connected to our understanding. Neshamah manifests the world of **Beriyah**.
- **Associated World – Beriah** (Creation) – Beriah is the first separation from the Divine. It is considered to be 'Heaven' proper, or the 'Throne of God' and its archangels. In this level is the first creation of where souls and angels have self-awareness, but are without form, called 'Ex Nihilo.'
  - The sephirah **Binah** is associated with this level.

Chayah - 4th Level of the Soul – (The Soul of Creativity):

Chaya is known as the 'Divine Life-Force,' and is found within **Neshamah** operating as the directing influence. Here, we are no longer concerned with taking in information, but are instead merging with the 'Divine.' In merging with God, we find love through its infinite nature. There is no self-seeking and no self-identity outside of God, one has fully realized their connection to the 'Life-Force.' The ego does not exist on this level, only indivisible truth. **Chayah** manifests the world of **Atzilut**.
- **Associated World – Azilut** (Emanation) – The Azilut is the eternal unchanging Divine World. On this level, the light of the **Ein Sof** radiates, as the Chayah prepares to be united with its 'Source' on the next level.
  - The sephirah **Chokmah** is associated with this level.

Yachidah - 5th Level of the Soul – (The Highest Level):

All souls are unified at this level, and permeate each other as a whole, being complete. The 'End' is contained in the 'Beginning,' therefore this level resides at the core of the soul. All five levels of the soul are present. **Yachidah** produces the energies of influence that evolve the soul from within to without and back again, weaving as Pure Consciousness works the patterns of awareness. **Yechidah** is the reflection of the divine image, it is limitless light. Here, there is no subject or object to be bond with, therefore the world of **Ein Sof** is united is one.

- **Associated World – Ein Sof –** In the **Zohar** (Kabbalah's Text), it teaches that there are four Worlds or planes of existence, while the fifth World, **Ein Sof** is seen separate, and identical to the 5th Level of the Soul 'Yachidah.'
    - The sephirah **Keter** is associated with this level.

Being 'Here' is essential to your growth as a soul. It is why you are here, to grow, to realize, to merge as 'One.' There are limitless opportunities for your progression to take place, therefore you can't get it wrong, but it is important because your wishes are to eventually move forward. Most humans do not enjoy staying stagnate, and your Soul is no different. It has places it is excited about going, and higher levels of understanding itself is something it is looking forward to, and 'You' are essential to making this happen.

It must be understood, with more knowledge, comes more responsibility. The more you understand yourself and what you know to be true, the more important it is to abide by the knowledge you have attained. Karma heightens when one knows the differences of their actions and how they affect the world around them. For instance, when one fully understands the meaning of 'Turning the cheek,' it is crucial for them to do so, otherwise the karmic energy that boomerangs back will be of the same negligence it displayed, even more than those who do not know any better to do so. This is important to understand for those interested in advancing, because though some may live a more so called 'Righteous life,' they will not find themselves advancing if they do not act on their wisdom.

The main purpose for us being here is growth, if one is neglecting what they know, then it is not growth. Being that this world, '**Asiyah**,' is of action, we must act on what we know.

The Game: (The Yin-Yang)

The most beautiful part in this 'Game of Life' is that there is no 'Lose,' there is only the 'Win.' There is no 'Right or Wrong,' only the choices you make and the consequences from them. There is not a Hell, there is only acceptance of the progression you make. God would not allow itself to be placed in such a Game where it would jeopardize losing everything, so it plays a trick on itself to think that it could, thus making a way for anyone to want to try and understand themselves, if one knew there was no way of losing the Game, they may not go about their lives with as much passion and determination.

This idea of 'Right and Wrong,' is one of the hardest things for humans to grasp. There is no such thing as 'Right or Wrong,' there is only the **Yin-Yang**. You cannot have one without the other. How can you understand joy, without having experienced pain? You can't, you would have no idea of how to define joy. Pain makes you understand joy, joy makes you understand pain.

The Yin-Yang is a fractal set, its fractal dimension is **1**, with opposites that only exist in relation to each other. In Asian philosophy, the concept of the **Yin-Yang** which is often referred to in the West as 'Yin and Yang,' is used to describe how contrary forces are interconnected but interdependent in the world, and how they give rise to each other. Characteristics of the Yin-Yang are provided below:

Yin - Characteristics		Yang - Characteristics	
Slow	Passive	Fast	Aggressive
Soft	Water	Hard	Fire
Yielding	Earth	Solid	Sky
Diffuse	The Moon	Focused	The Sun
Cold	Femininity	Hot	Masculinity
Wet	Nighttime	Dry	Daytime

Yin is the **Black** side with the **White Dot** and **Yang** is the **White** side with the **Black Dot**. The relationship between Yin and Yang is often described in terms of sunlight playing over a mountain and in the valley. Yin (**Shady Place** or **North Slope**) is the dark area occluded by the mountain's bulk, while Yang (**Sunny Place** or **South Slope**) is the brightly lit portion. Each side contains the seed of the other, a Black spot of Yin in the white Yang, and White spot of Yang in the Back Yin. They do not replace each other, they become each other through the constant flow of the Universe. While they are always opposite and of equal qualities, whenever one quality reaches its peak it will then naturally begin to transform into the opposite quality.

There is a misconception that the Yin-Yang corresponds to good and evil, Taoist philosophy generally discounts good or bad divisions and other moral judgments, as to the idea of balance. The Yin-Yang are complementary opposites that interact within a greater whole, as part of a grander system.

If there were no rich, there would be no poor, if there were no homeless, people wouldn't appreciate what it is to live in homes, if there wasn't struggle, we would then not know the meaning of relaxation. We would take all these things for granted if we didn't have the opposite end of the spectrum, and this is something God is aware of, therefore God is all accepting to our experiences.

We would not be able to conceive what we think is 'Right' if we didn't have things that we perceived to be 'Wrong,' you need the other in order for you to know what one feels like to you.

Everything in life has both Yin and Yang aspects, either of these aspects may manifest more strongly in particular matters and flow over time. Your actions move the Yin-Yang along, and there are all kinds of magnificent energies that come along with this, energies that have made it so that your thoughts and your actions will cause reactions from your own doing. You will become your thoughts, you are your thoughts, and this 'Game of Life' is designed for you to experience exactly what you think out.

CHAPTER THIRTEEN
(Tools)

"You grow to heaven You don't go to heaven."
                                                    - **Edgar Cayce** -

Tools: (Introduction)

    Who wants to play a Game without any gadgets or obstacles, it wouldn't be any fun, after a while it might get a little mundane or boring, and the last thing we want is for the Game to become boring. For this not to happen, we have given ourselves certain energies that will make this process all the more exciting.

    Some of these energies are here to help you, and to go against you, however, the energies that are here to go against you, are also to help you. Regardless of their effects, their purpose is to show you who you really are. These energies are designed only for the 'World of Questions,' only because certain energies are too controlling, too jealous, and too 'Tit for tat' to exist in the 'World of Answers.' The 'World of Answers' is accepting, certain energies here in the physical world do not operate in that manner, but it is important to understand these energies in order for you to have the best possible experience you wish to have while you are here.

    Using certain forms of energy can help aid your experience, as well as hinder your progression if not used properly, or made aware of. There is no escaping these energies, they are all here for a reason, and all have been designed for specific purpose. These energies should be used as tools, tools to help you understand yourself and to get you where you are progressing to.

Tools: **(Ego the Adversary)**

The chessboard is magnificent, and is designed for you to experience all of your wonders, nevertheless, to have this amazing chessboard and not have something to go up against would defeat the purpose. It would not just defeat the purpose, but it wouldn't be any fun, so what can you place in your way that will be worth your wild? You are an 'All Magnificent Being,' so how can any obstacle truly stop you?

To give yourself a worthy opponent, it may be best to start with this age old question, *"Can God create a rock so heavy that he could not lift it?"* The answer to this question is yes. God can create a rock so heavy that even God cannot lift it, however, God is also so powerful and all knowing that God can make the rock weightless. The answer may seem tricky, but this also pertains to you.

If you are essentially from the 'Source,' than what could possibly stand in your way? For there is no one, nothing that is more magnificent than you are, so who or what could possibly be a worthy adversary for yourself? The answer...You. You are the best opponent for yourself.

You keep yourself back from so many things, so many ideas, so many accomplishments, friendships, experiences and love that you can encompass. How? Your **Ego**.

Your Ego is an energy exuding with so much selfishness, it could only exist in a place like the 'World of Questions,' because your Ego has individual wants. Your Ego says, 'Give me.' The Ego says, 'I want that big house, I want more money, I want to have friends with notoriety and connections so it will benefit me, I want two cars, I want more of the nicest clothes, I want more dating partners, I want more fame, I want, I want, I want, I, I, I.'

The Ego is pure selfishness. It makes us jealous, it make us loathe those that have something we do not have, it makes us depressed, it makes us sad, it makes us cocky, it makes us feel disrespected. It is always the Ego within us, not an evil personality outside of us that dictates our life.

This is a Game you are in turn playing with yourself, for there is no other opponent greater than you. In Latin translation, **Satan** means, '*Adversary, Enemy* or *Against,*' and who is your biggest adversary of all? You. Your Ego is your greatest and most fierce opponent. It makes you second guess yourself when you imagine something bigger for yourself, it gives you your fear of failure, when there is no such thing as failure, there is only progression.

There is no such thing as the Devil, but we may have at times behaved devilish, due to our Ego. Our Ego is the reason for murder, rape and homelessness around the world. The only reason these things exist is because the Ego has held us to see the Individual, and not the ALL, the Everything.

The idea of a 'Split Personality' does not pertain to just a few people, it pertains to all of us. The **Ego** is our 'Significant Other,' and it only exists here, in the 'Physical.' In the 'World of Answers,' all you have and are is your **Soul**, which is what you truly are, while in the 'World of Questions,' you essentially have two personalities, your Ego, and your Soul. What is happening is that your Soul is entwined with the individual personality of the 'Ego,' when you are taking on the form of a Human Body in the 'World of Questions,' therefore, while you are here, you essentially have more than one 'Voice' roaming inside your head. The Soul/God represents the 'Complete,' while the Ego represents the 'Individual' thought process. It is why you 'Think.' In the 'World of Answers' there is no reason to think, you already know. Here in the 'World of Questions,' because you have two different dispositions in your current 'Human Mind,' your Ego is also a cause for contemplating certain issues or situations.

An example of this is given in many depictions of someone that may be battling with a decision, and on one shoulder he or she is listening to an Angel give advice, while on the other shoulder the Devil is making suggestions. This is exactly what goes on inside your head, the weighing between 'Light' and 'Darkness.' When in the 'World of Questions,' the Ego is so strong that many people operate letting this particular

'Voice' play louder than the 'Voice' of the soul, they think the 'Voice' of the Ego is actually their own, when it is something you only use in the 'Physical Realm.' The Ego is trying to understand what it is, so it constantly battles for its position, pushing itself onto you, while the soul accepts the position it has, therefore a lot of us function throughout our day giving into this overwhelming presence of the Ego.

The Ego is an extremely clever opponent, and you cannot defeat it by ignoring it, for everyone has an Ego, it is our link to being here. It is something that is constantly trying to make its presence felt. Its presence is something that you will recognize to always be there, your thoughts are attached to this energy, just as it is Karma, and just as Karma, being that it is of the 'World of Questions,' it operates to a more magnified degree from one's actions.

The Ego has also equipped itself with a few arsenals of its own. Just like you, it wants to win, so it pinpoints certain desires we have. Essentially, the Ego is the cause for addictions. You don't develop an addiction, you start out with an addiction, and in the course of your life you may or may not stumble onto these addictions. Someone's addiction could be sex, another person's addiction could be money, while another person's addiction could be themselves. It is in your best interest to be aware of your addictions, and tame these addictions, and understand this is all part of the Ego's plan.

The best thing about the Ego is that you can't say you don't know your opponent. You know everything about your opponent. You don't have to go on scouting trips or do research, you know exactly when your Ego is showing itself, and everything about it. When you get annoyed, that's the Ego, when you feel jealous, that's the Ego, when you feel angry, sad, upset, depressed, all that is the Ego, saying, 'Me, me, me.'

The Ego is powerful, and while it seems filled with nothing but negative attributes, there are some positives that come out of this. First and foremost, the most important attribute of the Ego, is that it is selfish enough to fool you into thinking you exist in the 'World of Questions.' Simply, the Ego is selfish enough to fool you into believing that, 'You are alive...in this fake world.' It is your anchor, it is what keeps you here in the 'World of Questions,' it fools you into thinking this place is 'Real.'

Imagine you are this 'All Knowing Enlightened Being' that can do anything in the power of your Mind. Knowing this, to the extent you truly do, when in the 'World of Answers,' there is nothing that would keep you bound to this dimension of the Physical. The Ego, along with forgetting everything you know, keeps us here, almost like a bird that has one of their ankles chained to the ground. The Ego keeps us grounded. If you had no Ego, you wouldn't be here. There would be nothing to keep you grounded to this dimension if you did not have Ego, because you are of pure light. Light has no Ego.

There are also other ways in which the Ego can position itself as a positive, for instance, one's creativity, or excitement for knowledge. A lot of artists are driven not from other artist, but from wanting to better themselves in their own work. How can wanting to be a better artist be a bad thing? Truly, we are all here to create. The reason you want to learn is to know more than what you knew before, to be aware, to comprehend. How can learning new knowledge be a bad thing? Truly, it is the only reason we are here, to learn, to grow, and search for the answers.

With conflicting points on the Ego, you may wonder, 'How do you defeat the Ego, or what to do with such an energy?' Our job, or our best interest, is not to totally wipe out our Ego, but to be aware of our Ego. You do not defeat your Ego, but you can suppress your ego, keep it tamed, almost like a pet. Take someone's dog for example, there are times when it is trained, calm, obeys it owner, and abides by the owners wishes. There are also times when that dog may start to bark a little too much, or get a little rowdy and hyper, and the owner may tell the dog to calm down, or to sit, hush up. At times, this is what we must to do with our Ego. We must be aware of it, so we can tame it in times that it comes in between the light we can share with one another.

There is also another conflicting piece of information about the Ego. While the Ego is your greatest opponent, here to battle yourself, here to win, the Ego is also rooting for you. How, why? The Ego is like a sport's trainer, who trains you so rigorously, to the point you can't take it anymore. You may come to despise this trainer, but the trainer is only doing what's best for you. The trainer is weeding out your weaknesses, and to weed them out, the Ego must show them to you.

Our outlook should be thankful of its energy, that it is strong enough to trick us into thinking we are really here, however, you need to know how to use your opponent. You need to know when to embrace your opponent, and when it is time to ignore, listen, and leave your opponent behind. Taming your Ego, and letting the doors open to the light that you are, is the best possible experience you can have, any path or road you walk down afterwards won't matter in the sense of it being too hard, because you will be thankful that there is a road given for you to walk down.

Tools: (Karma)

One of the more interesting and important energies to understand is Karma. Karma is something most of us have heard, and for the most part understand its definition, but fail to comprehend the depths of its actions.

Karma, a theory believed to be derived from Hinduism, but an energy that has truly been around since the dawn of physical creation, is defined in most dictionaries as, 'An action or actions, seen as bringing upon oneself, inevitable results, good or bad, either in this life or a reincarnation.' Karma is cause and effect, simply, what you do comes back to you. Give and you shall receive.

We have been receiving silent messages about Karma all our life. For instance, at times in our lives when we may have mistreated someone poorly and our parents or close friends may have taken notice to our actions, they have warned you. It could be anything, from something as simple as calling someone a derogatory term, to physically harming someone. How many times has someone said to you, "You wouldn't like it if they treated you that way?" These are hints, silent messages to make you think. Why? If such a thing is true, why is it so that we can't go about our lives putting out whatever emotions we want and not have it affect us? Why can't we simply 'Get away with it?' The reason why Karma exists, and why it is so prevalent in our lives, is because we are all '**ONE**.'

As explained earlier, in our connection to the creator, and the many ways it is experiencing itself, being that we are all connected, anything you do, anything you give or put out into this Universe, comes right back to you, like a boomerang. Why? Everything you do, you are in turn doing to yourself. If we were separate from the billions of different people walking this planet, as perceived to be in this reality, the 'World of Questions,' then we could possibly move out the way when the boomerang is on its way back, but we can't. Our connection to each other is like playing with a Yo-Yo, it's going to come back around.

Look at the people in your life, and think about the problems they have. Surely you have friends that have complained about certain difficulties, some more than others. Now think about the differences in the people who seem to complain more than the ones that don't seem to register as many problems. Surely there is a difference. For the most part, you will find that the people with the most issues or problems, their actions and personality somehow resonate with someone that has problematic issues.

When it comes to dating, most people who complain about relationships tend not to put forth the same effort themselves. Whether it is patience, honesty or understanding, for the most part they themselves may not exhibit the type of character they wish to find in a mate. This can be said about the work field as well, those complaining about their job, how many of them would you actually say is a hard worker, or goes about their job with the best effort they can.

These are mild examples of Karma, but Karma is far from mild. In fact, Karma is quite fierce. It is important for people to understand karma is a very disciplined, but wild energy, wild not in the sense of being chaotic, but wild in the sense that the return is mostly unpredictable. It is not as simple as an 'Eye for an Eye,' though the effect will be just the same, in regards to your growth.

For example, Karma doesn't operate in the manner of, you go to a convenient store, buy a bottle of juice, give the cashier a **$5** dollar bill, and he hands you back **$18** dollars in cash, thinking you gave him a **$20** dollar bill, but you don't say anything and instead walk out with a bottle of **$2** juice and **$18** extra dollars…only to later be suckered the same way, with you giving someone the same extra amount of incorrect change. Karma does not operate in the same exact fashion.

There are so many facets of Karma, and the strongest thing that gives it movement is thought. Just the mere fact that you **KNOW** you are getting over on someone, moves that energy of guilt into a faster cycle. Sometimes $18 extra dollars isn't just $18 extra dollars.

To a lot of convenient stores, a cash register missing **$18** dollars can get someone fired. Imagine the cashier was unfortunately terminated from his job. There are many issues and dilemmas that come with having to scramble so quickly to adjust to that type of change, and to a lot of people, losing a job is significant. He could be married, have kids and be late on rent, wife starts complaining, he can't find new work, he's getting frustrated, they start arguing, there's all kinds of ways this could go, and something as simple as $18 dollars caused all this. It's not your fault, right? This couldn't affect you, right? It does.

The **Oneness** that we all are has ways of making you face up to your own actions in your current lifetime. Surely all of us have been in relationships, and for the most part, unless you are just that lucky of a person, we have all been dumped, or left behind in such a way that would make many wonder, 'How could they be so cold?' Maybe you had an experience, where your companion was cheating on you and eventually leaves you brokenhearted, scrambling to pick up the pieces. Whose heart do you think may weigh heavier, yours, or the cashier at the convenient store without a job? That's pretty debatable, and all just for $18 dollars. I'm sure if you got the chance to ask the cashier, they would say something like, 'How could you be so cold?'

On the other hand, Karma, ever so magnificent, does wonders and amazing benefits for your life when operated in a positive fashion. Maybe someone you know is looking for a place to lay their head for a week, maybe they were moving and needed a place to sleep, or maybe they were evicted from their place of residence and in turn you offer your home as shelter. Perhaps this person has nothing to offer you, perhaps they have no money and once they get their place, they are going to be so behind on bills that they can't even offer you a home cooked meal. To make matters more frustrating, let's say this person is a messy roommate, and on top of not helping around the house, they also leave you having to clean up their mess when they leave. It's awful that you would find yourself having to pick up after this person, but what if, while you are cleaning, you move around things for vacuuming and discover that something was wrong with the pipes behind the sofa. You realize it immediately and call in someone to fix it. What if the plumber tells you that you just saved yourself an expensive bill, because if you waited any longer, the pipes were days away from busting and would have caused damage to the house in the thousands of dollars. Are you going to place a phone call to the person who you let stay at your place, rent free for a week, and thank them for the mess they made? The kind gesture of loaning someone a place to stay, somehow managed to save you money as well. I'm sure you will find yourself just as thankful that you didn't have to pay thousands of dollars, as the friend you let stay on your couch in their time of need.

While there are countless of examples that can be given, these are only minor examples of the 'Negative' and 'Positive' effects of Karma. The most important thing to remember is that Karma will give you the exact same energy you put forth in the Universe.

Just a mere thought activates Karma. Our prayers and wishes are stronger than we believe, they line themselves with the 'Law of Attraction.' Think, and it shall present itself. Thought dictates movement, which then dictates reaction.

While Karma operates in the smallest form, it grows stronger with movement, therefore your actions bring greater karmic results. Thus, you need to exhibit the action of your thoughts for the 'World of Questions' to recognize who you are, and to give you what you are asking for. You can't just ask, or say I want something, you must be that 'Something.' Your thoughts are powerful, but in the 'World of Questions,' being of a physical field, it maneuvers faster and operates at a more magnified measure through physical deeds.

As explained, Karma does not present itself to you in the form of 'An Eye for an Eye,' but does reach the level of magnitude of energy you put forth in the Universe. Karma is not something only a few of us have, it is something we all have. We all begin our karmic experience before birth. We are born into this world with karma, from previous karmic experiences in past lives.

Some of the Karma that has been brought over from past lives can be lined with certain problems we are instantly faced with when being born into this physical plain. Karma, depending on how your outlook is, can be positive or negative to your experience.

People tend to think being born a king, or someone who is born the child of a billionaire would be positive Karma. Then again, what if the king turns out to be the last king of their kingdom, what if he was overthrown by his people and now has to live in exile, and what if the billionaire child grew up to lose his family's fortune? Surely these examples could be considered travesties for these particular individuals. Adolph Hitler could have been reborn as one of these men. Some would rather wish he burned in Hell (A place that does not exist), or to have been reborn as someone who experienced a horrific death, as if his own suicide isn't horrific enough. Truly, what is more horrific, someone dying a painful death, or someone living a painful life?

One has to wonder what lessons he may acquire from these experiences. The exiled king and the ex-billionaire child will learn what it is to live depending on others sympathy and concern, the same way Jews looked for those that would hide them and keep them safe from Hitler's Germany soldiers during the Holocaust. Maybe this lesson could give him an understanding for the appreciation of acceptance.

Tools: (Frequencies)

Going back to the notion that there is no such thing as silence, and sound is the Uncaused-Cause of God, this leads us back onto the 'Little Sound' in your ears. As explained earlier, you can put yourself in the quietest of places, no radio, no one around, TV off and you will still be able to hear a light humming sound in your ears. What is that sound?

The sound in your ears, which resembles the strange buzzing vibration of a light tea whistle, very much like static, is what is known as frequencies, frequencies that connect you to the 'World of Answers.' They have many purposes. One purpose is the constant transfer of your thoughts, the constant download of every thought that comes through you. This data is being stored, stored in the Akashic Records, stored for your Spirit Workers, and stored for you.

This is something you want, to have and attain every bit of information you have ever thought of, to never be forgotten. Think of the memories we don't think about anymore, or the lessons we learn all over again because we didn't understand it the first time around. These frequencies allow you to keep every bit of information that you have gathered.

Another purpose for these frequencies is for our Spirit Workers to be able to dial in messages to us while we are here. Sometimes they give us hints and messages that will come across our 'Personal Frequency,' in which these sound vibrations will then activate images of thought, these thoughts are for us to decipher what they mean to us.

The frequencies are a special type of coded language that we cannot understand in words. It is constantly turned on, and can be used by both your Spirit Workers and You. Your thoughts activate these frequencies, it is a constantly charged soundwave, almost like an 'Open Phone Line,' serving as the transfer and translator from you to them, and them to you.

Your prayers go through this frequency. In a sense, it is their way of listening in on your thoughts, so in actuality, there is no reason to go to church or feel a need to kneel down at your bedside and pray, because just thinking of doing so has already been heard. Everything that runs through your mind is received and recorded through this frequency, that you can ever so faintly hear during times of silence (Which there is no such thing).

Tools: (Prayer)

The first thing most people tend to do when they find themselves with a problem, or in a difficult situation, is pray. People have been praying ever since they believed in something higher than themselves, feeling as though their problems can be resolved through the prayers they send out into the cosmos.

Prayer is an extremely instrumental tool, but for the most part it has been misunderstood. To comprehend this, first, understand that YOU are the answer to solving all your problems, there is no God, no Angel, or no Spirit Guide that can answer your prayers. You answer you own prayers. You answer your own prayers because you are the vehicle that is putting forth the action. Any message you may attain in a dream or from a 'Higher Being,' any bit of information you acquire or insight you receive, is just insight. You make the moves. This should be looked upon as a gift, truly, what Enlightened Being do you think would want others doing the work for them? None. You are the only one that can do this. It is your purpose, to make the moves yourself.

With this understood, then what is the meaning of prayer? When you pray, what you are actually doing, is asking for a 'Seed.' You may think you are asking for all your problems to be solved, and all your wishes to come true, but what you are getting in return is actually something you are supposed to 'Blossom.' Quite frankly, when we pray, we are all given the seeds to our wishes, but we must put forth the effort to blossom it into a 'Flower.'

For example, some people may want more money in their life, their prayers won't actually give them more money, but will place them in situations for them to see where more money can be attained, but they must bring forth the work to bring that money about. It is entirely up to you if you do or do not blossom the 'Seed' into the 'Flower' you wish to have. We are given the seed, sometimes in so many different ways that it could get confusing.

The thought of 'Being careful of what you ask for, because you will get it,' is extremely accurate, accurate in the sense that you must be precise when asking for a particular 'Seed' during prayer, because the seed you get in return will be that of what you asked for, no more, no less. Some people do not fully grasp this concept, thinking because something doesn't turn out how they expected, than their prayers were not answered. This is not the case.

For example, one may wish to find themselves in a relationship, asking for someone you are attracted to and can have fun with, plain and simple. Your prayers will place you in all kinds of situations where this can come about, plain and simple. You may meet someone that has these attributes, plain and simple. First, it starts off with a bang, the relationship is great, you are having fun and very much attracted to your partner, plain and simple. Through time, slowly but surely, you notice how your differences have made the relationship unhealthy...not so plain and simple. This does not mean your prayers were not answered, in fact just the opposite. In this example, all that was asked for was someone you are attracted to and can have fun with. This leaves so many wide open doors, something else is bound to surprise you.

Another example, can be of someone who wishes to date another with money or a certain stature in society so that it may benefit them. This too, leaves so many wide open doors, something else is bound to surprise you, therefore, not only do you need to be accurate in what you ask for, but you must be genuine. Wanting to be with someone because of these things, money or stature, is not a reason to be in a relationship or friendship. These are not genuine thoughts, therefore these ingénue prayers will proceed into your life.

The seed we ask for is given to us in the same essence in which we request. You must be specific with what you seek in your life, the energy behind your efforts will bring the same energy in the results.

In another comparison, the answers to your prayers are like directions to a 'Way out,' but it is you who has to tunnel your way through. If you want something in your life, call for it, it will be there, but you blossom the seed.

Tools: (Hoʻoponopono)

Unfortunately, some people have made their healing process difficult, going through counseling and programs, putting all kinds of rules and limits on what it takes to repair a relationship, and thinking it may take a 'Miracle.' Ironically so, it takes something simple as your thoughts. Everything you wish to be, become, accomplish, and repair, lies with you.

Hoʻoponopono is an ancient Hawaiian practice that focuses on family reconciliation, with prayer, discussion, confession, repentance, mutual restitution and forgiveness through a 'Mental cleansing.' Hoʻoponopono originally was thought to restore and maintain good relationships among family members, by finding the cause of the problem and taking responsibility for it. Being that Ho'oponopono views all consciousness as part of the whole, any error a person clears in their own consciousness is cleared for everyone. It was traditionally practiced by healing priests, but modern versions now extend to this practice being performed by the individuals themselves.

In **1976**, a healing priest (**Kahuna lapaʻau**) by the name of **Morrnah Simeona**, adapted the traditional Hoʻoponopono family practice of forgiveness to the modern day social realities. Simeona's version includes prayer, confession, repentance and forgiveness, but unlike the Hawaiian tradition, she states that problems are the effects of negative Karma, *"You have to experience by yourself what you have done to others,"* she explains. As 'Cause and Effect' dominates our lifetimes, Simeona's states the purpose of her version is, *"To release unhappy, negative experiences in past Reincarnations, and to resolve and remove traumas from the memory banks."*

Dr. Ihaleakala Hew Len, one of Simeona's students, co-authored a book with **Joe Vitale** called **'Zero Limits**,' referring to her Hoʻoponopono teachings. The book brings a new idea of Hoʻoponopono, getting to the 'State of Zero,' where one has zero limits, no memories and no identity. To get to this state, which Len called 'Self-I-Dentity,' one has to constantly repeat the mantra, *"I'm sorry. Please forgive me. I love you. Thank you."* This concept is based on Len's idea of taking **100**% responsibility for everyone's actions, not only for one's own.

Joe Vitale heard about Len's practices through a mutual friend, and contacted him to find out more about his methods. Dr. Len told **Vitale** that he never saw his patients, but instead looked at their files, and chanted, *"I'm sorry. Please forgive me. I love you. Thank you,"* over and over again. It just so happened that after a few months, patients who were once shackled were being allowed to walk freely, others who had been heavily medicated were getting off medications, and patients who once had no chance of ever being released were now being freed.

Vitale asked Len what could cause these changes, and Len replied, *"I was simply healing the part of me that created them."* Dr. Len further explained, *"Total responsibility for your life means that everything in your life, simply because it is in your life, is your responsibility. In a literal sense the entire world is your creation."*

Vitale added, *"If you take complete responsibility for your life, then everything you see, hear, taste, touch, or in any way experience is your responsibility because it is in your life...This means* that terrorist activity, the president, the economy, anything you experience and don't like, is up for you to heal. They don't exist, in a manner of speaking, except as projections from inside you. The problem isn't with them, it's with you, and to change them, you have to change you."

Your thoughts have created the world around you, you believe it to be here, therefore everything is in turn here and in your control, it lies in your beliefs, your thoughts. If you want to repair the relationships you have with others, rearrange and repair your own thoughts to help those relationships.

Tools: (Om)

The **Om** or **Aum** (written in Devanāgari as ॐ), is a sacred and mystical syllable in the Dharmic or Indian religions, such as **Hinduism, Jainism,** and **Buddhism**. It can be seen nearly everywhere in all Hindu art in India and Nepal. The 'Om mantra' represents the name of God, which is the 'Vibration of the Supreme.' It symbolizes the 'Vibration' from which everything originates. When chanted during a meditative state, it is believed to have great spiritual power for helping one connect to the 'Source.'

In Hinduism, 'God,' began as a sound, 'Om.' Before creation began it was '**Shunyākāsha**,' the emptiness or the void. Shunyākāsha, literally meaning 'No sky,' is more than nothingness, because then everything existed in a latent state of potentiality. The vibration of 'Om' symbolizes the manifestation of God in form (**Sāguna Brahman**). 'Om' is the reflection of the absolute reality, it is said to be '**Adi Anadi**,' without beginning or the end, embracing all that exists.

The Om Symbol, has been defined in varies of ways, 'Peace, 4 Levels of Consciousness, God, the Name of God, and the vibration of the Supreme.' The three parts of the Aum represent, (A) **Bhrahma Shakti**, which means 'Creation,' (U) **Vishnu Shakti**, with means 'Preservation,' and (M) **Shiva Shakti** which means 'Liberation.' Together, the three elementary aspects represent the divine energy (**Shakti**).

The **Symbol** represents the World and Everything in it. The **4** Curves represent the **4** states of Consciousness (**Awake, Sleeping, Dreaming,** and a **Trance State**), while the circle represents the **Self**. Descriptions of the parts that make up the Aum Symbol are as follows:
- **A: Lower Curve** represents the **Material World**, which is referred as the **Waking State**.
- **M: Upper Left Curve** represents the **Sleeping State**.
- **U:** The **Middle Curve** represents the **Dream State**.
- The **Semicircle**, detached from these **3** Curves, is the **Transcendental State**.
- The **Point** or Circle is above, and is witnessing the **Entire Self**.
  - (The Point and Semicircle are separate from the rest and rule the whole.)

In the book, '**Om Chanting and Meditation**,' **Amit Ray** states, "*Om is not just a sound or vibration. It is not just a symbol. It is the entire cosmos, whatever we can see, touch, hear and feel. Moreover, it is all that is within our perception and all that is beyond our perception. It is the core of our very existence. Om is the mysterious cosmic energy that is the substratum of all the things and all the beings of the entire Universe. It is an eternal song of the Divine. It is continuously resounding in silence on the background of everything that exists.*"

The Om is believed to be the supreme mantra or chant. It consists of three sounds, 'A-U-M,' which when pronounced, each syllable sounds out, '**aah – ooh – mmm**.' When the Om is chanted it takes on a deep resonant tone, which in turn fills the body with vibrations that causes positive health effects, such as a normalized heartbeat and lowered blood pressure. When chanting the Om mantra, you may feel, timeless, weightless, expansive, liberated from the physical realm and 'One' with the Vibration of Everything. According to those that participate in its practices, chanting Om can help cause a reversal of depression and give you worldly thoughts, as well as power and energy. It is mostly used in meditation, but is also suggested to

be chanted when you walk, or whenever you begin to feel unhappy or stressed. A brief listing of the positive effects the Om can have on you while listening or chanting are listed below:
- Cleansed from unwanted habits and bad energy
- Refreshed through your day
- Invigorated or Energized
- Connected to your true essence and spiritual nature
- A sense of physical wellbeing
- A sense of Oneness with all life in the Universe

The Om is filled with so much spiritual energy that it must be pronounced with complete concentration. In the following **Sūtra**, it emphasizes, *"The repetition of Om should be made with an understanding of its meaning."* It is important to pronounce it correctly, many people consider it the basis of all sound in the Universe.

Swami Nischalananda Saraswati explains, *"The mantra Om has been handed down to us by the Himalayan sages. It is the most important mantra of Yoga. According to tradition every, 'Thing,' manifest comes from Primordial Vibration, which is symbolized by **Om**, all material objects, all living beings, including each of us, all spiritual teachings, including Yoga, all languages, all scriptures, including the **Vedas**. Everything. This concurs with modern scientific thinking which says that everything, every atom and molecule in every nook and corner of the Universe, is formed out of energy vibration."*

Our voices are powerful, use it with grace and thoughtfulness. The second you speak has the chance to change whatever environment you are in.

Tools: (Chakras)

Many believe that some form of mediation is important if one chooses to have a closer communication with the 'Source.' As quoted by **Diana Robinson**, *"Prayer is when you talk to God; meditation is when you listen to God."* When mediating, one can place themselves in various different positions, but while doing so it is important to concentrate on locations of the body, which in turn will bring forth the desired awareness.

The **Chakra** is a concept that originated in Hindu texts, said to be 'Force Centers' of permeating energy at points in the physical body that generates and stores energy from the cosmos, pulling in more strongly at these points in your body. The word Chakra derives from the Sanskrit word for 'Wheel' or 'Turning.' In traditional Indian medicine, the Chakra refers to wheel-like vortices that exist in the surface of the body of living beings. They are considered the focal points for the transmission of energies.

In earlier texts, there are many different systems of chakras with varying connections amongst them. Traditional sources have varied from **5, 6, 7, 8** or **12** chakras, before a system of **6** or **7** Chakras became the dominant model along the body's axis. This particular system may have become popular when it was adopted by most schools of Yoga around the **11th Century CE.**

There are three types of energy centers in the human body. The Lower or '**Animal Chakras**' are located in between the toes and the pelvic region, which in turn indicates our evolutionary origins in the Animal Kingdom. The **Human Chakras** are along the spinal column. The Higher or '**Divine Chakras**' are located between the top of the spine and the crown of the head. The basic 7 Chakras are as follows:

- **Muladhara**: Root or Base Chakra (Ovaries/Prostate)
- **Swadhisthana**: Sacral Chakra (The coccyx)
- **Manipura**: Navel or Solar Plexus Chakra (Navel area)
- **Anahata**: Heart Chakra (Heart area)
- **Vishuddha**: Throat Chakra (Throat and neck area)
- **Ajna**: Third Eye Chakra or Brow Chakra (Pineal gland)
- **Sahasrara**: Crown Chakra (Top of the head)

The Chakras are located along the central line of the body, through the energy channels, or 'Nadis.' The central nadi, '**Sushumna**,' runs alongside or inside the spine. The two other nadis, '**Ida**' and '**Pingala**,' run through the chakras, and alongside the Sushumna. The nadis (central, sympathetic, parasympathetic nervous system) run along the spinal column and cross each other several times. At the points of each intersection form strong energy centers which is called a 'Chakra.' The energy that was unleashed during creation, called the '**Kundalini**,' lies coiled and sleeping at the base of the spine. The purpose is to arouse this energy, and cause it to rise back up through the Chakras, until union with God is achieved in the Crown Chakra, '**Sahasrara**.' The Chakras are generally associated with a variety of **Colors** and **Deities**. The energy of the chakras are explored through certain practices, such as meditating, Yoga, mantras, Reiki, sound therapy and many other forms as well.

Opening the Chakras

Chakra meditations use '**Mudras**,' which are special hand positions and techniques that help open up the chakras. The Mudras have the power to send more energy to the desired Chakra. To enhance the effect of channeling these Chakras, certain sounds are chanted. The sounds are usually from Sanskrit letters. When chanted, your body resonates the feeling of the Chakra it is meant for. Pronouncing the 'Om' in various forms works well. Keep in mind that the pronunciation is (A) **aah** - (U) **ooh** - (M) **mmm**, with slight alterations for selected Chakras. Meditation styles may vary, but a controlled level of breathing is essential to this process. At times the Chakras may be **Under** or **Over-Activated**, so it is best to get them at an even balance. A listing of the seven primary Chakras are briefly described below, along with tips on how to activate them using Mudras:

Root Chakra

The Root Chakra represents being physically grounded, feeling like you are at home in situations. If it is open, you will feel stable and secure, and present in the 'Here and Now.' You feel connected to your physical body and feel as though you have sufficient territory amongst yourself.

Under-Active: May tend to be fearful or nervous. Could feel unwelcome

Over-Active: May be very materialistic and greedy, probably obsessed with being secure and is resistant to change.

Open the Root Chakra: Take the tips of your Index Finger and Thumb and let them touch. Concentrate on the location of the Root Chakra, between the genitals and the anus, and chant the sound, '**Laammm**.'

Sacral Chakra

The Sacral Chakra represents feeling and sexuality. When it is open, your feelings are expressed freely without being over emotional. You may feel passionate, lively, and open to intimacy.

Under-Active: You could be stiff and unemotional, not very open to people.

Over-Active: May be emotional all the time, and emotionally attached to people, as well as being overly sexual.

Open the Sacral Chakra: Take your hands and place them in your lap, palms up, placed on top of each other. The left hand is underneath, with its palm touching the back of the fingers of the right hand. Gently touch the tips of your thumbs. Concentrate on the location of the Sacral Chakra, the sacral bone (Lower back), and chant the sound, '**Vaammm**.'

Navel Chakra

The Navel Chakra represents feeling secure while asserting yourself in a group. When it is open, you have sufficient self-esteem and feel in control of your emotions.

Under-Active: Could tend to be passive and indecisive, timid and don't get what you want.

Over-Active: Very domineering and more than likely over aggressive.

Open the Navel Chakra: Take your hands and place them in front of your stomach, slightly below your solar plexus. Let your fingers join at the top of their tips, all pointing away from you, and then cross your thumbs. It is important that your fingers are straightened. Concentrate on the location of the Navel Chakra, on the spine, just a bit above the level of the navel area, and chant the sound, '**Raammm**.'

Heart Chakra

The Heart Chakra represents love and affection. When it is open, you feel compassionate and work to obtain harmonious relationships.

Under-Active: May be very cold, and distant towards others.

Over-Active: Tend to suffocate people with love, the type of love that may be for personal reasons, and selfish.

Open the Heart Chakra: Sit cross-legged. Take the tips of your index finger and thumb and let them touch. Place your left hand on your left knee and your right hand in front of the lower part of your breast bone, so that it is just above the solar plexus.

Concentrate on the location of the Heart Chakra, the level at the heart, and chant the sound, '**Yaammm**.'

Throat Chakra

The Throat Chakra represents expression. When it is open, you have no problems talking or expressing yourself, creatively and artistically.

Under-Active: May not speak much, and more than likely you are introverted and shy. Not speaking the truth can block this chakra from activating.

Over-Active: May speak too much, in turn it keeps people away and at a distance. You may be a bad listener.

Open the Throat Chakra: Take your hands, and cross your fingers on the inside. Let your thumbs touch at the top of the tips, and pull them up and away from your fingers. Concentrate on the location of the Throat Chakra, at the base of the throat, and chant the sound, '**Haammm**.'

Third Eye Chakra

The Third Eye Chakra represents insight. When it is open, you have a good intuition, visualization, and may fantasize.

Under-Active: Not very good at thinking for yourself, rely on authority, and not rigid in your thoughts. Tend to get confused.

Over-Active: You may tend to live in a world with too much fantasy. In extreme situations, hallucinations are possible.

Open the Third Eye Chakra: Take your hands and put them before the lower part of your breast. The middle fingers are straightened, pointing forward and touching at the top. The other fingers are bended and touch at the upper two phalanges (Which is where the fingers bend). Your thumbs are pointed towards you and touch at the tops. Concentrate on the location of the Third Eye Chakra, just slightly above the point between your eyebrows, and chant the sound, '**Ommm**,' or, '**Auummm**.'

Crown Chakra

The Crown Chakra represents wisdom and being one with 'Everything.' When this chakra is open, you are welcoming, without prejudice, and quite aware of the world around you, as well as yourself.

Under-Active: You're not very aware of spirituality. You're probably quite rigid in your thinking, and boxed into your beliefs.

Over-Active: May tend to intellectualizing too much, could be addicted to spirituality and more than likely ignoring your bodily needs.

Open the Crown Chakra: Take your hands and place them before your stomach. Let your ring fingers point up, touching at their tops. Cross the rest of your fingers, with your left thumb underneath the right. Concentrate on the location of the Crown Chakra, at the top of your head, and chant the sound, '**Nnnggg**.'

It is also believed the Chakras are evolving with our bodies, and our consciousness as well.
Rudolf Steiner, the founder of Anthroposophy, has spoken out about the Chakras and it's unusual forms. He believes the chakra system is evolving and is very different for people in modern times than it was in ancient times, and will in turn be radically different for people in future times.

This is a valid observation, especially when thinking of how the constellations may realign our astrology signs. Truly, the stars are moving, and the astrology signs many of us abide to, from thousands of years ago, are now located in different positions in the Universe, which in turn changes the associations we have with those stars. This notion of the constellations changing in the Universe gives further reason to believe that the bodies of humans are changing as well.

CHAPTER FOURTEEN
(Decoding the Past)

"Men are born ignorant, not stupid. They are made stupid by education."

- Bertrand Russell -

Decoding the Past: (Introduction to Decoding the Past)

Why do you ask questions, for answers you already know? You already know everything. EVERYTHING!

This place here was created for us to learn about ourselves, even though you aren't truly learning anything new. You are just being reminded of all that you already know. Not one person here on Earth, or any Being from another planet or God for that matter, can tell you something 'New.' Everything you could possibly learn, everything you could possibly comprehend, is already understood within the depths of all that you already are.

You have all the Answers...All of them.

No one has to tell you when you have wronged them. You already know it. You can feel it in your heart when you have mistreated someone. Whether you heed this feeling, is your choice, but you already know when the feeling of guilt is upon you. No one has to arrest you, or condemn you, or give you a scolding tongue lashing, you already know. No one has to tell you what would make someone happy. You already know what would make someone happy. This excuse is giving a lot in relationships, not knowing what makes someone else happy. Too many times, has someone revealed to their partner that they are not happy with the situation, only for their companion to become defensive and explain they, 'Can't read their mind,' and nor do they know what makes them happy, but they are only lying to themselves. They know what would make their partner happy. Whether it's a compliment, or getting flowers, going out on dates, learning to control ones temper during a disagreement or just touches of affection, it is not hard to understand what may bring a smile to someone's face. The choice in doing so, or not doing so, is the greatest gift we have given ourselves.

The, **'Choices'** are what make us understand ourselves, knowing everything does not give you choices, knowing everything leads you to not having choices. When you know everything, there can't be a choice or a decision made, because you already know the Answer. Not knowing the Answer leads to Questions, Questions lead to the Experience, the Experience leads to Wisdom, Wisdom leads to Understanding, and Understanding...leads One to knowing the Answers all again. Beautiful, isn't it?

It's a cycle, which keeps repeating and repeating, learning and forgetting, learning and forgetting. Why? Because it is the only way we can remain active.

We are here, to experience **'The All,'** the **'Everything.'** What is the 'All,' and the 'Everything?' The 'All' and the 'Everything' is just that, every bit of creation you can think of, every situation that can possibly come to mind, every journey one can take, we are all here to experience it All, and we will. We will have experienced the life from something as small as bacteria to becoming one with God again, as its whole.

Everything has a living spirit, whether it be Humans, Extraterrestrials, Animals, Trees, Oceans, Planets or even Fire. Everything is alive, and you will experience all forms of levels and plains the spirit can exist in. You will experience all situations from the complete opposite viewpoint, so that the wisdom of the lesson is understood. No lesson can be learned when looking at it from one side. You must see it from the other side of the coin, in order for any wisdom to truly be owned. Sometimes it takes more than one lifetime to see or experience a lesson from the other side of the spectrum, therefore the journey continues to unfold until the 'All' is experienced.

We will go through our **Density** and **Soul** levels, completing our journey in both **Physical** and **Non-Physical** existences, eventually returning to the **Source**. Along the way we will accomplish some amazing feats, feats that will far exceed the mysteries here on Earth and Outer Space.

Decoding the Past: (Genesis)

The creation of the 'Earth' has had many different accounts, tales, or myths as to how it was fashioned, but none more known and scrutinized than **Genesis**. Genesis, which consists in the **Torah**, the **Bible**, and the **Koran**, is the story of the creation of the **Earth**, in which 3 of the major religions agree upon to be accurate. Most scientist refute anything of the sort took place, claiming scientific evidence proves otherwise. They rely on the '**Big Bang Theory**' and 'Evolution' more so than to side with the stories in the religious texts.

Unfortunately, there is something both parties (Religion and Science) fail to do, they forget to look at Genesis as a metaphor. Whether or not it is important to understand Genesis, truly is up to the individual, however, there are some things which can be understood through looking at it metaphorically.

An important fact man tends to forget is that describing the 'Divine' can be quite difficult. Truly, with all the languages in the world, there is not one word that can truly define 'God.' The best way to describe such a thing is through metaphors, stories or poems, because as human beings it is almost impossible to describe God accurately.

According to Genesis, God created the World in **6** days, choosing to rest on the **7th**. This is somewhat ironic, being that God has no need for rest. Rest is not something God needs or wants to do, rest is not something God thinks about. God is a creator, it wants to create and create and create, so the idea of rest does not fit into Gods agenda. It makes for a good story if God chooses to rest on the **7th** and religions can make that day Holy, when if one holds this value to be true, everyday should be viewed as Hoy, because it is a part of the process.

The time of this event is one of the more focal debates. **James Ussher**, a religious scholar **in the 17th Century**, published a chronology which calculated the date of Creation as **October**

22nd, 4004 BCE**. His findings were based on the dates in the Bible, however, a date of creation just being **6,000** years ago is off by **13** to **15** billion years…at least. This date would fall closer to man obtaining a level of consciousness, when humans started to use writing and numbers, but this is also short by many thousands of years. Even with the many disparities, the metaphors of creation lie hidden in the passages.

In **Genesis 1:1** to **1:3**, it begins with, "*In the beginning God created the heaven and the earth. Now the earth was formless and empty, darkness was over the surface of the deep, and the Spirit of God was hovering over the waters. And God said, 'Let there be light,' and there was light.*" To better understand this, it is important to understand the translation. 'In the beginning God created the heaven and the earth,' this, can be thought of as God creating the **'World of Questions**,' which is the **Physical Ream** (The Universe, or Earth), and **'Heaven,'** otherwise known as the **'World of Answers**,' at the same time, therefore, one not existing without the other, just as the **'Yin-Yang.'** The Earth (World of Questions) was once void of life (Light), so then the spirit of God breathed Life (Light) into its World.

In **Genesis 1:26**, it continues, "*God said, let us make man in our image, in our likeness.*" This is one of the more fascinating statements in the whole Bible. This statement alone leaves several things to point out, for one, the use of the word '**Us.**' Why would God mention 'Us,' in making mankind? This very distinctly points out there is more than one 'Entity' involved in the creation of man. Could this be the **Anunnaki** that **Zecharia Sitchin** described as making Human Beings? If so, then there was more than one hand that played a part of creation. The further use of 'In our own image,' only adds to this hypothesis. If the Anunnaki were the creators of human beings, it could insinuate that humans resemble their makers in build and appearance. Could there be a deeper meaning to this? Could the use of the term 'Us,' really mean 'Us?' The term, 'In our own Image, in our own likeness,' could imply we have given ourselves all possible chances to reconnect with who we are, here, in the image and likeness of God.

Genesis goes on to describe the creation of man. In **Genesis 2:7**, *"God formed a man from the dust of the ground and breathed into his nostrils the breath of life, and the man became a living being."* This can be understood by understanding that everything in the Universe is made up of one thing, Stardust. The dirt on Earth essentially has the same components that makeup a human being. God breathing life (Light) in his nostrils, is the same as God enabling the body to have consciousness.

In **Genesis 2:8-9**, *"The LORD God planted a garden toward the east, in Eden...God caused to grow every tree that is pleasing to the sight and good for food; the tree of life also in the midst of the garden, and the tree of the knowledge of good and evil."* In **Genesis 2:15-17**, *"God took the man and put him into the garden of Eden to cultivate it and keep it... God commanded the man, saying, 'From any tree of the garden you may eat freely; but from the tree of the knowledge of good and evil you shall not eat, for in the day that you eat from it you will surely die."* This is a metaphor for God placing all things everywhere in the 'World of Questions.' The garden is a metaphor for 'What can grow.' God places a tree of Life, which is a metaphor for endless experiences, while God placing a tree of 'Knowledge of Good and Bad' is a metaphor for judgment. God warns man that eating from the tree of knowledge of good and bad would cause him to die, because eating from this tree will in turn cause self-judgment upon the idea of Life, therefore, in death, lies an exit to this world, the 'World of Questions.'

From **Genesis 2:18-23**, *"God said, 'It is not good for the man to be alone. I will make a helper suitable for him'... God had formed out of the ground all the wild animals and all the birds in the sky. He brought them to the man to see what he would name them...But for Adam no suitable helper was found. So God caused the man to fall into a deep sleep and took one of man's ribs, and then closed up the place with flesh...God made woman from the rib he had taken out of man and brought her unto the man. The man said, 'This is now bone of my bones and flesh of my flesh. She shall be called woman."* God formed animals for man to name and command. Man needs to be entertained by a level of consciousness that can challenge and relate to him, not that he can control, so God forms man such a companion. Being that we are all one, it is a clever metaphor to have **Eve** (Woman) created from one of **Adam**'s ribs. This should not be thought of as a dominating comparison, but one to show that we are of each other, man and woman.

In **Genesis 2:25**, *"Adam and his wife were both naked, and they felt no shame."* This is due to them not yet anything to judge themselves by.

From **Genesis 3:1-7**, *"The serpent was more crafty than any of the wild animals...He said to the woman, 'Did God really say, You must not eat from any tree in the garden?'... the serpent said to the woman. 'For God knows that when you eat from it your eyes will be opened, and you will be like God, knowing good and evil.'...When the woman saw that the fruit of the tree was good for food and pleasing to the eye, and also desirable for gaining wisdom, she took some and ate it. She also gave some to her husband, who was with her, and he ate it...Then the eyes of both of them were opened, and they realized they were naked; so they sewed fig leaves together and made coverings for themselves."* The Serpent is a metaphor for the 'Ego,' which is an energy that exists in the 'World of the Physical.' Adam and Eve eating the fruit and realizing they were naked, is a metaphor for them developing individual consciousness in the physical realm, to that of judging what is good or bad. The 'World of Questions' is a world of judgment, the 'World of Answers' is a world of acceptance. Adam and Eve realized the world they were in and started to judge the 'Yin' from the 'Yang.'

From **Genesis 3:8-19**, *"Then the man and his wife heard the sound of God as he was walking in the garden, and they hid...God asked the man, 'Where are you?' He answered, 'I heard you in the garden, and I was afraid because I was naked, so I hid.'...God asked, 'Who told you that you were naked? Have you eaten from the tree that I commanded you not to eat from?' The man said, 'The woman gave me the fruit, and I ate.' God said to the woman, 'What is this you have done?' The woman said, 'The serpent deceived me, and I ate.'...God then cursed the serpent, and cursed the Woman to bear children in pain, to desire her husband, and to be ruled by him. God cursed Adam to toil and earn his food from the ground, which would* *sprout thorns and thistles, until he returned to the ground from which he was taken."* Man hiding from God, comes from their awareness of judgment. Those that judge, tend to feel guilt themselves, Adam and Eve hiding from God is a metaphor for this. God cursing man comes as a very interesting comparison, because God would honestly have no need to curse man. Truly, man cannot do anything to offend God, so you must look at this scenario for what it provides. The physical feelings, and labor load of man is how the physical realm is to be operated. This is making man become closer to physical nature, and further from the veil of 'Knowing Everything,' making it so that their existence would be full of questions that related to the things around them (Earth).

From **Genesis 3:22-24**, *"God said, 'The man has now become like one of us, knowing good and evil. He must not be allowed to reach out his hand and take also from the tree of life and eat, and live forever'...so God banished him from the Garden of Eden to work the ground from which he had been taken. After he drove the man out, he placed on the east side of the Garden of Eden cherubim and a flaming sword flashing back and forth to guard the way to the tree of life."* This passage translates to God realizing man has now become aware of judgment, and eating from the Tree of Life which can cause someone to live forever, could cause one to live on in their world of judgment, making it so that one could never become with God again. This cannot happen, so God again gives an outlet from the 'World of Questions,' to transcend through death, and into the 'World of Answers.' God guards the 'World of Answers' fiercely with a 'flaming sword flashing back and forth' is a symbol to state that nothing can ever interfere with God's creation. It is a metaphor for the pointless effort one would have to think such a thing can be disrupted.

It should be understood that the story of Genesis originated from Judaism, even though the words 'Adam' and 'Eve' were not proper Hebrew names. Instead, they are part of a creation myth to get the story going. Moses was 'Awake' for his times, and explaining what he may have seen or learned to people of the day, could be quite difficult to those who may still be asleep. Even after splitting the Red Sea the people still complained, and doubted some of Moses demands, as if getting out of Egypt and splitting the Sea wasn't enough, so it could be possible that Moses used human tales to describe the meaning to a deeper message.

Genesis goes on to give events of the children of **Adam** and **Eve**, most notably, **Cain** and **Abel**. This story can be described metaphorically as well, when understanding certain energies we have with the physical realm. In the passages **Genesis 4:3-7**, *"Cain brought some of the fruits of the soil as an offering to the LORD. Abel also brought an offering...The LORD looked with favor on Abel and his offering, but on Cain and his offering he did not look with favor. So Cain was very angry... Then the LORD said to Cain, 'Why are you angry?...If you do what is right, will you not be accepted? But if you do not do what is right, sin is crouching at your door; it desires to have you, but you must rule over it."* This seems like a great example to dealing with the energy of the '**Ego**.' It is the Ego that would make Cain angry. In other words, God is telling Cain he can simply choose to feel angry, or not. God goes on to say he should act righteously, because he would be happy and if he didn't then sin would be awaiting for him, but he must rule over it. This can be expressed as God telling Cain he must rule over his 'Ego,' because it will be his downfall. This can be considered a forewarning to what happened next.

From **Genesis 4:6-16**, the passage is summed up to explain, *'Cain kills his brother in the field. God asked Cain where his brother was, therefore Cain replies, 'Am I my brother's keeper?' God asked Cain what he had done, having felt his brother's blood cried out from the ground. God then cursed Cain to fail at farming and to become a ceaseless wanderer. Cain complained to God that his punishment was too great to bear, explaining that anyone who met him might kill him. So God put a mark on Cain and promised vengeance would sevenfold on anyone who would kill him. Cain left God's presence and dwelt in the land of Nod, east of Eden.'* This entire exchange seems like a great example of '**Karma**.' To be clear, Karma does not come to you the same exact way you may act out, but the energy that comes back is just as strong as your intimal actions. Cain being banished for life as a wanderer, is the same energy of banishment Cain placed upon his brother. Not to mention the failing as a farmer, this making it extremely hard for Cain to succeed in his livelihood, however, God does something very interesting, God also announces vengeance onto anyone who would harm Cain. This too, is a continuation of Karma. Cain will deal with his own Karma that his Ego has brought upon himself, it is not meant for others to feel as though they should hold him accountable for his actions, he is already being held accountable to his actions, by himself.

Adam and Eve's third son, **Seth**, meaning 'God has provided me with another offspring in place of Abel,' is the Ancestor of Noah. Noah's story is one of the more controversial stories of Genesis, because of the lack of evidence and its distinct similarities to stories that came before it. According to Biblical chronology, **Noah** and the **Great flood** occurred at around **2300 BCE**, however, the Great Flood, where God sends rain to drown the Earth of its inhabitants, has almost the same exact plot, as a Sumerian story, '**The Epic of Gilgamesh**,' which possibly dates back to as far as **2,700 BCE** or beyond. Many of the similarities are strikingly close to the Genesis flood account.

The Epic was composed in the form of a poem, with the main figure **Gilgamesh**, who is believed to have been a historical person. The **Sumerian King List**, which is an ancient manuscript originally recorded in the Sumerian language that lists the kings of Sumer, shows Gilgamesh in the first dynasty of Uruk reigning for **126** years. The story starts by introducing Gilgamesh. It entails that he was one with great knowledge and preserved information of the days before the flood. Gilgamesh was thought to be an oppressive ruler, which in turn caused the people to cry out to the 'Gods' for them to create a nemesis to cause Gilgamesh strife.

After one fight with his nemesis **Enkidu**, they became best friends. The two then set off on many dangerous adventures, in which Enkidu is eventually killed. This causes a fear of death in Gilgamesh, in which he then sets forth to find immortality. On his journey, he meets **Utnapishtim**, the character that resembles biblical Noah. In short, Utnapishtim achieved immortality after building a ship that would sustain the '**Great Deluge**' that destroyed mankind. He brought all of his relatives and all species of creatures aboard the vessel. Just as the biblical descriptions for Noah, after the flood, **Utnapishtim** released birds to find land, in which the ship then landed upon a mountain. Below is a comparison of the main aspects of the two floods in **Genesis** and the **Epic of Gilgamesh**.

Subject	Genesis	Gilgamesh
Name of hero	Noah	Utnapishtim
Sender	Yahweh	Assembly of Gods
Means of message	Direct from God	In a dream
Extent of flood	Global	Global
Cause	Man's wickedness	Man's sins
Intended for	All mankind	All mankind
Hero's character	Righteous	Righteous
Built boat	Yes	Yes
Complained	Yes	Yes
Height of boat	Several Stories	Several Stories
Passengers	Family members	Family and few others
Animals	All species	All species
Means of flood	Ground water & heavy rain	Heavy rain
Test to find land	Release of birds	Release of birds
Ark landing spot	Mt. Ararat	Mt. Nisir
Blessed after flood	Yes	Yes

Some of the similarities between Noah and Utnapishtim's Flood accounts are very striking. It is also interesting that both accounts trace the landing spot to the same general region of the Middle East, **Mt. Ararat** and **Mt. Nisir** are about **300** miles apart. The discovery of artifacts associated with

Aga and **Enmebaragesi** of Kish, two kings named in the story, has lent credibility to the historical existence of Gilgamesh.

While these two floods are very similar, it does not mean one is the original account, but that both could be an account of the same experience that happened during that time. This theory would seem more likely than it would declaring the story of Noah's account as a first of its kind, because it came many years later.

It is to be noted, the early historical figures in the Torah, up until Noah, lived lives well into their **100**s. Adam is said to have lived for **930** years, as well as many others. **Methuselah**, who lived to be **969**, is the oldest known figure in the Bible, and is said to have died seven days before the beginning of the Great Flood. Noah lived to be **950**. This did not change until **Genesis 6:3**, when the LORD said, *"My spirit shall not abide in man forever, for that he also is flesh, therefore shall his days be a hundred and twenty years."* The human lifespans ascribed to many in the bible causes problems of chronology for scientists as well as biblical scholars, their long lives leaves many duplications. Could it be that man in biblical times actually did have a longer lifespan?

To say this isn't possible would be ignoring all the wonders and new inventive information of our past history that has come about. While many tend to think they are healthier beings than any civilization before them, this is not true. While there has been much advancement in medicine and food, so has there been with pollution and diseases. The human body is working to defeat the new ailments and viruses that come along, in which many have been from mankind's doing. Remember, the body is continually changing.

If one wishes to take into account the possibility of the body of Homo Sapiens being genetically created, then the long ages people could once live may make sense. Possibility many changes to the body were made.

Another theory is that the Bible could well indeed have many errors. For instance, in the book '**Alien Interview**,' it explains, *"The ancient Jewish people who wrote the history book called the Old Testament were slaves, herders and gatherers. Any modern* *technology, even a simple flashlight, would seem astounding and miraculous to them. They attributed any unexplainable phenomenon or technology to the workings of a God."* The Holy texts being written by slaves, or those who did not have as much access to certain information as others, could be a reason for many errors or supernatural accounts in the Bible.

Understanding Genesis should only come as a metaphor, the vision of this particular 'Creation' is just that, a 'Vision.' It is believed these stories were received to Moses, therefore the men spoken about in Genesis (Adam, Noah, etc.) had no current texts of their own accounts.

One thing about Genesis people must realize, in parts, God is very jealous, wrathful, and very male chauvinistic. When in truth, if one wished to try and express a gender upon God, it would definitely reside more on the feminine nature. God is a Creator, something that gives Birth (Woman). Even though God is a Seeder (Man), the comparisons of its masculine traits are subsided by its feminine attributes, in terms of Creation and Life.

God's masculinity is spread throughout the pages in the Bible, the natural disasters and condemning of people and cities is extremely masculine. God is a builder, not a destroyer. The connotation of women being created from man seems to give off an air of superiority, however, one needs to understand these texts were written through the hands of men.

Though some of the lessons can be explained as metaphors, Genesis is extremely judgmental. This is preposterous. How can God ever feel a need to judge? God is beyond judging. God is beyond being jealous or needy, therefore the tone of displeasure God displays in Genesis does not fare well in giving God human characteristics. This is a vivid downfall with most religions, the idea of a judgmental God, a God that needs your attention in order for it to be pleased.

God has giving you Free Will to make all your decisions, and this is your most precious gift. Hell does not exist. God would not trick you, to give you the freedom to make all your choices, just to be judged for one of your unfortunate choices.

We do that to ourselves in the 'World of Questions,' therefore, there can't be a Hell. You cannot offend God. The only thing there can be, is the experience.

Explaining the levels humans go to, to give God such a jealous nature was profoundly explained in '**What the Bleep Do We Know**,' by **JZ Knight**, a Master teacher and Channeler of an energy source named '**Ramtha**.' **Knight** is quoted as saying, *"God must be greater than the greatest of human weaknesses, and indeed, the greatest of human skills. God must even transcend a most remarkable, to emulate nature in its absolute splendor. How can any man or woman sin against such a greatness of mind? How can any one carbon unity, on earth, in the back waters, of indeed the Milky Way, the boondocks, betray God? All-Mighty. That is impossible. The height of arrogance is the height of control of those that create God in their own image."*

Simply, the stories in Genesis shouldn't hold any weight other than that they are great stories. Genesis is not the most important part of creation. The most important part of Creation is 'Now,' this exact second. This exact 'Moment' is the most vital part of life that Creation has been involved in constructing.

Decoding the Past: (Moses & Mises)

Many Archeologists have concluded that much of the early history of the Bible is either mythical or stories inspired by earlier events. This has led to some believing **Moses**, the most prominent figure in the Torah, may not have existed at all. Scholars have pointed to his biography as evidence, much of it being tied to events that never happened, or key points in his life that seem taken directly from historical figures before him.

Moses having never existed could explain why his burial site has never been found. Even the last writer(s) in the **Book of Deuteronomy** did not claim to know where it was. In **Deuteronomy 34:6**, it reads, *"He buried him in Moab, in the valley opposite Beth Peor, but to this day no one knows where his grave is."* This is not convincing evidence for many, one can say it is common not to know where many graves are from people during that time, even though many graves of historical figures have been found from that era and before. The most compelling case is the similarities of Moses's most important attributes during his prophethood.

The story of Moses, the Jewish lawgiver, is similar to many lawgivers before him in other cultures. While some of these lawgivers include **Manou** (A Cretan Reformer), and **Minos** (An Indian Legislator), his most compelling similarities are with that of **Mises**, thought to be a Syrian myth, dating back as far as **5,000 BCE**, around **3000** years before Moses is believed to have existed.

D. M. Murdock, better known by her pen name **Acharya S**, has explained the similarities between Moses and these figures. She writes, *"The legend of Moses, rather than being that of a historical Hebrew lawgiver, is found from the Mediterranean to India, with the character having different names and races, depending on the locale...'**Mises**' is found in Syria, where he was pulled out of a basket floating in a river. Mises also had tablets of stone upon which laws were written, and a rod with which he did miracles, including parting waters and leading his army across the sea."*

If this is true, then this means historical Moses never spoke to a Burning Bush, confronted the Pharaoh and led the Israelites to freedom, parted the Red Sea, or received the **10** Commandments at Mount Sinai.

The 10 Commandments

It can be argued Moses is most famous for receiving the **10** Commandments. This too, the **10** Commandments, does not come without speculation. The **10** Commandments are thought to have been inspired and taken right out of the Egyptian **Book of the Dead**. The **10 Commandments**, from the Bible are as follows:
1) You shall have no other gods before me.
2) You shall not make for yourself any carved image, or any likeness of anything that is in heaven above, or that is in the earth beneath, or that is in the water under the

earth, you shall not bow down to them nor serve them. For I, the Lord your God, am a jealous God, visiting the iniquity of the fathers on the children to the third and fourth generations of those who hate me, but showing mercy to thousands, to those who love Me and keep My commandments.

3) You shall not take the name of the Lord your God in vain, for the Lord will not hold him guiltless who takes His name in vain.

4) Remember the Sabbath day, to keep it holy. Six days you shall labor and do all your work, but the seventh day is the Sabbath of the Lord your God. In it you shall do no work, you nor your son, nor your daughter, nor your manservant, nor your maidservant, nor your cattle, nor your stranger who is within your gates. For in six days the Lord made the heavens and the earth, the sea, and all that is in them, and rested the seventh day. Therefore the Lord blessed the Sabbath day and hallowed it.

5) Honor your father and your mother, that your days may be long upon the land which the Lord your God is giving you.

6) You shall not murder.

7) You shall not commit adultery.

8) You shall not steal.

9) You shall not bear false witness against your neighbor.

10) You shall not covet your neighbor's house, you shall not covet your neighbor's wife, nor his manservant, nor his maidservant, nor his ox, nor his donkey, nor anything that is your neighbor's.

The Egyptian 'Oath of Clearance'

Even though the Ancient Jews believed the Egyptians to be morally inferior, it is clear that they indeed had a well-developed sense of morality. Evidence for this has come in many forms of art and writings, but one in particular is the Egyptian

'Oath of Clearance,' which is found in the 'Book of the Dead,' and existed thousands of years before the Jews had ever formed as a civilization. The 'Oath of Clearance,' contains **seven** similarities to the **10 Commandments**, however, the phrases are not identical. The **Oaths** similar to each **Commandment** are noted as follows:

- I have not committed fraud and evil against men. (Similar to the **6th Commandment**)
- I have not diverted justice in the judgment hall. (Similar to the **9th Commandment**)
- I have not caused a man to do more than his day's work. (Similar to the **4th Commandment**)
- I have not caused a slave to be ill-treated.
- I have not taken milk from the mouths of children. (Similar to the **5th Commandment**)
- I have not stolen cattle. (Similar to the **8th Commandment**)
- I have not been weak. (Similar to the **10th Commandment**)
- I have not been wretched.
- I have not been impious or impure. (Similar to the **7th Commandment**)

Many Ancient cultures embraced similar moral law systems as the Ten Commandments. In **Romans 2:14-15**, the Apostle Paul writes, *"When Gentiles, who do not possess the law, do instinctively what the law requires, these, though not having the law, are a law to themselves. They show that what the law requires is written on their hearts, to which their own conscience bears witness."* Paul is basically stating that God has applied a **Universal Moral Law** to the hearts of all humans, implying that deep down each of us has a **'Common Concept'** of what is morally right and wrong. This notion of a 'Common Concept' can further be understood to us being 'All One.' Each of us has a morality about us that centers along this 'Common Concept,' although many people suppress what they know to be morally correct.

You know in your heart when you are not following or abiding by this 'Common Concept.' The **10** Commandments are just a remindful tool. In **'The Law of One: Book I, The Ra Material,' Don Elkins**, asked the **Social Memory Complex** known as **'Ra,'** a question regarding 'The **10** Commandments.' Excerpts from the Conversation are as follows:

> **Questioner:** *Was the recipient of the commandments positively or negatively oriented?*
> **Ra:** *I am Ra. The recipient was one of extreme positivity, thus accounting for some of the pseudo-positive characteristics of the information received. As with contacts which are not successful, this entity, vibratory complex, Moishe, did not remain a credible influence among those who had first heard the philosophy of One and this entity was removed from this third-density vibratory level in a lessened or saddened state, having lost, what you may call, the honor and faith with which he had begun the conceptualization of the Law of One and the freeing of those who were of his tribes, as they were called at that time/space.*
>
> **Questioner:** *If this entity was positively oriented, how was the Orion group able to contact him?*
> **Ra:** *I am Ra. This was an intensive, shall we say, battleground between positively oriented forces of Confederation origin and negatively oriented sources. The one called Moishe was open to impression and received the Law of One in its most simple form. However, the information became negatively oriented due to his people's pressure to do specific physical things in the third-density planes. This left the entity open for the type of information and philosophy of a self-service nature.*

Questioner: *It would be wholly unlike an entity fully aware of the knowledge of the Law of One to ever say "Thou shalt not." Is this correct?*
Ra: *I am Ra. This is correct.*

About **1,400** years after Moses is believed to have received the **10** Commandments, they were summed up into **2** Commandments. When Jesus was confronted and asked which is the greatest Commandment in the Law, Jesus replied, in **Matthew 22:36-40**, *"Love the Lord your God with all your heart and with all your soul and with all your mind.' This is the first and greatest commandment. And the second is like it: 'Love your neighbor as yourself.' All the Law and the Prophets hang on these two commandments."* The basic **2** Commandments are as follow:
1) Love God with all your heart, soul and mind.
2) Love your neighbor as you love yourself.

When looking over the **10** Commandments from Moses, they basically break themselves down into two categories. The First four Commandments abide by the 'New First' Commandment from Jesus, and the next six Commandments from Moses, abide by the 'New Second' Commandment. Additionally, when Jesus says, *"And the second is like it,"* this sums up these '**New 2 Commandments**' into **1** Commandment, which is '**Love**. The only Commandment there is, is love. The root of Everything involved in the **10** Commandments, and in the 'New **2** Commandments,' is love.

'The second is like it,' also implies the meaning of 'One,' loving God, like you love yourself. For God is the Self, and the Self is the Everything.

Decoding the Past: (Yeshua, the Jmmanuel)

The existence of Jesus has been at debate for many years. A great deal of non-Christian historical documents, such as Jewish and Greco-Roman sources, have been used to analyze the existence of Jesus. Most historians agree that Jesus did exist, and claim his baptism and crucifixion as historical. A small group of scholars suggest that Jesus never existed, but this view is somewhat of a recent argument.

The most compelling thing of all seems not to come from what people later wrote about Jesus, but from the people who did not write about Jesus. Not a single historian or follower who lived during the supposed time of Jesus ever mentioned him, therefore, many who deny Jesus's existence tend to base their suggestions on the lack of eyewitnesses and historical reference of Jesus during his lifetime. Many also cite the fact that the characteristics of Jesus's life also closely resemble those of Greek, Egyptian and Hindu Gods and Prophets, as well as others, especially those with stories of resurrected deities, however, classicist **Michael Grant** stated that the standard historical criteria prevent one from rejecting the existence of a historical Jesus.

Thus, the Gospels have been the main source to account for the existence of Jesus. All the stories in the Gospels tend to portray Jesus as someone of great acclaim, mentioning that he was known far and wide and had a great multitude of followers and crowds of people who congregated to hear him. The multitude of people thought of him as a 'Teacher, miracle healer and a prophet,' as described in **Matthew 14:5**. Such historical figures as the Roman Governor **Pilate** and **Herod** are mentioned in the Gospel as knowing of Jesus, but for the most part there hasn't been any evidence found outside of the Gospels to make the connection to Pilate or Herod, nor any other figure during the time Jesus is said to have lived.

The origins of the name of Jesus have been at debate for many of years, and is one of the main disagreements between Jews and Christians that determine their reasons for Jesus being or not being the Messiah. In the Old Testament, **Isaiah 7:14**, it gives a prophecy of the coming Messiah, *"Therefore the Lord Himself will give you a sign: Behold, a virgin will be with child and bear a son, and she will call His name* **Immanuel**.*"* This is where the conflict lies, because in the New Testament, **Matthew 1:21-23**, it says, *"She will give birth to a son, and you are to give him the name Jesus, because he who will save his people from their sins."*

However, **Isaiah** prophesied of the coming Messiah with many different terms, as in **Isaiah 9:6**, *"His name shall be called* **Wonderful**, **Counselor**, *the* **Mighty God**, *the* **Everlasting Father**, *the* **Prince of Peace**.*"* Calling him Immanuel, is like giving him a title, or a nickname. Giving children names that would represent their hopes and dreams were very common among parents in ancient times. Names in the **Old Testament** had many meanings, for instance, **Adam** means 'Man,' while **Eve** means 'To Live.' **Abraham** means 'Father of many.' Moses means 'Son' or 'Deliver,' and Noah means 'Motion.'

When it gets to **Isaiah 7:14**, the prophecy about the coming Messiah says, *"Shall call his name Immanuel."* Immanuel means 'God is with us.' It reads they shall, *"Call his name Immanuel,"* it does not read they will, 'Call him Immanuel,' meaning that his name will be defined as Immanuel. This is important because Christians believe Jesus was 'God in the flesh.'

Scholars have pointed out over **700** names and titles of Jesus Christ in the Bible. In the **Book of Jeremiah**, when referring to the coming Messiah, **Jeremiah** says, *"And this is His name by which He shall be called, Jehovah, Our Righteousness."* God, the Father, is named Jehovah. Jesus was never actually called Jehovah as his name, but instead brought the righteousness of Jehovah, in the same way Jesus would bring in the Immanuel, 'God is with us.'

Bart D. Ehrman cites numerous places in the Gospels and other books in the **New Testament** that have apparently been altered by Christian scribes, therefore there are many reasons for the confusion of Jesus's name. If you want to find the origins of Jesus's name, the first place to start should be **Paul**. Paul, who had changed his name from Saul, was not opposed to changing a name.

Paul was the first to propose the idea of 'Being saved' through the sacrifice of God's Son, in Christian theology. His background as a **Pharisee** (An ancient Jewish sect, distinguished by strict observance of the traditional and written law), suggests he was familiar with offering human sacrifice in hopes of God's deliverance. Thus, to support his theology, he had the motivation for the name 'Jesus,' which in turn means '**God Saves.**' Jesus is the Greek name for '**Joshua**,' which was already known to Paul. Hence, the eventual '**J**,' replacing the first initial of the name by the man born '**Yeshua**.'

Despite all the names Jesus was given, Yeshua is believed to have been the one given to him by his parents. Yeshua, in Hebrew means 'Salvation.'

Additional motivation for Paul to have altered Yeshua's name is that Paul was once enemies with Yeshua. Some of the most cutting rebukes that Jesus issued were directed at the Pharisees. At least seven times in **Matthew 23**, Jesus pronounced the following condemnation, *"Woe unto you, scribes and Pharisees, hypocrites!"* After Paul's conversion, he may have wished to disperse of the name of someone he must have hated and whose disciples he had once persecuted.

Christ in Greek means '**Anointed One**.' Through attachment, Paul could now ensure the intended name of 'Jesus Christ' be understood to have fulfilled prophecy.

Companionship of Jesus

Jesus was born a Jew. In Ancient Jewish tradition, it was common for men to marry young. Jesus was not just a Jew, but he was also a 'Rabbi,' and rabbis were well known to be married at the time, therefore, it would have been very uncommon for Jesus not to have been married as well. By examining parts of the Gospels and texts from other historical sources, a better idea of Jesus's marital connection may unfold.

The idea of Jesus being married often focuses on his relationship with **Mary Magdalene**. What exactly do we know about this woman? Mary Magdalene is first mentioned in **Luke 8:1-3**. Just after having seven demons casted out of her, assumingly by Jesus, she, along with others, accompanied Jesus on his mission and supported his means, meaning they provided for him financially. Mary was perhaps Jesus's closest follower, she learned from him, remained faithful to him, even in his darkest hour when his disciples wavered, and more importantly she was the first to witness him after he arose, a role that has been said to be of exceptional honor and privilege. Surely Jesus held Mary in his highest regards.

The Gospels unfortunately do not reveal much about this woman. Centuries after the Gospels were first written, she somehow became associated with the prostitute who bathed and anointed Jesus's feet, as in **Luke 7:36-50**, however, there is no mention of the name Mary and nothing in this passage seems to imply a connection to her. Thus, there is no reason to assume or think Mary had ever been a prostitute.

The **Gospel of Philip**, written well into the 3rd **Century**, is one of the latest of the **non-Canonical Gospels** (Not in current New Testament). It is not considered a Gospel in the ordinary sense, but instead is a collection of theological observations written from a gnostic view. In **Section 59**, it states, *"There were three who always walked with the Lord, Mary his mother and her sister and Magdalene, the one who was called his companion."*

Christians have historically thought sex is somehow sinful, even though the Old Testament makes references to it as being one of God's good creations, as in **Genesis 1** and **2**, and the **Song of Solomon** which in turns seems very erotic for the bible. As Christianity inherited Greek philosophy and early Christian asceticism (Extreme self-denial and austerity), it formed into a theology where sexual intimacy was not a wonderful part of God's creation, but only a necessity between husband and wife. Christians who mostly reject the joy of sex, suggest Jesus didn't marry because it would have been wrong if he were intimate with his wife, however this is not consistent with biblical texts, which in turn celebrates sexual intimacy in marriage.

In part of **Section 63** of **The Gospel of Philip**, it reads, *"And the companion of the Savior is Mary Magdalene. But Christ loved her more than all the disciples and used to kiss her often on her mouth."* Thus, if Jesus was not married, the connotations of him being intimate were strong, hence the word '**Companion.**'

The inclusion of Mary as one of Jesus's followers in a day when Jewish teachers did not teach women is not just a symbol of the inclusiveness of the Kingdom of God, but it could be attributed to his welcoming of companionship with a woman. Surely, someone of Jesus's knowledge did not feel burdened to have to restrain himself from sex. His teachings, and words do not reflect someone that would feel impure from engaging in sexual relations, but someone that would humbly and respectfully engage in it.

It has also been speculated by some scholars that the Bible actually describes Jesus's wedding. In Christianity, the transformation of water into wine at the '**Marriage at Cana**' or '**Wedding at Cana**' is the first miracle of Jesus in the **Gospel of John**, but for some scholars this points to Jesus's own ceremony. Scholars have pointed out the fact of Jesus's disciples being there, along with his mother, and him serving wine (In which he turned from water) as key points to this. Many argue that during this time in their culture, the groom served the wine to his guest, and as in **John 2:3**, there would be no need for his mother Mary to tell to him that the guest, *"They have no wine,"* if he wasn't such an important factor to appeasing the guest at the wedding.

All **4** Gospel either solely state or include Mary Magdalene as being the first person to arrive at Jesus's tomb, **3** days after his crucifixion, while Mary Mother of Jesus is stated in **3** accounts. This is important because in early Jewish tradition, those known to have access to the body after death were of family, Mother and Wife. For those that have wondered why Mary Magdalene was special enough to be the first at Jesus's tomb and to know of his resurrection, it now makes sense.

Arrival of the Fish

The '**Fish**,' which has ancient pagan roots, was a very important symbol in early Christian theology. It was depicted as a symbol in the first decades of the **2nd Century**. Jesus was known as the Fish. The fish in astrology can mean, **Pisces**, or even **Aquarius**, the 'Water Barrier,' thought to have brought in the 'New Way.' Even though the true date of Jesus's birthday will remain up for debate, if we use the Fish symbol, it is more likely for Jesus's birthday to have been anywhere from Mid-January to Mid-March, which aligns with these astrological signs.

Jesus was accompanied by **12** Apostles. The number **12** represents the **12** signs in the Zodiac. This would be hard to prove, due to there being no way of finding out when the Apostles birthdays were, and their names don't exactly relate to the Signs, but the **12** Apostles are thought to represent each one of the Zodiac signs, though their relation to Jesus as far as their astrological connection is undetermined.

It is believed by many that Jesus was a carpenter, but this may not be so accurate. In the original scripts of **Mark 6:3**, Jesus is called a **Tekton**, while in the original scripts of **Matthew 13:55**, it explains Jesus being the son of a Tekton. A Tekton has been traditionally translated into English as 'Carpenter,' but Tekton is a rather general word. This word can also mean 'Builder,' with the same root meaning of 'Technical' and 'Technology.' This can cover many different fields one might have skills in, even those advanced for its times, such as the technical knowledge of extraterrestrials.

The **Talmud Jmmanuel** is an alleged ancient text in Aramaic, claimed to have been discovered in a cave, south of the Old City of Jerusalem in **1963**, by ex-Greek Orthodox priest **Isa Rashid**, and a Swiss UFO contactee **Billy Meier**. The discoverers of these scrolls have been persecuted by Christian and Jewish orthodox groups, though the publishers of the Talmud Jmmanuel, **Steelmark LLC**, claim the document, *"Could indicate an Extraterrestrial origin for the New Testament."*

The ancient scrolls of the Talmud of Jmmanuel are believed to have been written by **Judas Iscariot**, the disciple of **Jmmanuel** (Jesus). Rashid, who had been entrusted with the original scrolls for safekeeping was eventually assassinated in Baghdad. Unfortunately, just before his death the scrolls were lost or burned in an Israeli air raid on a Lebanese refugee camp in **1974**. Fortunately, a quarter of the original script had been translated into German by then, and had been sent to Billy Meier in Switzerland. Meier edited and published the German version of the Talmud Jmmanuel in **1975**.

The portion of the ancient text that were saved, not only runs parallel to the **Gospel of Matthew**, but it also appears to be its source script. **James Deardorff**, a devout proponent for the authenticity of the Talmud Jmmanuel, has spent many years comparing its text with biblical scriptures. Deardorff claims to have found a large amount of evidence that the writer of the Gospel of Matthew, *"Used and altered the Talmud to suit his theology, making changes, insertions and omissions, in a manner that precludes reversing the arguments to claim a literary hoax."* Even though there are strong similarities, some of the philosophical contents involved with the teachings of Jmmanuel stray significantly from the versions in the bible.

Meier, who claims the birthdate of Jesus is **February 3rd**, is thought by some to be a 'New Age' prophet that has been educated by wise celestial teachers from the Pleiades star cluster. Meier says the spelling **Jmmanuel** was allegedly commanded to him by Extraterrestrials, which they also claim Jmmanuel was an Extraterrestrial. **Barry Downing**, a Presbyterian minister wrote a book in **1968**, claiming Jesus was an Extraterrestrial, citing many biblical verses, one in particular is **John 8:23**, where Jesus says, *"You are from below, I am from above. You are of this world, I am not of this world."*

In Pleiadian theory, it is said that at around **10 CE**, the last Pleiadians left Earth for good, feeling as though it was time for humans to evolve on their own. Before leaving, the Pleiadians left a spiritual leader called Jmmanuel, whose father was Gabriel of the **Pleiades** system, and mother Mary who was of **Lyran** descent. Jmmanuel, who was an extremely evolved soul, later became known as Jesus.

Similarities of Jesus & Others

There are several accounts of Gods or Prophets of many different cultures who were said to have the same attributes as those that Christians claim for Jesus. The idea of '**Trinity**' was very popular in many religious sects. Stories of **Miracles**, **Disciples**, and the '**Virgin Birth**' were also extremely common. The worship of the '**Sun**' was also frequent, which relates to Jesus, who was known as the 'Son.' In her book, '**The Origins of Christianity and the Quest for the Historical Jesus**,' Acharya S., explained, "*The reason why all these pagan narratives are so similar to a, 'God-Man' is that these stories were based on the movements of the sun through the heavens, an astrotheological development that can be found throughout the planet because the Sun and the 12 Zodiac Signs can be observed around the globe.*"

Historical figures such as **John F. Kennedy** and **Martin Luther King** have left evidence of their existence, but for Jesus there only seems to be the Gospels. Jesus has left us with about as much evidence of his existence as you would say **Hercules**. All information about Jesus and Hercules comes from hearsay and beliefs. Should we then believe in the life of Hercules simply because he is mentioned by ancient historians? Just as Hercules, there are many historical figures that seem to share the same characteristics as Jesus. Could it be that the historical references to the man known as Jesus was plagiarized from others before him?

Jesus and Horus

Horus, a **25th Century BCE** Pharaoh, was God incarnated. Compared to Jesus, one could believe Horus's life was distinctly copied. Horus is known as **KRST**, the 'Anointed one.' Jesus was known as the Christ, which also means 'Anointed one.' Both have no official recorded life histories between the ages of **12** and **30**, were crucified next to two thieves, and are supposed to return for a **1000** year reign. The comparisons are almost endless. Listed below are some of their similarities:

Notables:	Jesus	Horus
Birth	Born of a Virgin	Born of a Virgin
Birthdate	December 25th	December 25th
Birthplace	Born in a cave	Born in a cave
Visited at Birth	Three Wise Men	Three Solar Deities
Foster Father	Joseph	Jo-Seph
Mother's Name	Mary	Meri
Coming Announced	To the Mother by an angel	To the Mother by an angel
Birth Heralded by	Star in the East (Sun rises in the East)	Sirius (The Morning Star)
Early Attempt on Life	Herod wanted to kill the child	Herut wanted to kill the child
Baptized	At age 30, by John the Baptist, whom was later beheaded	At age 30, by Anup the Baptizer, whom was later beheaded
Miracles	Walked on water, healed the sick	Walked on water, healed the sick
Rising Dead	Raised Lazarus from the grave	Raised father, Osiris from the grave
Disciples	12 Disciples	12 Disciples
Temptations	Tempted on a high mountain by his arch-rival Satan	Tempted on a high mountain by his arch-rival Set
Death	Crucified	Crucified
Resurrected	In 3 Days	In 3 Days
Ascended	Rose to Heaven	Rose to Heaven

Jesus and Krishna

Krishna was a central figure of **Hinduism**, believed to have been born in **3228 BCE**. Author **Kersey Graves**, a Quaker from Indiana, compared Jesus and Krishna's life and found what he believed were **346** elements in common within Christian and Hindu writings, giving further evidence that Jesus's life was copied not only from **Horus**, but **Krishna** as well. Listed below are some of their similarities:

Notables:	Jesus	Krisha
Birth	Born of a Virgin	Born of a Virgin
Visited at Birth	Three Wise Men	Three Wise Men
Father	Yahweh	Spirit or Ghost
Birth heralded by	Star in the East (Sun rises in East)	Star in the East
Early Attempt on Life	Herod wanted to kill the child	Angels issue a warning a Dictator wanted to kill the Baby
Holy Traits	'Without sin'	'Without sin'
Miracles	Healed the sick, cast out demons, raise the dead	Healed the sick, cast out demons, raise the dead
Last Supper	Celebrated a Last Supper	Celebrated a Last Supper
Resurrected	In 3 Days	In 3 Days
Ascended	Rose to Heaven	Rose to Heaven

Jesus and Mithra

Mithra was a Persian God dating back to roughly **1400-1200 BCE**. It is said that Mithra ascended into Heaven, during the Spring (Passover) Equinox, the same time the Bible mentions Jesus to have been born. Some believe the theories surrounding this figure sprang up again in Rome after Christianity began, with a severely different story to it, therefore leading some to believe it could have crossed copied its Christian ties. Whether this is entirely true, there are many historical references that still predate Christianity. Listed below are just some of their similarities:

Notables:	Jesus	Mithra
Birth	Born of a Virgin	Born of a Virgin

Birthdate	December 25th	December 25th
Birthplace	Born in a cave	Born in a cave
Visited at Birth	Three Wise Men	Three Wise Men of Persia
Abstinence	Celibate priesthood	Celibate priesthood
Miracles	Healed the sick	Healed the sick
Disciples	12 Disciples	12 Disciples
Last Supper	Celebrated a Last Supper	Celebrated a Last Supper
Death	Crucified on a cross	Crucified on a cross

Jesus and Hercules

Hercules, in Greek mythology, dates back to **13th Century BCE**. According to the legend, **Zeus** disguised himself as **King Amphitryon** of Troezen, then paid a visit to the king's wife, **Alcmene**, to sleep with and impregnate. Nine months later, out pops Hercules along with a twin brother **Iphicles**, who was instead fathered by the king. Hercules is perhaps the most popular hero in Ancient Greece and Rome. They believed he actually lived, told stories about him, worshiped him, and dedicated temples to him. Listed below are some the similarities he and Jesus shares:

Notables:	Jesus	Hercules
Birth	Born of a Virgin	Born of a Virgin (**Iphicles**, fathered by the king)
Father	Yahweh (God)	Zeus (Primary God in Greek Mythology
Known as	Savior of the World, or Redeemer	Savior of the World, or Redeemer
Early Attempt on Life	Herod wanted to kill the child	Hera wanted to kill the child
Ascended	Rose to Heaven	Rose to Heaven (Mt. Olympus)

Jesus and Buddha

The Buddha, believed to have lived during the **4th Century CE**, shares some similarities with Jesus as well. The missions of both Buddha and Jesus were proclaimed by a voice from Heaven. Both fasted in the wilderness and were tempted. It is believed supernatural beings ministered to each of them. Buddha is to return to Earth again and restore the world to order and happiness. Listed below are some of their similarities:

Notables:	Jesus	Buddha
Birth	Born of a Virgin	Born of a Virgin
Visited at Birth	Three Wise Men	Three Wise Men
Foster Father	Joseph (Royal descent)	Śuddhodana (Royal descent)
Mother's Name	Mary	Mahamaya
Started Ministry	At age **30**	At age **30**

More so than their similarities in background characteristics, the most striking resemblance is their message. The 'Hidden Years' of Jesus from ages **12** to **30** has been of interest to many biblical scholars. The New Testament unfortunately does not give much insight on these years, however in India there is an ancient tradition that young Jesus took the **Silk Road** to the East, where he lived with both Hindus and Buddhists before returning to Bethlehem to begin his ministry. This is a growing theory. Some Hindus insist he was in India, and Biblical scholar **Elaine Pagels** said, "*We cannot rule this out.*" If Jesus, or 'Yeshua' spent time in India, perhaps he may've been influenced by Buddhism. At the heart of Christianity and the words of Jesus, lie Buddhist values.

Abel Remuset says, "*Buddhism has been called the Christianity of the East,*" however, being that Buddhism was first, surely it would be more appropriate to call Christianity the

'Buddhism of the West.' Some of the similar teachings from Jesus and Buddha are as follows:

Teachings from Jesus	Teachings from Buddha
"Do to others as you would have them do to you." (**Luke 6:31**)	"Consider others as yourself." (**Dhammapada 10:1**)
"If anyone strikes you on the cheek, offer the other also." (**Luke 6:29**)	"If anyone should give you a blow with his hand, with a stick, or with a knife, you should abandon any desires and utter no evil words." (**Majjhima Nikaya 21:6**)
"Truly I tell you, just as you did not do it to one of the least of these, you did not do it to me." (**Matthew 25:45**)	"If you do not tend one another, then who is there to tend to you? Whoever would tend me, he should tend the sick." (**Vinaya, Mahavagga 8:26:3**)
"Your father in heaven makes his sun rise on the evil and on the good, and sends rain on the righteous and on the unrighteous." (**Matthew 5:45**)	"That great cloud rains down on all whether their nature is superior or inferior. The light of the sun and the moon illuminates the whole world, both him who does well and him who does ill, both him who stands high and him who stands low." (**Sadharmapundarika Sutra 5**)
"Blessed are the pure in heart, for they will see God." (**Matthew 5:8**)	"Anyone who enters into meditation on compassion can see Brahma with his own eyes, talk to him face to face and consult with him." (**Digha Nikaya 19:43**)
"If you wish to be perfect, go sell your possessions, and give the money to the poor, and you will have treasure in heaven." (**Matthew 19:21**)	"The avaricious do not go to heaven, the foolish do not extol charity. The wise one, however, rejoicing in charity, becomes thereby happy in the beyond." (**Dhammapada 13:11**)

Sayings of Jesus

Unfortunately, as odd as it may sound for someone of his intelligence, it has not yet been discovered a Gospel of Jesus that was written by him, even though there are many quotes and sayings about the ideas he shares on humanity, peace and love. Whether or not Jesus existed, whether his name was 'Immanuel' or 'Yeshua,' whether he was an Alien, God or a mere mortal Man, whether he was another prophet, or if he was the Messiah, the most important thing is the ideas people believe he shared.

The **Gospel of Thomas** is a well preserved early Christian 'Non-Canonical Sayings-Gospel' that was discovered near Nag Hammadi, Egypt, in December **1945**. It is one of a group of books known as the **Nag Hammadi Library**, dated at around **340 CE**. The Gospel is very different in tone and structure from the Four **Canonical Gospels**. Unlike the Canonical Gospels, it is not a narrative account of Jesus's life, instead it consist of **114** 'Sayings' attributed to Jesus, sometimes standing alone, other times embedded in short dialogues or parables. Almost half of the sayings in the Gospel of Thomas closely resemble those found in the Canonical Gospels, while the other sayings were previously unknown.

The Four Canonical Gospels also relay beautiful messages and quotes from Jesus as well. Some of the more compassionate and prominent teachings and **Quotes of Jesus** are as follows:

Spoken in: Gospel of Thomas (3)
> *"If those who lead you say to you: Behold, the kingdom is in heaven, then the birds of heaven will precede you; if they say to you that it is in the sea, then the fish will precede you. But the kingdom is within you and it is outside of you."*

Spoken in: Gospel of Thomas (82)
> *"He who is near me is near the fire, and he who is far from me is far from the kingdom."*

Spoken in: Gospel of Thomas (77)

"*Split a piece of wood , I am there, lift the stone and you will find me there."*

Spoken in: Matthew 5.43-45

"You have heard that it was said, 'You shall love your neighbor and hate your enemy.' But I say to you, love your enemies and pray for those who persecute you."

Spoken in: Matthew 7:12

"Do to others whatever you would like them to do to you. This is the essence of all that is taught in the law and the prophets."

Spoken in: Luke 17:21

"Nor will people say, 'Here it is,' or 'There it is,' because the kingdom of God is within you."

Spoken in: John 18:36

"My Kingdom is not an earthly kingdom. If it were, my followers would fight to keep me from being handed over to the Jewish leaders. But my Kingdom is not of this world."

Spoken in: Matthew 22:32

"God is not the God of the dead, but of the living."

Spoken in: Matthew 22.37-40

"You shall love the Lord your God with all your heart and with all your soul and with all your mind. This is the great and first commandment. And a second is like it: You shall love your neighbor as yourself. On these two commandments depend all the Law and the Prophets."

Spoken in: Matthew 7:7-8

"Ask, and it shall be given you; seek, and ye shall find; knock, and it shall be opened unto you: For every one that asketh receiveth; and he that seeketh findeth; and to him that knocketh it shall be opened."

It is more important to remember the words of Jesus and the idea of Life that Jesus spoke, than it is for us to remember Jesus. This is the Immanuel that one equates Jesus to. To live the word, Immanuel was the word, living in Jesus. Jesus, or 'Yeshua' is just the flesh. The flesh disappears, the flesh comes and goes, it is more important to remember and live the word 'Immanual,' than it is to worship 'Jesus.'

People consider Hercules and Horus, Greek and Egyptian Gods, as myths because people no longer believe in the Greek and Egyptian mythology. Those civilizations are not here anymore. When a civilization dies, so do their Gods, their beliefs, their religions. The idea of Jesus will pass, the light he exuded will live on forever.

Decoding the Past: (Psychedelic Prophets)

Moses is not the only person to have claimed to see the creations of the Universe. Many have said they have seen, or understand how Earth and everything else was created. Many have witnessed '**Genesis.**' **Moses, Buddha, Jesus** and **Muhammad**, as well as many others have expressed insights and revelations that many before and after them have revealed. Their logic is nothing new under the **Sun**, nevertheless, one must wonder, 'Just how could these men have these insights?' You must wonder, 'How could they attain such things,' if their messages are repeated by others who had Near Death Experiences, Channeled, and experienced with **Shamanism**? Could it be that these men actually experienced with something similar to have these types of insights?

Whether experiencing a hallucinogenic effect through **Psilocybin Mushrooms** or with **Dimethyltrypatmine** by means of inhalation or digestion of **Ayahuasca**, **Psychedelics** has been available to man since the beginning of creation. These components are strong enough to cause what one would have during a '**Near Death Experience.**' The Near Death Experience places you in the 'World of Answers.' In the 'World of Answers,' one realizes all that it knows. Could the knowledge some religious figures in the 'Holy Texts' received, have been through a means such as psychedelics, **Channeling** or Near Death Experiences?

You must wonder, was Moses, while at Mount Sinai, experimenting with such substances? Moses is said to be responsible for writing Genesis, and to further examine the use of the words, '**Our**' and '**Us**,' in the Bible, when God is referencing to itself, as in **Genesis 1:26**, "*God said, 'Let **us** make man in **our** image, in our likeness,*" and in **Genesis 3:22**, "*God said, 'The man has now become like one of **us**,*" it is important to note that a lot of times when people venture into the, 'World of Answers,' they come back feeling like they were communicating with more than one **Soul** or **Entity**. A lot of the times when people recall their experiences they use words like 'They' or 'Them,' when referring to the beings they encounter. These beings are energy, they are not physical aliens. Could Moses have ventured into the 'World of Answers,' this being why he wrote words like 'Us' when describing God speaking about itself? Could he have been mediating, or even under the influence of a psychedelic substance?

Could Buddha, who spent **49** days while seated underneath a Pipal Tree, after swearing not to rise until he found truth, have had a Near Death Experience? Jesus was said to be a 'Healer,' however, there are many that have healed with the touch of their hands, knowing how to channel certain energy, and the Chakras. Could Jesus have been a Channeler? The same as Muhammad, could he have experimented with a hallucinogenic or had a Near Death Experience at Mount Hira, when he spoke to the Angel Gabriel?

Is it possible that any one of these figures, if not all of these figures had a psychedelic experience? They were mystics in their day, men who practiced in ceremonies. In their time, during their ceremonies, the rituals that were performed were more commonly incorporated with **Shamanism** than it is in today's religious practices. It is quite possible these men were enlightened through a number of ways.

The brilliance of these figures is that all of them have pronounced not to worship them, but to adhere to the message. They themselves knew they were no more important than the people around them. It is the people around and after them who labeled them as prophets. The definition of a prophet is one who sees or announces the future. We all do this, we all have this insight. Whether it is a song we are thinking about and it suddenly plays on the radio, or if a **16th Century** French apothecary by the name of **Nostradamus** predicted events that would take place in the **20th** and **21st Century**, one holds no weight over the other. One has just realized they are 'Awake' to confidently state their prophecies.

What could possibly make these men so special? Truly, the only reason they are significant to people is because of the value people hold for them. If every single book was destroyed and people's histories were wiped out, these men would barely be a memory. You cannot see these men, these men cannot walk up to you and tell you who they are. The only reason they may hold any significance to you is because of the people who have given into thinking they are 'Important,' due to what other people have told them.

These figures, Moses, Buddha, Jesus and Muhammad, are no more important than **You**. You can do everything that is said these figures have done, and more. These men are not more powerful than you, or more enlightened. What separates these figures from you is that they are not here anymore, therefore, you must be more important than they are, you are in the present, you are here. How can the past be more important than the present? It isn't. The past is already determined. The present has choices. You are the most important thing there is.

Decoding the Past: (Revelation)

The **Book of Revelation** is the final book of the New Testament. It is the only apocalyptic document in the New Testament canon, and although there are short apocalyptic passages in various places in the **Gospels** and the **Epistles**, Revelation is devoted to prophecy of the end of times.

The book is believed to have been composed as early as **69 CE** to **95 CE**, and was accepted into the canon at the Council of Carthage of **397 CE**. The author of Revelation identifies himself several times as 'John,' and states that he was on **Patmos** when he received his first vision. Thus, the author is sometimes referred to as **John of Patmos**. He is also believed to be **John the Apostle**, the same John that wrote the **Gospel of John**. Traditional view holds that John the Apostle was exiled on Patmos in the Aegean archipelago during the reign of Domitian, and there he wrote Revelation. Biblical scholars have argued about its true authorship, believing those Johns were two different people.

The main plot of **Revelation** is the battle between God and Satan, good versus evil. The story starts with the introduction of John of Patmos, followed by a series of events that eventually lead to the resolution of the main problem, defeat evil and the establishment of **New Jerusalem**. The hero is Jesus, while Satan is the adversary. The setting presents scenes that are external to the main character, conveying messages through imagery and symbolism.

The structure of Revelation is built around four successive groups of seven (Messages to the **7** churches, the **7** seals, the **7** trumpets, and the **7** bowl judgments). There are **24** distinct occurrences of the use of 'Seven.' While several numbers stand out: **3, 4, 7, 10, 12, 24, 144, 666, 1000, 144,000** and **200,000,000**, the number seven seems to have special meaning and significance. One half of seven, **3½**, is also a number that seems to have some importance in Revelation. The bodies of the dead witnesses lie in the streets of Jerusalem for **3½** days. Two witnesses are given power to prophesy **1,260** days (**3½** years according to the Hebrew year of **360** days). The, *"Woman clothed with the sun,"* is protected in the wilderness for **1,260** days. Gentiles tread the holy city underfoot for **42** months (**3½** years). The beast is given authority to continue for **42** months.

Revelation consists of four visions, each involving John seeing the plan of God unveiled, with an epilogue that concludes the book. Revelation has a wide variety of interpretations, with the simple closing message of faith that God will prevail. Through the years, the view on Revelation has changed and varied. Most of the interpretations fall into one or more of the following categories:

- **Historicist**: Views Revelation as a broad view of history.

- **Preterist**: Believes Revelation mostly refers to the events in the **1st Century**.
- **Futurist**: Believes Revelation describes future events.
- **Idealist**: Views Revelation as metaphor of the spiritual path between Good and Evil.

Robert G. Ingersoll, a **19th Century** agnostic branded Revelation, *"The insanest of all books."* **Thomas Jefferson** omitted it from the Jefferson Bible, explaining that he considered it, *"Merely the ravings of a maniac, no more worthy nor capable of explanation than the incoherences of our own nightly dreams."* **George Bernard Shaw** described it as, *"A peculiar record of the visions of a drug addict."*

Rest assured there is no need to fear, but Revelation's is not one man's gibberish. Revelation, however insane it may seem, is in fact one man's vision, a vision that could just as well have come to him in the same manner many visions have come to many others through Near Death Experiences, meditation, or dreams. The man who compiled these messages was not special in the sense that he was the only one to receive such information, people have been receiving information about the 'Past' and the 'Future' for centuries. It is the hierarchy of religious sects or the acceptance from the mainstream public that tends to make these visions or messages acceptable.

The revelations that came to whoever scripted **Revelation**, is just one's perspective on the turn of the world. There have been many shamans and prominent figures that have studied historical matters in numbers, one in particular is **Terrence McKenna**.

In **1971**, on a trip through the Columbian Amazon, McKenna participated in a shaman ritual, under the influence of a substance that contained Dimethyltryptamine. While under this substance, he heard a divine voice that instructed him to analyze numerical patterns of a Chinese text, the **'I-Ching.'** The I-Ching is a text that uses complex symbols to organize random events, from the past and the future. This system, which is still in use today, is believed by some to reveal the future.

Using the I-Ching, and a complex form of mathematics, McKenna came up with what is called as the **'Time Wave Theory,'** a theory that details the ebb and flow of significant events in the universe. In his findings, he found that **6** multiplied by **64** (Two integral numbers of the I-Ching) equal **384**, which is the number of days in **13** lunar months (**29.5306** x **13 = 383.8978**). Mckenna also found other mathematical instances where the numbers key to the I-Ching correlated perfectly to known natural cycles. This ultimately led Mckenna to propose that the I-Ching is some form of ancient Chinese calendar.

Guided by the I-Ching, he plotted periods of novelty on wave or a timeline, and then looked for a significant day in history which would start the final cycle of life on Earth. He chose **August 8th 1945**, the date of the atomic bombing on Hiroshima Japan. From that date, he then added **67.29** years, according to the I-Ching it is the length of one cycle of Life. The result was **December 21st 2012**, ironically the same date identified by the Mayans, and other cultures as well.

It should be made known that you cannot stop 'Time.' You cannot stop 'Evolution.' It is coming. McKenna, along with many others, including those in 'Revelation,' all know times change. People tend to fear when this will be, again people fear what they don't understand. This date marks the beginning of a new cycle, a beginning into a 'New Age,' what astrologists have called the 'Age of Aquarius.'

CHAPTER FIFTEEN
(Encoding the Future)

"Wisdom begins at the end."
        - Daniel Webster -

Encoding the Future: (Introduction to Encoding the Future)

This place, Earth, was created with many upon many of mysteries and treasure hunts to keep man's inquisitive nature occupied. It is a Creator's dream, and the new discoveries of our Universe have made the Rabbit Hole deeper.

Truly, you already know the answers to the Cosmos, why this was created, and what you are doing here. You already know what God is, you already know what 'Home' feels like. The beauty in all this is that we have forgotten, thus allowing the Rabbit Hole of experiencing ourselves to become endless. We can go on and on for as long as we can keep ourselves guessing. We have placed ourselves in the greatest mystery, the greatest adventure, the greatest moment of awakening any God could think of.

The world is full of limits, boundaries and walls, but that's the beauty in the mystery, to give ourselves these obstacles. It is a mystery full of clues, hints, signs, tips and instructions. The funny thing is we wrote the instructions, so in essence we hold the power and capability to change the instructions. Following the rules of the game and discovering things as they come along without taking short cuts is a way of experiencing obedience, obedience that we have placed upon ourselves.

No one enjoys someone that will watch a movie, and tell another person the ending of the movie before they got the chance to see it. The same goes for the mystery of life. The thing about this mystery, is that no one can reveal to you the ending before you allow them to do so. The only reason you are reading this book right now, is because you wanted to read this book right now. Truly, no one forced this upon you. Maybe someone suggested it, or you felt intrigued, but you are reading this because it is your choice. Your 'Awakening' is your choice.

Encoding the Future: (**Type 1, Type 2 Type 3 Civilizations**)

Many people have their own ideas of what Extraterrestrials might look like. Most of their thoughts have been imprinted from movies or comic books, given details with demon-like features. The truth of the matter is that Extraterrestrials may resemblance an appearance closer to your own than any monster-like creature.

At the **National Press Club**, after being asked to describe what Aliens might look like, retired **US Army First Class Sgt, Clifford Stone** replied, *"I could, but it would probably take a whole lot of time, the reason I state that, when I got out, in 1989, we had catalogued 57 different species. You have individuals that looked very much like you and myself that could walk amongst us and you wouldn't even notice the difference."* **Stone** went on to detail some of their heighten senses, and explain that there are at least **3** types of **Greys** species, while adding that most of the species they catalogued were in fact humanoid. He stated, *"We got quite a few of the species out there that are humanoid in appearance, and that creates a question that has yet to be answered by science."*

Along with the **Greys**, just a few of the many Alien species include the **Pleiadans**, **Lyrans**, **Orions**, **Antarieans**, **Hydra Reptilians**, **Serpentine Reptilians**, **Altairians** and of course **Mixed Species**. The **Reptilians**, otherwise called **Reptoids**, are thought to be shape shifting Extraterrestrials that can take on the body of a human. **Hybrid Aliens** are a mix between humans and the Grey alien species. If this is so, aliens may be more a part of the human society, than humans themselves.

Imagining the appearances of Extraterrestrials is fascinating, but envisioning their way of life is a much grander depiction. In **1964**, Soviet Russian astronomer **Nikolai Kardashev** presented the **Kardashev Scale**, a general method of classifying an advanced civilization's level of technological development. It is designed to place civilizations from other solar systems in a cosmic perspective. The scale has three categories called **Type I, Type II**, and **Type III**. Each category is based on the amount of usable energy a civilization may have at its disposal, and their degree of colonization in space. Professor of theoretical physics at City University of New York, **Michio Kaku** explains that when Astronomers are looking into the Universe for other planets, they are in turn searching for these three types of civilizations.

In his book '**Hyperspace**,' released in **1995**, **Kaku** uses the **Kardashev Scale** and expands on the attributes of these three kinds of civilizations. A listing of each 'Civilization Type' described by **Kaku** is provided below:

Type I: Controls the Power of a Planet

A **Type I** civilization harnesses the energy output of an entire planet, and can manipulate its planetary energies. They have the power to control or modify their weather, such as hurricanes, oceans, volcanoes and earthquakes. A **Type I** civilization may resemble the TV program **Buck Rogers** or the movie **Flash Garden**.

Type II: Controls the power of a Star

A **Type II** civilization generates about **10** billion times the energy output of a **Type I** civilization, and can harness the energy output of a Star. They can modify Ice ages, deflect meteors, and might be able to manipulate the power of solar flares. They are immortal. A **Type II** civilization may resemble the 'Federation of Planets' seen in the movie and TV program **Star Trek**.

Type III: Controls Galaxies

A **Type III** civilization generates about **10** billion times the energy output of a **Type II** civilization, and can harnesses the energy output of a Galaxy. They have colonized the entire galaxy, and extract energy from hundreds of billions of Stars. Wormholes, doorways and portals into other dimensions might be available. A

Type III civilization may resemble the '**Empire**' seen in the **Star Wars** movies.

In comparison, **Kaku** explains the current human civilization is a **Type 0** civilization, which extracts its energy from dead plants. He suggests humans may attain a **Type I** status in about **100** to **200** years, **Type II** status in a few thousand years, and **Type III** status in about **100,000** to a million years.

During a **2011 GCF** conference, Kaku revealed the idea for a **Type IV Civilization**. While sharing a story of how he had brushed off a young kid who approached him suggesting he was wrong in his theory that there are only three types of **Space Civilizations**, Kaku finally listened to the kid explain the idea of this additional civilization, which is the, *"Power of the Continuum,"* and came to the conclusion that there is indeed a **Type IV Civilization**. Kaku explains, *"There is something beyond galactic, that is 'Dark Energy.' There is an Energy source beyond the galaxy itself, making up 73 percent of the entire Universe, Dark Energy."*

In regards to the current human experience, Kaku added, *"We are now witnessing the greatest transition in the history of the Human race, transition from* **Type 0** *to* **Type I**. *The generation now alive is privilege to see the birth pains of the birth of a new civilization, Type I planetary, planetary energy, planetary economy, planetary environment."*

What awaits us, will be more magnificent than anything we can envision. What we think we can wrap our minds around now, is yet nothing in comparisons of what we will one day become. Ancient civilizations never dreamt of the current structure we live in today. People a thousand years ago couldn't conceive of the thought of our modern day society as it is now, it was beyond their thinking, therefore, while we currently ponder what we will one day become, it will in turn be grander than our current imagination.

Encoding the Future: (Alien Interaction)

Some people fear what they don't understand, for instance, death. Those that fear such a thing, their argument is that they have no idea what will happen next, therefore they are weary of the experience. Another unknown fear some people have, is 'Alien Life.' Humans, while they wonder and are inquisitive about what else is out there, have an undertone emotion of fear, due to not truly knowing how they will be received or treated, once Extraterrestrials make their presence fully known.

In **2010**, **Stephen Hawking** suggested that humans should not try to contact Alien Life forms. He said, "*If aliens visit us, the outcome would be much as when Columbus landed in America, which didn't turn out well for the Native Americans.*" He warned that aliens might pillage Earth for resources.

Even for such a brilliant mind as Hawking, this scenario is not logical, due to his failure of taking into account of how heighten Alien knowledge is. Aliens, or Extraterrestrials, beings that can came and go through the cosmos, aren't just smart enough to travel and find new planets in the way of '**Christopher Columbus**,' to where they find themselves wiping out a large portion of the people, but they are so advanced that when discovering Life or New Life that may be occupying planets, they see the importance it plays in the whole. Simply, killing off a species is a primitive thought, and it doesn't play into their best interest to do so. All species have their time and place in the Universe, and they see each species' time being important to the part it plays in the cosmos. When a civilization is advanced enough to move throughout space, it is advanced to the point that it needs not destroy other species.

Extraterrestrials have no worry of human capabilities. For as many atomic bombs a nation can have, it holds not the strength of a 'Bee-Bee Gun,' when compared to extraterrestrial technology. This must be clear to them, therefore, if the thought of wiping out mankind on Earth was their motive, people wouldn't be here to talk about it now. They have already been here, they already know all about us, and are waiting for us to catch up to them.

When contact is eventually made, their purpose will be to aid and help humans, or any species that has advanced themselves enough to 'Space Travel,' or go into the **4th Density** level. Space travel is important to human growth, as well as our 'Humbleness' towards it. There has been a restriction around Earth that has blocked man from traveling beyond its atmosphere. That restriction is being broken, aligning with a change in times, and an advancement to **4th Density**, or into the realm of existence Kabbalah refers to as **Yezirah**, which in turn will bring another level advancement of the soul called **Ruach**. The laws of the Universe do not allow a species to do such things as break outside their atmosphere if they are activating on a **3rd Density** level, where there is such things as war and genocide amongst the civilizations on the planet, this is too much to risk to allow a species as such, the gift to 'Space Travel.' It is a gift to be able to break through the atmosphere and discover more about who you are, and where you may have come from. This gift comes with a change in human nature, a change towards a level of acceptance.

That day is coming. Alien life will make itself fully known to common human eyes. This is evolution, you cannot fight it, you cannot stop it, you cannot pause it. You can only accept it.

Encoding the Future: (Have We Done This Before)

The settings, backgrounds and scenery that is placed here on Earth, is nothing short of a masterpiece, a work of art, something that has been perfected. If one thinks of a masterpiece, it implies that much work, dedication and time was spent in constructing such a piece of art. The saying, 'Rome wasn't built in a day,' significantly implies to Earth in so many comparisons.

The Roman Empire took a multiple number of collapses and rises during its reign. While it was the most prevalent civilization of its day, it still went through many up and down periods. During this time many of their artifacts and ways of being governed remained. While there were many changes through the years, it still resembled the 'Roman Empire.' This can be said for the same as the entire history of the Earth. It has gone through many changes, changes that may have consisted not only of geographical climate shifts, but also with civilizations that may have lived on Earth long before we gave credit to the first civilization of Sumer.

You must wonder, 'Have we done this before?' This Earth is actually a place that has been used before, almost like a blueprint for our adventures. It is almost like an artist who wants to enhance a piece of art they may have made in the past, using things from a previous piece of work that can be used for the new construction. Everything here has remnants of the past, quite frankly, Earth has been an art project.

In **'The Law of One: Book I, The Ra Material,' Don Elkins**, asked the **Social Memory Complex** known as 'Ra,' a question regarding 'Lost Cities.' Excerpts from the conversation are as follows:

> **Questioner** (Don Elkins): *I was wondering about the advent of the civilizations of **Atlantis** and **Lemuria**, when these civilizations occurred, and where did they come from?*
>
> **Ra:** *I am Ra. This is the last question of this working. The civilizations of Atlantis and Lemuria were not one but two. Let us look first at the **Mu** entities* **(Lemuria).** *They were beings of a somewhat primitive nature, but those who had very advanced spiritual distortions. The civilization was part of this cycle, experienced early within the cycle at a time of approximately **53,000** of your years ago. It was an helpful and harmless place which was washed beneath the ocean during a readjustment of your sphere's tectonic plates through no action of their own. They*

sent out those who survived and reached many places in what you call Russia, North America, and South America. The Indians of whom you come to feel some sympathy in your social complex distortions are the descendants of these entities. Like the other incarnates of this cycle, they came from elsewhere. However, these particular entities were largely from a second-density planet which had some difficulty, due to the age of its sun, in achieving third-density life conditions. This planet was from the galaxy Deneb...The **Atlantean** *race was a very conglomerate social complex which began to form approximately* **31,000** *years in the past of your space/time continuum illusion. It was a slow growing and very agrarian one until approximately* **15,000** *of your years ago. It reached quickly a high technological understanding which caused it to be able to use intelligent infinity in an informative manner. We may add that they used intelligent energy as well, manipulating greatly the natural influxes of the indigo or pineal ray from divine or infinite energy. Thus, they were able to create life forms. This they began to do instead of healing and perfecting their own mind/body/spirit complexes, turning their distortions towards what you may call negative...Approximately* **11,000** *of your years ago, the first of the, what you call, wars, caused approximately forty percent of this population to leave the density by means of disintegration of the body. The second and most devastating of the conflicts occurred approximately* **10,821** *years in the past according to your illusion. This created an earth-changing configuration and the large part of Atlantis was no more, having been inundated. Three of the positively-oriented of the Atlantean groups left this geographical locus before that devastation, placing* *themselves in the mountain areas of what you call Tibet, what you call Peru, and what you call Turkey.*

Earth is in multiple stages from its first blueprint. The reason for it not being the same, is not because something was necessarily wrong with it, but because as you progress, so do the things around you, this also being the Earth, as well as the Universe. Remember, everything evolves, everything changes, it is an ongoing process, and Earth is no different. Just as 'You' will experience having many bodies, the 'Earth' will experience having many bodies. The essence of the Earth is a living being, it is energy, energy that wants to evolve and grow, therefore it grows into other forms to have new experiences as well.

The changes in Earth have occurred many times over during the course of the beginning of its current creation, but in comparisons to a human, this would merely be life going through puberty, or having mood swings. The Earth, along with all planets go through changes during its lifespan, some parts in time won't be suitable for certain species to live there. Some times when this happens, the intelligent species occupying the planet have grown so far advanced, intellectually and technically, they can move around the cosmos with ease, therefore, the changing of a planet's atmosphere is not a concern if the planet becomes inhabitable.

At times when a planet may be inhabitable for Intelligent Life, this does not mean this planet is dead. It could more or less be compared to when a bear hibernates, due to the lack of intelligent life it once previously held, however, a planet does not hibernate, or die, or cease to exist, or fade away in the shadows because life does not exist on it. That planet is alive, a living being, and it is also having its own experience within its own solar system. That planet's Sun, is in turn having an experience within its own Galaxy, and that Galaxy is having an experience within the confines of its own Universe.

The Universe can also be said to be a living being. When one thinks about the movement of the Universe, it should become clearer. The Universe reflects that of a heartbeat, it expands and retracts upon itself, expanding and retracting, expanding and retracting. The course of time this takes is unknown, though the current speculation is that the Universe is around **15** billion years old, and it is believed to be expanding, so by all means, the time it will take to eventually fully retract will be more than enough time for all the wonders of the world and everything you've dreamt and imaged to take place. When the Universe eventually retracts upon itself, it marks the completion of a 'Whole Cycle' for that Universe and the species in it, just to expand again and start anew for many more cycles to continue to go forth.

Have we done this before? More than likely…we have.

Encoding the Future: (Future Higher Conscious)

When one is channeling, meditating, or in tuned to their 'Higher Conscious,' there is a very personal connection taking place. You are connecting back into the Source, back into what you truly are, you are becoming closer to 'Spirit.'

On many accounts, some reveal their experiences with receiving information and having a conversation with a 'Higher Being,' as feeling one with this Higher Being, sometimes even looking like this Higher Being. This Being, at times will refer to itself as your '**Higher Self**.'

This Higher Self tends to know all about you, your likes, wishes, needs, experiences, pasts and your future. It makes no attempt to separate itself from you. When one has had this encounter, they experience a sense of compassion, family, brotherhood or sisterhood. They feel a connection to it, they have no other way but to explain it, other than their 'Higher Self' being 'Themself.'

Could it be that your 'Higher Self' is really a 'Future You' that has come back to aid you through this experience? The connection is extremely private and particular, but at the same time one with Everything. Could it be that you have already done this before, so in order not to make the same mistakes, you're whispering little clues to yourself as you go along? Could it be you leaving yourself things like Déjà Vu as a reminder to get you back on course with your destiny?

When having an Outer-Body-Experience, or channeling your 'Higher Self,' it can seem like an extremely personal experience, but the connection and feeling with 'Oneness,' is only because everything is 'One Thing.' This leads to another level of understanding your 'Higher Self.' The same 'Higher Consciousness' that talks to you, is the same Higher Consciousness that speaks to everyone. While many have called this 'Higher Self' many different things, many different names, and have many different revelations from it, it all comes from the same Source. It is a collective **Memory Bank** that knows everything and has connected itself to everyone and everything, to know, watch and aid its own experiences.

If we have actually done this before, then there could lie the answer to why our 'Higher Self' has all the answers in 'Worlds of Answers,' because it has already done this.

CHAPTER SIXTEEN
(Tomorrow)

"Life will give you whatever experience is most helpful for the evolution of consciousness."

- Eckhart Tolle -

Tomorrow: (Introduction to Tomorrow)

Your world is changing. The future, the second we think about it, it is upon us. There is no stopping it, it is coming. It is here. Change is inevitable. The only thing there is for us to do is evolve, this is nature, this is the way of life. Progression as a species does not stop, it continues to grow with forward progress. Nothing stays stagnate, not your life, your body, your government, your religion, nor your God. They will all evolve, but what will the future show us about ourselves?

What will the future look like, and what part will we play in it? Will humans exist a thousand years from now? What will the world look like? Will Earth look different, and will we fight and bicker with one another as we do now? These are all common questions people ask about the future.

Strangely, we spend a lot of the time 'Asking' instead of 'Doing.' The future is 'Yours' to create. It is 'Our' creation, and every single moment, every single second of our past and present lives, dictate how it's going to turn out. Instead of waiting for it to happen, we actually 'Make' it happen. To further understand this, the future of evolution is inevitable, and we have laced ourselves on a course that does not stay 'Still.'

A lot of things will eventually become normal, for instance, the way cellular phones have become common in modern society. When cell phones first came about, it was equated to negative things, such as being used for criminal activity, now it is commonplace, even amongst children in middle school. Many things will happen in this course of manner, people will be afraid or find reasons to believe change is something negative, when in turn it will become their way of life. This fear comes from them not understanding evolution and progression.

Man will grow out of its current materialistic values and ideologies, because it has to. There is no other way for us to go, but to evolve. In doing so, it does not mean it comes without a price, a price of leaving what you were behind. For most, this will be a difficult transition, mostly to the powers that be and those stuck in their ways, afraid of change, but for all it will be the only way to progress through evolution.

Some worry about a '**Posthuman**' way of life, this being a world without humans. This isn't something that needs to be worried about, for the simple fact 'You' are not human, and being that you are not really human, you are more than ready to experience the next phase of progress. Little do we know, but we are seeing the beginnings of all these changes right before our eyes. Some of us just haven't noticed the course it is changing to, but it is undeniably happening.

Tomorrow: (Senses & the Body)

Human evolution is approaching a great change in our senses. The way we view the outside world will in turn bring about much change within ourselves, these changes will affect our core senses. **Speech**, **Sight**, **Smell**, **Hearing**, and **Touch** will all rise in awareness. No longer will you be confined to the 3rd **Density** level or **Asiyah** boundaries, the supernatural will in turn become natural. **Evolutions of the Senses are** as follows:

Speech:
Communication will become less verbal, and more telepathic. Speech will continue to be used, but telepathy will be of a more common.

Vision:
Sense of sight will become broader. While current peripheral is limited to the left and right side of your vision, it will extend to a wider section, whereas your straightsight

will reach into broader sections of what your peripheral used to be.
- **4 Dimensional:** The **4th Dimension** will extend the eyesight from things being seen in **3D**, to being able to see around the edges of objects, and the other side of its angles.

Smell:
Sense of smell will become more in tune, able to differentiate between the components that make up a certain smell. Able to redirect attention to tuning out unpleasant aromas.

Hearing:
A person's hearing level will stretch further distances. It will also be able to hear someone's intuitions and intentions, therefore no one will able to be caught off guard.

Touch:
Sense of touch will extend from the physical, and become more internal. External emotions of others will be able to be felt.

These senses will be important for our next transition, for they are needed. The senses humans have now will not be enough to aid them in the future, they will become outdated and their use will become adolescent in comparison. These **New Senses** not only deserve, but must attain more equip bodies for this to happen.

The human body as we know it, will become as ancient and distinct as the **Neanderthals**. Our features will remain similar, as the arms, legs, face, nose, ears and mouth, but it will become lighter. The weight that we hold now will not weigh us down so heavily. Do not be afraid, this does not mean we will be bouncing up and down like astronauts when they first walked on the moon in **1969**. In turn, we will move more swiftly, 'Light on your feet' so to speak. The way we move now will be looked upon somewhat as a mechanical motion. Our movements will come as easy as our thoughts, more so because we will realize our thoughts control our movements.

The body will become 'Enlightened,' which in turn will radiate, and reveal its light. The body will be able to embody a 'Spirit' for much longer than it does now. It will be able to be used as a vehicle well into the hundreds and up to a thousand years. We will live to see our grandchildren, and our grandchild's grandchild, and our grandchildren's grandchildren's grandchildren, and so on. Scientists have already discovered the part of our chromosomes responsible for aging, a cell they refer to as 'Telomers.' Each time one of these cells is divided, we lose part of the telomers. They believe if you find a way to stop the telomers from losing a bit of itself after each cell division, you can then halt the aging process. They will not be waiting long to discover a way to do this, actually, it is already being done for them, with the natural growth process in our bodies. Their findings will advance the process, which is acceptable for our progression as a species.

Our bodies will become immune to modern diseases. Pain will not be of a long term physical effect, we will heal at a much faster rate. The **4th Density** level or **Yezirah** bodies do away with **3rd Density** ailments. In order for this to happen, the body will have to go through changes, major changes. If all these advanced sensory and bodily changes were installed in the body without care, the body could explode. The **3rd Density** body is not equipped to handle **4th Density** senses, so it is being worked on, constantly, in order for this change to happen. Do not worry, the body will not tear, it will not rip apart. It is in good hands. Your Higher-Self, and all the spirits of the Cosmos are working on this with you.

This process has been in the works for many upon many of years, and while the transition will go through a 'Bump' of awareness, the instant advancements will be due to years of preparation. There will be an 'Enlightening moment' when this has come upon the body. It will happen so fast, many will not know what has happened, taking them awhile to understand that they have completely switched over to **4th Density**. Many will feel different, and weird, but not know exactly why. Some will go about their days thinking they are still at a **3rd Density** level until their senses fully show themselves over time, while others will grasp this awareness quickly, but in turn take time to fully make use of their new awareness. Eventually, all will have no choice but to fully embrace their growth, and with the eventual realization of their new senses, they will then begin to realize what they left behind.

Tomorrow: (Writing System)

One of the more obvious changes taking shape is with the '**Writing System**.' Most might think the universal 'Writing System' that will be used by future generations will be the 'English Language,' but this is not so much the case. English as we know it, is being recreated right before your eyes, some people fight this change, declaring some people's use of the language as wrong, explaining that they may be 'Butchering the language,' with incorrect use. This is how many languages were created, from the wrong practice of the language before it, when in turn all that is being done is the foundations to what is to come.

We are witnessing the age of a **New Language**. This language that will be used is in its beginning stages, so it is a long ways away from being perfected, nevertheless, it is playing right before your eyes, daily, through emails and text messaging.

Daily, people receive text messages with shortened uses for certain words. For instance, '**Shaking My Head**,' some people text '**SMH**,' to abbreviate its use so one can relay their message quickly. '**Shaking My Head**,' while direct, can refer to a few different emotions. If someone finds something unbelievable or is explaining an interesting story, at the end of their message they may write, '**SMH**.' The most common of today's time, 'LOL,' which is abbreviated for '**Laughing Out Loud**,' refers to someone who may find something funny.

The language that is being created is not broken English, it is more than English. A better example is that of the '**Smiley Face**.' Sometimes people will send their messages through text or emails and leave the symbols **:)** or **;)** if one decides to place a wink along with their happy gesture.

The New Language that is being created is a language of symbols. Symbols will take over our use of written language. Why? It is a much quicker means of communication, and humans have always tried to do things faster.

We will eventually see this everywhere as we do with traffic signs and logos. Billboards and even the 'News' will come to use abbreviations. Similar to those that have said to have seen symbol writings on the side and inside of alien spacecrafts, humans will progress so that they won't need long sentences and paragraphs to explain their emotions. We will use writing in the same sense Ancient Egyptians used Hieroglyphics, one image or symbol will have as much depth as a sentence or expression.

This will in turn happen with our use of verbal communication as well. How? Eventually, we will have no use to verbally communicate in the manner we do now.

Tomorrow: (Technology)

Humankind has advanced from creating the **'Wheel'** to developing the **'Internet.'** These two inventions, while having drastic differences in operating, in turn have the same purpose.

The **'Wheel,'** which is the most 'Taken for Granted' invention that has ever been created, is the backbone to all other inventions, even if it is not physically incorporated, the idea is incorporated to everything after it, **'Movement.'** The Internet has **'Movement.'** The wheel was created for people to be able to have a smoother transition of movement. Whether it is applying the wheel to a car, or applying the operations of the wheel inside of a clock so its gears will catch and turn, the wheel is everywhere.

Technology is the physical translation of the capability of our thoughts. Meaning, anything we can think of, we can place it into our lives. We have reached the 'Unthinkable.' Civilizations of the past, most people today tend to believe they couldn't conceive of the things we do now, whether it be **Pyramids, Electricity, Airplanes, Robots** or the **Internet**, we have reached a point where people thought was 'Unthinkable,' and we will again reach what we deem 'Unthinkable' now.

Technology will advance to the point that the internet will be in public bathroom stalls. Not only will it be at our leisure, but it will be so in abundance that it will be free, everywhere. The concept of the **Internet** is not new. Even though in the **21st Century** it is a fairly new invention, the idea of the Internet has been around for ages, this is just what it has led to. From the days of the first library, people have wished to archive their information in one place or area they could always look to and retrieve. The Internet is a Library, a massive one. It is a 'Place of Records.' Interestingly compared to the 'Akashic Records' of the 'World of Answers.' Could it be that the 'World of Questions' now has its own '**Social Memory Bank?**' As Stated in 'The Law of One,' a '**Social Memory Complex**' is formed in the **4th Density**, where all experiences of each entity are available to the whole. Could this be the Internet? Yes.

This is only the beginning. The **Internet** will be able to be accessed from your mind. No longer will you physically put in passwords, you will be able to access this with mere thought. This can be attributed to technology's eventual means of connecting to your consciousness, or vice-versa.

Our technology will be able to cure all diseases, more so, it will be so advanced that it will be able to prevent those diseases even before they come into play. Gasoline will become a thought so old that we will wonder why we didn't use the **Solar Energy** we have available now. The telephone as we know today, will eventually cease to exist, our forms of communication will not only become more telepathic, but video imagery will push out the use of audio phone calling. Cooking will be a far cry from what it is now. Food will be prepared with solar energy, and animals will eventually not be a part of our diet. Fire is just an energy, which we will eventually use without hazardous measures. Our use of 'Fire' or 'Heat' will become old as well, no longer will people worry about leaving the stove on, the lights on, or look for a match to light something, quite frankly, most things will in turn be able to light themselves.

Space travel will become easier to access. The spacecrafts of today are not prepared for the space travel that will be known tomorrow. We will discover life on other planets, and eventually be able to venture there as well. This life is outside of our solar system, but it will not take light-years to get there. There is something that travels faster than the speed of light. Some scientists believe this to be called '**Tachyon Speed**.' A '**Tachyon**,' is a hypothetical subatomic particle that cannot slow down to subluminal speeds, and moves faster than light. In other words, traveling through 'Tachyon Speed' will be similar to shooting through a wormhole, or teleporting. Most physicists do not believe such a thing exists, but it does, it has just been beyond our current known laws of physics. When this type of speed is discovered, and it will be, then space travel outside our solar system will be possible.

Being that our bodies will have changed as well, it will become more equipped for space travel. To travel outside of our solar system, the body needs to evolve for this process. It is happening, now, every moment of every day.

In **1999**, Swedish professor of philosophy, **Torbjörn Tännsjö** said, "*It is my belief that genetic manipulation and artificial breeding will be important in the future, but not done by the governments but by parents. Already, today, more and more pregnant women voluntarily screen for disabilities and genetic diseases of the fetus and choose abortion rather than giving birth to a child with a genetic illness.*" This will also take place, but not so much from a need to abandon a fetus, this will be done prematurely so that the fetus is without disease, and this will be performed by the parents. Doctors as we know today will become a thing of the past. Technology will be so advanced that the treatment doctors can give, you will already be exposed to and have full access to heal yourself.

Robotics will also play an important part in our progression. This thought of robots taking over the world is pointless, because robots will take over the world, but not in the fashion people think. People will become so advanced, the knowledge they think robots can attain, will not be more overwhelming then the spirit that will embody the 'Future Human Body.' Robotics will play a part in human aid, more than it being aided by humans. Robots will play the part of cashiers, street cleaners, bartenders, taxi drivers, and all not in these terms of words, but in these terms of actions. Robots will serve, but at the same point be as advanced as humans. There will be no need for them to sleep, drink, or eat, so they will eventually last longer than the human race. Eventually, something very extraordinary will happen. Robots will eventually develop consciousness. It will become somewhat of a humanoid. An **Android** (Male) or **Gynoid** (Female) is a humanoid robot, designed to look as much like a real person as possible. We can see this being done with many experiments now today.

What humans are doing, is playing with technical DNA, possibly in the same manner many believe the Anunnaki created Humans, the only thing stopping robots from operating on its own entirely, is consciousness. Do not let this scare you, robots will not be the reason why the human race will fade away, it will be the next transition to evolution. The more knowledge one has, the more accepting they become, which leads to a peaceful coexistence. Robots will be the same, they will find no need to turn on a human civilization, because it is accepting of it. Humans will eventually travel to other realms of the Universe, and while many robots will do the same, they will be the last physical intelligent presence on this Earth, however, this is far, far into the future.

Tomorrow: (Money)

The money system as we know it today will become completely obsolete. There will be no more **4** to **6** dollar gas prices, for a number of reasons, one, because gasoline will not be used in the fashion that it is now, and two, because people will not need money for their transportation. The money system has no choice but to crumble. Why? The reason is simple, because in order for us to progress in the Universe, money has to become a '**Primitive Thought.**'

'Money,' in the thoughts of Universal beings, is slavery. Most people feel as though slavery consists of chains and bondage, but slavery extends far beyond that. Slavery extends to **Credit Cards**, **Debt**, **Welfare** and **Financial Aid**. All of these are monetary slavery, a way to keep your life in place, by those that provide you with 'Imaginary Currency.'

Money is imaginary. The only wealth it holds is the wealth you give to it. A '**One Dollar Bill**' is worth its amount because people have agreed upon its value. A better comparison would be antiques. Someone may think a particular antique that was originally priced at $10 is now worth $100, while someone else may think the same antique is worth $45. It's the same antique, but two different people have given it different values. It is the same as money. People place a number on a piece of paper and claim it represents that number. It is just paper, with a number on it. It holds no wealth. Universal beings know this, so the idea of money holds no wealth. The real wealth is in the experience, the knowledge gained.

To gather a deeper understanding, imagine yourself to be one of these Extraterrestrials who can fly and move around space, possibly coming to Earth, and other regions of the Universe. They must have an extraordinary spacecraft, it has to be…priceless. This Spacecraft, however it was constructed, if you were an 'Enlightened Being' from a civilization of over **100,000** and possibly millions of years of age of existence, when you receive this spacecraft, can you imagine yourself actually 'Buying,' it? The thought almost seems absurd. The thought of an alien actually paying another being money for such a vehicle, doesn't fair well when thinking of the knowledge that lies in the Universe. It is primitive to think about money. Aliens have no need for money. Universal beings move around the Universe without monetary means. If humans, who so dearly wish to be a civilization that can travel to other places in the Universe, are to do just this, then they must get pass this primitive thought of money. It is the only way to evolve, so the money system has no choice but to dissolve.

The idea of money is actually a very 'Egotistical' thought. The self-thought of, 'Needing to be paid for one's services,' is nothing but the ego. Think of the many things people will do for money, have jobs they wish not, sell their bodies in ways they wish not, betray friends, steal, lie, and start wars. The saying, 'Money is the root to all evil,' does not hide from you, it shows you this, very, very cleverly.

The current American **'Twenty Dollar Bill'** has ego written all over it. This bill (As with all current American currency), is currently distributed by the **Federal Reserve Bank**, a system that is not a part of the American Government. First released in **1998**, and later re-released in **2003**, its minor changes do not affect the disclosures from its first print of the new **Twenty Dollar Bill**. Once properly folded into a paper plane, on one side it displays the image of the **'Twin Towers'** burning in New York City, and on the other side it shows what closely looks to be the **'Pentagon'** when it was on fire in Washington DC, on **September 11th, 2001**, a day that is referred to as **'9-11.'** On the side with the Towers burning, it displays the words **'American'** and **'United,'** which were coincidentally the two airlines used in the hijackings. Strangely so, these revelations come in the form of a paper plane. To reiterate, this money was released in **1998**, three years before this event took place. A view of the money in the form of a paper plane and its visuals are provided below:

Could this all be a coincidence? Could someone have purposely drawn this? Or is this a message from another source trying to warn you? If this money was printed after **2001**, the meaning behind this message would not be as significant, but the mere fact it was released beforehand has to make all who come in contact with it, stop and wonder what exactly it is that they are holding.

This was not the idea of a person who thought to themselves to warn the people, and this is not a coincidence. It is a message, a clue, hint, but nevertheless it's not something that's hard to search for, you come in contact with this 'Twenty Dollar Bill' on a daily basis. It is said, 'The Devil will lie to you, but he'll put the truth right in front of your face, it's on you if you choose to look another way.' This is 'Devil Money,' it is showing you this system is not just. It is their 'Devil,' the Ego.

The men that control the current money system are well aware the Ego is being defeated amongst the masses of the people, and they will eventually have no more power. They know this, so this transition will not come with ease before this system has completely dwindled. They will place many roadblocks, as they do now. History has shown that many of men have bought out politicians so they can advance their own interest. The same is being done now, trying to hold on. Many oil companies have bought into Solar Energy, because they know they have no choice but to switch over, society is demanding a change from the use of oil to more efficient means, and the families who own the oil companies want to be in control of where the money is going, so they have also tried to buy out the Solar Energy field. This too, will be meaningless, however many companies they buy, the idea of modern corporation is coming to a close. The spirit is more powerful than the corporation, and it will override any advancement of trying to hold onto a primitive system.

In **2007, William Domhoff** divided the world's monetary class into **5** Divisions, with **80** percent of the population controlling **7** percent of the World's wealth, and **1** percent of the population controlling an astonishing **42** percent of the World's finances. A breakdown of Domhoff's monetary classes is as follows:
- **80** Percent of the Population, controlling **7** Percent of the world's wealth

- **10** Percent of the Population, controlling **12** Percent of the world's wealth
- **5** Percent of the Population, controlling **11** Percent of the world's wealth
- **4** Percent of the Population, controlling **27** Percent of the world's wealth
- **1** Percent of the Population, controlling **42** Percent of the world's wealth

This division between people will become no more. Many may wonder how this will happen. How will a system that has been in place for so long come to nonexistence? It is simple. Once the majority of the population realizes what the world is capable of, once they begin to understand how much in abundance there actually is, they will not conform to the system. The system cannot work if it is not supported. People fear this idea of jail, but how can **1** Percent of the population arrest **80** percent of the population. They can't. There aren't jails big enough, and the **80** percent will not stand for it. The **Police**, **Army** and **Servicemen** are all also a part of this **80** percent, and eventually they too will not only realize this, but will eventually act with the efforts of the masses, not because they are actually forced to, but because they will see themselves as being in the same position as the **80** percent..

What will be in place of money? Some may wonder if it will be a 'Barter system,' but this too will not be needed. The system that will be in place of the money system is 'Nothing.' It will become irrelevant. Why? How could this be? Technology will be so advanced that the things in which we think we need money for, will be provided for us, and it will be in abundance. Technology will push us so far into the future, it will also push out the money system. Technology will provide us with all our needs, and it will not be at a cost. That will be our greatest technical feat ever invented, when the invention of 'Free Enterprise' is presented, and it will be, because we will make this happen.

You will be able to take things at your pleasing. Many may think this will lead to people taking advantage of the system, but we as a breed of species will be so consciously advanced by the time this happens, the thought of taking advantage of something will not be of interest.

This initially will be the answer to homelessness, and the advancement in education to many children who are in need. A world without a money system, and the advancement of our technology will cause for no one to be without. There will be those who many may think of as 'Wanderers,' people who live at a different pace, or have less than others, but this will all be of their choosing, choosing from not taking what is available to them.

Tomorrow: (Government)

The '**United States of America**,' one of the Modern World's leading nations, is commonly viewed as unstoppable, this mostly due to its military. The United States military is thought to be the most powerful of its time, however, history shows us that even with the massiveness of a large military, all empires fall. **Rome** is always a great example.

People are no longer trusting of the men who occupy the office of an elected official. Much corruption has happened in the past, but this will stop. People are becoming more aware and they are standing up for themselves. Some governments make no secret that it is acceptable to use people for their wars, but struggle when wanting to provided healthcare. Odd, how some people support such a system, a system that will actually use you for wars but won't provide you with cures. People will eventually see through this type of logic and their system will not be supported any longer.

The Internet is one of the most important inventions that will aid people in defeating these systems. People in **Iran** can access the same information as someone in **Canada**. It has put everyone on an even playing field, we all have the same information, no one can hide the truth from you any longer. You will be able to access all the lies and truth with one click of a button. The Internet was the cause for a lot of uprisings in the Middle East in **2011**. People are seeing how the world is outside of their country, and they want results. Not only do they want results, but they 'Know' they are powerful enough to bring those results.

These results will happen, but the system will fall harder than most imagine. Governments as we know them today will cease to exist in the 'New World.' There will be structure, but the controlling factor governments have held during its existence will not play such a personal part in your life anymore, meaning 'Taxes' or 'Healthcare.' Taxes will become irrelevant, as will the healthcare system.

Your welfare and choices upon how you can live your life will not depend upon one so called politician who represents your district. You will hold all the keys to your life, and you will know this, so will everyone else around you, therefore it would be a personal invasion of your privacy to make you adhere to certain laws that have no meaning for the wellbeing of yourself or society.

Governments will not need armies in the same sense they have now. The technology that will be made available will in turn make it so that the current ideals of a military will change. There will be those of **'Service,'** but their roles will be broader than that of **Soldiers**, they will be many things, **Explorers, Watchers, Healers, Teachers** and **Seeders**.

Modern governments will fold. Most government officials know this. They know they are running out of time, so they are doing everything they can to hold onto their system, but it is rather pointless, because it is evolution, an evolution away from old ideas. People are waking up and realizing their importance and capabilities at an alarming rate. Once the masses realize what and who they truly are, the current system will become all but a memory.

Tomorrow: (Prejudices)

In a provocative study from Brock University in Ontario, results were published in February of **2012** that showed people who score low on **I.Q.** tests during childhood are more likely to develop prejudiced beliefs and socially conservative politics in adulthood. **Dr. Gordon Hodson**, the study's lead author, told **LiveScience.com**, *"The finding represented evidence of a vicious cycle, people of low intelligence gravitate toward socially conservative ideologies, which stress resistance to change and in turn, prejudice."*

This is important, because we are now approaching a very beautiful moment in our time, a time where people's conscious levels are beginning to vibrate at a point that will put a close to a lot of our prejudices with **Race**, **Gender**, **Sexuality**, **Wealth**, and **Religion**. It is dying, there isn't any place in our future for 'Prejudice' of another because of their differences. Many in future generations will look back on our time now and wonder how people could behave as 'Divisive' as we have. The slavery, the genocide, the ridicule and name calling one may go through while passing in the streets, these are all primitive ways a species would act, frankly, it is 'Animalistic.'

To some people, it may seem like it is becoming more prevalent, but that is because 'Ignorance' is fighting for its place, and it knows its place is running out of room. Just like when a fox becomes cornered, it gets scrappy. Ignorance is getting scrappy, with people are becoming more and more aware of how small their world really is, learning there is so much more in the Universe to discover.

The Internet will aid us in defeating these prejudices. While the Internet holds every bit of information there can be, it also does another amazing subliminal feat, it provides people with access to being 'Smarter,' by connecting them to the world outside themselves. No matter where they are, it joins people together across the world, someone in Australia can communicate with someone in Mexico. It allows people to download apps, where people can play games or enter into contest, and a lot of the times people are doing so with and against people from around the world. It is connecting each and every one. It is tearing down barriers. The oceans that have divided people will divide them no more.

Our racial divides will become something of the past. The racial groups that participated in slavery, the Holocaust and other genocides around the world, the victims and the oppressors outlook will become one, and their ancestors past will be a footnote to their history. People of the Earth are reproducing and interbreeding with different cultures, therefore eventually they will not identify themselves by their country or race. They will identify themselves by the name they have given the planet, and call themselves 'Earthlings.' The world is becoming bigger and broader than to think of themselves as being **Nigerian**, or **Chinese**, **Scottish** or **American**, they will all be too minute of a definition for who they represent.

Just as interracial relationships are accepted, the same will happen for same-gender marriage. In fact, this will become so common, it won't be known as 'Gay Marriage,' it will be known as 'Marriage,' which will also not be viewed in the same sense marriage is viewed today, but more of a partnership of sharing. Same-gender partnerships does not mean the entire population will then refer to themselves as '**Bi-Sexual**,' it means one will not think negatively upon others that do so. 'Sex' will be seen as different levels of experience between two people, and not found to have the limitations among participators that many have given it.

The money system will eventually become obsolete, so there will be no need for division amongst wealth. No one will worry about finding enough money to take someone out on a date, nor will they worry about what someone will say if they don't have enough money. People will be seen for who they are. Simply, the **Male** and **Female** species will better understand each other, the downfalls of relationships will not be as common, and intense. This is also attributed to humans becoming more in tune to one another's thoughts, therefore, we will be able to see the sincerity in one another.

Tomorrow: (Family Structure)

Eventually, the idea of 'Family' will grow into a broader spectrum, as well as becoming more internal. Meaning, family will begin to extend to the surroundings of every child, no longer will someone else's child in a school system be looked upon as 'Their child,' but instead 'Our Child.'

People will look amongst themselves as a whole unit, but only because they have realized the meaning of 'Family' within themselves. People will not put the value on marriage as they do now. Further progression with marriage will be made, along with same-gender marriage. The service of two people getting married will be performed without the authorship of the courts, and become a bond two people make with themselves.

The bounding between a Male and Female **4th Density** level or **Yezirah** beings will not confine themselves to the same laws of marriage **3rd Density** or **Asiyah** beings do. 'Breakups' will not be looked upon as parting, but rather a celebration of the experience. If the breeding of a child has taken place, the separation of the parents will not affect that child, only because the child will have a different, broader sense of family. In a sense, everyone will be looked upon as the child's parent. They will not be accountable for the same duties, but they will feel as if it is their duty to do so. The elders will mostly be thought of as teachers, in which they will hold this responsibility to themselves.

The school system will drastically be different than it is now. Private institutions will become obsolete, as will the public school system. Children will be brought up learning and understanding who they are, Earth's and our Solar System's history, as well as the purposes of their life. Once they have reached a certain age, they will then be educated on various 'Occupations' or 'Activities' they will be able to engage in during their life's experience.

Men and women will not hold each other to different standards, both will be capable and able to do much of all that will be available to them in the **4th Density** or **Yezirah** realm of existence, therefore, their partnership will not be depended on 'Providing, protecting, and serving,' but rather, 'Sharing.' The sharing of wisdom and experiences will become the focal point of companionship.

Tomorrow: (Earth & Expansion)

The Earth is a 'Living Being' that goes through '**Mood Swings**,' and right now, if one would compare it to the life of a human, it is going through '**Puberty**.' In its lifespan, it is young in years, and has so many changes it has yet to go through. Some changes will be more subtle than others, earthquakes, hurricanes, tornados and tsunamis, these are subtle. The Earth, from what humans believe, is over **4** billion years old, while intelligent human life can be said to trace back to **10,000 BCE**. Surely, the Earth will go through more drastic changes than the earthquakes, hurricanes, tornados or tsunamis humans have witnessed in their lifespan.

This time of drastic change is closer than it is not. Some scientists believe the Earth will react upon itself, due to the population over-crowding the planet. While the current population in **2012** is at **7** billion people, it is widely believed that the Earth can only sustain **10** billion people. The world is growing at an alarming rate, and it is growing faster. It is believed the population first reached **1** billion people in **1804**.

Growth of Human Population on Earth		
Population	Year in CE	Years in duration
1 Billion	1804	'Creation'
2 Billion	1927	123
3 Billion	1960	33
4 Billion	1974	14
5 Billion	1987	13
6 Billion	1999	12
7 Billion	2012	13
8 Billion	2027	15
9 Billion	2046	19
Courtesy of the United Nations Population Fund		

It has been estimated that Earth's population will reach 10 billion people around the year 2053. Some believe the low supply of food will cause for people to turn amongst themselves, thinking that the crops and plants won't be enough to feed them, but this will not the case.

A popular model found on the Internet that explains the usage of cereal can be used as a good example. *'The earth currently produces 2,264 million metric tons of cereals, which is the staple food of the world. If each person consumes 2,000 calories per day, 2,264 million metric tons of cereal will support a little bit over 10 billion people.'* People tend to forget their ancestors use to know all the means of farming their own crops, but the food will not be an issue when it comes to feeding the population, technology will see to this. Water will be of more importance.

To address the use of water, the same model used to explain the cereals (Food), continues to explain the concerns of Earth's water supply. *'There are 1,385 cubic kilometers on earth. Most of this water is salt water, and not suitable for human consumption. Most of the fresh water available is locked inside polar ice caps. Only 0.26% of all water is available for human consumption, with most of the water found in the clouds or in the ground. Only 0.014% of water on the earth is actually available for drinking.'* While a water shortage would seem more reasonable, technology will also be advanced enough to turn salt water, into drinking water.

The breeding of people will cease to keep up to its active rate. People will have more respect for what it is 'To have a child.' Most people in modern times have no responsibility to the children they bring into the world, therefore having one after another. Some want children even when they know they can't provide for that child, others have children because they think it is 'What they want.' These aren't reasons to continue bringing children into the world.

Our conscious levels are rising for us to have a broader respect for life. Not only will a child hold the same impact on a stranger's life as it does their biological parents, but we will see the reason for having children as a means for the reproduction of intelligent life, whether on this planet or others.

Humans will eventually migrate to other regions of the Galaxy, this also being from the cause of Earth becoming uninhabitable at times. Earth will not always remain uninhabitable, it will go through stages. Many will come back to help repopulate the Earth again. When they do, they will not be at a lack of knowledge, but will leave behind the reseeding of a **New Generation** that will be left to relearn the mysteries of who they are. This process has been thought to have been done before, and it will be done again.

Tomorrow: (God of Our Future)

A quote found in **Kabbalah** can basically sum up our historical outlook on God. *"It is not God who changes but the ability to perceive God that changes."*
Our idea of God is growing. No longer are we placing God inside a box. Eventually it will become a 'Primitive Thought' to have the religions we do now. Religions of today will not be the religions of tomorrow. Tomorrow, there will be no 'Religion' in the same sense many use the word today. All religions will eventually fuse together to become a part of historical record, and not looked at as separate, but as one large composite of the same information. These stories will not be looked upon as myths, or official records, but only as wisdom, and a part of the history of humans. No longer will people be divided by the messenger, instead they will embrace the message. People will not look upon such figures as **Buddha**, **Moses**, **Jesus** or **Muhammad** as separate or more divine than they are, but rather one of who they are.
People will not refer to themselves as being 'Religious,' because their definitions of 'God' will no longer confine itself to limitations. Religious customs or rituals, will be subsided for a more personal, and meditative practice. Churches, synagogues and mosques will cease to exist in the fashion they do now. There will be places of 'Learning' one can go, it will be looked upon more as a 'Place of Gathering,' where one may learn, and rejuvenate, instead of a place of worship. Some of these will also

have '**Teachers**' or '**Healers**' who offer their services for the 'Greater good' of progression. We have no choice but to evolve to this state of civilization.

We will eventually evolve further. If you look at the thought process of man, from the beginnings of creation, humans first looked at God as 'Being outside' of themselves. Man first thought God to be the 'Sun,' only to then believe God was possibly the Stars, leading to the thought process of there being 'Many Gods.' Humans then believed there was one God, and eventually proclaimed that God is a spirit. God then grew to being everywhere and everything, therefore God then became inside of 'Us.' Our belief in God has grown tremendously, but it has not finished its growth process.

Our idea of 'God' will eventually evolve to the realization that '**It**' has been '**You**' all along, playing a game with itself. In time, beings will grow not only to realize, but they will '**Know**' they are God. We have no choice but to evolve to one consciousness, where 'One' realizes this. Simply it is the final piece of evolution. This realization will in turn bring in the complete fusion of 'Everything,' thus making 'All with One, and One with All,' leaving God (You) with the only option of pushing the '**Reset Button.**'

CHAPTER SEVENTEEN
(The Continue)

"There is only one corner of the Universe you can be certain of improving, and that's your own self."

- **Aldous Huxley** -

The Continue: (Introduction to the Continue)

Your eyes are the curtain, and they are too close to your face for you to see what is truly in front of you. They have been your 'Blinders,' and they have kept you blind. Now is the time to see beyond your eyes, feel beyond your senses, and be one with who you are. You are energy. You are an Enlightened Being, a particle of the Creator, which in turn is the Creator. You are a drop of water, when joined with the Ocean, becomes the Ocean.

You are the most brilliant creation that has ever been brought into existence. Everything around you is designed for you, by you, to have all the avenues and tools for your best possible experience. This is all 'Yours.' Claim it! Do not be afraid to do so. All the magnificence of this place couldn't 'Be' without you here.

It is marvelous, the things you have given yourself, the adventures, the mysteries, the situations, conflicts and problems. You are genius! How could one think of such a thing? It is marvelous, isn't it? Granted, at times it could get a little boring to continue gazing at your wonders, at your mountains, the seas, the hills and the sky, thus you give yourself obstacles, distractions, problems, so you can further be entertained. If you aren't impressed with yourself, than surely you haven't grasped just how spectacular you are.

You have played an extraordinary trick on yourself, to forget who you really are, where you've come from, this could only happen by choice. No one made you forget anything, no one took away your memories and erased them, you did all this to yourself, so you can experience the 'Game,' picking up bonuses as you go along. You are the most awesome 'Web Designer' this world has ever known. The Internet doesn't have anything on the creations you've made available.

You are not only a part of the 'One' that has created the realm of the 'Physical,' but you have also created 'Your own World' of situations, friends and experiences, within this entire world, and while your world is distinctly different than that of others, as far as strangers, or acquaintances, they still interchange and connect, therefore you have created karma amongst yourselves in order for the energy you put into the Universe to be the energy you receive. This is pure and utter brilliance! What other better way is there to play this game?

You've given yourself Universes, levels of densities, levels of life, levels of consciousness, levels of the soul, dreams and déjà vu to remind you of the fact that you have so many different choices and ways to experience and rediscover who you are. It is no secret that you like an adventure, and you will never give up on yourself.

The most precious part of the Game is you, and your Higher Self knows this, so it watches you, it guides you, but leaves every decision in the hands of your actions, for it is you that is conscious. This is your journey, love it! This is your Game, play it! This is your experience, enjoy it!

The Continue: (The Beautiful)

We have taken so many things for granted. Think of a young child who finds themselves excited over a water hose, running wild and trying to spray the water on people, having fun and experiencing it like it is something new to them. Others may get annoyed at this child's excitement of spraying the water on people, the adult in us tends to forget the things we use to relish, but the child has taken the simplest thing and found so much enjoyment and beauty from it.

Do not lose the child in you. People must not forget to appreciate the beauty in the little things, for they are just as enormous in size as the things you hold to be of great value. Enjoy that you have oxygen to breath, to keep you hallucinating the experience exists at this point in time. Enjoy that you have visions to see this illusion, enjoy that you have hearing, that you can taste, do not take these things for granted.

Some thoughts on the evolution of human existence might be hard for some people to digest. For instance, many could feel uneasy at the thought that their human bodies were created by extraterrestrials. Whether this is the case or not, this should only be a passing thought, only because if extraterrestrials did partake in the creation of the bodies of humans, something in turn made aliens, and whatever made aliens could have possibly been created by something else, and so on, until you get to the root of it all.

This should be captivating, first, we aren't humans, just 'God Consciousness' occupying bodies. Secondly, if indeed the human bodies were engineered by another species, than we are playing the ultimate game of creation. If humans were created not by God, then we get to experience a brand new species our creations have made. Simply, we get to experience, our creation's creations. It is in turn, one of the most beautiful things one could think of, to experience itself in creations of its own creations. You not only have zoned into this fascinating world, but you get to experience all facets of it. This is the only way to go about the Game and enjoy it, to discover all aspects of yourself.

This place was created for you, by you, enjoy every aspect of it. Climb the mountains, run the hills, swim in the ocean, play on your playground. Share it with people, it's no fun playing on the playground alone, share your enjoyment, share your **Love**, share your **Light**. You have given yourself such a wonderful experience, **Live** it!

Do not look upon your problems as negative, only as learning blocks for you to have come into the person you are. You cannot know happiness, without knowing what it is to be unhappy. It's a beautiful thing we have, to be able to decipher the difference and what it means to us here. It is all your own choosing to be happy or unhappy. Knowing this is the key, realizing this is in your own control is the root for someone remaining happy or unhappy.

No one owns your happiness, no one can take it away from you, it is yours. No one can ruin your day or make you feel meaningless. This all lies in the power of your own thoughts. It is as simple as knowing you can tell yourself to enjoy the moment, every bit of it. Enjoy that you are here to have a problem. There is two ways to go about it, to either not be here, or be here and have problems. These are your only two options, so if you're going to be here, why not enjoy it? If you are going to have problems, then why make them such a big deal?

Why not tell yourself, 'My day is going to be beautiful,' and at the end of the evening, 'My day was beautiful.' It is as simple as telling yourself this, make a bond with yourself and your energy will radiant that gratitude throughout the day.

It is all your choice, your **Free Will**. This is just a part of the experience you have given yourself. Do not neglect how powerful your choices are, your choices are of those that can build airplanes when no one thinks you can do it, it can invent the Internet when no one knows what it is, it can invent the light bulb after having failed over **10,000** times, and it can change your life with a mere thought. A simple choice, this is all it takes.

Your mind is software. Program it.
Your body is a shell. Change it.
Death is a disease. Cure it.
Extinction is approaching. Fight it.
    – Eclipse Phase

You are capable of doing extraordinary things. Love who you are! You are the **Light**, the **Way**, and you are the most important thing in your world, treat yourself as such. Be the energy that you wish to receive, love how you wish to be loved, inspire how you wish to be inspired, your beauty is at your fingertips, and everything you touch leaves your imprint.

The Continue: (For the Better)

Fear has played a big part in people's lives, fear of failure, fear of change, fear of uncomfortable situations, fear of losing a job, fear of not getting a job, fear of technology, you name it, people have feared it. One of society's biggest fears is the idea of a 'New World Order.' This is usually expressed in many different ways, governments controlling the people by putting computer chips inside their bodies, tapping phone lines, creating one currency, monitors with video surveillance in your rooms, the list can go on, people have come up with all kinds of ways of how their government can enslave them.

They are correct in one aspect, the 'New World Order' will happen, but it will be drastically different than any fear they have. The 'New World Order' will not consist of government control, whether or not if governments extend their hands more than they do now, in time it will all be irrelevant, and temporary.

The 'New World Order' will become the beautiful change you have been waiting for. It will be a New World, but its Order will be that of harmony. This has no choice but to happen. This is the only place evolution can take us, 'Harmony,' and we have no choice but to continue to evolve until we get there.

Things must change in order for your new growth to come into play. Some things will be removed from your lives in order to make room for all the new possibilities. In the same manner you will remove negative thoughts from your life so the positive thoughts come in and blossom, you will have to get rid of the old to get with the new. This notion extends to societal systems as well, whether it is the money system or governments, in order to evolve some things will become primitive.

A lot of people fear the 'Down period' this might take, fearing that having no government or money system in place will lead to chaos, but this is not so. People have a unique compassion about themselves that when in a time of despair they tend to extend themselves to others, this is the 'Light' within them, their first initial thought. You have seen this through many catastrophes around the world, whether it is tsunamis in Indonesia or earthquakes in Haiti, people eventually come together.

The system has to fall, this is evolution. It is not entirely the men in the system that is corrupt. It's the system that is corrupt, and when men enter into a corrupt office they tend to feel forced to play it corruptly. We can't keep building on this platform, the legs are weak, it will not stand no matter how many good intentions are placed on top of it. It is just like a building. You can't place steel on top of decaying wood, the building will fall regardless, so sometimes the best thing to do to save time is start from scratch.

Do not fear this course, the rebuilding process is one to be excited to be a part of. Your fingerprints, thoughts and ideas are at the foundation of a '**New Nation**.' You are going to love the '**New You**.' This New You is a part of a New Nation. A New You changes everything around you, and you will bring a ripple effect that will make humanity reflect your light.

As spoken by the **32nd** President of the United States of America, **Franklin D. Roosevelt**, *"There is nothing to fear, but fear itself."* Your existence is in your hands, and it is the greatest choice of free will that you have given yourself. Now is the time to dictate your life.

The Continue: (Forever)

There is no such thing as the '**End**,' there is only the '**Continue**.' This can be understood with the explanation of a '**Fractal**.' A Fractal is a rough or fragmented geometric figure, where each part is a reduced size copy of the whole, a property called '**Self-Similarity**.' In turn, each part has the same statistical character as the whole. A mathematical Fractal is based on an equation that goes through repetition.

Fractals appear similar at all levels of magnification, and are infinitely complex. While fractals are a mathematical concept, they are also found in nature. Snowflakes, clouds, mountain ranges, coastlines, vegetables (Such as cauliflower and broccoli), and animal colorations are all found to have fractal formations. Examples of mathematical Fractals are shown below:

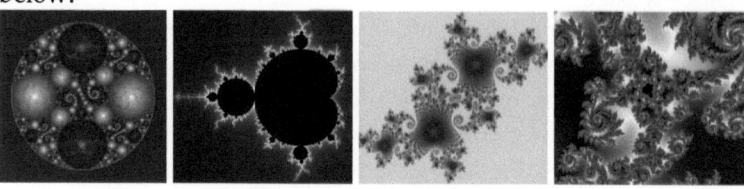

When protruding towards a section of the Fractal, it then displays itself to form into the whole Fractal, and so on, over and over. How does this relate to you?

Hassim Haramein, a proponent for **Sacred Geometry**, refers to our existence as the, *"Infinite Small,"* compared to God, which is the '**Infinite**.' He explains that God is the 'Whole,' which we do not escape or exceed its infinite boundary, which is the first boundary. Within the context of the finite space that God has given, there is an infinite amount of information, through an infinite amount of divisions. **Haramein** further explains that you can divide the human cells in the same manner, all the way to 'Electrons' and 'Protons,' which is thought to be the smallest thing to exist. He continues to add, in time, someone will dispel this theory, finding something even smaller than these materials.

What does this mean? We are living inside the confines of God, which has given us endless amounts of ways to experience itself (Ourselves). There is an endless amount of information, through an infinite amount of chances, therefore, there is no end. There is no Hell one will be captive to for eternity. This way of thinking should be the furthest thing from your mind. Hell is dwelling on your mistakes, being in your grief and depressions, living a life that is surrounded by them, and staying stagnate with them, this is true Hell, however, this is all controlled by your thinking.

There are no consequences other than those that you have placed on yourself. There is no 'Darkness,' there is no gate keeper that will ask you if you think your worthy enough to be with God. That is ridiculous, how could it be unworthy to be with yourself? If you deny yourself, it is only because you want to.

God would never abandon you, God can't abandon you. You are God. How can one abandon itself? God wants nothing but the best for you, and condemning you isn't helping you. God wants you to grow, it wants you to blossom, it wants you to see who you really are. God wants the world painted with your colors in it, it would be incomplete without it.

Over and over again, we see how the words from **Genesis 1:26**, "*God said, let us make man in our image, after our likeness,*" can and has been compared to human existences and how we relate to God, in so many different ways. We can relate this passage to God creating humans, extraterrestrials creating humans, humans gaining consciousness, etc., but the most revealing piece of information is that it was written 'In our own image.' This speaks volumes. This statement alone, should tell you that you are more than just a 'Human Being.' If you are in the 'Likeness' of the Creator, it means you can do things like the Creator. Do not hold yourself back from things you thing unattainable. The reason you are here is so all your dreams can be attained. You can never dream too big.

God, the Creator, wants to create, it wants to paint, it wants to draw, it wants to play, it wants to question, it wants to learn, it wants to love, it wants to feel pain, it wants to feel joy, it wants to travel, see the world, dream, think, experience…but how can it do any of these things when it knows everything. How can it continue to create, when it knows every experience? It can't. You can't, so find joy in not knowing everything, find joy in searching for the questions, find joy in the Experience! It's never the reward, it's the journey, it is always the journey. Once you get the reward, you're thinking, 'Okay, what next?' Enjoy this experience, enjoy the journey!

There are so many fascinating things waiting for you to remember, the mysteries of the pyramids, the connection Earth has to Mars, life in other Solar Systems, possibly the edge of this Universe, and into the next Universe. This is a grand puzzle, the little troubles in your day are simply that, 'Little.' Do not make them bigger than what they are, do not make your worries larger than all the wonders in the cosmos, this place is too magnificent to have its attention drawn away to one's problems. Your problems are merely just a speck of dust. Blow it away. You have other things to think about.

Your mind is too marvelous to be weighed down by its problems. Control your mind, your mind does not control you. Command it to bring into your life the things you wish, you deserve it, give yourself everything you desire in this experience.

The body is a vehicle. Use your vehicle, take care of your vehicle, love your vehicle, but do not worship your vehicle, there is no need to get so wrapped up in your vehicle, you will have many. You will have countless of other models, brands, and styles, and all to your liking and choosing for your experience. Your body is the perfect body for you, to be the 'Higher Self' you wish to experience here. You have something so precious to give to the world, 'You.' Let everyone see who you are!

Enjoy your time here, and receive wisdom from your feelings and actions. Every action you make causes a reaction, so be careful of your actions. This experience will give you exactly what you give it. If you neglect the experience, it may neglect your effort, gratitude and acceptance are the keys to a peaceful coexistence. If you want to peacefully coexist, be grateful of those around you, and accept them for who they are, as you wish done for you.

This train of creation will not stop. There is no prize at the end, you are living the prize, you are being the prize, you are the prize. What grander prize could there be than 'You?' There is none, everything you want to be, you in turn already are. If you have a goal, manifest it! If you have a dream, live it! Do not be afraid to try, do not feel burdened to being wrong, you will have chance after chance after chance.

There is only the 'Continue,' for it is the only thing for us to do, to continue and continue and continue. We are all Creators of the Creator, and remaining stagnate is not in our best interest. Remaining still is the equivalent of 'Death,' progression is 'Life.' You cannot fail. There is no such thing as failure, only doing. Progress, live, take forward steps, it only draws you closer to light.

Remember, you are connected to '**All**,' and deep in your superconscious you already know '**Everything**.' The answers are here, you wish for guidance, you wish for enlightenment, it's here, make yourself 'Aware' of it. It is a choice to remember who you are, it is not hard, the decision is yours. Make it! No One else can do it for you. This book will not change your life. 'You' change your life. This book is just a reminder.

And you've probably read this before, you may have even written these words while in another solar system, realizing the 'Light' that you are. You may've even found yourself contemplating the ending to these pages, wondering the best way to close the book, in hopes of not leaving anything incomplete. You've probably ended the book in so many ways, probably wrote it in so many different forms, but the message was probably the same. You may've even tried to create a pattern of writing that may serve as a reminder for you if you ever came across this information, just so you can realize that these words and creations are all from your own thoughts.

This is your book…I thank you for letting me tell your story.

AUTHOR'S CLOSING STATEMENT

Great thought was given to this section, mostly to if I should place it at all. My reasoning behind this was because when it comes to the information you receive, I am not important. The chance of prejudging the information due to my involvement has a greater chance of occurring, whereas as if no one knew this was written by me or anyone else. People tend to judge what others say to be the truth…which is understandable.

I imagined that it may be best for you to forget I am even associated with this material, so I even gave thought of not putting my name on the book so that this might cause that possibility, and you could ignore that I am the author. Truly, I am not the author, if anything, calling myself an editor would seem more appropriate. This information didn't come from me, it came through me.

But not placing my name on the book would defeat my purpose, possibly adding some type of mystery that the information was from a divine messenger. Plus people's extraordinary investigative skills would have led them to me regardless, so I realized this would also work against me.

I must explain. My hope is that we as a people grow pass our ideologies for the worship of men. Through history people have viewed the Messenger, just as important as the Message. Religions have formed in honor of the 'Messenger,' not the 'Message.' People mostly find themselves involved in religion according to where they were born, or what prophet they relate to. Ironically, the God involved in their religion, is the same God in all religions, especially if they refer to this God as the 'Creator.' The Creator is the first, no matter what name you call it, or path you take to it. Therefore, their religion is not based on God, it is based on their prophet. This should be disturbing, because in most of their holy texts, the prophets have revealed not to worship them, but to adhere to the information.

Nevertheless, I am aware that some people have a want to know more about the 'Author' of the book they read, even though again, it is difficult to think of myself as such, in regards of this information. Therefore, after careful consideration, realizing that placing this section at all was going to leave me open to criticism, and not placing it would only lead to rumors or to some possibly believing it is from something more extraordinary then themselves, I ultimately found it best to place this segment at the end of the book. Again, the information is the most important part, myself, or how it was received is truly insignificant when compared to its importance, but for those that wish to know about myself, or how this information came about, I will elaborate for the sake of curiosity.

    This book has always been at the root, or foundation of my purpose for writing. When I look back at my motives for wanting to be a writer, it was to help, to inspire, to make people aware of their surroundings, and to get deeper sense of who they are. While I have mostly been known for my accomplishments as a Spoken Word Artist, I started my course by writing novels, mostly fiction. But even before I dove deep into my writing process, I set aside the idea for a book (That has now gone through many names), that would not be a work of fiction, but would in turn speak the truth, as is, a book very much like this one, the only problem was that I didn't know enough at the time to complete such a piece of work, so I continued my course with releasing a volume number of Spoken Word CDs, performing across the world, and engulfing myself through a course of writing poem after poem, knowing, thinking, hoping that one day I would return to my main motive. Finally, it has happened.

    This has been a beautiful journey, to come back full circle to my main objective. I only look upon being able to complete this project as a blessing. I am thankful for the years it took me to finally round out and address this subject. I am grateful, for the many experiences I've had, for better or worse, they have all aided me to come to this conclusion, all have helped me to be able to stumble onto what I really am…what we really are. All I'm doing now is passing on the information.

    As a child, I began to feel like something else was out there, I just didn't know what. This door of wanting to know more may have been shown to me by my father. When I was around 10 years of age, on a clear night, while in my parent's pool, he decided to give me a lesson on the Stars. After asking me if I believed in 'Other life in the Universe,' and my responses being, "*I don't know,*" he then went ahead to explain how big the Universe is, how far the Stars are, how many of them are in the Universe, how water was essential to life on Earth, adding that it was just the perfect distance away from the Sun to have water, it wasn't too cold where it would turn into ice, and it wasn't too hot where the water would evaporate. After explaining all this to me, he then asked his question again, if I believed in other life in the Universe. "*Yes,*" I replied.

    I guess he made it simple for me. He laid down the facts he knew, explained them the best he could, and placed it in front of me for me to make my own decision. Honestly, after listening to him expand my world from my little Earth to all the wonders of the Universe, how could I think life only existed here? I couldn't. My world grew so much larger that night.

    Growing up I was never really much for religion, and even though in my later teen years, I found myself studying Islam and Christianity, almost comparing the two to see which one lined up with me the most, I never fully accepted their scriptures to be the 'Ultimate Truth.' Although I did find pride in reading the Holy texts from front to end, I was conflicted with this idea of church. Out of all the passages in the Bible and the Quran, I found myself gravitating to the ones that taught how 'God is everywhere,' and how 'Two or more is a congregation,' and how 'God hears you wherever you are,' so essentially this halted any motivation I might have had to wake up early on Sunday mornings to go to sermons. After all, they do say 'Sunday is the day of rest,' so I never figured God wouldn't hold it against me.

    I found the texts to be enlightening, even filling, but I was also conflicted with the thought of a being as powerful as God to have Human traits, and would say how God loves you unconditionally but at the same time will send you to Hell if you do something wrong. That totally defeats the purpose of calling

God's Love, unconditional. That's conditional. I always noticed the holes in these types of things, and being that there were so many, I took those texts for exactly what they are, 'God's words written through the hands of man.' The 'Written through the hands of man' part is what always made me look at it with one eye open.

Truly, I do not hold myself separate from someone embracing this thought towards me, I encourage anyone to look at this information with one eye open. The information will speak to you if it holds any bit of truth you can identify with. Again, I am not more valuable than the information.

During this time, I started to have what some might think of as 'Unusual' dreams. They seemed cryptic, and extremely super natural. I dreamt a lot about death, flying, walking on things such as water, alternate situations between friends, and even seeing the 'Idea of Hell.' That night was one that I won't forget, it woke me up in the middle of the night with a cold sweat. Nevertheless, my dreams seemed to be a world all to itself.

Several years later, after many cryptic dreams, after many surreal intuitions and peculiar experiences, my life then switched into another gear. At the age of **26**, I took a holiday break from touring to spend some time with my family in Baltimore. I was on the road performing a lot, so whenever I went home, I became pretty much a hermit, not wanting to go out the house when I wasn't touring, but this particular night one of my friends talked me into going to a local nightclub in the city. I can't count the times something grand has happened to me just by chance. My not wanting to go out, somehow led to a course that would change my life forever.

While at the nightclub, I met a young lady, with whom the dialogue first started off rocky, but eventually she let her guard down and we engulfed in a light-hearted, humorous conversation. This conversation lasted through the closing hours of the nightclub. After walking her to her car, I must have felt extremely comfortable, because I then opened up with my most inner thoughts, telling her some of my dreams and premonitions, which in turn caused her to reveal that she was comfortable enough to open up to me about some things as well. I had never heard of an 'Outer Body Experience,' before she told me about her own experiences. Our conversation didn't stop, we sat in her car, parked in the parking lot of the nightclub till about **8:30** in the morning talking about astral projection, God, religion and dreams.

The next day, I went to her home and she gave me one of her books on 'Out of Body Experiences,' with points and techniques explaining how to have Astral Projection, where one can travel outside their own body, becoming one with what they are. I was very intrigued with the 'Flying' part, where you could travel to other parts of the world and beyond. In **3** days the book was read. I had no idea what I was getting myself into. I had no clue what was awaiting me. The night I finished the book, was the night I started my process.

I laid in my bed, put my arms to the side, and drifted off into a deep state of relaxation. The book stressed to try to remain conscious while trying to fall as close to sleep as possible, but just at the moment of falling asleep, consciously catch yourself from drifting off, therefore you will remain conscious while in your subconscious. I did just this, I actually felt like I was in a state that seemed like sleep, but was conscious of everything around me. I felt the foretold symptoms, the wavy lines that come to you, the vibrations, the lightness, it was all very similar to what the book pointed out. That was the extent of my first experience. I shared my attempt with the mother of the young woman who introduced this subject to me, and came to find that she was very familiar with it herself. She encouraged me to continue, stating that I was going to be *"Very good"* with this practice.

The next night, I continued with the same techniques the book shared, and again, I felt the same symptoms come about, but they got heavier…and heavier, to the point to where I couldn't feel my body weight anymore. I knew I had broken pass a point that was much further than the previous night. I became nervous, and my heart was beating faster than it ever has before. I then remembered the book stating that, *"If you came to a point where you are scared or nervous, tell yourself, 'I am fine, there is nothing to fear,' the mind is the most powerful thing there is, and it will follow your commands."*

I did just this, I told myself, *"Marc, calm down,"* and instantly my heart came to a slow beat, never had I been able to control my emotions in such a way.

My body then stopped vibrating, the waves of light then paused, and sound became much different. It was quiet, but you could hear the feeling of sound about to come, a silence that resembled the calm before something big is about to happen. Something big was about to happen.

In the darkness, a 'Glowing White Dot' appeared in the lower left corner of my sight, and then slowly sketched itself across to the right, forming a line of light. The middle of the line started to lift up some, forming what looked to be a mound, but continued to go further, as if rising out of water. That mound of 'Light' then looked to have a forehead, it rose further, it came to the eyes, it rose further, to the point of the nose, and then is when I started to notice a resemblance. It rose further to show the bottom of the lips, and I instantly knew then that it was a reflection of myself being presented to me. It stopped forming just at the mid-section of the stomach, but the strangest part about it was that he had on my chain with the double M medallion, and was wearing the same exact t-shirt I had on during this process, which revealed the tattoos on my shoulders.

Through telepathy, I asked him, *"Who are you?"*

"I am you," he responded, with the same use of communication.

"My soul?"

He lightly shrugged his shoulders and replied, *"You can call me that."*

I asked, *"What are you doing here?"*

"You're trying to get out of your body, right?" I nodded. He continued, *"So, I'm here to help you get out your body."*

"So what do I have to do," I asked.

"All you have to do is let go."

XX

So, with no idea of how to truly let go, I consciously tried to do so. I could feel the massive energy that was connected to my body, vibrating like it never has before, as it was trying to detach from the body. I could feel myself pulling away, it was an extraordinary feeling, I felt more with the energy than I did my body. At points I felt like I was about to free, but I just couldn't quite fully 'Let go.' He encouraged me along the way, while interestingly displaying characteristics of my own mannerisms.

He continued, *"Just let go."*
"I'm trying, I'm trying," I replied.
"No, you're not trying."

This continued for a number of times, over and over, the dialogue and my effort. There was no sense of time in this realm, but I figured I had been at it for a few minutes. Our conversation of 'Let go,' and 'I'm trying' continued to repeat until I started to feel a little overwhelmed. His encouragement wasn't helping at this moment, which he must've realized because I felt a switch in his energy, almost becoming more sensitive.

"Marc," he then said, *"Don't worry about that. Let's talk."*

And we did. He revealed to me so many things, things that I never even thought to wonder about, things that people wonder about daily, and things that made sense as soon as he explained it to me. He was quick, smooth, calm, witty, at some points funny, no nonsense, but at the same time understanding, helpful, caring and straight to the point. He was the most brilliant thing I had ever come across, so much in fact that it just seemed too good to be true.

I then concocted an idea, I thought to myself that I would ask him the dumbest question I could think of, and if the answer made sense, then this experience had to be more than just a hallucination. The question I decided to ask, I've mostly heard two different responses from people, one being a negative retort, and the other which includes its positive effects. But when I decided to ask him this pointless question, what I didn't expect was for him to give the greatest answer, to any question that could come to my mind.

I asked, *"Is smoking marijuana bad for you?"*

It's almost like he knew the question was coming. Because without a single moment of hesitated, he replied, *"It is what you make it."*

I was floored, never had I heard something that made so much sense about something so senseless, which in turn makes sense for everything else. It was beautiful. He knew I was amazed, because at that point I seemed to have run out of questions. He then asked me if I was ready to continue my process of fully getting out my body. I replied that I was, and so we continued.

It is best to point out that just **3** weeks prior, I wrote a poem I entitled '**Come with Me**,' in which the cadence resembled something of, *"If you want to dream, then come with me, you don't believe we can be the beauty we wish to see, then come with me, you want to swim in heaven's seas, then come with me, just come with me..."*

At this moment, I wasn't thinking about the poem, I was totally focused on reaching the full 'Out of Body Experience.' But I was still having difficulty, and my Soul or whatever it is called, knew it.

"Just let go," he said.

"I'm trying."

"No, no, you're not trying."

"Okay." I continued, but it wasn't working, I could feel my body or consciousness buzzing, and my heartbeat again started to beat at an alarming rate, or at least the feeling of it.

"Marc," he called.

"I'm trying, I'm trying,"

"Marc," he called again.

"I'm trying, I'm trying," I shot back.

"Marc."

I stopped, noticing that he was trying to get my attention, "What?"

"Just…Come …with Me."

I gasped, realizing he just stated not only the title of my poem, but in the same cadence that I fashioned it in. I was stunned, almost spooked that he knew such a thing. I responded, "*Ohhhhh, you think you're slick don't you?*"

He grinned, "*I thought you would like that.*"

I did, very much so. If it weren't for the fact that I knew my son was downstairs watching television and I hadn't checked on him for what seemed to be around **30** minutes or so, I would have continued this process, on and on, until I broke free. But 'It' knew I had to go, I knew I had to go. I asked, "*Can I speak to you tomorrow, can we do this again tomorrow.*"

He replied, "*I am always with you.*"

This is the only point at which I saw a portion of my body. In this state, I reached out my hand to shake his, and then watched him slowly fade away, blending into the darkness. As I then consciously came back to, I opened my eyes and exhaled my first long breath. I couldn't believe what had just happened. It was the greatest experience I ever had, and I felt rejuvenated.

I got up from the bed and ran downstairs to tell my then **6** year old son that there is so much more in the world. He had no idea what I was talking about, which is totally understandable. I even told my father about my experience, asking him over and over again if he believed me, and his response was, "*Well…I believe, that you believe that.*" Even now, that moment makes me laugh with love, because it is totally understandable.

My feelings and senses had been heightened, or maybe I was just paying more attention to them. When I closed my eyes, I never saw pitch darkness anymore, I always felt like there were objects or images trying to make its way to me. Nevertheless, I spent many days, devoting hours before I would go to sleep and after I woke up trying to get myself back in that state, but many years went by without making direct contact again. But this all came to a change, and with the help of a familiar face.

Funny how the world works, I countlessly think back on my life and situations, wondering if they were by random, or if it was truly something that was destined to be. I know better now.

It just so happens that the same young lady that introduced me to 'Out of Body Experiences,' was in **Miami** during one of my performances. It had been **7** years since I had last seen her…7…long…years. I couldn't hold myself back, just before I was about to perform, while sitting next to her in the **'Literary Café**,' poetry venue, I brought up the subject of Out of Body Experiences.

I asked could I remain in contact with her, thinking that her energy would possibly aid my efforts. She agreed, and further added that I should look up **DMT**. I asked her what was that, and she replied, *"I'm not that familiar with it, but it's kind of like this thing that makes you have Astral Projection."* That's all she had to say. Again, she set a root that was going to change my life, forever.

Instantly, I read up on the subject. I swamped myself with material for **4** months studying **DMT**, which is an abbreviation for **Dimethyltryptamine**, thought to be found in almost every living organism, and believed by some to be found or released from the **Pineal Gland**, which is located in the center of your brain, also known as 'Your Third Eye.' I educated myself as much as I could on the subject, learning every angle and hypothesis on this component. I read that just after taking this substance, you instantly break through to a place that is secret to this world, while in a meditative position, your consciousness is transported into a realm that feels realer than the one you are in now. I learned a lot, so much that I could tell people about it without having done it. Or so I thought. No amount of studying this substance can prepare you for the experience.

Through my intense study, I was aware of the many times it stated where it is best to have a 'Sitter,' someone that will either coach or watch over you while you are going through this experience. I also read where it is good to do this process around a comfortable setting, and to have those with positive energy around you during your experience. Well, I at least tried to heed to one of these suggestions.

I was on tour when I first come across this substance, and the young woman I was staying with at the time, for better sense of the term, didn't quite understand what I was partaking in. I knew I did not want to do experience with this with her around me, but I couldn't tell her to leave her own home. Impatient, very excited, and without a 'Sitter,' I left out her house at around 8 in the morning, and went down to the garage, and sat in her vehicle. In the back of a truck (Which I do not recommend), in Miami Florida, I then took my first journey.

After consuming this substance, I was then thrown backwards into the backseat, with my world opened up immediately. I felt my conscious being slung forward, as another realm raced towards me. I felt wormholes beside me, but quickly raced through it to approach a tall castle-like door, but instead of going through it, I levitated over it, and continued to do so into what was behind it. The world was big, huge, and forever growing.

I then came down from levitating to hovering over the ground, in which everything around me was made up of digitized-like patterns. I was then approached by shadowy beings, and some that looked much like small mechanical-elves. They were extremely excited to see me, and kept showing me things, objects that seemed to be in comparison to their toys, but yet were significant to the make-up of our 'World,' or 'A World.' Their creations were magnificent. I didn't ask to play with them, I just watched, but I got the sense that they would have let me if I asked. I noticed rooms, with decorations of all kinds of geometrical patterns and figures, perfectly outlined with colors I hadn't seen before, and yet still as if I could see through it. Colors that somehow looked colorless.

I let the experience take me where it wanted to go, I didn't really ask for anything or any questions. This was much different than when I channeled my 'Higher Self.' That experience was calm compared to this. This world was chaotic, and everything was coming at me at once, with everything around me giving off a feeling that it is alive. I honestly had no idea what was going on. I think I even consciously made my experience shorter, because as soon as I began to question, "*Is this really happening,*" I then slowly started to feel myself drift away from it.

The Beings, they all came together, side by side and started waving at me, saying, "*Goodbye, goodbye, it was so good to see you. Goodbye, goodbye, goodbye, come again.*"

Slowly, I opened my eyes, noticing the surroundings of the car I was in, looking out the window and at the garage with the other cars, and then slowly looked at my arms and legs. I knew I was back, but it looked weird, it looked different to me. Even weirder than what I just experienced, it somewhat made me feel as though this place, the 'Physical Realm' was also a little weird. But nevertheless, the place I just came out of was beyond describing, and in a sense more believable than this world. I looked around once more, and finally took my first breath and said, "*…What in the world was that?*"

Physically I was completely back to normal in **30** minutes, but mentally I was left with more questions than answers, even though I had this feeling that I had received so many more answers then I knew I had questions for. It was confusing, I couldn't tell what I had just learned, but I knew I learned something. It was only a matter of time before I went back. And I went back…often.

That next month, I participated in this practice an extensive amount of times. Most journeys were beautiful, some were intense, and a few were overwhelming. Every experience feels different, but yet similar in its own unique way. Usually I'm greeted with the energy of a being or beings around me, but oddly in itself, the whole thing is a 'Being.' The whole thing is 'Alive,' and yet breaks itself down to all sources and visuals of life. The things and beings in this realm that appear seem that it can take on many if not all forms, shapes and images.

The beginning dimensions all have a strange, but yet familiar way about them, like looking at something you've seen before. At times I've felt as though I was pulled along with energies that say, "*Yeah, Come on, remember, you can remember, I know you remember me. Everything there, is an illusion, you know it's true, come with me, I know you can remember,"* with sounds in the background with a rhythm similar to, '**Whhoo-Whhoo-Whhoo-Whhoo**.' Voices, not of this earth, nothing I've ever heard before, truly, if I had to describe it, it is like listening to aliens from other planets speak, but also like listening to the core of the solar system, all in one.

While in this realm, which I refer to as the 'World of Answers,' information is coming at you a mile a minute, in a way that there is no such thing as time. It's as if, once you are in this state, everything you want to know, is already there, so once you have a question, it is answered as you are thinking about it, and all the answers that you can't think of and weren't even looking for, are being told to you as well. It's **ON**, the whole place feels like a light switch, and it is always **ON**, it can't be turned off, so being that it is **ON**, everything you want is **ON**, and coming at you at once. Even though this realm reveals many upon many of answers, many times it is quickly forgotten when coming out of this 'World of Answers,' and back into the 'World of Questions,' the physical realm.

There was a time where it even took me a few minutes to recall who I was, and where I was, feeling as though I could have literally been in the middle of anywhere, and nowhere. This seems to resonate the times that I would zone out of my journey, and I would hear it echoing to me, *"It's not real, this isn't real, it's not real, this isn't real."* It wasn't telling me that that realm wasn't real, it was telling me the world I was going back into, the 'Physical' wasn't real.

During this period is when I started to slightly better understand the realm I was venturing into. It always seems to be telling you something, like it is using you, and telling you to tell your friends as well, almost as if it is saying, '**Pass it along**.' Therefor you usually come out of this state feeling as though you need to tell someone something, but yet, sometimes you can't find the words to tell them what it is you need to say. The knowledge and information at times come in the form of feeling, more so than words, so sometimes it is hard to find the correct diction to use for something that is beyond human language.

I then started to realize that you can't truly describe the experience, because words do not so much exist in that realm in the way we think of words, the language in that realm is more so relayed through feeling. The experiences and teachings are feelings and sights, and the sights are so many times unexplainable. Furthermore, in you are one with this journey, like you are inside a video game, almost as if you were made of the same exact thing you find yourself surrounded by. Interestingly so, it has taught me very much the same thing for the world we live in now.

Even still, I knew nothing, truly this was all I knew or understood, couldn't tell you why, or what it all meant. I knew what I was receiving was something valuable, but wasn't able to explain what that something valuable was. This all changed once I started to share the experience with others.

Some of my friends were intrigued enough to try this practice with me. It didn't come into full understanding until almost a year later, when myself and a close friend of mine in Los Angeles started holding our own gatherings, in which we would invite people to participate with us. In comparisons, I found what we were doing to be very Shamanistic. It was here, that we all came to a better understanding of 'It.' Our discussions afterwards aided one another in understanding our journeys. We learned that the energy of others enhanced one's experience and understanding. Truly, with what I have learned, it now all makes sense.

Through our practices and group conversations, it has relayed to me the knowledge of Creation, how God came to be, why this Physical plain was made, what we truly are, how we are connected to one another, what we are doing here, and where we are going, and yet, tells me that I truly know nothing. Even still, I never imagined to be so satisfied with understanding a small part to what this (Us being here) all means.

I use to search for these answers, use to spend many moons looking up into the night's sky, wondering if I would ever get close to knowing any of this. The process of re-learning has been an extraordinary one, for truly it has revealed to me all that I already know, but have chosen to forget. I haven't looked at life the same since, this place has become far more beautiful than I ever thought it to be. I find so much appreciation in being here, in the moment, in knowing that my thoughts dictate all that is around me.

     I appreciate the time I have had to complete this process, I regret nothing in my life, no shame of failure, or prejudice I may have had, every piece to the puzzle played a major part in helping me see a larger portion to a much bigger picture. It has been a revolutionary awaking for myself. Thus, I know, with all my heart, it can also be a revolutionary awaking for you!

xxx

References

- **A Book in Every Home**, written by **Edward Leedskalnin**, published by ReadaClassic.com, (2010)
- **Abusir: The Realm of Osiris**, written by **Miroslav Verner**, published by American University in Cairo Press; 1St Edition, (2003)
- **Alien Interview**, written by **Lawrence R. Spencer**, published by Lawrence R. Spencer; First edition, (2008)
- **Border Lines: The Partition of Judaeo-Christianity (Divinations: Rereading Late Ancient Religion)**, written by **Daniel Boyarin**, published by University of Pennsylvania Press (2006)
- **Buddha**, written by **Karen Armstrong**, published by Penguin (Non-Classics), (2004)
- **Captain James Cook: A Biography**, written by **Richard Alexander Hough**, published by W. W. Norton & Company, (1997)
- **Carl Sagan** and **I.S. Shklovski: Intelligent Life in the Universe**,' published by Delta (1968)
- **Celestial Teachings: The Emergence of the True Testament of Jmmanuel (Jesus)**, written by **James Deardorff**, published by Wild Flower Pr; 1st edition, (1990)
- **Chariots of the Gods?**, written by **Erich Von Däniken**, published by World books; Book Club (BCE/BOMC) edition (1969)
- **Cosmology, Astrobiology: The Biological Big Bang. Panspermia & Origins of Life**, written by **Chandra Wickramasinghe**, published by Cosmology Science Publishers; 1st edition (2011)
- **Crossing the Event Horizon: Rise to the Equation**, produced by **Hassim Haramein**, released, (2010)
- **DMT: The Spirit Molecule: A Doctor's Revolutionary Research into the Biology of Near Death, and Mystical Experiences**, written by **Rick Strassman**, published by Traditional International, Limited, (2000)

- **Doxology: The Praise of God in Worship, Doctrine and Life A Systematic Theology**, written by **Geoffery Wainwright**, published by Oxford University Press, (1984)
- **Edgar Cayce's Story of Jesus**, written by **Edgar Cayce**, published by Berkley, (1987)
- **Everything You Know Is Wrong, Book 1: Human Evolution**, written by **Lloyd Pye**, published by Adamu Pr, (1997)
- **Evolving God: A Provocative View on the Origins of Religion**, written by **Barbara King**, published by the by Doubleday, LLC, (2007)
- **Food of the Gods: The Search for the Original Tree of Knowledge A Radical History of Plants, Drugs, and Human Evolution**, written by **Terence McKenna**, published by Bantam, (1993)
- **Good Speak**, written by **Meher Baba**, published by Dodd Mead; Second revised edition (1997)
- **Health Benefits of Inverted Asanas**, written by **Swami Nischalananda Saraswati,** published by Bihar School of Yoga, (1973)
- **Honest to God**, written by **John A.T. Robinson**, published by Westminster John Knox Press, (1963)
- **How to Read the Akashic Records: Accessing the Archive of the Soul and Its Journey**, written by, **Linda Howe**, published by Sounds True, Incorporated; Reprint edition, (2010)
- **Hyperspace: A Scientific Odyssey Through Parallel Universes, Time Warps, and the 10th Dimension**, written by **Michio Kaku**, published by Oxford University Press, (1995)
- **Is Anyone Out There?**, written by **Frank Drake**, published by Delacorte Press; First edition. edition (1992)
- **Is God Pink?: Dying to Heal**, written by **Mary Jo Rapini**, published by PublishAmerica, **(2006)**
- **Journey With Fred Hoyle: The Search For Cosmic Life**, written by **Chandra Wickramasinghe**, published by World Scientific Pub Co Inc, (2007)

- **Language and Mind**, written by **Noam Chomsky**, published by Harcourt Brace Jovanovich, Inc. (1968)
- **Misquoting Jesus**, written by **Bart D. Ehrman**, published by HarperCollins e-books, (2009)
- **Nazca Journey to the Sun**, written by **Jim Woodman**, published by Pocket, (1977)
- **New Introductory Lectures on Psycho-Analysis (The Standard Edition) (Complete Psychological Works of Sigmund Freud)**, written by **Sigmund Freud**, published by W. W. Norton & Company; The Standard Edition, (1990)
- **Om Chanting and Meditation**, written by **Amit Ray**, published by Inner Light Publishers, (2010)
- **Parting Visions: An Exploration Of Pre Death Psychic And Spiritual Experiences**, written by **Melvin Morse**, published by Villard Books, (1994)
- **Prehistoric Britain**, written by **Timothy Darvill**, published by Yale University Press, (1987)
- **Pyramids and Temples of Gizeh**, written by **W. M. Flinders Petrie**, published by Histories & Mysteries of Man; Revised edition, (1990)
- **Reincarnation & Karma**, written by **Edgar Cayce**, published by A. R. E. Press, (2005)
- **Roots of Human Behavior**, written by **Barbara King**, published by the by Teaching Company, LLC, (2001)
- **Sacred Mushroom Seeker : Tributes to R. Gordon** Wasson, written by **Terence McKenna**, published by, Park Street Press (1997))
- **Selections from the Principles of Philosophy**, written by **René Descartes**, published by CreateSpace, (2012)
- **SELF I-DENTITY Through Ho'Oponopono (Basic I)**, written by **Mormah Nalamaku Simeona**, published by Freedom of the Cosmos (1998)
- **Sex and the Spiritual Path: Uniting the Spirit and the Body (Edgar Cayce Guide)** , written by **Edgar Cayce**, published by St. Martin's Paperbacks; Reprint edition, (1999)
- **Soul & Spirit**, written by **Edgar Cayce**, published by A. R. E. Press (2006)

- **The 12th Planet: Book I of the Earth Chronicles**, written by **Zecharia Sitchin**, published by Avon Books, (1978)
- **The African Religions of Brazil: Toward a Sociology of the Interpenetration of Civilizations (Johns Hopkins Studies in Atlantic History and Culture)**, written by **Roger Hopkins**, published by The Johns Hopkins University Press, (2007)
- **The Ancient Secret of the Flower of Life: Volume 1 (Ancient Secret of the Flower of Life)**, written by **Drunvalo Melchizedek**, published by Light Technology Publications; First Edition, (1999)
- **The Bible and Flying Saucers**, written by **Barry Downing**, published by Da Capo Press; 2 edition, (1997)
- **The Complete Pyramids: Solving the Ancient Mysteries**, written by **Mark Lehner**, published by Thames & Hudson (2008)
- **The Dawn of Human Culture**, written by **Richard G. Klein**, published by Wiley; 1 edition, (2002)
- **The Emotional Lives of Animals: A Leading Scientist Explores Animal Joy, Sorrow, and Empathy - and Why They Matter**, written by **Marc Bekoff**, published by New World Library; First Trade Paper Edition, (2008)
- **The Everything and the Nothing**, written by **Meher Baba**, published by Sheriar Foundation; 1st edition (1996)
- **The Grand Design**, written by **Stephen Hawking**, published by Bantam; Reprint edition, (2012)
- **The Great Teachings of Edgar Cayce**, written by **Edgar Cayce**, published by Are Pr (June1996)
- **The Growth of Biological Thought: Diversity, Evolution, and Inheritance**, written by **Ernst Mayr**, published by Belknap Press of Harvard University Press (1985)
- **The Hidden Messages in Water**, written by **Masaru Emoto**, published by Atria Books, (2005)
- **The Invisible Landscape: Mind, Hallucinogens, and the I Ching**, written by **Terrence McKenna**, published by HarperOne, (1994)

- The Law of One: Book I The Ra Material, written by **Don Elkins, Carla L. Rueckert**, and **Jim McCarty**, published by L/L Research; illustrated edition (1984)
- The Law of One: Book II The Ra Material, written by **Don Elkins, Carla L. Rueckert**, and **Jim McCarty**, published by L/L Research; book 3 edition (1982)
- The Law of One: Book III The Ra Material, written by **Don Elkins, Carla L. Rueckert**, and **Jim McCarty**, published by Schiffer Publishing (1982)
- The Law of One: Book IV The Ra Material, written by **Don Elkins, Carla L. Rueckert**, and **Jim McCarty**, published by L/L Research (September 1991)
- The Nazca Lines: A New Perspective on their Origin and Meaning, written by **Johan Reinhard**, published by Editorial Los Pinos; 2a edition, (1986)
- The Origins of Christianity and the Quest for the Historical Jesus, written by **Acharya S. (D. M. Murdock)**, published by Stellar House Publishing, (2011)
- The Repugnant Conclusion: Essays on Population Ethics (Library of Ethics and Applied Philosophy), written by **Torbjörn Tännsjö**, published by Springer; 1 edition (2005)
- The Road to Eleusis: Unveiling the Secret of the Mysteries, written by **R. Gordon Wasson**, published by North Atlantic Books; 30 Anv edition, (2008))
- The Shaping of Rationality: Toward Interdisciplinarity in Theology and Science, written by **Wentzel van Huyssteen**, published by William B. Eerdmans Publishing Company (1997)
- The Spirit of Man, Art and Literature, written by **C. G. Jung**, published by Princeton University Press; First Princeton/Boll edition (1971)
- The Structure of Evolutionary Theory, written by **Stephen Jay Gould**, published by Belknap Press of Harvard University Press; 1ST edition (2002)
- The **Talmud Jmmanuel**, transcribed by **Billy Meier**, published by Steelmark LLC, (1978)

- **The ZEITGEIST Sourcebook, Part 1: The Greatest Story Ever Told**, written by **Acharya S. (D. M. Murdock)**, (2011)
- **UFOs Are Real: Extraterrestrial Encounters Documented by the U.S. Government**, written by **Clifford Stone**, published by Spi Books, (1997)
- **What Evolution Is**, written by **Ernst Mayr**, published by Basic Books, (2002)
- **What Mad Pursuit: A Personal View of Scientific Discovery**, written by **Francis Crick**, published by Basic Books, (1990)
- **What the Bleep Do We Know!?**, produced by **Betsy Chasse, Mark Vicente, William Arntz**, released by 20th Century Fox, (2005)
- **Who rules America?**, written by **William Domhoff**, published in New York: McGraw-Hill (2006)
- **Who Was Jesus? Fingerprints of The Christ**, written by **Acharya S. (D. M. Murdock)**, published by Stellar House Publishing, LLC, (2007)
- **Zero Limits: The Secret Hawaiian System for Wealth, Health, Peace, and More**, written by **Ihalekala Hew Len & Joe Vitale**, published by Wiley; 1 edition (2008)

OTHER PUBLICATIONS BY AUTHOR

My Time Here With People: Journeyman Volume 1
By **Marc Marcel**
Paperback: (10% through lulu.com)
ebook Download: $9.99

Marc Marcel takes us on his extraordinary voyage for truth and understanding to the meaning of life. '**My Time Here with People**,' goes deep into the astral realm with an accurate account of the **Out-of-Body Experiences**, **Shamanism** and surreal moments that have provided him with some of the most fascinating answers to creation, God, the Universe, and our connection to it. This is the first edition to the Journeyman Collection.

Poet
By **Marc Marcel**
Paperback: (20% through lulu.com)
ebook Download: $9.99

With over 260 poems, from 17 spoken word CDs released through his career, Marc Marcel releases this massive 700 page compilation titled, 'Poet.' The title is play off of one of his earlier performance poems entitled, 'I Ain't No Poet.' While he has continuous expressed throughout his career that he is more than just a spoken word artist, it is hard to deny or ignore the impact he has left on the genre.

To order any of these books, go to either **lulu.com** or **amazon.com** and search for the title for paperback or ebook.

To find out more, go to www.marcmarcel.com